New Business for Old Europe

Product-Service Development,
Competitiveness and Sustainability

New Business for Old Europe

PRODUCT-SERVICE DEVELOPMENT, COMPETITIVENESS AND SUSTAINABILITY

EDITED BY ARNOLD TUKKER AND URSULA TISCHNER

Greenleaf
PUBLISHING

2 0 0 6

This book is based on the outcome of SusProNet (www.suspronet.org), a Thematic
Network supported with funding from the European Community's 5th Framework
Programme (1998–2002) under contract no. G1RD-CT2002-05079.

Published by Greenleaf Publishing Limited
Aizlewood's Mill
Nursery Street
Sheffield S3 8GG
UK
www.greenleaf-publishing.com

Printed in Great Britain on acid-free paper by Antony Rowe Ltd, Chippenham, Wiltshire.
Cover by LaliAbril.com.

British Library Cataloguing in Publication Data:
New business for old Europe : product-service development,
    competitiveness and sustainability
    1. New products   2. Sustainable development
    I. Tukker, Arnold   II. Tischner, Ursula
    658.5'75

ISBN-10: 1874719926
ISBN-13: 9781874719922

Contents

Foreword

Bas de Leeuw
UNEP DTIE, France

It is a shame that the product-service systems (PSS) concept did not end up with a different name. At first sight, it is just one among a host of three-letter abbreviations in the environmental field—and with less of a ring to it than most.

However, if we allow ourselves to fully understand the concept, then we might come to realise that PSS could well be one of the most promising ways of approaching the worldwide quest to achieve sustainable consumption and production patterns. Going several steps beyond concepts such as eco-efficiency and ecodesign—which never really managed to escape the purely technical engineering spheres—PSS enables the building of linkages between environmental, economic and sociological ways of looking at society. And these are powerful bridges, since the concept is deeply rooted in the commercial world. Rigorous consumer research, combined with creativity and a refreshing desire to earn money in a different way, is what it takes to make sure that planet, people and profit are compatible ideas.

This is why the United Nations Environment Programme (UNEP) is among the most active organisations promoting the concept at a global level. We focus our efforts on keeping it practical, simple and understandable. And we do our best to prevent the emergence of a new divide between developed and developing countries. PSS should allow poor communities to leapfrog towards more sustainable consumption and production patterns. Transfer of knowledge should not be restricted to hardware only. This is a very important condition for global success.

Our efforts towards this end are reflected in publications, including *The Role of Product-Service Systems in a Sustainable Society*[1] and *Product-Service Systems and Sustain-*

---

1 United Nations Environment Programme, Division of Technology, Industry and Economics, *The Role of Product-Service Systems in a Sustainable Society* (brochure, 2001; www.uneptie.org/pc/sustain/reports/pss/pss-brochure-final.pdf).

ability: Opportunities for Sustainable Solutions.[2] And we have promoted related concepts—such as the function-based approach—in the preparatory process of the World Summit on Sustainable Development (WSSD), held in 2002. This led to the current Marrakech process through which the international policy-makers' community is developing and promoting a worldwide ten-year framework on sustainable consumption and production (SCP). International Marrakech Task Forces (MTFs) are now investigating issues such as sustainable lifestyles, sustainable product policies, sustainable procurement and co-operation with Africa aimed at leapfrogging to SCP. UNEP's Production and Consumption Branch is committed to making the Marrakech process meaningful, different and acute. PSS and the system innovation concept, discussed in this book, fit very well within this context.

Over the last decade many researchers, institutes and programmes have been looking at product-service systems (PSS). The European Union funded the Sustainable Product Development Network or SusProNet, which formed the framework for this book. We commend the European efforts in this field, which we welcome in the broader context of our strategic partnership agreement with the Commission, with SCP as one of the priorities.

This publication presents a number of interesting innovations in comparison with earlier publications. It is one of the few that pay significant attention to the business side of the concept. It contains targeted discussions on the potential for PSS in five areas: materials and chemicals, information and communication technology (ICT), offices, food, and households. And a simple, easy-to-use manual is annexed to the book.

All of which makes *New Business for Old Europe* one of the most interesting publications since the Johannesburg Summit. A 'must-read' for all stakeholders in the Marrakech process and a 'must-read' for other individuals, in business, government and civil society. *New Business for Old Europe* is aimed at those who want to make a difference in this world. Whether one is motivated by the environment or by concern for other people or by concern for oneself is unimportant, as long as PSS becomes a much wider reality. Ultimately, PSS may well prove to be nothing less than the dawn of a strategy to optimise happiness for all with zero negative environmental and social impacts. And who will care then about what the abbreviation sounds like?

Bas de Leeuw,
Head, Strategy Unit
Sustainable Consumption and Production
UNEP DTIE, Paris, France
www.unep.fr/sustain
email: sc@unep.fr

---

2   Ezio Manzini and Carlo Vezzoli (eds.), *Product-Service Systems and Sustainability: Opportunities for Sustainable Solutions* (United Nations Environment Programme, Division of Technology Industry and Economics, Production and Consumption Branch; Interdepartmental Research Centre, Innovation for the Environmental Sustainability, Politecnico di Milano University, 2002; www.uneptie.org/pc/sustain/reports/pss/pss-imp-7.pdf).

Part I
Product-services:
the context

1
Introduction

Arnold Tukker

TNO, The Netherlands

1.1 From products to solutions or product-services

Selling products used to be the standard way of doing business. A company makes a product, sells it to a user, receives compensation, and that is it. It is up to users to finance their purchase, learn how to use it, arrange maintenance for it, insure it if needed, buy any consumables and auxiliary materials the product needs to be operational, discard it after its useful lifetime and, above all, apply the product for a useful purpose. In one sentence: it is left to the user to transform the purchase of a product into something that fulfils effectively a final user need.

Two streams of research, which normally have very distinct perspectives on the world, in the last two decades surprisingly converged to a common conclusion: selling products is old-fashioned business. Companies should switch their focus to selling need fulfilment, satisfaction or experiences (e.g. Pine and Gilmore 1999). Or, in other words: sell integrated solutions or product-services.

Which two knowledge streams are we talking about? The first is of course the business management literature. 'Go downstream' stated Richard Wise and Peter Baumgartner (1999). 'Skate where the money will be' suggest Clayton M. Christensen and colleagues (2001). 'Deliver integrated solutions', is the message of Andrew Davies *et al.* (2003). 'Turn ordinary products into extraordinary experiences' is the advice of Diana LaSalle and Terry Britton (2003). All these messages have one thing in common. With a true focus on the integrated, final client needs, and delivery of integrated solutions fulfilling these needs, companies will be able to improve their position in the value chain, enhance added value of their offering and improve their innovation potential. In a business world where many products are becoming equally well-performing commodities, this strategy is one of the ways to avoid a competition on price alone—a type of competition that Europe can never win against emerging and low-cost economies such as China (Manufuture 2003). In that sense, product-services can mean new business for old Europe.

The other knowledge stream has a totally different starting point. In the early 1960s it became increasingly clear that human production systems could be a significant threat to the health of ecosystems. Initially, the focus in this debate was on toxic emissions to water and air (including the use of certain pesticides; e.g. Carson 1962). However, over the years it has become clear that the sheer mass of resource flows through our economy is an important driver for the volume of emissions and waste flows (e.g. climate change-causing CO_2; Adriaanse *et al.* 1997; Matthews *et al.* 2000). Additionally, it was realised that most (80%) of these materials were used by just a small percentage (20%) of the world population (i.e. in the USA, Europe and Japan). The combined effect of the world's population growth from 6 billion to 9 billion people in 2050, and wealth growth in the still under-developed world, could increase the volume of the world economy four- to tenfold. Without a change in production and consumption systems, resource use and emissions would rise by similar factors. This, it is believed, will cause a near-certain disaster. Hence, ways have to be found to de-link economic growth and environmental pressure: 'doubling wealth, halving resource use' (von Weizsäcker *et al.* 1997). Many authors in this essentially environmentalist-driven arena quickly understood that, if one could really take final consumer needs (rather than the product fulfilling the need) as a starting point, the degrees of freedom to design need fulfilment systems with Factor 4–10 sustainability improvements are much higher.[1]

The idea that need-focused solutions could be inherently more sustainable than products was born. Product-services would offer the value of use instead of the product itself, such as a 'clean clothes service' versus a washing machine, or a 'mobility service' rather than a car. Making the value of use the centre of business could decrease its environmental load in two ways. First, companies offering the service have all the incentives to make the (product-)system efficient, as they get paid by the result. Such a company would probably use an efficient washing machine, or a light and economical car. On the other hand, consumers would alter their behaviour as soon as they gain insight into all the costs involved with the use. For each kilometre in a car from a car-sharing company, one would pay the actual costs. With one's own car, this is much more difficult, as the purchasing costs, taxes and fuel costs all add to the total costs. Fuelled by these ideas, a string of research activities by mainly environmental scientists and (eco-)designers on this theme followed suit (e.g. Schmidt-Bleek 1993; Stahel 1998; Meijkamp 2000; Charter and Tischner 2001; Mont 2004).

Until today, the connections and interchange between the two research streams have been quite limited. Each group works mainly in its own arena, with its own institutions,

---

1   In general, one sees in environmental policy a downstream shift in focus through the production–consumption chain. The first-generation environmental policies focused on remediation and emission reduction via end-of-pipe technologies. The second generation paid more attention to inherent cleaner production. The third generation included an attention to products. And the fourth generation takes final user needs as a starting point, looking at how production–consumption systems can be organised so that these needs can be fulfilled with the least environmental impact (Simons *et al.* 2001).

journals, funding sources/clients and, indeed, basic goals.[2] In the business management stream, several theories with explanatory and predictive power about the (business) sense of servicing seem reasonably well established (e.g. Wise and Baumgartner 1999). In the sustainability stream, this point has not yet been reached (e.g. Hockerts and Weaver 2002). There is some conceptual integration and co-operation between the different research groups, but research still focuses too often on individual empirical case studies without striving for a good theoretical foundation. Whether product-services truly are the avenue to a sustainable world is still under discussion and this book develops a systematic and clearer view on this issue.

1.2 SusProNet

1.2.1 EU-funded product service research

This potential of product-services to enhance competitiveness and contribute to sustainable development prompted the EU to invest heavily in the theme of product-services. Under the EU's 5th Framework Programme (FP5; 1997–2002), a variety of research and development projects in the field were supported. These include:

- MEPSS (Methodology development and Evaluation of PSS; van Halen *et al.* 2005)

- Homeservices

- HiCS (Highly Customerised Solutions; Manzini *et al.* 2004)

- ProSecCo (Product-Service Co-design)

- Innopse (Innovation Studio and Exemplary Developments for Product-service)

Most projects were performed by a mix of European research institutions and companies. Some of these projects focused on developing methods that could help industries to change their offering from a product to a service (MEPSS), others focused on method development and development of new product-services or solutions (HiCS, ProSecCo, Innopse), and again others tried to analyse under which circumstances product-services are likely to be implemented and accepted by consumers (homeservices). One project focused on dissemination of the PSS (product-service system) concept to SMEs (small and medium-sized enterprises) (lean services). Other projects focused purely on PSS development, such as Brainfridge (an intelligent fridge managing its supply chain), ASP-NET (application service providers), Protex (intelligent enzymes) and IPSCON (receivers for wireless telephones). Apart from these research and business development projects, a network project was also supported, which served as a platform for experience exchange on product-service research. This network was called the Sustainable Product Development Network or, in brief, SusProNet. This book is the main outcome of SusProNet.

---

2   For instance: journals such as *Harvard Business Review* and *Sloan Management Review* versus the *Journal of Cleaner Production* and *Business Strategy and the Environment*; business schools versus environment and design schools; major industries versus sustainability research programmes; and improving competitiveness of business versus reducing environmental impact.

1.2.2 The network

As a thematic network under FP5, SusProNet had the following aims:

- Exchange, analyse, complete and make easily available information on best practice on development of product-service systems (PSS)

- Identify research needs to create excellence in PSS development in Europe

Additionally, SusProNet aimed to create a strong network of all EU experts in this field, as well as from industry, research institutes and others. Overall, by achieving these goals, SusProNet wanted to support various EU policy objectives, such as competitive growth, integrated product policy and sustainable development.

Table 1.1 and Figure 1.1 give an overview of the structure of SusProNet. The network involved some 50 core participants, with the following roles:

- Seven network partners, including the network co-ordinator. These institutions took the lead and primary responsibility for all activities (laid down in work packages) related to preparation and management of the network. Together they formed the steering committee of the network

- More than 30 network participants, mainly from industry and their representative organisations and governmental institutions. They brought in their current experience and were able to apply the lessons from the network in their daily practice

- About 15 participants from other research projects on PSS in the EU's FP5, which formed a 'cluster' with SusProNet. In these cluster projects, about 17 new product-services were developed

Since product-services have a clear focus on final client needs and consumer satisfaction, it was decided to organise SusProNet around five 'need areas'. Each need area formed a work package (WP7–11), and was allocated to a SusProNet partner. Each of the 40 other participants took part in the need area group that was most directly related to their business, interest and market field. The need areas were defined somewhat pragmatically in order to ensure that each group would have a similar number of participants and indeed would deal with topics of common interest. Eventually, need area groups were formed on base materials, information and communication technologies, office work, food and households. During the time that these need area groups were operational, five workshops and conferences were organised (WP12–16). Each workshop dealt with a specific step in PSS development (analysis, idea generation, implementation). The two conferences focused on agenda setting/validation of the analysis phase (Conference), and dissemination and policy implications (Conference 2). These conferences were open to any person interested in PSS, even if they were not part of SusProNet or its cluster. A cluster dissemination (WP2) event finalised all work in the cluster.

Furthermore, SusProNet organised an overall work package on PSS methodology and market potential (WP1), in which representatives of the more methodologically oriented cluster projects, Innopse, ProSecCo and lean services, participated. Work packages on overall management and cluster co-operation (WP3/4), network communication and website (WP5 and WP6) and network heritage (WP17) completed the structure of SusProNet.

WP leader*	Need area	WP	SusProNet participants	Participating cluster partners
P7-INETI	Materials	WP7	Dow Corning Europe	Protex 1 (enzyme application)
			Ecobouw C.V.B.A	Innopse 3 (teleservice for machines)
			Green alliance	Innopse 4 (online inspection)
			Johns Manville	
			Product-Life Institute	
			Redco/Eternit	
			SECIL	
P5-CfSD	Infor-mation	WP8	Alcatel	Brainfridge 1 (automatic display)
			Bespak Europe Ltd (for IEE)	Innopse 1 (price strategy calculations)
			Crawford, Hansford & Kimber Ltd	
			IBM (for IEE)	
			Orange UK	
			Recyclingpartner e.G. (RPG)	
			Thames Valley Technology Limited	
P4-econcept	Offices	WP9	AGFA Gevaert AG	Innopse 2 (facility management)
			Hewlett Packard	ASP-NET 1 (e-messaging)
			Pars Pro Toto	ASP-NET 2 (project management)
			Samas Benelux	ASP-NET 3 (HR management)
			Veldhoen & Company	
P2 TNO Industry	Food	WP10	Apetido	Brainfridge 2 (supply management)
			Apintech Ltd, the Daedalus Group	ProSecCo 2.1, 2.2 (remote patient monitoring)
			ETNA PelgrimHome Products BV	ProSecCo 3.2 (food chain monitoring)
			Food and Drink Federation	
			Siemens Nederland BV	
P3 Vito	House-holds	WP11	Ecofys Energy and Environment B.V.	Protex 2 (carpet cleaning)
			JAGA NV	ProSecCo 1 (culture on demand)
			Nokia Mobile Phones	
			Philips Consumer Electronics	
	Free role[†]		Alliance for Global Sustainability	
	Free role[†]		European Environmental Bureau	
	Free role[†]		INSEAD	

* Other partners in SusProNet were TNO-STB (management and, together with econcept, PSS Methodology), and O2 Global Network (website and external communication)

† These organisations (a university network, business school and NGO) are mainly involved for their dissemination potential and are free to participate in the need area they want

TABLE 1.1 Partners and participants in SusProNet per need area

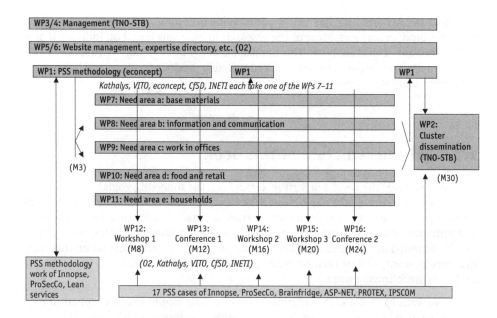

FIGURE 1.1 **Structure of SusProNet**

1.2.3 Goal of the network

Essentially, thematic networks are meant to collect and evaluate the existing knowledge in a specific research field, to describe the state of the art and best practice, to coordinate research, and to develop a research programme highlighting the existing gaps in knowledge. The SusProNet approach allowed us to do this in the following ways:

- By collecting, analysing and discussing the research results of the projects in the SusPronet cluster and other product-service projects (WP7–11 and WP1)

- By an in-depth exchange of experiences with the 40 mostly industrial participants that followed a product-service development trajectory during the workshop series, with a focus on specific need areas (WP7–11)

- By connecting all this information with a focused literature search (WP1)

- By collecting a large set of case studies (about 200) in a structured database (WP1), which allowed for analysis of, among others:
  - Indicative environmental gains of the product-service compared with a regular product
  - Economic advantages and disadvantages of the product-service compared with a regular product
  - Other drivers/barriers for implementation

The database, in particular, has a clear added value over most research to date on (sustainable) product-services. Most of the research to date was based on individual or a limited amount of case analyses. This database made it possible for the first time to do research into specific patterns related to sustainable product-services, and hence contribute to theory development.

1.3 Goal and structure of this book

This book bundles the results of SusProNet and has the following goals.[3]

First, it aims to bridge the gap between the largely business-oriented literature from the first research stream, and the largely normative/sustainability and design-oriented literature from the second research stream mentioned in Section 1.1. This must lead to a better-founded understanding of the business drivers for embarking on product-service development, and its relation with sustainability. For this purpose, Chapters 2–4 deal with the following issues:

1. We want to give a clear definition of product-service in relation to both the sustainability-oriented and the business-oriented literature (Chapter 2)

2. We want to understand what drives the competitiveness of business systems, and how product-services can contribute to competitiveness (Chapter 3)

3. We want to understand if and, if they do, how product-services can contribute to more sustainable production and consumption systems (Chapter 4)

Second, a large number of studies have developed tools, methods and approaches that can support marketers, product developers and strategists in business to develop product-services. This book will review this information, select the best-practice approaches from it, and analyse any gaps in view of the more theoretical review of business management and competitiveness in Chapter 3. This work is presented as Chapter 5.

Third, we want to show what opportunities there are for product-service development in a variety of need areas. For this purpose, after a common introduction in Chapter 6, Chapters 7–11 give the results of SusProNet's need area-oriented activities. Each chapter discusses the need area, developments that will stimulate or hinder the market opportunities for product-services, product-service examples, and typical implementation challenges for product-services in that need area. These chapters can serve as a quick introduction for companies interested in developing product-services in a specific area.

---

3   Underlying research reports, conference proceedings, and even an extensive database on product-service literature are available via the SusProNet website: www.suspronet.org. In due time, the information on this website will be redirected to the website of a follow-up project, www.score-network.org.

Fourth, we want to translate all the lessons gathered from the former chapters into suggested approaches for product-service development by companies. This reflection is presented in Chapter 12. A lightweight 'product-service development manual' is presented in Annex 1, with an alphabetical list of useful underlying tools in Annex 2.

Finally, Chapter 13 ends with conclusions about:

- The market potential of product-services
- The sustainability potential
- Gaps in knowledge
- Policy implications

Part II
Fundamentals concerning competitiveness and sustainability

2
Product-services: a specific value proposition

Arnold Tukker and Christiaan van den Berg

TNO, The Netherlands

Ursula Tischner

econcept, Germany

One of the surprising findings in the SusProNet project was that much of the theory development on what has been termed (sustainable) product-services is not well linked to business literature. Indeed, we found that many of the company members in Sus-ProNet had never heard of the term 'product-services'. At the same time, this was the header under which the EU funded more than ten major projects, and the activities of many of the firms surely could be classified as putting product-services on the market. Hence, there is a clear need to define the term 'product-services' in more detail, preferably in a terminology that is usually applied by business and/or the business literature. We will first review terms and definitions mainly used in the sustainability-oriented literature. After that, we will review how the business literature tries to describe business systems. On this basis, we will choose a descriptive model and terminology that suits this book best, and introduce a classification of product-services.

2.1 Product-service systems in the sustainability literature

2.1.1 Definitions

Table 2.1 shows some definitions for product-services or product-service systems given in the sustainability-oriented literature. All these sources acknowledge that products and services are linked. In practice the provision of services involves a number of tangible and intangible elements, while the supply of products relies on the culmination of a long chain of services. The idea of serviceless products or productless services is thus flawed (Cooper and Evans 2000). In reality there is a spectrum from product-dominant entities (e.g. an apple) to service-dominant entities (e.g. serving apple pie in a restaurant). Having identified this common feature, it is also clear that definitions may differ on the following points:

1. The central term varies. Authors use, for example, one of the following terms:
   - Product-service systems
   - Product-service combinations or mixes, in short: product-services
   - Eco-efficient services

2. The parameter indicating whether and to what extent products and services are 'mixed' varies. Most authors do not make this parameter explicit, and just talk about mixes of products and services. The initial definition used by the SusProNet team saw product-services as an offer where the *value* consists of both a (tangible) product and (intangible) service element. Hockerts and Weaver (2002) speak of product-services when the *property* rights related to a product are distributed between user and provider. Such property rights include:
   - The right to retain profits/the obligation to cover losses
   - The right/obligation to maintain and operate a product
   - The right/obligation to dispose of a product
   - The right to exclude others
   - The right to use a product

3. Some definitions include the normative demand that a lower environmental impact should be reached, while others do not (e.g. Brezet *et al.* 2001; James *et al.* 2001; Mont 2004)

4. Some definitions are purely related to what the provider offers to the client. In this context, the word 'system' is only used to indicate that the offer consists of a mix of products and services (e.g. Manzini 1996; Goedkoop *et al.* 1999). In other cases, the term also includes the organisation of the production network as being the 'system' that puts the 'product-service' on the market (Mont 2004)

5. Some definitions seem to cover any business process, or any offer a firm can put on the market (e.g. Mont 2004). Others try to indicate that a 'product-service' should fulfil a specific, integral client demand (e.g. Manzini and Vezzoli 2002)

We think this short overview already gives some indications of how this set of defini-tions can be better aligned and made more precise. First, we think that a clear differ-ence should be made between the *offer* to the client, and the *organisational structure* (often involving a network of firms) providing it. Second, we think that a term should not implicitly include the normative notion of sustainability but, if relevant, that this should be indicated specifically. And, finally, it should contain the notion that the prod-uct-service tries to fulfil an integrated, final client need. The following set of definitions could align the language on product-services in the sustainability literature:

1. Product-service (PS): a mix of tangible products and intangible service designed and combined so that they are jointly capable of fulfilling final cus-tomer needs. NB: this concerns only the *offer* to a client. Terms such as 'mix' or 'combination' might be added, but this is not necessary

2. Product-service system (PSS): the product-service including the network, infrastructure and governance structure needed to 'produce' a product-ser-vice

3. Eco-efficient (PS or PSS): (a PS or PSS) causing minimum negative environ-mental impact while having maximum economic added value

4. Sustainable (PS or PSS): (a PS or PSS) causing minimum negative environ-mental and social impact while maximising social well-being and maximising economic added value

2.1.2 Visualisations

The sustainability-oriented literature has made relatively few attempts to come to a structured visualisation of PSS. Currently, there are two important approaches.

The first approach was developed in the context of environmental evaluation meth-ods of production–consumption chains (e.g. life-cycle assessment [LCA]). Such meth-ods break down the production–consumption chain into unit processes. The material flows between unit processes, and the input of primary resources and output of emis-sions of unit processes are mapped. This gives a good insight into the unit processes and material flows that take place in the system that provides the product-service (see e.g. Fig. 2.1).

A second approach was developed by François Jégou in the HiCS project, and later used in a variety of other projects dealing with product-services (Jégou and Joore 2004). His 'Design Plan' approach grew from the well-known 'blueprinting' techniques from the design field (e.g. Maylor 2000 and Zeithaml 1996). It aims to visualise the business relations in a system providing a product-service. The method uses standard-ised icons to indicate specific roles of actors in the system, and gives a structured overview of (aggregated) physical flows, financial flows and information flows between them. In this way, a simple figure should be produced that reviews in one A4 page the most important organisational characteristics of a product-service system (see for instance Fig. 2.2).

Both methods have been developed for different uses. The first comes from a scien-tific/engineering tradition and was developed to support transparency and under-

PSS definitions and connected terms	Source
The configuration (quantity and quality) of products and services supplied to meet the demand for well-being may be described as a product-service mix or product-service combination	Manzini 1996; Goedkoop *et al.* 1999
A product-service system is defined as 'a marketable set of products and services capable of jointly fulfilling a user's needs'	Goedkoop *et al.* 1999: 18
PSS is a system of products, services, supporting networks and infrastructure that is designed to be competitive, satisfy customers' needs and have a lower environmental impact than traditional business models	Mont 2004
Eco-efficient services are systems of products and services that are developed to cause a minimum environmental impact with a maximum added value	Brezet *et al.* 2001
An eco-efficient service is one that reduces the environmental impact of customer activities per unit of output. This can be done directly (by replacing an alternative product-service mix) or indirectly (by influencing customer activities to become more eco-efficient)	James *et al.* 2001
A product-service system can be defined as the result of 'an innovation strategy, shifting the business focus from designing and selling physical products only, to selling a system of products and services which are jointly capable of fulfilling specific client demands'	Manzini and Vezzoli 2002; Definition in the EU FP5 project MEPSS
A pure product system is one in which all property rights are transferred from the product provider to the client on the point of sale . . . A pure service system is one in which all property rights remain with the service provider, and the clients obtain no other right besides consuming the service. A product-service system is a mixture . . . of the above. It requires that property rights remain distributed between client and provider, requiring more or less interaction over the life time of the PSS	Hockerts and Weaver 2002
A product-service system consists of tangible products and intangible services designed and combined so that they jointly are capable of fulfilling specific customers needs*	Initial definition used in SusProNet

* The SusProNet definition also included some aspects that describe the consequences of PSS development: 'As most of the business focus today is either on product manufacture or on service provision the strategic design of Product-Service-System shifts the business innovation focus from mainly product or mainly service design to an integrated product-service design strategy. This can result in the involvement of additional stakeholders and even the customers in the PSS development and design process.'

TABLE 2.1 **Definition of product-service (systems) in the sustainability-oriented literature**

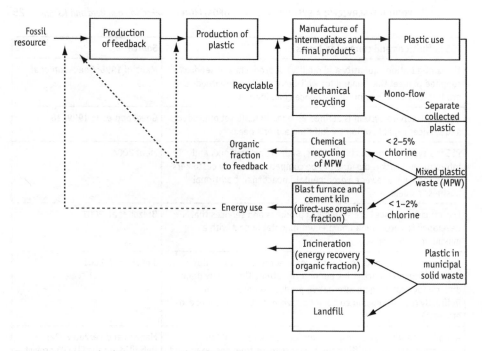

FIGURE 2.1 A typical process tree in life-cycle assessment

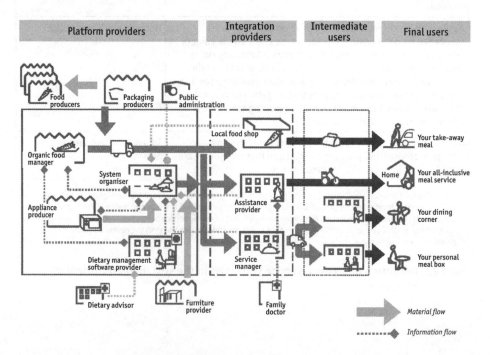

FIGURE 2.2 A business system presented via the 'Design plan' method

Source: Manzini *et al.* 2004

standing of the often complex calculations needed in LCA, for example. The second was developed by designers, mainly to support a process of PSS design. Given these different applications, it is not very useful to strive for harmonisation.

2.2 Value propositions and their production in the business literature

2.2.1 Definitions

'Product-service' and 'product-service systems' are terms that are hardly used in the mainstream business literature. Usually, what business puts on a market is described as an 'offer', 'offering' or 'value proposition'. This can be anything from a product, a service, to whatever else a client is willing to pay for. For value propositions that fulfil specific, integrated client needs, the following terms have become quite common:

- Functional sales: this concerns value propositions where the unit of transaction is the *function* of the product, rather than the product itself

- 'Experiences' and/or satisfaction: this term, particularly used for the business-to-consumer market, seeks to shift the business focus from the actual good or service sold to the 'need behind the need' that is fulfilled (cf. Pine and Gilmore 1999; LaSalle and Britton 2003)

- Integrated solutions: these can be defined as value propositions that bring together products and services in addressing a customer's business or operational needs in an integrated way (Davies *et al.* 2001, 2003)

Several authors have developed structured ways of describing a business network that puts the offering on the market. One of the most influential is the 'value chain' concept of Porter (1985: 33). It illustrates how a firm designs, produces, markets, delivers and supports its value proposition, and disaggregates 'a firm into its strategically relevant activities in order to understand the behaviour of costs and the existing and potential sources of differentiation'. The value chain displays the total value (defined as the 'amount buyers are willing to pay for what a firm provides them'), and is divided into nine—technologically and strategically distinct—value activities and a margin: maintaining a firm infrastructure, human resource management, technology development, procurement, inbound logistics, operations, outbound logistics, marketing and sales, and service (Fig. 2.3). Though initially developed for an individual firm, the concept could be fruitfully applied to business chains as well.

In the 1990s, owing to the increasing complexity and flexibility of business, scholars started to argue that the linear value chain concept should be replaced by a more fluid 'value network'. In such networks, roles and functions can be combined in different ways by different actors.[1] The networks would further be described in terms of their

---

1 Interestingly enough, this concept has many similarities with the 'platform' approach used in the PSS project 'Highly Customerised Solutions' (HiCS); see Chapter 5 and Manzini *et al.* 2004.

Definition and elements	Source
A description of how a company or a set of companies intend to create and capture value with a product or a service. A business model defines the architecture of the product or service, the roles and relations of the company, its customers, partners and suppliers, and the physical, virtual and financial flows between them	Ballon and Arbanowski 2005
A term that is often used to define the key components of a given business (a firm, normally) or to describe a particular business . . . we would propose a generic business model that includes the following causally related components, starting at the product market level: (1) customers, (2) competitors, (3) offering, (4) activities and organisations, (5) resources and (6) factor and production inputs	Hedman and Kalling 2001
The functions of a business model are to: • Articulate the value proposition, i.e. the value created for users by the offering based on the technology • Identify a market segment, i.e. the users to whom the technology is useful and for what purpose, and specify the revenue generation mechanism(s) for the firm • Define the structure of the value chain within the firm required to create and distribute the offering and determine the complementary assets needed to support the firm's position in the chain • Estimate the cost structure and profit potential of producing the offering, given the value proposition and value chain structure chosen • Describe the position of the firm within the value network linking suppliers and customers, including identification of potential complementors and competitors	Chesbrough and Rosenbloom 2002
'[A business model] elucidates how an enterprise works with those external stakeholders with whom it engages in economic exchanges in order to create value for all involved parties. [It is] a unit of analysis that centres on a focal firm but that also extends its boundaries'	Amit and Zott 2003

TABLE 2.2 Definitions of business models

'business model' (e.g. Ballon and Arbanowski 2005). The definitions of what a business model is diverge quite a lot, and some are extremely loose (see Table 2.2).[2] The interesting point for this chapter is that it tries to untangle the activities in a business network that puts a value proposition on the market. In doing so, most authors (Hedman and Kalling 2001; Chesbrough and Rosenbloom 2002; Amit and Zott 2003; Davies *et al.* 2003; Ballon and Arbanowski 2005)[3] discern elements such as:

2   The fact that business modelling was a concept developed by scholars that focused on 'new economy' businesses emerging in the 1990s made it even a little controversial. The term was almost inevitably caught in the discussion about whether this 'new economy' indeed created new rules of the business game, or was merely the same play in a new technical context (e.g. Porter 2001).

3   We use here mainly the terminology proposed by Ballon and Arbanowski (2005).

- The value proposition

- The value network (actors involved in producing and using the value proposition)

- The revenue model (which reflects the formal [contractual and governance] relations within the network, essentially dividing the costs and revenues between the actors in the value network)

- The technological infrastructure (the 'hardware' needed to produce the value proposition, generating the costs that have to be covered by revenues received by selling the value proposition)

Specific business models cannot be regarded as inherently 'good' or 'bad'; their performance depends on how successfully the business model creates a 'fit' between different interests in the value network, at all relevant levels: the functional, strategic/organisational and financial (e.g. Ballon and Arbanowski 2005).

2.2.2 Visualisations

In the business literature, simple actor-process chains (as already shown in Fig. 2.1) or blueprint-like techniques (compare Fig. 2.2) are a common way of visualising (activities in) a business network (e.g. Fitzsimmons and Fitzsimmons 1994; Gattorna and Walters 1996; Kaczmarek and Stüllenberg 2002).

However, when describing the system that creates the offering, business literature is not only interested in the actors and the physical flows between them, but also in monetary flows, activities, mutual agreements, and so on (see for instance Porter's [1985: 33] value chain approach illustrated in Fig. 2.3). The literature on business modelling goes a step further than describing just the structure of the network in terms of value. Using the work of Ballon and Arbanowski (2005) as an example, Figure 2.4 visualises the value proposition, technological architecture, value network and revenue model

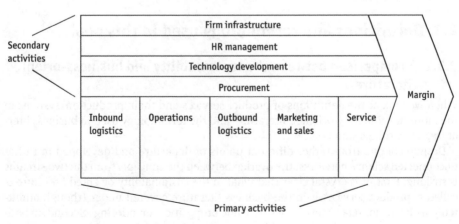

FIGURE 2.3 The generic value chain

Source: Porter 1985: 37

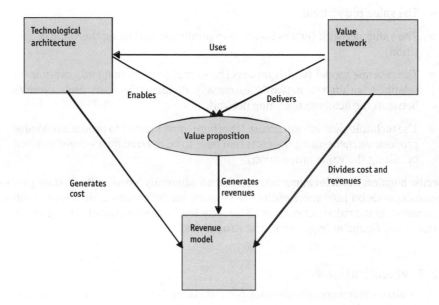

FIGURE 2.4 Elements in a business model as proposed by Ballon and Arbanowski
(2005)

(i.e. the business model elements described above). It basically differentiates between
the value proposition and three different elements (technical, actor-related and gover-
nance-related) of the system putting the value proposition on the market.

2.3 Definitions and terminology used in this book

2.3.1 A comparison between the sustainability and business-oriented literature

When we look at the definitions of product-services and their 'production' systems in
the more sustainability-oriented literature, and the terminology used in business literature, a few things stand out.

Despite coming from rather different points of departure and developed in rather
unconnected science networks, the overlap between the concepts from the two streams
is striking. First, it is crystal clear that what in the sustainability-oriented literature is
called a 'product-service', is in the business literature covered under (though admit-
tedly with a wider reach) terms such as 'value proposition' or 'offering'. Second, in both
streams a structured way of describing the system (co-)producing this value proposition is developed. And particularly the visualisations from the 'blueprinting' tradition
and the business modelling approach describe the systems in almost similar compos-

ing elements (actors, financial flows, material flows and information flows versus the value network, revenue model and technological architecture). Furthermore, the philosophy that business models are the result of a negotiation and alignment process between actors in a network in the best fit with regard to the elements of the network structure is well in line with the PSS concept. After all, due to their part service and part product character, most PSSs will be put on the market by a network of businesses that negotiated a form of collaboration beforehand. We hence think that it is useful to conceptualise PSS in terms of a business model approach. This implies that the PSS has to be described in terms of the following questions:

● What is the offering or value proposition?

● Which parties in which roles make up the value network?

● Which revenue model is used?

● How is the technological architecture organised?

The conclusion is now straightforward. What the sustainability-oriented literature calls a 'product-service' is nothing more and nothing less than a specific type of 'offering' or 'value proposition'. What the sustainability-oriented literature calls the 'system' is nothing more and nothing less than the combination of the value network, technological architecture and revenue model. Putting a product-service on the market rather than a product hence implies first and foremost an innovation of the value proposition. Changing this value proposition might have implications for how to organise the value network, technological architecture and revenue model, but this is no automatism.

2.3.2 Definition of product-services

On the basis of Section 2.3.1 we can now refine the first definitions given in Section 2.2 of this chapter:

● Product-service (PS): a value proposition that consists of a mix of tangible products and intangible service designed and combined so that they jointly are capable of fulfilling final customer needs

● Product-service system (PSS): the product-service including the (value) network, (technological) infrastructure and governance structure (or revenue model) that 'produces' a product-service

The definition of product-service in particular deserves a few remarks. As indicated, one has to acknowledge that products and services have always been linked. With 'product-service' we simply want to indicate a value proposition that derives its value from a significant part of both the product and service element (see Fig. 2.5).

Second, it is also clear that the definition we decided to use is not often applied in the business literature. This is of course a severe drawback. After all, in essence we are writing a book on value propositions, which is at the heart of business strategy and management. However, generic terms such as 'offerings' or 'value propositions' cover everything that a business can put on the market and hence seem too broad. The term 'functional sales' is, as we will see in the next section, more limited than the term 'product-service'. The term 'solution' might be the only viable alternative, but this also has a generic character and does not reflect the fact that the object of analysis is a mix of products and services.

2.3.3 Types of product-service

Various classifications of product-services have been proposed (e.g. Brezet *et al.* 2001; Zaring *et al.* 2001; Behrend *et al.* 2003). Most classifications make a distinction into three main categories of PSS. Product-services are literally seen as a mix of a (tangible) product and a (intangible) service; the different types of product service differ in the extent to which their value is determined by the product or the service component (see Fig. 2.5).[4] They are also a more radical deviation from the traditional product sales concept:

1. **Product-oriented services.** Here, the business model is still dominantly geared towards sales of products, but some extra services are added

2. **Use-oriented services.** Here, the traditional product still plays a central role, but the business model is no longer geared towards selling products. The product stays in the ownership of the provider, and is made available in a different form, and sometimes shared by a number of users

3. **Result-oriented services.** Here, the client and provider in principle agree on a result, and there is no predetermined product involved

In the SusProNet work it appears that each of the main categories defined above still covers product-services with quite different economic and environmental characteristics. Elaborating on typologies in PSS literature and previous studies[5] we will discern the following more specific types:

Product-oriented services

1. **Product-related service.** In this case, the provider not only sells a product but also offers services that are needed anyway during the use phase of the product. This can imply, for example, a maintenance contract, a financing scheme, the supply of consumables, but also a take-back agreement when the product reaches its end-of-life

---

4   Hockerts and Weaver (2002) argue that the value of the product and service component should not be the determining factor for classification, but the extent to which the property rights of the product are transferred from the provider to the user. Though the basis for classification is hence different, their classification criterion leads to the same categories as in Figure 2.5. For product-oriented services, the property rights of the product are transferred totally to the user; for use-oriented services, the user buys access to a product (which stays in the ownership of the provider); and for result-oriented services, the user buys a result (without any predetermined product, let alone property rights involved).

5   The typology presented here was mainly inspired by those given in Zaring *et al.* 2001 and Tukker and van Halen 2003. See among others Hockerts *et al.* 1994, Behrendt *et al.* 1999 and Prepare 2000 for similar classifications.

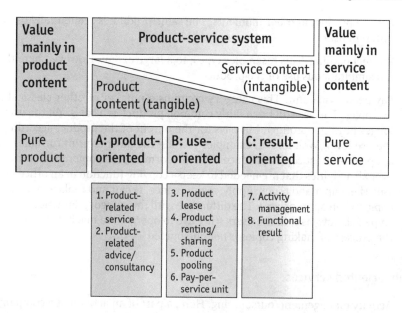

The classification in this figure allows for a logical grouping of virtually all types of value proposition that one can think of, including 'non-material' offerings such as (non-product-related) advice and consultancy (which is a pure service). However, as with any classification system, there are exceptions for which this classification does not work well. The classification assumes that 'products' by definition have a material character, and for some products—most notably software—this is simply not the case.

FIGURE 2.5 Main and sub-categories of product-services

2. Product-related advice/consultancy. Here, in relation to the product sold, the provider gives advice on the most efficient use of it. This can include, for example, advice on an organisation structure of the team using the product; or optimising the logistics in a factory where the product is used as a production unit

Use-oriented services

3. Product lease. Here, the product does not shift in ownership. The provider keeps the ownership, and often is also responsible for maintenance, repair and control. The leaser pays a regular fee for the use of the product; in this case normally he or she has an unlimited and individual access to the leased product

4. Product renting or sharing. Here, the product in general is in the ownership of a provider who is also responsible for maintenance, repair and control. The user pays for the use of the product. The main difference with type 3 is, however, that the user does not have unlimited and individual access; others can

use the product at other moments. The same product is sequentially used by different users

5. Product pooling. This resembles type 4 to a large extent. However, here there is a simultaneous use of the product

6. Pay-per-service unit. This category contains a number of other classical PSS examples. The PSS still has a fairly common product as a basis. Yet the user no longer buys the product, but pays for the output of the product according to the use level. Well-known examples include the pay-per-print formulas now adopted by most copier producers. In this formula, the copier producer takes over all activities that are needed to keep a copying function in an office available (i.e. paper and toner supply, maintenance, repair and replacement of the copier when appropriate). The difference with the category 'Functional result' (type 8, below) is that the users still have to operate the machine themselves: the process of making copies is *not* outsourced

Result-oriented services

7. Activity management/outsourcing. Here, a part of an activity of a company is outsourced to a third party. Since most of the outsourcing contracts include performance indicators to control the quality of the outsourced service, we group them in this chapter under result-oriented services. However, in many cases the way in which the activity is performed does not shift dramatically. This is reflected by the typical examples for this type, which include the outsourcing of catering and office cleaning that is now commonplace in most companies

8. Functional result. Here, the provider agrees with the client to deliver a result. We use this category, in contrast to type 6, for a functional result in rather abstract terms, which is no longer directly related to a specific technological system. The provider is in principle fully free to choose the means to deliver the result. Typical examples of this form of PSS are companies that offer to deliver a specified 'pleasant climate' in offices rather than gas or cooling equipment, or companies that promise farmers to keep harvest losses to an agreed minimum level rather than selling pesticides

After this basic introduction into the concept of product-service systems the next chapter will discuss the economic side of this concept.

3
Product-services and competitiveness

Arnold Tukker and Christiaan van den Berg
TNO, The Netherlands

Many examples of potentially sustainable product-service ideas have been described in the literature, which—supposedly—could also be profitable for companies (e.g. Goedkoop *et al*. 1999; Kazazian 2003). Probably one of the most influential books in this area is *Factor 4: Doubling Wealth, Halving Resource Use* by von Weizsäcker and the Lovinses (1997). The book gives some 50 inspiring examples, including many product-services, which can greatly reduce material flows without true loss of wealth. However, von Weizsäcker and his co-authors could not escape posing themselves the question: 'If all this is so smart, then why hasn't it already happened, with a whole raft of billionaires to boot?' In the meantime, almost ten years have passed, and the first billionaire who used a 'Factor 4' case as a starting point for his business development is yet to be seen.

According to Hockerts and Weaver (2002), such examples indicate how immature theory development in the field of (sustainable) product-services still is. The past decade saw many conceptual studies, some integration of concepts and largely isolated case research. But most of these studies suffered from the problem that they were either based on normative 'wishful thinking', or did not attempt to develop theories overarching the different individual cases. A theory with explanatory and predictive power is hence still lacking. Even worse, though product-services basically form a specific business value proposition, the (sustainable) product-service community has largely neglected theories and case studies from the field of business management research.[1] All this has prevented the (sustainable) product-service community from succeeding in forming a science field in its own right.

1   Even what we regard as the high-quality research of e.g. Mont (2004) and Goedkoop *et al*. (1999) only very partially embodies literature from business management research.

In our view, the first pillar of a sound theory on (sustainable) product-services is to understand when business wants to put such a value proposition on the market. One has to acknowledge that a business's reason for being is to create added value—preferably over a longer time period. Hence, industry's new business developers will embark on PSS (product-service system) models, when that is the key to (lasting) competitive advantage and value creation, but use other models when that better helps to beat competition. In this analysis, an important factor is, of course, how radical a switch to product services is for a firm. For instance, a very product-oriented firm may relatively easily embark on product-oriented services, but changing its business model to result-oriented services would be a radical organisational change. The first question to be answered in this book is hence: *Which factors determine whether a (sustainable) product-service concept helps to achieve lasting competitive advantage?*

We will answer this question in three steps. First, we will review perspectives on business strategy (Section 3.1) and business system dynamics (Section 3.2) as described in business literature. Second, on this basis we will describe which factors determine the competitiveness of business systems, and how different PSS types can contribute to this (Section 3.3). Section 3.4 suggests how to manage risk factors and barriers to PSS, as identified in Section 3.3. Section 3.5 ends with an overview of barriers and drivers and conclusions.

3.1 Some perspectives on business strategy

In principle the goal of almost any firm is to create value over the longer term.[2] Hence, managers and business scientists alike want to understand how a firm can reach long-term success. This has led to a quest for the holy grail of what has been termed 'sustained' or 'sustainable competitive advantage' (Hoffman 2000).[3] In essence, this question has been the central one for business strategy scientists since the inception of this field in its own right (compare Alderson 1937). The term 'sustained competitive advantage' was first used in the mid-1980s by authors such as Day (1984) and Porter (1985). In the early 1990s, Barney (1991: 102) suggested that:

> A firm is said to have a *sustained competitive advantage* when it is implementing a value creating strategy not simultaneously being implemented by any current or potential competitors *and* when these other firms are unable to duplicate the benefits of this strategy (italics in original).

---

2   This seems to us also true for authors who claim that, for long-term survival of firms, management should not focus on (short-term) profit, but other parameters such as learning capacity (e.g. de Geus 1997). These authors basically have found that too narrow a focus on short-term profitability might harm the resource base of the firm, impairing the ability to sustain its existence (and hence creation of value) over the longer term.

3   Note that 'sustainable' is used here in the meaning of 'keeping up' or 'prolonging', and hence does not explicitly include the social and environmental dimensions of sustainability (see Chapter 4). To avoid confusion, we will use the term 'sustained competitive advantage'.

In the last 50 years, a variety of theories has been developed that contribute to the understanding of how a firm should approach its strategy development process to reach (sustained) competitive advantage. Most of these theories analyse the organisation and development of business (networks) from a different perspective, and hence emphasise different sources of value creation and competitive advantage. We discuss here (e.g. Mintzberg *et al.* 1998; Hoffman 2000; Amit and Zott 2001; Grant 2002):

- Early strategy theories
- The industrial organisation/value chain perspective
- The resource-based view
- The learning school

Each section ends with a text box indicating the main lessons for PSS development.

3.1.1 Early strategy theory

In the 1950s and 1960s, through the work of, for example, Chandler (1962), Andrews (1965) and Ansoff (1965), business strategy became a field in its own right. In this period, two dominant schools of thought emerged: the so-called 'Design school' and the 'Planning school' (e.g. Mintzberg *et al.* 1998; Grant 2002).

At the heart of the strategy development approach of the design school is the SWOT (strengths, weaknesses, opportunities and threats) analysis. The world is divided into external factors that a firm has to take for granted and internal factors that a firm can influence. An external appraisal identifies in a firm's environment threats and opportunities that can be transformed into key success factors. An internal appraisal leads to an insight into strengths and weakness of the organisation. From this, a firm's distinctive competences can be identified. Strategy, then, becomes the art of identifying the best *strategic fit* between the opportunities and threats in the external environment, and the firm's resources, capabilities, organisation, systems, goals and values (Fig. 3.1).

The planning school is in a way a logical follow-up of this design school. The planning school basically formalised the relatively simple, informal approach of the design school in an 'almost mechanically programmed'[4] system (Mintzberg *et al.* 1998: 57; Grant 2002). Via setting of objectives and an extensive SWOT a strategy was developed, which should be implemented via an elaborated and detailed 'master plan'. But eventually this led to slow, inflexible and expensive bureaucratic systems, in which the strategy 'planners' and 'implementers' were largely detached from each other. Learning from and quick adaptation to changing situations in the real world was made difficult. All these aspects are at odds with a business environment that more than ever requires a flexible interaction with a fast-changing reality. Most firms, including the pioneer of planning systems (General Electric) hence dismantled their planning systems in the 1980s.

---

4   In the words of Mintzberg *et al.* (1998: 57), who, as we will see later, are not so enthusiastic about bureaucratic systems that oppose learning.

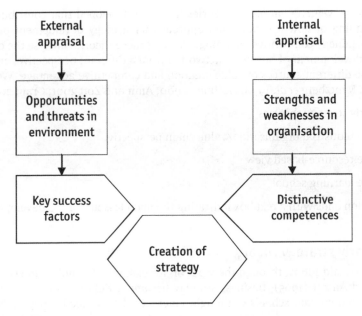

FIGURE 3.1 SWOT

- The product-service offered should fit better with the opportunities in the market than a competing product offer. This is often the case since product-services can be better tailored and customised to client needs
- The production of the product-service should fit to a reasonable extent with the firm's capabilities, resources and organisation. This depends on the organisation (product-oriented or already with experience in service-related offers) and how radically the envisaged product-service differs from the normal offering a firm puts on the market. In several cases, the firm may solve capability gaps by partnering with others

Box 3.1 Lessons for PSS development from the design and planning school

3.1.2 The industrial organisation/value-chain perspective

The planning and design schools primarily focused on the individual company. Michael Porter (1985) shifted the focus to the structure of an industry (the so-called industrial organisation (or I/O) perspective). According to Porter, the attractiveness of an industry is defined by five external forces:

1. Competition between present firms
2. The threat of new entrants

3. The bargaining power of suppliers

4. The bargaining power of consumers

5. The threat of substitute products

In 1985 Porter complemented this with the value-chain model, in which he mapped all activities within a firm that together build the value of a firm's offer (see Fig. 3.2). All activities should be optimised in line with the chosen strategy. The five forces, and the structure of the value chain, are to be analysed and acted on. A company can flourish if it is able to fend off new entrants and substitutes, and if its bargaining power *vis-à-vis* customers/distributors and suppliers is high. Threats of new entry depend, for instance, on the extent to which entry barriers are present in an industry. Entry barriers can be economies of scale, capital requirements, access to distribution channels and so on.

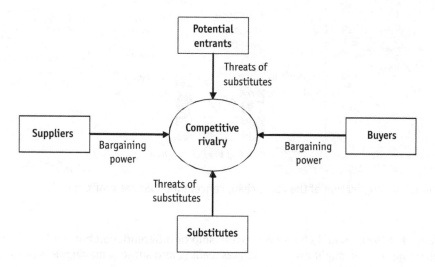

FIGURE 3.2 Porter's five competitive forces model

Source: Porter 1985

To reach competitive advantage, Porter claimed that firms have only three 'generic' strategies to choose from:

1. To offer products at the lowest price (cost leadership)

2. Differentiating its products in order to receive higher margins (differentiation)

3. Focus on one clearly defined market segment (focus)

Porter's approach has been termed 'outside-in' since it emphasises the external environment of a firm in determining its strategy. His work has gained enormous popularity, but also encountered criticism. Clear counter-examples have been found to Porter's

Gadiesh and Gilbert (1998) give a practical example how Porter's value chain concept can be used to analyse which value proposition can best be offered. They developed the concept of the 'profit pool'—basically a visualisation of the value chain that reflects the percentage of the added value of a set of offerings fulfilling an integrated need, and the profit margin market per offered element (see the figure below which gives an imaginary profit pool for car driving). The surface of each square is the total profit per element. If the analysis shows that the market, profits, etc. related to, for example, maintenance and servicing of products are more attractive than offering these products as such, companies should expand their product offer with these elements (which implies de facto offering a PSS).

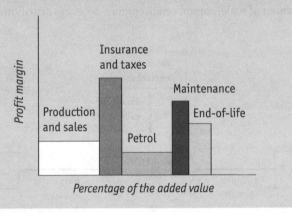

Box 3.2 An application of the value chain concept for PSS: the profit pool

claim that firms should choose cost leadership or differentiation but not both.[5] And, where his toolbox might provide analyses feeding into strategy making, it is not strategy making in itself (Mintzberg *et al.* 1998: 112).

3.1.3 The resource-based view

The resource-based view of the firm became popular in the 1990s. Where Porter put the emphasis on analysing firm-external forces, this theory gave the pendulum a full swing back by focusing on the firm itself.

The resource-based view of the firm points to resources as the main source of competitive advantage. In an unstable industry environment, with rapidly changing consumer preferences and evolving technologies, a firm can find its best sense of direction by looking at, and being faithful to, a well-defined set of internal capabilities. Various

5   For instance: Caterpillar, the example of a differentiator, making the highest-quality earth-moving equipment in the world, was eventually surpassed by (cheaper) Japanese competition (Miller 1992). Benetton succeeds in differentiating itself from competitors, in combination with low-price offerings (Baden-Fuller and Stopford 1992).

- Offering a product-service should be a means that allows for differentiation. This is often the case since product-services can be better tailored and customised to client needs

- Offering a product-service should be a means for (radical) cost reduction. This depends of course on the costs of putting the product-service on the market, but cost-cutting options usually do exist. Product-oriented services help clients to use the product more efficiently; use-oriented services result in a more intensive use of capital goods, and result-oriented services open totally novel perspectives to reach the same result

- Offering a product-service should be a means to improve the bargaining power towards buyers and/or suppliers and fend off substitutes and potential entrants. One of the advantages of all product-services compared with product sales is that usually a more prolonged and intimate interaction with the client is organised, which can reduce the threats of new entrants and substitutes

Box 3.3 Lessons for PSS development from the industrial organisation/value chain perspective

successful firms appeared to have emphasised developing a set of unique resources, which could not easily be copied, enabling them to serve a string of often quite different markets from there (Grant 1991). For instance, Canon's core competences in fine optics, precision mechanics and micro-electronics allow it to operate in seemingly disconnected markets such as photo cameras, laser printers, copiers, faxes and notebook computers. Since its founding in 1948, Honda has built its strengths around developing and manufacturing engines and subsequently developed clip-on engines for bikes, small motorcycles, larger motorcycles, marine engines, generators, pumps and finally even cars. 3M is in the business of sandpaper, adhesive tapes and floppy disks, and tens of thousands more products—all possible through the combination of key technologies in the fields of materials science, micro-replication and health sciences in combination with elaborated capabilities of developing and marketing new products (Grant 2002: 134-46).

Resources can be categorised in many ways. Barney (1991) distinguishes physical (capital) resources, human capital resources and organisational capital resources. Other authors make a distinction into tangible, human and intangible resources (Grant 2002: 139) or tangible assets, intangible assets and capabilities (Fahy and Smithee 1999). Table 3.1 gives some examples of resources.

Whether a certain set of resources forms a sustained competitive advantage for a specific firm depends on whether or not potential competitors are able to duplicate the benefits of the chosen strategy. In this context, Barney (1991) stressed that resources must have the following characteristics to be a source of sustained competitive advantage:

	Tangible	Intangible	Human
Examples of resources/ assets	● Financial ● Physical	● Technology, IPR ● Databases, blueprints ● Reputation ● Brand names ● Networks	● Individual skills ● Organisational skills; capacity for teamwork and communication ● Organisational culture ● Motivation ● Mutual trust
Visibility	Easy	Some easy (brand name), others not	'Invisible' and 'tacit'
Measurability	Easy (book value)	Difficult but done (e.g. 'goodwill')	Very difficult
Potential for imitation	Relatively easy	Difficult to copy in the short run	Most difficult to copy (Collis 1994)

TABLE 3.1 Types and examples of resources

Sources: based on Amit and Schoemaker 1993; Fahy and Smithee 1999; Grant 2002

● A firm should consider outsourcing activities that are not relevant core competences, since usually there will be others who can do the job better and more cost-effectively. This usually implies that another firm will have to offer activity management or result-oriented services to the firm that has outsourced its activities

● Offering a product-service rather than a product should fit with the existing resource base or allow for contributing to the resource base of a firm. Whether this is the case depends on the existing competences of the firm and how radically the product-service idea deviates from the existing way of doing business. An alternative to in-house development is partnering with other firms

● The resources developed via offering a product-service should ideally be valuable, rare, inimitable and non-substitutable. Usually, product-services contribute to a more intimate and unique relationship with clients, which can become a source of sustained competitive advantage in itself

Box 3.4 Lessons for PSS development from a resource-based view perspective

- Valuability. The resource must have the capacity to improve the organisation's efficiency and effectiveness

- Rareness. The resource must be rare and in high demand

- Inimitability. It must be difficult or costly to imitate the resource

- Non-substitutability. It must be equally difficult or costly to find a substitute for the resource

3.1.4 The learning school

Closely related to the resource-based view is the strategy school that propagates *learning* as a main source of competitive advantage. Yes, developing a bundle of unique and valuable resources is a good start. But real competitive advantage is created only if one has an eye on the market and learns what of real value can be produced making use of the resources—and which resources in the future might be needed.

The learning approach has roots going back to authors such as Simon (1957), who launched the concept of 'bounded rationality', and Lindblom (1959), who coined the phrase 'science of muddling through'. The world is assumed to be too complicated to be fully understood, and the only solution is to 'learn by doing, and do by learning'. Arie de Geus (1997), who was co-ordinator of the Group Planning (!) department at Shell, even claimed that the 'only method to achieve sustained competitive advantage is learning faster than your competitor'. The learning school is quite sceptical about an extensive use of analytical tools and planning. Analysis and planning lead to an idea of the world outside and a sense of direction that is usually no longer open for discussion. This is fine for a world that sees little change and in cases where (almost) full knowledge about relevant parameters is achievable. But it can be disastrous in situations where only keeping your eyes open really tells you what to do.

In particular, Gary Hamel and C.K. Prahalad stressed the importance of learning and creating dynamic capabilities (Hamel and Prahalad 1994). Dynamic capabilities are rooted in a firm's managerial and organisational process, such as those aimed at co-ordination, integration, reconfiguration or transformation, or learning. Such capabilities are particularly relevant in relation to product development, strategic decision-making, alliance formation, knowledge creation and capabilities transfer (Eisenhart and Martin 2000). Hamel and Prahalad (1994) state that firms need to build on well-selected core competences, which are the consequence of effective, collective learning of the organisation. Furthermore, they need strategic intent: a sense of direction of where the development of the firm should lead.[6] A firm should also not just seek a 'fit' between capabilities and the environment, but rather 'stretch' itself to aspirations that go beyond what is directly feasible with its present resources. In relation to this, firms should also learn to leverage their limited resource bases by concentrating, accumulating, complementing, conserving and recovering resources where possible. Firms

6 Note that it does not concern a pre-described path or goal, but more a sense of direction that can be adjusted when needed. This sense of direction is needed to overcome one of the pitfalls of a learning approach: at best nicely wandering around in circles accumulating experience, but with no real progress forward; and at worst leading to total chaos.

- If a firm developing a product-service offer has to seek partnerships with other firms, the firm develops a dynamic capability that goes well beyond the individual case (i.e. the capability of developing partnerships in general). This makes the firm much more flexible and makes it possible to leverage resources with others
- The more intimate client contacts that are usually at stake in product-service business models give a better opportunity for learning about client needs, product performance, etc.

Box 3.5 Lessons for PSS development from a learning perspective

A much-cited case in the debate on learning versus planning is two accounts of how Honda conquered the motorbike market in the US in the 1960s. Faced with a disastrous decline in export of motorcycles to the US, the UK government commissioned a study from the Boston Consulting Group (BCG) on why the Japanese were so successful. BCG basically came up with a story about a brilliant series of rationally planned moves by Honda: entering a market by developing a new niche (small motorcycles to middle-aged customers), using the large production scale in the home country to sell large volumes at low prices, thereby moving quicker through experience curves, etc. But, when Richard Pascale (1984), a business researcher, took the trouble of going to Japan to ask Honda managers what had really happened, a much more prosaic truth arose. They had sent some people over to the US with little more plan than 'to see if there was something to sell in the US'. Actually, top management was quite sceptical and only allowed a very limited budget. Initially, they tried to target the existing market of motorcyclists, mostly men with somewhat rough and alternative lifestyles driving around on big machines. A market for commuting or small motorcycles was non-existent. However, the Japanese happened to have some small 50 cc Supercubs that they used for their own transport—since they were on a tight budget. These got a lot of attention—and since by chance the larger bikes they had sold broke down due to heavy use, they had no option but to give the Supercubs as replacements. From then on, the story became history: via the small motorbikes Honda was able to create a wholly new market segment and entered the market in force. Adherents of the learning school find this a fascinating story, since the Japanese did not plan the big assault in Tokyo, but went with their eyes wide open to the place where it had to happen and developed the winning formula while working on the job.

Box 3.6 Example: Honda motorbikes conquer the US. A case of planning or learning?

mastering such dynamic competences will be much more capable of dealing in a timely and appropriate manner with disruptive changes in their environment, or to embark on disruptive innovations and hence shape the future themselves (Gibson 1998).

3.2 Some perspectives on business system dynamics

The above sections discussed strategic approaches to develop competitive advantage from a business perspective. Another way of looking at this issue is to look at developments in the economy from a higher level, and to draw lessons on how competitive advantage can be achieved from there. Some perspectives that in our view deserve attention include:

- An evolutionary perspective on (socioeconomic) development

- Stages in the industry life-cycle

- Shifts in the mode of value creation

- Transaction costs as a factor in business system organisation

3.2.1 An evolutionary perspective on (socioeconomic) development

Highly relevant for analysing the competitiveness of business systems is the basic view one has on economic development. Neoclassical economic theories, probably still providing the mainstream view for this, traditionally saw (technical) innovations as being autonomous and exogenous processes. Of course, it became clear that actors in the economic system could have influence on innovation, by investing in human capital and research and development. Which investments to make, and which innovations finally are adopted, depends on whether such innovations help a firm to compete better on the market. All this assumes that firms are relatively 'free' to adopt innovations, and the consequence is that a rather gradual technological progress will take place. The process of change is—essentially—seen as a rather smooth and even predictable path close to equilibrium. This view of the economy hence tends to emphasise the relevance of efficiency (and hence often uniformity) of business systems, with a conscious and targeted investment in innovative technologies, selected via cost–benefit analyses.

An alternative view is provided by a string of theories that can be labelled as 'evolutionary economics'. These theories, simply stated, see development of technology as a Darwinian process of variation (determined by heuristics in research and development) and selection (by e.g. market forces, existing physical infrastructure but also other contextual factors such as existing institutions, culture and societal habits), leading to preferred trajectories, which in turn influence the context of technology (cf. Dosi 1982; Nelson and Winter 1982). Scholars hence now prefer to speak about socio-technical trajectories (rather than technology development), in which different dimensions of the system (e.g. technologies, knowledge, markets, infrastructure, culture and symbolic meaning, etc.) co-evolve (Rip and Kemp 1998; Geels 2002a; compare also Berkhout *et al.* 2004; Elzen *et al.* 2004).[7]

Next to the regime, which can be seen as a development at meso-level, niches can be discerned. These niches are relatively limited areas, in which new technologies can be developed and tested under relatively protected circumstances. Examples are specific market niches (where protection is provided by a specific market demand), or technological niches (where a specific actor network is willing to create the financial and other boundary conditions that make experimenting and learning possible). And, finally, a socio-technical landscape can be discerned. These are a set of fairly stable factors that are in principle external to the regimes and niches, and can only slowly be influenced. Examples include the existing material infrastructure, but also the existing culture, lifestyle, demography or trends therein. The landscape basically 'channels' the direction of the socio-technical trajectories (see Figs 3.3 and 3.4).

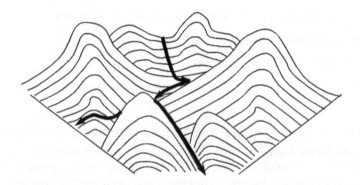

FIGURE 3.3 Topography of a socio-technological evolution: how the 'landscape' channels a 'socio-technical trajectory'

Source: Sahal 1985: 79, as reproduced in Geels and Kemp 2000

These different views on economic development have important implications for how companies should organise and stimulate innovation. In the neoclassical approach, it is of utmost importance to organise existing production structures as efficiently (and often hence as uniformly) as possible, and to analyse carefully which developments to invest in.

The evolutionary approach emphasises much more the problem of 'lock-in': that is, that a business system may be in a development trajectory that is largely historically

---

7 Some of the most famous examples: the QWERTY keyboard was developed for mechanical typewriters—the rationale behind it being that the metal arms for the letters most used were separated as much as possible. Nowadays, with computers ubiquitous, this argument is no longer valid and much more ergonomic keyboards allowing for faster typing are possible. However, since everybody is used to QWERTY all alternative keyboard layouts have failed thus far. Also, magnetic trains have had a hard time breaking through despite their superiority over traditional high-speed trains—the traditional high-speed trains have the enormous advantage that they can also use existing rail tracks to reach city centres. And, so, a basically 19th-century transport system defeats something much better.

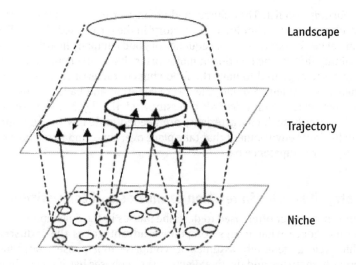

Landscape

Trajectory

Niche

FIGURE 3.4 A multi-level perspective on innovation

Source: Geels and Kemp 2000: 17

predetermined and from which it cannot easily deviate—even if more efficient technical systems become available which would have been applied without hesitation if a 'greenfield' situation existed. The problem for companies facing such a 'lock-in' is that competitors from totally different fields may arise that master in the end the more efficient system. We refer to the extensive discussions in the business literature on 'disruptive innovation' (e.g. Christensen 1997; Christensen *et al.* 2001; Rafii and Kampas 2002). Here, the recipe should be to keep options open, to allow for diversity in the firm in order to maintain flexibility for future change. Hence, what from a static viewpoint probably is not the most efficient strategy may be the most efficient one from a dynamic perspective. Indeed, in his influential book *The Living Company*, de Geus (1997) showed that many firms in fact are unable to survive much longer than 40 or even 12.5 years—even if they are at one moment strong and big enough to be part of major stock market

The evolutionary economic perspective has two implications for PSS development. First, like the resource-based view and the learning school, it points at the limitations of change in business models that a company can go through. It may actually be best that a radical new PSS concept is developed by a separate business entity, which is not hindered by the culture, structure or market drivers ('socio-technical regime') of the mother firm. Second, for many companies, embarking on PSS is something new, which will widen their horizon, sensitivity for clients and environment, dynamic capabilities and flexibility (see Section 3.1.4). These are all factors that seem to contribute to the long lifetime of a firm.

Box 3.7 Implications of an evolutionary perspective on PSS development

indices or the *Fortune* 500 list. They simply had no answer to major shifts or crises in society ('the landscape' and 'technological trajectory' in the terms used above). De Geus saw good financial performance as a consequence of good company health, rather than being a determining factor. The few dozen major firms that really managed to survive for a century or more appeared to have the following characteristics. First, they were sensitive to their environment. Second, they were coherent and had a strong sense of identity. Third, they were tolerant towards diversity. And, finally, they were financially conservative. Apparently such characteristics are needed to deal with the sometimes radical shifts in business environment that take place over time, and to manage related shifts to a totally new competence base.

3.2.2 Industry life-cycles in relation to the basis of competition

Another dynamic parameter often used to describe phases in the development of business systems (and hence what brings competitive advantage) is the **industry life-cycle**.[8] This life-cycle is generally assumed to comprise four phases: introduction/emergence, growth, maturity and decline. Each of these phases has its own characteristics when it comes down to type of market, size of market and emphasis of the innovation effort (Grant 2002: 305, 375; see Figs 3.5 and 3.6):

1. **Introduction/emergence.** In this stage, the market is small and penetration is low. The products produced by the industry are just doing their job, quality is low and prices are high. This, in relation to the newness of the product type, leads to a slow growth rate. Design and technology can be heterogeneous. The effort of the company is mainly focused on improving product quality and improving its functionality—which in this stage is a main source of competitive advantage

2. In the growth stage, market penetration accelerates and the product technology becomes more standardised. In relation, prices are becoming lower and the product type enters the mass markets. The shift from stage 1 to 2 also marks a shift from radical to more incremental innovation of products

3. In the maturity stage, market saturation slows sales growth to a virtual standstill. New demand becomes a replacement demand and companies start to compete on costs rather than functionality or quality. This usually shifts the emphasis from product innovation to large-scale manufacturing and process innovation

4. Finally, the industry enters the decline stage once it can no longer keep up with challenges posed by new industries that produce substitutes with superior functionality, performance and price

So, in principle, an industry life-cycle starts with an emphasis on product innovation, and later on shifts towards process innovation. In the stages between 3 and 4, however,

---

8   By 'industry' we mean a business sector that puts a more or less uniform type of product or product-service on the market. The life-cycle discussed here (of e.g. the automotive industry) hence goes beyond the life-cycle of an individual product (e.g. an individual car model).

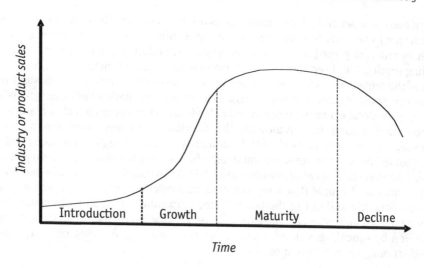

FIGURE 3.5 The industry life-cycle

See e.g. Grant 2002

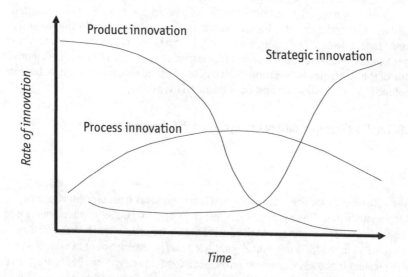

FIGURE 3.6 Innovation per industry life-cycle stage

See e.g. Grant 2002

when both product and process innovations are to little avail, the only viable alternative seems to be what has been termed 'strategic innovation'. This involves activities such as redefining markets and market segments, embracing new customer groups, adding products and services that perform new but related functions or reconfiguration of the sequence of activities in a new format. Reconciling multiple (opposing) performance goals is often the key to strategic innovation. Baden-Fuller and Stopford (1992) have done extensive research into this issue. They concluded that maturity is more a state of mind than an industry characteristic that binds a firm; that an entrepreneurial, learning and experimental culture is key; that strategic innovation needs to be endorsed by top management and needs the creation of suitable boundary conditions; and that with all creativity one has to be selective in choosing its new territory.

The catch is of course that a rejuvenating 'strategic innovation' approach requires entrepreneurship and out-of-the-box thinking, capabilities that so easily might have been neglected and even become extinct in phase 3, when all focus had to be on cost reduction by upscaling, volume growth, detailed planning, forgoing costly (production-disrupting) experimentation, etc.

At the start of an industry life-cycle, superior performance of products and later superior and more cost-effective production are the key to realising differentiation or cost leadership. Hence, a firm must be superior in technical product and process development. Using a PSS business model can still be useful, but is a secondary issue. In the maturity and decline stage, however, the tables are turned. Products and processes are mature and no longer a source of differentiation or cost leadership. Then, using a PSS business model can be one of the strategies for creating new sources of added value: for example, because of its potential for customisation and close client relationships.

Box 3.8 Implications of industry life-cycles on PSS development

For the consumer as for the industrial market, refrigerators have probably become rather commoditised. There is little room left to compete on quality or performance of the product. One of the projects in the SusProNet cluster, Brainfridge, developed an innovative PSS in the form of an intelligent fridge with advertisement capabilities. The service element is the advertisement provided to food suppliers. The clients are both the retailers (subsidised owners of the fridge) and the food suppliers who are using the fridge as an advertisement board. The service invites people to purchase products produced by the specific food suppliers from the specific retailer where the advertisement is displayed.

Box 3.9 Example: Brainfridge

Source: case presented by Mr Vargadis during the SusProNet–MEPSS Dissemination Conference, 13 October 2004, Brussels; www.suspronet.org

3.2.3 Societal megatrends and shifts in the mode of value creation

Another notion relevant for this chapter is the shifting basis for competition and hence the goals companies should pursue. This has in part to do with the industry life-cycle notion discussed in the previous section, and developments in society in general. In most Western economies, services now count for 70% of the GNP (gross national product). One could arguably maintain that the (mega)trends of globalisation, informatisation, move towards a network economy, lean and 'just-in-time' production, concentration on core businesses, the shift to two-income families, more single-person households, time pressure on citizens, and individualisation inherently will lead to a greater demand for product-services rather than products. Customers simply do not have the time, the skills, or do not want to devote resources to integrate all kinds of products and services from individual suppliers to an integrated solution for their needs. They will prefer suppliers that can provide an integrated fulfilment of needs.

This message is probably most eloquently given in *The Experience Economy*, written by Pine and Gilmore (1999). Pine and Gilmore argue that, over time, the characteristics of economic supplies have shifted from commodities or materials, to products, and further to services, to finally experiences. Each of these economies leads to its own basis for competition (see Table 3.2). The key message of Pine and Gilmore, but also authors such as LaSalle and Britton (2003), is that society is shifting to an experience economy. In an affluent (Western) society consumers generally can take basic Maslowian[9] needs such as food, shelter and safety for granted, and will be more geared towards realisation of higher needs such as affiliation, love, esteem and self-realisation. The trick then becomes to satisfy needs on these higher levels in conjunction with the offer of a material artefact: *Turning Ordinary Products into Extraordinary Experiences*.[10] By creating such intangible added value, the provider makes the client willing to pay more than would be justified on the basis of 'rational' calculation.

3.2.4 Transaction costs as a factor in business system organisation

Transaction cost economics tries to understand why in some cases firms internalise activities and related transactions, whereas in other cases these are outsourced and transactions are conducted in markets as a consequence.

Transactions executed in a market are not free of charge; there are costs included related to planning, adapting, executing and monitoring the transaction (e.g. Williamson 1979). Essentially, transaction cost economics seeks to flesh out the most efficient

---

9 Abraham Maslow (1943), an American psychologist, developed a highly influential hierarchy of five levels of basic human needs. Basic or lower need levels need to be fulfilled before humans become interested in fulfilling higher-level needs. The most basic needs are the physiological needs, essential for keeping a human alive (food, water, oxygen). Next comes the need for safety. After that, the need for love, affection and belongingness follows. The need for esteem is the following step in the hierarchy. And, finally, the need for 'self-actualisation' is the ultimate need level to be fulfilled.

10 As LaSalle and Britton subtitled their book. The main title, *Priceless*, was taken from a Mastercard commercial, which goes roughly like this: 'Matches: 10 cents. Candles: $8. Relaxation in the atmosphere created: priceless.'

Type of economic offering	Commodities	Goods	Services	Experiences
Economy	Agrarian	Manufacturing	Service	Experience
Economic function	Extract	Make	Deliver	Stage
Nature of offering	Fungible	Tangible	Intangible	Memorable
Key characteristics	Natural	Standardised	Customised	Personal
Delivery	Bulk	Per piece	Made on demand	Shown during a specific period
Seller	Trader	Manufacturer	Provider	Stager
Buyer	Market	User	Client	Guest
Factors influencing demand	Characteristics	Features	Benefits	Sensations

TABLE 3.2 Shifts in the basis of competition

Source: Pine and Gilmore 1999

form of governance of a given transaction in a specific context. Factors affecting these costs include (e.g. Klein *et al.* 1978; Williamson 1979):

- Uncertainty (and hence the level of standardisation of the object of transaction)
- Exchange frequency and volume
- The assets and procedures enabling the exchange

Reducing uncertainty, complexity, information asymmetry and small numbers bargaining conditions can reduce cost and hence enhance value. In the case of special and irregular transactions, reputation, trust and experience in organising transactions can reduce costs (Williamson 1975, 1979). Transaction costs are probably also relatively low when the business system is mature, since then the transactions concern well-defined, standardised and modularised building blocks of the overall value proposition.

The above text mainly aims to understand transaction costs in static terms: the costs of doing a transaction have to be offset by savings due to outsourcing the (often more

Society is becoming much more specialised, individualised and busy. Such developments favour PSS rather than products. Neither consumers nor businesses want to spend time or resources in combining products and services into a final result, but are looking for integrated offerings fulfilling their needs. And, particularly in a B2C (business-to-customer) context, consumers are moving away from standardised, mass-produced products in favour of unique and personalised experiences.

Box 3.10 Implications of societal developments on PSS development

Product-services are usually put on the market by a network of firms (see Chapter 2), and require application of more complicated revenue models than product sales (where there is just payment at the point of sale). Transaction costs hence can be a determining factor if a PSS is value (delivered to the client) for money (in terms of production costs). The transaction costs in a PSS can be kept relatively low when the elements of the PSS are well standardised and the need for mutual adjustments of product parts, service elements and production processes across firm borders is low (or, in sum: when the business system is mature).

Box 3.11 Implications of transaction costs on PSS development

expensive) in-house production. However, if one looks from a more dynamic perspective, another form of transaction costs can be identified as well. This is closely related to the life-cycle stage of an industry (see Section 3.2.2). In the early stages of the life-cycle, product and later process development is quite rapid. In such stages, there need to be very close and frequent interactions between the actors dealing with different stages in the product and process chains. The system is not yet optimised and continuous improvement and learning 'to make things better' has to take place. This learning can usually take place faster and more efficiently if the different elements of the product and process life-cycle are not separated by commercial firm boundaries. Historically, firms in sectors in such relatively early stages of development, which integrate activities under one umbrella, appeared to outperform firms that relied on buying in other capabilities from third parties.

3.3 Competitiveness of business systems and the contribution of PSS

On the basis of the sections above, we will now describe how business systems can enhance their competitiveness by a move to PSS, and which trade-offs can be at stake.[11]

The work of de Geus (1997) in particular, discussed in Section 3.2, indicates that a mere focus on financial parameters may be insufficient if a firm wants to survive in the long term. However, inevitably, financial parameters will play a dominant role in the decision if a business wants to pursue a move to PSS. We hence prefer to see a firm (net-

11 We concentrate on business systems or networks rather than individual firms since, as we showed in Chapter 2, product-services are combinations of products and services and hence their 'production' usually demands close co-operation of a network of firms with different competences. There are other arguments for looking at the level of systems rather than individual firms. Some authors suggest that competitiveness of individual firms is influenced, if not determined, by the networks or systems of which they are a part (e.g. Porter 1990; Castells 2000). And other authors argue that, since firms often already have optimised their performance, the next step is to look at optimisations at the level of business chains (e.g. Hammer 2001a).

work)'s ability to create and capture added value as a key factor for its competitiveness—though at the same time we acknowledge that this value-capturing potential must be sustained in the longer term. Value can be defined in a number of ways. Extending the concept of economic value added (EVA) as coined by Steward (1991)[12] with this longer-term perspective, we propose using the following determinants for the analysis of competitiveness of business systems:

1. The user value (co-)created

2. The (operational) system costs generated

3. The ability to capture value, now and in the future, determined by:
   a Power position in the system
   b The speed, ability and flexibility to innovate and shape the future

4. The investment needed and capability risk to develop the new (business) system

Points 1 and 2 in essence determine the added value that can be created in the system. Point 3(a) determines which part of this added value the firm (network) can direct to itself. But it also determines, in conjunction with point 3(b), whether a firm (network) is able to maintain its value-creating and -capturing potential in the longer term by continuing to deliver a better value proposition than competitors or providers of a substitute. Finally, point 4 concerns the investment that a firm considering a switch to PSS has to do—which has of course to be balanced by the future benefits determined by points 1–3. In the next three sections we will discuss first the issue of user value, then the system costs and finally the other issues. A final section draws conclusions on the competitiveness of the eight archetypical PSS discerned in Chapter 2.

3.3.1 Co-creating user value versus market risk

The essence

User value basically consists of two elements:

1. Tangible or objective value for the user (e.g. resources, time input and cost of capital saved)

2. Intangible or subjective value for the user (e.g. additional, 'priceless' experiences)

---

12 His definition is: 'A fundamental measure of corporate performance, it is computed by taking the spread between the return on capital and the cost of capital, and multiplying by the capital outstanding at the beginning of the year . . . It is the residual income that remains after operating profits cover a full and fair return on capital (i.e. the cost of capital). In theory, a company's market value added at a point in time is equal to the discounted present value of all EVA it can be expected to generate in the future.' Though maybe not meant like this by Steward, the literal text of his definition echoes a focus on short-time financial performance rather than long-term business success that is central to this book.

Point 1 is fairly straightforward. The value proposition of a provider can save the user resources, time input and costs of capital compared with a reference situation. The user can start to make a rational calculation of what the value proposition actually saves, including all kinds of 'hidden' cost, and that is in principle the maximum price he or she would like to pay for it. Take for instance the choice of a family to take their young children to a kindergarten, to allow both parents to work. The question of whether the cost of the kindergarten is lower than the extra salary gained is one (though certainly not the only) aspect that will be considered.

Point 2 reflects the extent to which the provider (system), in interaction with the user, delivers the most appropriate 'quality'. Such 'intangible value' related to image, brands and congruence of norms and values, etc., plays a role in the business-to-business context, but is particularly relevant in the consumer market. As indicated in Section 3.2, authors such as Pine and Gilmore (1999) and LaSalle and Britton (2003) argue that in (Western) society consumers become more and more geared towards realisation of intangible needs such as affiliation, love, esteem and self-realisation. Providers hence have to *Turn Ordinary Products into Extraordinary Experiences* to create extra, intangible added value above the 'rational' willingness to pay discussed under point 1.

Finally, Section 3.3.1 has—not without reason—the word 'co-creation' in its heading. Several authors point to the fact that the interaction between the provider and user can become a source of value in itself. This implies that one has to stop thinking in terms of a strict division between a firm network creating a value proposition and a client buying it, but rather to see the task of a firm network as creating a stage for a value co-creation process (compare Pine and Gilmore 1999). This strategy is of course most effective if a firm (network) is able to focus on the quality attributes of an offering: namely, a value co-creating process that users really see as making the difference (compare Kim and Mauborgne 1999, 2002). After all, providing other (unvalued) quality attributes is not worth the effort.

The advantage of product-services

It is essential to leave the product concept behind if one wants to define an appropriate output quality of a business system. The central point can be summed up in two words: Think Client! One has to understand the real need, function and satisfaction that have to be fulfilled. This is at the core of product-service development. The 'need behind the need' is the starting point for determining how satisfaction can be best realised: by delivering a product, a service, or a combination of the two, leading towards the ultimate experience of high satisfaction. Where this seems straightforward, it is astonishing how often firms still seem to focus on their product and its attributes, rather than working backwards from a deep understanding of what clients truly value. Indeed, the latter approach has been termed a radical new approach of 'value innovation' (Kim and Mauborgne 1997). Product-services also lead to a prolonged interaction with the client. This makes them a better stepping stone towards an interactive value co-creating process with a client than a business model purely based on product sales. Another advantage of the PSS concept is that it is in general relatively easy to combine the same product element with different service elements. This allows truly customised—and hence high-quality—value propositions to be made to different client groups based on the same product platform (compare Manzini *et al.* 2004).

Trade-offs: market risk

However, a move to product-services is not always a panacea:

- Where most PSS make life easier for the user, some also have a rather negative tangible added value. Compared with owning a product, in many cases renting, sharing or pooling a product implies that access becomes more difficult. It is not always available when wanted or not available on site. The user has to invest time or money to gain access

- Also, in taking satisfaction and experiences as a starting point, one can easily end up with a product as the offering generating the highest intangible added value:
    - Product-related service: consumers of products may value the freedom to choose their own service providers
    - Use-oriented services: often renting, sharing or pooling a product does not give the esteem, the sense of control, the experience of freedom, and hence the satisfaction of owning it (e.g. a car)
    - Result-oriented services: since the provider and user agree on a result, the user loses influence on which *means* are used to reach the result. This can be valued very negatively

- Also, in a more indirect way, the tangible added value of a PSS can be lower as well. If the industry is still in a life-cycle stage where traditional product and process innovations are the key to high-quality and well-performing products, a firm that diverts resources to developing a new business model such as PSS

Car-sharing systems may have become more professional over time, but even the most successful example (Mobility® Car Sharing in Switzerland with 60,000 members) is still responsible for a very small part of the overall mobility market (in terms of passenger-kilometres travelled). This is despite the fact that participation in a car-sharing system is in general considerably more cost-effective than owning a car. A key aspect is that users probably still do not have the same direct access or the direct availability that is experienced when one owns a car. It is still a bit more hassle to arrange a journey, which is at odds with the trend towards more convenience in society. And, also, taking pride in the fact that one drives one's own car is an important intangible value factor. The tangible and intangible value of a car share is hence much lower than a car in ownership. Car-sharing companies hence have to work on ways to reduce the aforementioned client sacrifices. Their competitive position may really change if, on top of this, they succeed in making the offer of a car-sharing system a true experience: for example, by taking advantage of the fact that for every journey in principle a dedicated vehicle according to the mood, goal and journey of the user can be offered (whereas those who own a car are confined for years to the vehicle they initially bought).

Box 3.12 Example: car sharing

Sources: SusProNet research; Meijkamp 2000; www.mobility.ch

may lose focus on what is the real key to value for the consumer. In the worst case, the firm may start to lose its focus on its core competences.

3.3.2 Minimising system costs versus financial risk

The essence

This point concerns the costs that the provider network and the consumer bear in realising the functionality, satisfaction or value that the final consumer experiences. It is the difference between the traditional 'tangible' production costs (e.g. resources, time input and cost of capital used) and the tangible or objective value for the consumer (e.g. resources, time input and cost of capital saved). Everything—and particularly the functionality or satisfaction delivered—being equal, in principle the system that generates the lowest integral costs will finally prevail.[13]

Many authors have written on operational excellence, leaner production, just-in-time management, and so on. Firms should standardise procedures, work on reducing their overheads, cutting out redundant activities and improving the communication between business units and departments.[14] They should carefully streamline the supply chain to minimise stocks, and they should carefully plan their staffing. And, by better controlling the internal production activities, or value chain, the total quality of their product/service should be improved and the number of deficient outputs produced minimised. Also, processes between companies need to be streamlined, such as ordering and supplying processes—a potential source of impressive productivity gains (Hammer 2001a, b). And, of course, firms should concentrate on what they are really good at: using their core competences to the fullest and outsourcing all non-core activities that can be done more efficiently by external suppliers. In a globalised world, this may imply relocation of production to or outsourcing activities to providers from low-cost countries.[15] Finally, firms should be careful when to buy assets, hire personnel, contract resources, and so on; they should do that when prices are (still) low.

The advantage of product-services

The above already indicates that outsourcing—which basically implies seeking a product-service provider to perform a non-core activity for the firm—can be an important mechanism to lower system costs. But also if one looks at the value proposition, a variety of mechanisms can make product-service systems more cost-efficient in generating the same output as a traditional product system:

13 This assumes a transparent pricing of cost elements over the life-cycle, and a rather rational behaviour of actors. In practice, such boundary conditions are not always met. Consumers often decide on the basis of a (clearly visible) purchase price of a product, and do not take the subsequent use phase costs into account.

14 Originally developed within the (physical) manufacturing industry, the theories on leaner production have also found their way to the service industry and have led to considerable productivity gains (Swank 2003).

15 Moves that have become known under terms such as 'offshoring': for example, the outsourcing of call centre activities to a firm in India.

1. Product-oriented services: the provision of additional services to the product, or advice and consultancy of use may lead to a more efficient use of the product

2. Use-oriented services: the same artefact may be shared or used by different users, leading to a lower capital need in the system. If the product is pooled, then also the use phase costs are shared by a number of users

3. Result-oriented services: with a user paying for a result or satisfaction, all elements in producing this result become cost factors whereas in a traditional product system the product is a profit centre. The provider now has the possibility (and in fact faces a very strong incentive) to reduce the overall integrated life-cycle costs of the production, use and waste management of the product

All these efficiency gains can be traced back to one basic cause. The activities in the system that lead to the final functional result are redistributed among actors in the production network and the user in such a way that all actors make most use of their core competences and that the use of material and human resources is minimised.

Trade-offs: financial risk

The above would suggest that product-services form a recipe to lower system costs. In practice, many trade-offs are at stake, which determine how activities should be distributed over the companies and users in a system to realise the lowest costs:

1. Each new inter-firm border creates (static) transaction inefficiencies: suppliers have to be chosen, contracts have to be agreed, cost compensation has to be transferred. Since a PSS is often put on the market by a network of firms, contractual relations and revenue sharing models will in general be more complicated than in the case of pure product sales. These transaction costs should be lower than the cost savings from enhanced efficiency (e.g. of an activity that is outsourced)

2. Each new inter-firm border also creates (dynamic) transaction inefficiencies. Particularly in not yet mature production systems (i.e. where product and process development is still rapid), learning across a variety of activities in the value system is often still needed. Such troubleshooting is normally more difficult across firm borders. Business systems that are not yet mature and standardised usually develop fastest when there is a high level of integration (e.g. Christensen et al. 2001, 2003)

3. In particular, use-oriented and result-oriented services have different financial profiles from pure product sales. In the latter case, the user pays the full value of the product at once. In the former case, the user pays for each time he or she uses the product or receives a result. The consequence is that the provider has to pre-finance the capital use related to the product(s) that play a role in the system

4. A switch from products to product-services not only redistributes activities in the system, but also influences risk profiles and feedback loops. For instance,

One of the success stories in the field of PSS is the emergence of chemical management services (CMS), a case of activity management. Many companies need to use chemicals for secondary activities such as degreasing and cleaning. Dealing with these chemicals can be difficult owing to environmental, health and safety, and waste management regulations. Handling chemicals is for most companies not a core competence, and so, particularly in the US, providers started to offer chemicals *and* their management: assistance in purchasing, managing and tracking chemicals. This shift to chemical services directly aligns the incentives of the service provider and manufacturer to reduce chemical use and costs. CMS providers are much more experienced in the management of chemicals than their clients, and also have greater bargaining power vis-à-vis producers of chemicals. Hence, both the CMS provider and the user can achieve bottom line benefits via reduced chemical use, costs and waste. So, CMS is an example where many factors work together in favour of this alternative model for chemical sales: costs savings by outsourcing a job to specialists (who in turn also have a higher bargaining power versus chemical suppliers), and an alignment of interests in the system that provides an incentive to find even more cost savings by using less chemicals.

Box 3.13 Example: chemical management services

Source: Reiskin et al. 1999; www.chemicalstrategies.org

a firm promising a result to another firm should be able to control—or at least predict—the (risk) factors that can jeopardise reaching that result, *even if they are in essence exogenous to the firm promising the result.* An example: if a firm just sells crop protection chemicals, it is the farmer who takes the risk of realising a sufficient crop yield. If a firm sells a pest control service that guarantees the result of a maximum of x% loss of crops due to pests, much more uncontrollable risks are taken. And this is an example where the result can still be defined in a meaningful way. There are also situations where it is very difficult to 'catch' the quality of the performance in meaningful indicators

5. Finally, the PSS may in the end require more or higher-priced human, capital and material input than the competing product system

3.3.3 Other benefits (power, innovation) versus investment and capability risk

The essence

Improving bargaining power and preventing development of substitutes
As more and more of our economy is made up of services, manufacturers of physical goods have a hard time keeping their businesses growing. Product markets become sat-

urated and, rather than market expansion, there are just replacement sales. Furthermore, in some areas manufacturing technology has matured. This implies that product performance and quality no longer form a source of differentiation. And it is of course such a type of uniqueness that gives actors in a value network the position and power to capture most of the value created. The result is value networks where the power to capture value must be searched for in nodes other than the manufacturing step. In the search for new value, many manufacturers hence move downstream, closer to the final user, for a very simple reason: that's where the money is (Wise and Baumgartner 1999; Davies *et al.* 2001; Sawhney *et al.* 2004).

Innovation
Though there are business sectors where changes are small, usually the business environment and the business itself is in a continuous state of flux. Companies hence ideally should be:

- Quick in picking up signals of change

- Flexible in adapting to change or even being the directors of change

This implies having an open-minded culture, an ability to 'think out of the box', an internal organisation that can bring new value propositions in a relatively short time to the market, options to change direction, and so on.

The advantage of product-services

Improving bargaining power and preventing development of substitutes
A downstream move in most cases implies not only that a (manufactured) product is sold, but also that the services, supplies, etc. needed downstream are included in the offering. This is in fact the case with all types of product-service:

- Product-oriented services: services needed downstream are included with the product in the value proposition

- Use-oriented services: the user buys access to a product, usually including all kinds of related service

- Result-oriented services: the supplier acts as system integrator, and creates a value proposition that encompasses all products and services needed to realise a result

In all these cases the provider ensures that the client has to purchase the (generally more profitable) downstream services in a combined package with the product. In short: the client is 'tied in'. The downstream move also allows the provider to create unique and customised client relationships, which become a form of unique knowledge to the supplier and hence a source of competitive advantage in itself. Offering a product-service in the main market rather than a product may create a contribution to the defence against the development of substitutes. Since product-services normally create contractual relations that last a longer time (particularly compared with a transaction at a point of sale), they make it more difficult for customers to switch providers.

Innovation

Product-services have a number of characteristics that in principle can improve speed, ability and flexibility to innovate:

1. Usually, there is more intimate contact with the client than in the case of one-off product sales. This usually allows for the development of a deeper understanding of the true needs and problems of the client, which is a good basis for a quick innovation of the offering

2. Product-services can be stepping stones for developing new competences or learning how to develop relationships with firms possessing complementary competences. They hence may generate a significant option value

3. Product-service development usually needs the use (and hence development) of dynamic capabilities related to product development, strategic decision-making and alliance formation. This will become a source of lasting flexibility and innovative power of the company (compare Section 3.1.4)

4. 'Soft' aspects of a value proposition such as services often can be innovated quicker than the hardware side (the products and processes producing them)

Trade-offs: investment and capability risks

There are, however, a number of reasons why a downstream move is not a panacea:

1. It may well be that excellence in traditional product development and manufacturing is still the key to uniqueness, and hence power and competitive advantage (e.g. in the introduction and growth stage of an industry life-cycle). Then, the clear priority for allocating resources is of course maintaining such excellence rather than diverting them to something new like PSS

2. The downstream move usually implies that the company needs to develop or marshal totally new competences. As explained in the previous section, this:
   - Diverts from existing core competences
   - May cause significant transaction costs (particularly if there is no mutual trust, quick connection, or mutual learning with partners)

3. Since for many firms PSS development is something new, investments may be rather high. Successful investments may be impossible if the company has a very product-oriented culture and the management has no real interest in PSS

4. Putting a PSS on the market may lead to a loss of synergies and cannibalisation of existing business. For instance, a business unit putting a use- or result-oriented PSS on the market may find that a product produced by a competitor fits better in the PSS offering. Existing business partners not part of the PSS may retaliate and frustrate its development

5. A specific problem related to the innovation issue is that in principle a product-service concept as such cannot be protected by copyright, and hence may be relatively easily duplicated by competitors. In some cases this may result in

Douwe Egberts (DE) was in origin a coffee supplier. Normally, clients in the out-of-home market (offices and the like) would buy a traditional hot plate-based coffee machine from a reputable supplier, buy consumables such as coffee and filters separately, and make pots of coffee in the traditional way. This system had a number of problems. First, particularly in the smaller offices, buying coffee and filters was often ad hoc, as was making the coffee, cleaning the coffee corner and dealing with coffee filter waste. Second, after some time on the hot plate the quality of the brewed coffee severely deteriorated. DE was actually in a fairly dependent position: clients in principle could switch coffee brands overnight. DE decided to switch this situation to its advantage by starting to offer a result-oriented PSS: coffee systems delivering freshly brewed, good-quality coffee per cup—of course making use of DE coffee. The offer of DE avoids a lot of fuss in offices, allowing DE to charge a price for that. And DE created a much more powerful position in the value chain: once a DE machine is in place, the client in fact is committed to the DE system for a long time. A marketing representative of a well-known traditional hot plate coffee machine producer confessed to one of the authors of this book that the company had missed the boat as a result of its highly product-oriented culture. It focused on improving its coffee machine, and did not look at new business models. And all of a sudden it was beaten out of the office market by a player that used to have low bargaining power in the value chain, and had little experience in making coffee machines. The move made by DE is in many ways an example of how to exploit the potential of PSS. DE's offering formed considerable added value for the user. And the company improved its strategic position in the value chain considerably.

Box 3.14 Example: from providing coffee to fresh-brewed coffee supply

Source: Goedkoop *et al*. 1999; SusProNet research

a disadvantage for first movers, since followers can learn from their mistakes and hence may be able to create the same value proposition with considerably less investment

3.4 Discussion per type of PSS

Table 3.3 gives a detailed summary of the previous sections. From it, we derive the following sub-criteria under the four main headings used in Section 3.3 (compare Tukker 2004):

1. The user value (co-)created
   - Tangible value
   - Intangible value

2. The (operational) system costs generated
   - Tangible costs
   - PSS specific attention points: risk premium, transaction costs, pre-financing costs

3. Dynamic value creation potential
   - The power position in the system
   - Defence against substitutes
   - ≠ The speed, ability and flexibility to innovate and shape the future

4. The investment needed and capability risk to develop the new (business) system
   - Investment in PSS development (building the structure, building core and complementary capabilities; overcoming opposition of suppliers and distributors and other existing business partners, etc.)
   - Other capital losses: cannibalisation, synergies, etc.

We will now discuss how the eight types of PSS discerned in this book score on these criteria (see Table 3.4).

3.4.1 Analysis per type of PSS

The analysis below cannot, by definition, give more than a generic list of attention points. Whether a PSS will be profitable business in a specific case will depend on (a) the characteristics (strength and weaknesses) of the firm and (b) the characteristics (threats and opportunities) of the market environment (e.g. the need area, characteristics of the PSS, for which [B2B or B2C] target group it is meant, etc). The need area chapters and final conclusions of this book will specify to some extent the generic analysis below, summarised in Table 3.4:

	Generic strategies	Potential advantages of a PSS value proposition compared with product sales	Potential risks and attention points of a PSS value proposition compared with product sales
Co-creation of user value versus market risk	• Creating tangible value: reducing client sacrifices or fulfilling unmet, tangible needs • Creating intangible value (brands, experiences) • Create diversified and customised offerings (e.g. via mass customisation)	• Inherent orientation on final client needs allows for developing innovative ways of function fulfilment (value innovation and value co-creation solutions) • Potential for customisation by combining the same product element with different service elements	• Tangible value: traditional product and process innovation are still the key to highly valued offerings and a shift to PSS distracts from the crucial focus • Intangible value: owning a product gives a better experience or quality than making use of a product-service (may particularly be relevant in B2C) • Value/cost ratio: added value above a product offer does not outweigh extra production costs and investment/capability risks (see below)
Minimising system costs versus financial risk	• Lean production and consumption: maximising the intensity of use of assets, optimising overheads, minimising stocks and gate-to-gate production times, often by standardising and modularising product platforms, build-to-order systems and TQM • Peak shaving (optimising in time): buying assets, covering capital needs, hiring staff, contracting resources, etc., at moments when markets are low • Globalisation (optimising in space): relocation/off shoring activities to places with the best factor conditions (including inefficiencies caused by any extra transport, storage, management, etc. needed) • Redistribution of activities and focus on core competences	• More efficient use of products (product-oriented services) • More intensive use of products (use-oriented services) • Life-cycle costs become the responsibility of one player who now can optimise over the life-cycle (result-oriented services) • Redistribution of activities in the value network so that each firm focuses best on its core competences	• Regular production costs: apart from PSS-specific factors below, the PSS may require more or higher-priced human, capital and material input than the competing product system • Transaction inefficiencies: 　– Static: contracting and revenue sharing is usually more complicated 　– Dynamic: in not yet mature, standardised systems often troubleshooting across activities is needed but difficult if these are separated by firm borders • Pre-financing product-related capital costs: the price of the product sold is paid in full by the user, but only recovered in instalments if one offers a use- or result-oriented service • Higher risk profile: particularly for use- and result-oriented services, the provider takes over responsibility of the use phase of the product. This can be risky if the provider cannot estimate or control costs or performance in this use phase • Higher ambiguity costs (particularly for result-oriented services): the result cannot be defined in sufficiently operational terms

TABLE 3.3 Enhancing value in business systems (continued over)

	Generic strategies	Potential advantages of a PSS value proposition compared with product sales	Potential risks and attention points of a PSS value proposition compared with product sales

Other benefits versus investments and capability risks	*Improving the power position (vis-à-vis clients, suppliers and substitutes)*
	• Create valuable, rare, inimitable and non-substitutable resources
	  – Develop relevant core competences
	  – Develop an IPR portfolio
	  – Set the standard for products with network effects
	• Focus on activities that are nodes in the value network
	• Block access of competitors to resources, distribution, sales and communication channels; create entry barriers by building size in assets, visibility, etc.
	
	Improving speed, ability and flexibility to innovate
	• Invest in dynamic capabilities
	• Create a foresight/scenario planning function
	• Invest in relevant niches to create and consolidate options
	• Ensure rapid product and service development processes (e.g. via rapid prototyping) and flexible production
		Improving the power position (vis-à-vis clients, suppliers and substitutes)
		• The offering usually includes more profitable activities in the system than product manufacturing alone
		• PSS builds unique client relationships that become a source of competitive advantage in themselves
		• Contracts are longer-term, which gives some protection against substitutes
		
		Improving speed, ability and flexibility to innovate
		• Intimate client contacts give a direct feedback on potential improvements in the offering and true underlying needs
		• PSS needs new competences which can be stepping stones for further innovations
		• PSS development requires and hence usually improves 'dynamic capabilities': alliance formation, reconfiguration, learning
		• 'Soft' aspects of a value proposition usually can be innovated faster than hardware (products and processes)
			Investment and capability risks
			• New core PSS competences (to be developed in-house): forms a capability risk and/or asks for high investments when there is:
			  – A low connection with existing core competences and unique selling points
			  – A product-oriented rather than client-oriented company culture and structure
			  – No interest from top management to invest in PSS
			• New complementary PSS competences (to be marshalled from partners): form a capability risk and/or ask for high investments when there is:
			  – No mutual trust
			  – No complementarities (in size, culture, capabilities, interests)
			  – No quick connection nor mutual learning
			  – The PSS is complicated; too many partners are needed; the network becomes unmanageable
			  – Current business partners or contracts block change
			• Other potential investment risks or risks on capital losses:
			  – Loss of synergies or cannibalisation: synergies between existing business units may get lost, or even internal competition is created, due to a switch of one unit to PSS
			  – First-mover disadvantage: a PSS cannot easily be copyrighted and followers may learn from a first mover's mistake

TABLE 3.3 (from previous page)

PSS type	User value/ market risk		System costs/ financial risks		Ability to capture value (now and in the future)			Investment and capability risk	
	Tangible value	Intangible value	Tangible costs	Risk premium finance, transaction cost	Power position (% value captured)	Defence to substitutes Client loyalty	High speed of innovation	Investment in PSS development	Other transition costs
1 Product-related service	0/+	0/+	0	0	0	+	0/+	–/0	0
2 Product-related advice and consultancy	0/+	0/+	0	0	0	+	0/+	–/0	0
3 Product lease	0/+		0/–	0/–	+	+/–	0	–	0
4 Product renting or sharing	!	!	+	–				–	–
5 Product pooling	!	!	+	–				–	–
6 Pay-per-unit use	+		+/0	!	+	+	+	–	0
7 Activity management	+	+	+/0	0/–	+	+	+	–	0
8 Functional result	0	!	+(?)	!			+	!	!

+ In general better than reference;   0 In general indifferent;   – In general worse than reference
! Critical factor for which a case-specific analysis is needed;   Blank: No judgement

TABLE 3.4 A discussion of the value characteristics of different types of PSS

1. Product-related services (1) and product-related advice and consultancy (2) usually provide additional tangible value for the user by enabling a more efficient use of the product. The provider makes more costs for material and human resources to provide the service, so it all comes down to the question of whether the provider can do the job more efficiently than the user. There is a lower client barrier (particularly if financing schemes are offered), a higher client loyalty and, due to more intensive client contacts, some increase in the speed of innovation. A product-oriented company embarking on these types of PSS usually has to make some investments in capital and organisational transitions. There is no cannibalisation since the original product is still offered. Since these types of PSS still give the product centre stage, they are excellent options for product-oriented firms to get started with PSS

2. Product lease (3) has a tangible value for the user, since various costs and activities (such as financing and maintenance) are shifted to the provider. User value via reduced transaction costs can be realised, too, if the leasing contract allows for an easy replacement of the product by another suiting a

changed need pattern (think of a growing family that needs a bigger car; compare Mont 2001a and Wong 2001). The provider might have to take provision for the fact that leased equipment tends to be used less carefully than products in ownership. Since the provider remains the owner of the product, it has to pre-finance capital costs. Barriers to attracting new clients are low owing to low initial investment by the client. User loyalty might improve (the product plus maintenance, etc. is provided), but the user can still easily switch to other providers. Since leasing companies use products provided by others, no influence on innovation is assumed. There is no cannibalisation if the lease is offered for the own product only

3. Product renting and sharing (4) can cut direct costs for the user considerably, particularly if it concerns a product that is not often used. It is also much easier to switch from the specific product model used. But, particularly in a B2C context, renting and sharing generates new 'costs': a user now has to put time and effort into getting access to the material artefact. In a B2C context, this PSS type is also likely to score poorly in terms of intangible value: rental equipment in many cases does not contribute to (self-)esteem, or 'priceless' experiences, though there are exceptions ('rent this BMW and be a king for a day'). Since the provider keeps on owning the product, it has a higher capital need. However, because of the shared use, the product is used much more intensively and the overall capital need in the system is considerably lower. Owing to the low initial costs, the access barrier for new clients is low. The provider has to invest in a system that manages access to the product. If the provider used to be a product producer, it cannibalises its own market. Implementing product renting and sharing systems hence seems to be more difficult in a B2C than a B2B context

4. Product pooling (5). The analysis is virtually the same as for renting and sharing

5. Pay-per-unit use (6). There is a clear tangible value for the user since various activities (maintenance, etc.) are outsourced as an integrated long-term package to the provider. The provider gets control over a larger part of the system, which gives it an incentive to look for efficiency gains that were not relevant in a business model based on product sales. Usually, this results in lower system costs.[16] The providers' position in the value chain becomes better, in relation to its direct access to clients and (enforced) client loyalty. The provider has to be able to predict the behaviour of the user, since otherwise no good cost calculation can be made and a risk premium has to be included. Since the product stays in the ownership of the provider additional capital is needed. There are low barriers for new clients and the good client contacts in principle lead to a better innovation potential

16   See for instance the business models of copier producers Xerox and Océ, which are based on pay-per-print. The incentive to sell copiers is now replaced by an incentive to take back old copiers and re-use and upgrade the still working parts into 'new' copiers to place with clients.

6. Activity management (7). Activity management shifts personnel and material costs from the user to the provider. Usually the direct operational costs in the system as a whole become lower since the provider makes (and has to make) gains by organising the outsourced tasks more efficiently by specialised knowledge. One aspect of this is that the outsourced task is now managed with much less effort by the user. It is important that good performance criteria can be defined, since otherwise discussion about the delivered result can arise between user and provider (risk premium and transaction cost issues). Since activity management is usually arranged via longer-term contracts and covers an integrated package of product-services, client loyalty is almost automatically embedded in the business model. The specialisation might lead to a high speed of innovation. Development costs of the PSS are probably low since for the provider it is probably already a standardised package; as activity (and hence personnel) transfer usually has to take place, other transition costs occur

7. Functional result (8). Since the same function is offered, in principle the user could give it the same tangible value. Intangible value is another matter, though, and cannot be judged without defining the specific system. In principle, the provider could try to provide a solution with much lower input of human resources and materials. Yet, since the provider promises a result at a high level of abstraction, here problems about the ability to agree about performance indicators, and the level of control in achieving this performance, can be an important (if not prohibitive) problem. It is often also complicated to estimate the costs that have to be made to realise this performance (which translates to a low score on the risk premium issue). This model leaves the highest degree of freedom with regard to innovation. For a producer of products, this switch implies a real turnaround of thinking and investing in a fundamentally different business model. Also, a product producer switching to a business model based on functional results may face the problem that cannibalisation of its existing business by the new concept may be at stake. For the best performance, a real functional result may require the use of product components that are made in other industries or, worse, by direct competitors

3.4.2 Conclusion

The overall picture is that product-oriented services are the least radical ones and are probably rather easily applicable by traditional product-oriented firms. Use-oriented services are now also common business models, offering greater flexibility, lower system costs, and lower upfront payments for the user. However, particularly in a B2C context, use-oriented services such as product renting, pooling and sharing seem to have a relatively high chance of creating tangible and intangible client sacrifices. Activity management (a result-oriented service) and pay-per-use (a use-oriented service) are becoming more and more common. They allow users to concentrate on their own core business, and the outsourced activities are usually performed much more cost-effectively by service providers than by users. The most important attention point for the provider of these PSS is the ability to agree with the user a set of good performance criteria, and to predict/influence the behaviour of the user within reasonable margins. This cost control/risk element is particularly relevant for the PSS type 'Functional result', since the provider takes over all liabilities that in a product-based system would fall to the user.

3.5 Conclusion: factors determining the business case for product-services

It is almost a truism that society has become more and more service-oriented: services make up some 70% of the GNP in most Western economies. This, and other societal megatrends such as specialisation, internationalisation, smaller and double-income families, clearly favours product-services. Innovation of the value proposition by offering a product-service rather than a product can help to:

● Adjust the quality of the offering much better to the needs of the client since:
  – Product-services demand an inherent orientation on the final client needs and the full business system fulfilling these needs. This creates a mind-set for developing truly innovative ways of function fulfilment
  – Products can usually rather easily be linked with a variety of service components, allowing for customised offerings

● Lower the costs in the system since:
  – Products are used more efficiently (product-oriented PSS) or intensively (use-oriented PSS)
  – One actor gets a full overview and responsibility for the total system costs related to fulfilling the final need or satisfaction, so that true cost optimisation becomes possible. This actor also now has a strong incentive to find radically more cost-effective ways of delivering the same result (result-oriented services)
  – Activities are distributed in such a way in the system that each actor makes best use of his or her core competences

● Improve the strategic position of the firm in the value chain, improve its innovation potential and create defence against substitution since:
  – The company moves (often downstream) to include activities in its offering that have a higher profit margin than traditional manufacturing (product-oriented, result-oriented and in part use-oriented services)
  – A more intensive (contractual) relationship with the client is arranged, which leads to higher loyalty, better insight into problems with the current offering, and insight into the true problems the offering has to solve for the client
  – In general a more intensive use of dynamic capabilities

However, it is by no means claimed that product-services in all cases deliver these attractive bonuses for providers. In a variety of cases, a product-service offering will have a significantly lower value than a product offering. People may like to maintain their product themselves. Hiring or pooling products can be awkward if fast and easy access is essential. Result-oriented services can be a horror if the provider all of a sudden uses a means to reach the result that the user does not like. Any efficiency that may be gained can be frittered away because of daunting transaction costs or uncontrollable risks in the use phase (in the case of a result-oriented offering). And sometimes focusing on excellence in product manufacturing and design is the key to uniqueness and hence power in the value network; diverting resources to PSS development may be the wrong way forward. And, on top of this, development of a PSS may come at a significant cost. The PSS may be complicated and require a lot of investment. Often, totally new competences need to be developed or marshalled. In the latter case, new business partners have to be found. It may also be that the PSS offering cannibalises existing business.

	Organisational strategies	Design strategies (offering)	Development strategies (process)
Market risk (will customers like it?)	● Focus on existing customers ● Train sales force to build on early adoption success stories while selling ● Train sales force to clarify return on investment ● Train sales force to manage customer expectations	● Use partners to fill in reputation gaps ● Offer trial periods ● Reduce customer adoption risk	● Prototype and iterate ● Blueprint carefully according to customer expectations
Capability risk (can we do it?)	● Incubate separately ● Create, acquire or partner with a company that has a service culture	● Design services that build on existing product platforms ● Design product architectures to support services ● Involve lead users	● Use partners to fill competence gaps ● Inventory new competences
Financial risk (is it profitable?)	● Use partner assets ● Use technology and internet to decrease labour costs and inconvenience by encouraging customer self-service and/or automated service	● For smaller customers create productised versions of services ● Use annuity payment model to obtain steady revenues	● Quantify economic value to customers and compare with service delivery cost ● Perform robust, early and frequent economic value analysis

TABLE 3.5 Risks and risk management of growth with (product-)services

Source: adapted from Sawhney *et al*. 2004

All and all, there is nothing magic about PSS. A company has to treat it like any idea for a new value proposition. It has to assess the market risk and opportunity, the financial risk and opportunity, and the capability risk and opportunity. But investigation of whether PSS has something for a firm should not be avoided. First, the business literature has developed scores of approaches for managing the risk factors related to PSS development (see Table 3.5); we will make our own contribution to this in Chapter 5. And, second, given the megatrends favouring PSS, sticking to the safe old business model of selling products has a clear danger. If there is better value to be created, or cost reductions to be realised by embarking on a PSS business model, sooner or later a company will find that out. And the question then is: will this company be you or your competitor?

In many cases, a thorough analysis will show that a PSS can form an interesting new way of doing business. But it may also be that traditional product-oriented systems appear to be the most efficient way of delivering the highest value for the user. Chapters 7–11 will offer a more dedicated analysis of the different need areas in which PSS makes good business, or not.

This balanced outcome may not be applauded by those who believe that PSS is the way forward to the Factor X world. But we cannot help it. The truth is that it is in some instances very logical, and from their perspective highly efficient, that firms still put products rather than results on the market. Such product-oriented business models may still flourish, even in a world where the megatrends indicate that in general the future for business in Europe probably lies in putting service- and product-service-oriented value propositions on the market.

4
Product-services and sustainability

Arnold Tukker

TNO, The Netherlands

Ursula Tischner and Martijn Verkuijl

econcept, Germany

It has become almost a platitude that radical innovations are needed to prevent nature from breaking down under the combined pressure of population growth and the growth in wealth per capita. In the next 50 years, the world population will rise from around 6 to 9 billion people (Lutz *et al.* 2004). The wealth per capita in areas such as China, India and Africa still needs to grow by a factor of five or more only to come close to the prosperity that Japan, Western Europe and the US currently have. This Factor 10 increase in combined population and economic growth will lead to Factor 10 more environmental pressure, if there is no change in the organisation of production and consumption patterns. Or, in reverse, if the environmental pressure is kept at the same level as it is now, a Factor 10 more effective fulfilment of needs should be reached (e.g. von Weizsäcker *et al.* 1997; Factor 10 Club 1997).

Some believe that the focus on function fulfilment that emerges from PSS (product-service system) thinking naturally leads to (absolute) decoupling of economic growth and environmental resource use,[1] since a function fulfilment service would be inherently lower in material usage (Schmidt-Bleek 1993; Stahel 1998). However, until now scholars from the sustainability arena have had little success in finding a structural foundation or explanation for the claim that product-services are inherently more sustainable than products. This, again, goes back to the situation that (sustainable) PSS

---

1 Economic growth while at the same time lowering the material flows through the economy.

research still lacks a coherent theoretical foundation, focuses too much on concepts, individual cases and normative desires, without developing an overarching picture (Hockerts and Weaver 2002). Indeed, some authors even doubt if a service-oriented economy will give the radical sustainability improvements desired. In an extensive input–output study, Suh (2004) showed that the life-cycle environmental impacts of services do not really differ significantly from those of products. His explanation is that what is sold as a service in practice is often an 'envelope' around traditional products, or that in earlier life-cycle stages traditional products are used to produce the service. This leads to another question we want to answer here: *Which factors determine whether a PSS generates fewer material flows and emissions than the competing product system, and which factors determine whether a PSS provides incentives for sustainable behaviour?* We will answer this question in the following stages.

1. The whole underlying assumption behind the Factor X debate is that it is essentially possible to realise a sharp decoupling of economic growth of material use. If—at abstract level—this is really possible, what kind of economic growth is one looking for? Is there any theory that can help us to understand the concept of decoupling?

2. The idea that product-services can contribute to decoupling has been discussed already intensively in the literature. What arguments have been brought forward in that debate?

3. We will try to understand in detail which mechanisms are relevant to describe the relation between product-services and sustainability. What is the inherent sustainability improvement? What is the change in system dynamics? What about rebound effects?

4. As a proof of the pudding we will show the results of a statistical analysis of 200 PSS cases: can they expect to reduce material flows? If so, to what extent?

4.1 Towards an understanding of decoupling

4.1.1 The need for Factor X

Decoupling can be defined as economic growth that does not cause a similar growth in environmental pressure (resource use and emissions). Generally, two forms of decoupling are discerned:

- Relative decoupling: the environmental impact grows, but less rapidly than the economy

- Absolute decoupling (such as the Factor 4/10 goal): the environmental impact diminishes while the economy as a whole grows

The need for radical 'Factor X' objectives seems to be accepted by many as a kind of general vision (e.g. Factor 10 Club 1997). But translating this notion to goals for specific sectors or impact categories generates much more discussion. Various authors—particularly from what can be called the 'Wuppertal school'—argue that ultimately material use drives all impacts caused by our economic system. Hence, each sector and activity has to contribute a radical reduction of material use per final consumption unit (e.g. Hinterberger *et al.* 1997). But others frame the problem differently. In its communication on a strategy for natural resources, the EU rejects the idea that the sheer input of resources into the economic system is invariably a problem. The real problems are the *emissions* related to resource use—such as CO_2 from fossil fuels (EU 2003). For many resources a direct link between resource use and emissions is absent (e.g. Nielsen *et al.* 2004). A similar position was taken by the Dutch Ministry of Environment Advisory Council. They see certain emissions (particularly of greenhouse gases), the use of certain biotic resources and biodiversity loss as problematic, but not the use of non-renewable resources in itself (VROM Raad 2002).[2]

In practice the difference between these positions may not be as large as it seems. For instance, it is unlikely that an emissions problem such as climate change will be solved without radical changes in our energy provision system that is now still largely based on fossil energy resources. Hence, at least for some types of impact, and for some resources, the need for absolute decoupling exists. For reaching absolute decoupling, two aspects are relevant, and are discussed in the following sections:

● Options for intervention in the production–consumption system that can contribute to a lower environmental impact

● The extent to which 'rebound effects' can occur: unintended consequences of the intervention, which cause developments that totally or partially annihilate its (initial) positive effect

4.1.2 'Enhancing quality of life, reducing resource use': intervention options for decoupling

In principle, the goal of consumption is to contribute to quality of life. Our primary interest is hence to see how final consumer 'quality of life' can be de-linked from environmental impact. Taking final consumer satisfaction rather than a seemingly 'neutral' parameter such as consumer expenditure as a final goal is of course a problem in itself. What is 'quality of life'? Can it be understood in a hedonic sense, such as 'satisfaction' or 'happiness'? Or should it be seen in a spiritual way: that is, that conditions are created that allow people to develop their capacities and potential, and hence grow to 'more complete' and 'mentally richer' human beings? Such questions have far from unambiguous answers, and indeed touch on normative questions such as what one sees

---

2   Another discussion is to what extent decoupling will occur more or less 'naturally'. The hypothesis of the so-called 'environmental Kuznets curve' postulates that in a growing economy the environmental impacts will first rise at the same pace as economic growth, but that later a relative and even an absolute diminishing of impacts will occur. Researchers such as de Bruyn (1999) and Chertow (2000) have shown that this has indeed been the case for emissions of substances such as SO_2, particulate matter and VOCs (volatile organic compounds), but not for CO_2—even in the former case the causes were targeted decoupling policies.

as the meaning of life.[3] But it is also obvious that just assuming that income (even if expressed in purchasing power parity terms) is a neutral determinant for quality of life would deny such value questions. It would also deny discussions among economic and other experts on whether national income is a true measure for wealth growth (e.g. Segal 1999; Jackson 2004).

An influential formula to describe the relation between production, wealth and environmental impact was first proposed by Ehrlich and Holdren (1971):

$I = P \times A \times T$, with
I = environmental impact
P = population (in capita)
A = affluence per capita
T = (technical) eco-efficiency of production

This so-called IPAT formula directly points at the three main drivers for environmental impact: population, affluence and technical efficiency. However, for the analysis of how to reach decoupling the formula is less useful. The product of P and A equals economic expenditure, leaving T as the (only) factor that can lead to decoupling. The reduction of neither population nor wealth is a viable strategy for reducing impact. First, population growth is currently not the key determinant for environmental impact, and is difficult to influence anyway.[4] Second, the whole concept of sustainability is based on improving quality of life, particularly for the world's poorer majority, within the Earth's carrying capacity (WCED 1987). Various authors hence have proposed formulas in which the 'T' factor is further decomposed (see e.g. de Bruyn 1998; Cleveland and Ruth 1999; Chertow 2000; VROM Raad 2002; Azar *et al.* 2002). We propose here the following decomposition and related decoupling strategies (see Box 4.1 for the rationale and mathematical approach):

1. The impact efficiency of technology (i.e. the emissions generated and resources used in a given technical production structure)

2. The product function efficiency of production (i.e. the output of a given production system)

3. The intensity of use of product functions

4. The product function composition of expenditure (i.e. to what extent income is spent on material artefacts)

5. The ratio of quality of life and expenditure

---

3 These examples were taken from the inaugural exhibition 'Happiness: a survival guide for art and life' of the Mori Art Museum, Tokyo, October 2003–January 2004. The exhibition discerned four ideal types of happiness: 'back to nature' Arcadia, 'spiritual' Nirvana, 'hedonic' Desire and finally Harmony, in a way a blend of the former types. See www.mori.art.museum/html/eng/exhibition/index.html.

4 Most forecasts now predict a world population of 9–10 billion people in 2050 (Lutz *et al.* 2004). Furthermore, about 70–80% of the current sustainability problems are driven by consumer expenditures of 1–2 billion people from developed economies and the (growing) middle class in emerging economies (compare Myers and Kent 2004).

The relation between impact and consumer expenditure (CE, which is the product of P and A) can be written as follows. What we call (after de Bruyn 1998) 'product composition of expenditure' (PCE) determines which fraction of the consumer expenditure CE is spent on the use of material products or immaterial value. The intensity of the use of products (IUP) determines how many products have to be produced. The (product) efficiency of production (PEP) determines how much production activity is needed to produce these products. The impact efficiency of technology (IET, the emission factors and resource intensity of production processes at a given output) determines how much impact per unit production occurs. Multiplication of consumer expenditure with these factors gives the total environmental impact (formulas a–c). In environmental input–output analysis, life-cycle impacts are calculated by multiplying a consumption vector, a technology matrix and an intervention matrix, which fits well with the structure proposed here. The product of CE and PCE is actually the consumption vector, which distributes the income in a region over different expenditure categories. The intervention matrix reflects emissions and resource use per unit process and equals IET. The technology matrix covers the two remaining factors (see e.g. Heijungs 1997; Suh 2004; Weidema *et al.* 2005; Tukker *et al.* 2006).

(a)

$$\text{Impact} = \frac{\text{Impact}}{\text{Production activity}} \times \frac{\text{Production activity}}{\text{Product output}} \times \frac{\text{Product output}}{\text{Product use}} \times \frac{\text{Product use}}{\text{Euro spent}} \times \text{Consumer expenditure}$$

(b)

$$\text{Impact} = \begin{array}{c}\text{Impact efficiency}\\\text{of technology}\end{array} \times \begin{array}{c}\text{Product efficiency}\\\text{of production}\end{array} \times \begin{array}{c}\text{1/Intensity of}\\\text{use of products}\end{array} \times \begin{array}{c}\text{Product composition}\\\text{of expenditure}\end{array} \times \begin{array}{c}\text{Consumer}\\\text{expenditure}\end{array}$$

(c)

$$I = IET \times PEP \times IUP^{-1} \times PCE \times CE$$

(d)

$$\text{Impact} = \text{Intervention matrix} \times \text{Technology matrix} \times \text{Consumption vector}$$

The relation with quality of life (QoL) and consumer expenditure (CE) can now be written as follows. First, many consumer expenditures are merely 'obligations' (Illich 1977; Segal 1999): without doing them, one cannot function normally in society (for instance, the need to drive a car to the shopping centre since there is no local village shop (anymore), or buying expensive suits since that is the dress code in one's job). We call them expenditures on obliged needs, CE_ON, which must be subtracted from CE. Second, much of people's quality of life is not directly market-related (e.g. friendship, a feeling of control over one's destiny, safety of the neighbourhood). Such quality of life from non-market sources (QoL_NM) must be added to CE. These two corrections lead to a true quality of life (formulas e–f) and allow for calculating the benefit of enlarging the consumer expenditure CE. If extra CE has no influence on the non-market quality of life

Box 4.1 Relation between quality of life and environmental impact (continued opposite)

(QoL_NM), and the same is true for the 'obliged expenditure' (CE_ON), all expenditure contributes to an improved quality of life. However, if the extra consumer expenditure goes at the expense of non-market sources of quality of life, or enlarges the expenditure on 'obliged' consumption, the net effect on quality of life is less than proportional (formulas g–h).

(e)

Quality of life = Consumer expenditure + Quality from non-market sources − Consumer expenditure on 'obligatory needs'

(f)

$$QoL = CE + QoL\_NM - CE\_ON$$

(g)

$$\frac{\delta QoL}{\delta CE} = \frac{\delta CE}{\delta CE} + \frac{\delta QoL\_NM}{\delta CE} - \frac{\delta CE\_ON}{\delta CE}$$

(h)

% change in quality of life per % rise of consumer expenditure = 1 + Change in quality of non-market sources by rise of consumer expenditure − Change in expenditure on obliged needs by rise of consumer expenditure

Box 4.1 (from previous page)

Enhancing the impact efficiency of production: 'reducing emissions factors'

This decoupling strategy is probably still the most applied and is generally referred to as the first or second generation of environmental policy (e.g. Simons *et al.* 2001). It essentially concerns reducing the resource inputs and emissions of the system without fundamentally changing the technology of production and products produced:

- Implementing end-of pipe measures (e.g. catalysts on cars)

- Implementing cleaner technology (e.g. a more efficient paint spraying technology in paint shops)

For small mass flows (toxic emissions, SO_x) this strategy has brought major emissions reductions (e.g. MNP 2005), but it influences fewer of the major mass flows.

Enhancing the (product) efficiency of production: output with less production

This decoupling strategy seeks to produce the same product functionalities as output with less production (and use phase) activities. This can take place in two forms:

- A (usually marginal) improvement of the production efficiency of the existing system (e.g. producing the same amount of goods in shorter production runs)

- A radical innovation of the system that delivers the product functionality; for example:
  - An energy supply based on the use of 'solar income' (solar, wind and water energy)
  - Radically improved production processes in sectors such as chemistry and agriculture by application of, for example, nano- and biotechnology

The latter form implies in fact that the (technology) structure in society undergoes radical changes. This form of innovation in particular (in part in conjunction with the following one) is seen by its advocates as the way to reach a 'Factor X' reduction of emissions and material use per functionality (see e.g. Weaver *et al.* 2000).

Enhancing the intensity of use of product: multiple use

This strategy seeks to enhance the intensity of use of product functions (in the form of material artefacts), once they are produced. Approaches that one can think of are:

- Designing products with multiple functionalities

- Developing systems of renting, sharing and pooling the same product

The work of Meijkamp (2000) and Mont (2004) shows that such measures typically can lead to a Factor 2 improvement of environmental impact.

Reducing the product composition of expenditure: spending with less impact

This strategy encompasses inducing a shift to expenditure on non-material value components:

- Shifting expenses to the purchase of *non-material* or *intangible value*. Such immaterial value is created when customers attribute an extra wealth and hence start to pay for value elements such as:
  - Experiences, atmosphere, etc.
  - Brand names, image, etc.
  - Intellectual property rights, such as copyrights and patents (compare e.g. legally downloaded music files and software, for which the price is mainly determined by copyright, and [almost free] illegal ones)

- Shifting expenses to or realising economic growth by products and services with a relatively low life-cycle impact (which is, in fact, a variant of the former point)

Some see such growth in 'quality' and expenditure of services such as culture, media and amusement as very promising (e.g. RMNO 1999; VROM Raad 2002). But this seems optimistic.[5] Figure 4.1 illustrates the life-cycle impacts per euro for the total final con-

---

5   For instance, much 'amusement' consists of TV watching—and TVs with a plasma screen, which compete with fridges as a major electricity user in the home, are now penetrating fast in the Western world.

sumption in the EU-25, split up into 280 expenditure categories (Tukker *et al.* 2006; Huppes *et al.* 2006). Neglecting the top and bottom 5%, the difference in impact per euro between the 'dirtiest' and 'cleanest' category is at most a Factor 4. Several services (e.g. outdoor eating places) are among the top 15%, since they are an 'envelope' around a product infrastructure. Even if massive expenditure shifts from the 'dirtier' to 'cleaner' categories were possible, this will at best give a Factor 2 net improvement in environmental impact. And, on top of this, not all shifts are possible. In Figure 4.1, food products have the highest impact per euro. Expenditure on food of course cannot be brought down to zero in favour of products with less impact: humans cannot stop eating.[6]

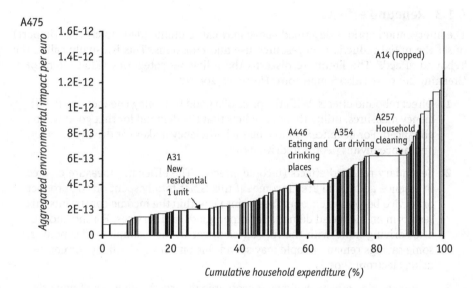

FIGURE 4.1 Impact per euro for 280 expenditure categories, EU-25

Source: Tukker *et al.* 2006

Enhancing quality of life per euro spent

This strategy focuses on two factors:

- Reducing 'obligatory needs' by creating 'no need' contexts: living conditions where one simply needs fewer material artefacts to reach the same result (e.g. a spatial policy planning that succeeds in reducing the need for commuting)

- Enhancing non-market-related quality-of-life factors

Various studies have plotted happiness of people (assessed via surveys) against income (e.g. between different countries or as change over time). These studies showed a

---

6   Of course, meat scores higher than most other foodstuffs, and a shift to diets with less expenditure on meat is not an impossible option.

rather mind-boggling result: once a certain threshold in income is surpassed, additional income has no influence on happiness (Veenhoven undated). There is also a considerable body of literature that suggests that fulfilment of basic needs in modern society is now possible only by using many material artefacts (Segal 1999). So, although the Japanese national income grew by a factor of five between 1959 and 1991, the increase in happiness was close to zero (cf. Hofstetter and Ozawa 2004). With all methodological discussions one could start, this suggests, at least, that the efficiency of income to create quality of life may show considerable room for improvement (Jackson *et al.* 2004).

4.1.3 Rebound effects

The intervention options described above may cause unintended effects that (in part) offset the initial reductions in resource use and emissions. This is usually called the 'rebound effect'.[7] The literature discerns the following categories (Khazzoom 1980; Greening 2000; see also Sanne 2001; Hertwich 2003):[8]

1. Direct rebound effects. With the price of a good becoming cheaper due to efficiency measures, utility theory predicts that the demand for that good will be enhanced. For instance: enhancing fuel efficiency makes car driving cheaper, and hence invites people to drive more

2. Secondary rebound effects (income effects). The efficiency measure creates in essence additional 'free income'. If this is not totally spent on the product or service becoming cheaper (see point 1), within the income constraints this results in an increased demand for other goods and services. For instance: if, after driving more with the fuel-efficient car in the example under point 1, some savings remain, people may spend this on package holidays or energy-using electronic goods

3. Economy-wide effects. Following economic theory, the changes of any price are likely to lead to readjustment of other prices and produced quantities at the macro level of the economy (also called the general equilibrium effect). For instance, fuel-efficient transport used in other production chains makes these products cheaper

4. Transformational effects. Changes in technology have the potential to change consumers' preferences, social institutions and the organisation of production. For instance, fuel-efficient and cheaper transport by cars may promote transport-intensive 'just-in-time' delivery in the production system

---

7   Some authors seem to consider as a 'rebound' general developments (e.g. growth of car traffic) unrelated to measures taken (e.g. introduction of car catalysts to reach lower NO_x emissions) (RMNO 1999). We do not favour this, since the word 'rebound' implies a relation between measure and (side-)effect.

8   Most literature uses economic mechanisms to explain rebounds. Other authors have suggested a 'rebound effect in time', since the available time is also a constraint for consumption activities (Binswanger 2001; Hofstetter and Ozawa 2004).

Not totally coincidental, the types of rebound effect listed here are in many ways the complement of the intervention options for decoupling in the former section. The same mechanisms are at stake, but work the wrong way around (see Table 4.1). The direct rebound effects, secondary rebound effects and economy-wide effects change the distribution and the volume of the basket of products that can be bought with the same income. The transformational effects play on the longer term, and are related to the notion of socio-technological change in Chapter 3, Section 3.2.1: eventually the production and consumption structure may change as such.[9]

Intervention mechanism	Rebound mechanism	
	Relatively short-term effects	Longer-term effects
1. Enhancing impact efficiency of production		
2. Enhancing product function efficiency output of production		
3. Enhancing the intensity of use of product functions		
4. Reducing the product composition of expenditure	• Direct and secondary rebound effect: – Savings consumed on the same product functionality – Savings consumed on other product functionalities • Economy-wide effects: new equilibrium changes available expenditure, prices, and hence total basket of product functionalities consumed	Transformational effects
5. Enhancing the ratio quality-of-life and expenditure	• Enhancing 'obligatory needs' • Reducing the 'non-market quality of life' – Shifting 'non-market quality-of-life factors' to the formal economy – Deterioration of non-market quality-of-life factors	

TABLE 4.1 Intervention mechanisms for decoupling and rebound mechanisms

9 This type of rebound is more difficult to quantify and predict than the former ones. An example: time-saving equipment in the household allowed women to work outside of the home—which in many countries was one of the driving factors behind the very rapidly rising house prices between 1985 and 2000, resulting in a situation that a family now *needs* a double income to buy a house of just average quality.

Surprisingly, the taxonomy above does not include rebound effects related to quality of life provided via processes that are not part of the formal economy. But these can be quite important (compare Segal 1999):

- Enhancing obligatory needs. A society that is not too careful about worker conditions may see a relatively high expenditure on healthcare. Safety in the neighbourhood, which in most European countries could be taken for granted 40 years ago, now needs continuous monitoring via camera systems, more intensive patrols and installation of burglar proof windows and doors

- Reducing non-market quality of life. Sometimes, 'economic growth' is little more than attaching a price tag to a 'service' that used to be for free. Taking care of toddlers, which was formerly done at home by a parent who was not involved in the formal economy, is now outsourced to a kindergarten.[10] And in the safety example above, despite all measures, the 'quality' experience may still be reduced

Quantifying the rebound effect is rather difficult, and heated debates have been going on about its importance (e.g. Lovins 1988; Khazzoom 1989). One of the most frequently quoted reviews (Greening 2000) shows, for a variety of energy reduction measures of electric end-use equipment, a (probably direct, secondary and economy-wide) rebound effect between 10 and 40%.

4.1.4 Conclusion: focal points for decoupling by PSS

Neglecting rebound effects, Table 4.2 reviews the potential for decoupling environmental impact from a growth in quality of life. So the potential for decoupling seems to be there. But the scientific jury is still out with regard to whether this will happen more or less automatically, as the theory of the 'environmental Kuznets curve' suggests. Historical studies have found examples of decoupling, but then mainly for substances such as SO_x and lead emissions to air, which could be reduced by targeted policy measures. For other (often larger) mass flows, temporary reductions were followed by re-coupling (e.g. de Bruyn 1998). As put by Cleveland and Ruth (1999):

> our knowledge of the extent of and mechanisms behind the patterns of material use are limited largely to individual materials or very specific industries, and most of those examples are metals . . . [T]he weight based material intensity of the economy may be falling, but it is unclear what, if any, significance this has. Despite claims to the contrary, there is no compelling macroeconomic evidence that the US economy is decoupled from material inputs.

All this seems to imply that one cannot bet that decoupling will arise more or less naturally. For sustainability problems where decoupling is seen as imperative, some kind of targeted intervention seems needed. Implementing PSS may be such a strategy—and an interesting one, since it potentially deals with the less traditional and more promis-

---

10   In their—otherwise very inspiring—book *The Experience Economy*, Pine and Gilmore (1999: 97) give in this respect a rather depressing quote: 'The history of economic progress consists of asking money for something that once was free.'

ing decoupling strategies in Table 4.2 (enhancing intensity of use, reducing product-related expenditure and enhancing quality of life). The next section discusses what the PSS literature has to say about this.

Intervention mechanism	Potential reductions of impact per unit quality-of-life (excluding rebounds)
Enhancing impact efficiency of production	● Small mass flows: several factors by end-of-pipe or cleaner technology ● Large mass flows: limited
Enhancing product function efficiency output of production	● Limited to intermediate, in case of incremental improvements and redesign ● Factor X in case of system innovation
Enhancing the intensity of use of product functions	● Factor 2 or more, depending on the sharing, pooling or function combination system
Reducing the product composition of expenditure	● Factor 2 (if limited to changes within existing product and service categories)
Enhancing the ratio quality-of-life and consumer expenditure	● Several factors?

TABLE 4.2 Ballpark data on the potential contribution of intervention mechanisms to decoupling of impact and quality of life

4.2 The contribution of product-services to sustainability

4.2.1 Environmental sustainability potential of product-service systems

Many authors suggest that a broad switch from product-oriented to service-oriented business models by industry could be such an intervention in support of decoupling.

Walter Stahel (Product-Life Institute, Geneva, Switzerland), one of the pioneers in this discussion, pleaded as early as the 1980s that we should 'Sell performance instead of goods'. This would move us from the industrial economy to the service economy, with the benefits of much higher resource productivity through (Stahel 2000):

● Longer utilisation of goods using techniques such as product life extension, remanufacture, re-use for furniture, automotive parts, etc. (which can be realised via product-oriented PSS)

● Systems solutions and more intensive utilisation of goods, which tend to go together and cover 'selling utilisation, results or function instead of goods': for example, leases, car-pooling, shared use of roads, railways (which can be realised via use-oriented PSS)

- Sufficiency solutions: organising operations so that need for a good or service is reduced or eliminated without compromising consumer demands (e.g. not washing unused hotel bath towels) (which can be realised via result-oriented PSS)

Discussion on the contribution of product-service business models to dematerialisation has emerged on many fronts. Heiskanen and Jalas (2000) identified two main mechanisms through which services may promote dematerialisation:

- Organisational opportunities. Services provide one way to organise a more efficient use of materials and products through shared product use, more intensive use, more professional use and better end-of-life management

- Economic incentives. Service providers may also have better incentives to economise in materials use; revenues are de-linked from material flows, and saving resources may actually become the principal source of revenues (e.g. energy services). However, there are also counter-incentives, and the strength and direction of incentives vary from one service type to another

Wong (2001), in his overview of the potential environmental benefits of PSS, points to similar mechanisms (see Table 4.3). Zaring *et al.* (2001), who studied product-services in a business-to-business context, discuss two other factors: the creation of intangible value and a change in user behaviour (see Fig. 4.2). In their view, product-service innovation can be related to an innovation of technology, the client interface, the service concept and the delivery system. Such innovations should lead to:

- An increased economic vitality (or added value; compare the issue of [intangible] user value discussed in Chapter 3, Section 3.3.1)

- A lower environmental impact, owing to:
  - A higher efficiency on the provider's side of delivering the same functionality (compare the issue of system costs discussed in Chapter 3, Section 3.3.2)
  - A change in behaviour on the user side (e.g. an incentive to minimise the use of the product since payment is now per unit of use or per unit of result)

The net effect could be the creation of higher added value (or economic growth) while lowering environmental impacts.

White *et al.* (1999), for example, mention three situations in which PSS arrangements lead manufacturers to reduce life-cycle environmental impacts:

- When servicing arrangements result in internalising the costs of use and/or disposal

- When servicing arrangements are driven by the economic value of the end-of-life good

- When servicing arrangements reconstitute the product as a cost rather than a profit centre

Lower materials and energy consumption during production and use phases of services compared with products
Lower stock of products in manufacturing as it encourages leaner manufacturing as products are more valuable (Hawken *et al.* 1999)
Potential for environmental benefits through economies of scale
PSS may be implemented as a method of encouraging firms to take greater producer responsibility over their product in a way that is palatable to the consumer, manufacturer and environment
More durable products, lowering the total stock of product required in the cycle to satisfy a specified need at any given time. Renting potentially opens up the possibility for more intensive use of the product, with the same environmentally beneficial outcome
Manufacturers may take more 'professional' care of the product over the use phase thus ensuring a higher quality end-stock and thus less *downcycling*
Manufacturers, which are also the main operators of the PSS, will have no incentive to sell excess material, will also be in a better position to optimise the products for their true function, will have far better knowledge regarding the true requirements and characteristics of the equipment
Collection of end-of-life products will be significantly easier thus increasing the rate of utilisation of end-of-life products
Development of better end-of-life disposal processes, as there will be clear pressure to design for this stage of the product life-cycle from the start of the concept generation phase onwards. Manufacturers incentivised to develop innovative uses for end-of-life products
Easier upgrading to more eco-efficient technologies

TABLE 4.3 **Potential environmental benefits of PSS**

Source: based on Wong 2001

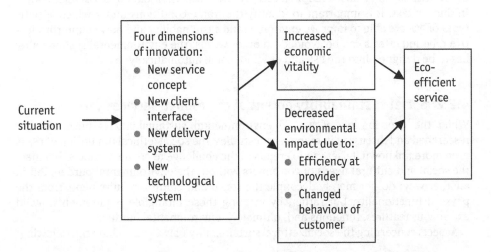

FIGURE 4.2 **Product service innovation and factors determining eco-efficiency**

Source: Zaring *et al.* 2001

The question of whether product-services are inherently more sustainable than products has generated much debate. Goedkoop *et al.* (1999) showed that the service sectors use over four times less energy than industrial sectors. However, most service sectors (e.g. insurance or financial service suppliers) do not deliver a final functionality themselves but provide a complement to a material offering (e.g. a car). Their analysis hence does not answer the question of whether the same functionality (e.g. transport from A to B) can be delivered better by a service than a product. Figure 4.1 showed just a limited difference in such life-cycle environmental impacts per euro value of different functionalities, whether products or product-services (cf. Suh 2004; Weidema *et al.* 2005; Tukker *et al.* 2006). Mont (2004) suggested an overall improvement of a Factor 2 at best. A massive switch to product-services (without other changes in the technological system) hence may not offer the radical improvements often suggested. Other counter-arguments against the environmental benefits of servicing include the following:

- Many services have high transport intensity. Other environmental benefits in the system may not compensate this (Ellger and Scheiner 1997; Graedel 1998)

- Many service suppliers see themselves as 'clean'. They hence often pay little attention to minimising the environmental burden of the infrastructure and products used to deliver these services (Charter 2001)

- Many product-services have been implemented for reasons other than environmental benefits (Maßelter and Tischner 2000). And since in our Western economy many materials and products are commoditised (compare Chapter 3, Section 3.2.2) the first focus in PSS development will probably be saving the relatively expensive human resources

Most authors hence conclude that the question of whether a PSS is better than a product system has to be answered on a case-by-case basis (Maßelter and Tischner 2000). In this context, it is important to identify the frame conditions under which specific types of PSS are able to improve environmental sustainability and how counterproductive rebound effects can be avoided. In other words: the environmental sustainability has to be designed into the PSS and does not come automatically.

4.2.2 Social sustainability potential of product-service systems

While the contribution of PSS to environmental sustainability is uncertain but researched and discussed in many recent studies, the social/ethical dimension of PSS is even more unknown. Lifset (2000) refers to the challenge to create products that meet the social and cultural needs of consumers without the environmental burden. Put in another way: do not merely decouple the social and cultural requirements from the physical functionality, but rather, by meeting those intangible requirements, avoid extraneous features, functions and, ultimately, environmental burden.

Aspects concerning the social/ethical sustainability of PSS can include the following:

1. PSS may focus much more on the needs and values of customers: for example, through the possibility of customising PSS offers individually and thus increase quality of life

2. PSS may integrate customers directly in the generation of the PSS and in this way increase the value of the offer and satisfaction of the customers by this participatory approach

3. Use- and result-oriented PSS have a revenue model that does not require payment for the full value of the product upfront—a relatively small payment is asked for every use or every time a result is delivered. This makes particularly high-quality and high-price objects accessible for consumers who could not afford to buy these objects

4. It is plausible that, in general, product-service-based business models come with better and more interesting jobs than in product manufacturing. The employees who deliver the PSS in direct contact with the customers are very important for the image of the PSS and thus have a high value and importance for the PSS provider

5. PSS can strengthen the role of the local economy because services are created at the same time and often at the same place when and where they are consumed. This may also contribute to enhancing social coherence in the region

6. PSS development, when making use of existing product concepts, can sometimes be done with limited investment. Some PSS may create new business opportunities for people who have been sidetracked in the regular economy, or fulfil needs that people cannot afford themselves in the regular economic system.[11] An example is the car-sharing system developed in Berlin that started as a relatively small, alternative initiative and over time was transformed into a 'normal' profitable business

7. As we will explain further in Chapters 5 and 12, PSS development in principle should use a broader perspective on the system and related need fulfilment than product development. In PSS development, it is hence more likely that yet untapped win–win solutions are found that limit negative externalities, and that are beneficial for all relevant actors in the system (rather than just the producer and its client)

So, PSS may contribute to social sustainability in two ways: they might either reduce negative social aspects such as unemployment, or increase the well-being of customers and participants in the PSS. However, PSS can also have a negative impact on social sustainability. For instance, some PSS may deliver services that the customers used to perform themselves, with the result that end-users lose skills and become dependent on market parties (e.g. some people no longer develop skills in cooking or car repair). Another example is the PSS 'activity management': this can be plain outsourcing (or even offshoring) activities of a company with the main aim of using a lower-paid workforce: for example, relocating a telephone service help desk to a call centre in India. Hence, as in the case of environmental sustainability, social sustainability is not an automatic feature of PSS. Again, it has to be designed into the system with care.

---

11   Compare the LETS (local exchange and trading schemes) systems where participants exchange services and offers outside the regular money economy; see www.gmlets.u-net.com.

The social sustainability aspects mentioned above are in essence all factors that have been included in Section 4.1.2 when discussing the relation between consumer expenditure and quality of life (2, 3, 4, 5, 6, 7), or the (intangible) value of the offering (1, 2). As stated above, a cleverly developed PSS can provide more interesting jobs, strengthen a local economy, create a greater local social cohesion and hence more pleasant local living conditions, among other things. This enhances quality of life in a way that cannot be bought on the market, and can reduce expenditures on 'obligatory needs'. In that sense, the framework developed in Section 4.1 for analysing decoupling includes social sustainability of product-services.

4.3 Factors determining sustainability per type of PSS

In this section, we aim to analyse the sustainability potential of each of the eight types of PSS discerned in Chapter 2. We will do so in two ways.

First, one can analyse the sustainability per PSS type via a deductive approach. Given potential mechanisms that enhance the sustainability of systems, one can analyse which ones in principle should be valid for a specific PSS. We will use the mechanisms identified in Section 4.1.2, and add the rebound effect as discussed in Section 4.1.3 as an extra factor in the analysis.

Second, one can also analyse a large number of individual PSS cases with regard to their contribution to sustainability. From such extensive case-study research, one can try to deduce generic patterns. Section 4.3.2 shows the results of the analysis of some 200 case studies that were filed during the SusProNet project in a relational database.

The two approaches are complementary. In essence, the case-study approach can be used to test the hypothesis developed via the first approach. This leads to final conclusions (Section 4.3.3).

4.3.1 Sustainability per type of PSS: hypotheses

The decoupling strategies discussed in Section 4.1.2 deal with either one or both of the following components: a (radical or incremental) change in the technical production system, and a (radical or incremental) change in the way in which consumers interact with the system. It is clear that, if the change is radical, and affects both components, the higher the potential is for radical sustainability gains. Figure 4.3 gives a matrix of these two types of change, and plots the different decoupling strategies from Section 4.1.2.

The same figure now allows us to analyse from a theoretical point of view the decoupling potential of different types of PSS. This is done below, addressing the different decoupling strategies in the discussion.

Product-related service

The majority of product-oriented PSS do not imply any change of the technological system or the way that the user operates it. Often, the user has already acquired the ser-

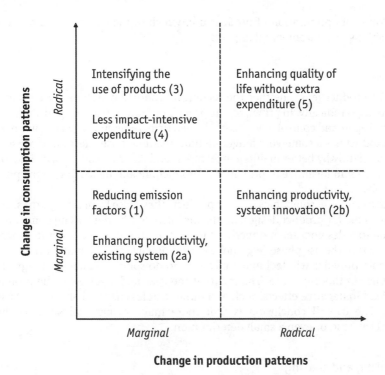

FIGURE 4.3   Change of production and consumption patterns in relation to different decoupling strategies

vice component (e.g. maintenance, supply of consumables) separately, so in such cases there are no shifts to more or less polluting expenditure categories. In many cases, one can hence not expect radical sustainability improvements, but just some incremental improvements since the maintenance is a bit more professional and regular, etc. In some cases, product-related services may lead to higher sustainability gains. If the product-oriented service is, for example, advice on how to reduce energy use in the use phase, or a take-back provision for waste components that leads to a much higher recycling rate, in some cases a Factor 2 may be reached. However, even in such cases it may have been that the user had already found out how to reduce energy use of the product by advice from third parties, or that a take-back scheme was already legally demanded and offered by a regular recycling company. The overall picture is that product-related services in general lead to only a marginal change in user behaviour and technical production systems. They can lead to impact reductions, but in most cases they are likely to be incremental at best.

Product-related advice and consultancy

The evaluation for product-related advice and consultancy is roughly the same as for the former situation. Again, the main value lies in the fact that the PSS provider might suggest all kinds of optimisation of product use, which in the end can lead to incremental reductions in environmental impacts.

Product lease

In the case of product lease, neither the technical production system nor consumer behaviour changes radically. In principle, the provider now also takes responsibility for maintenance, repair and control, and this could lead to incremental efficiency improvements: the product has a somewhat longer lifetime and might use energy and consumables more efficiently by better maintenance, repair and control. And, in principle, the provider also feels an incentive to prolong the product life and hence design the product accordingly.

Yet in most cases lease companies buy the products they lease from third parties, and are not responsible for product design. So the incentive felt by the leasing company is not passed on to a designer team directly. Furthermore, the lease does not in general cover many costs in the use phase (e.g. fuel consumption by cars), so neither the leaser nor the product provider will feel much incentive to do something about energy and consumable use in the use phase. The fact that the user no longer owns the product could even lead to negative effects, such as a rather careless use that shortens its useful lifetime. The overall conclusion is that there may be marginal sustainability improvements at best, or even a small deterioration.

Product renting and sharing

Product renting and sharing does not change the technical system radically, but does so with regard to the method of consumption. These PSS imply that the same product is now used more intensively. This can have high impact reductions, particularly if the life-cycle impacts are mainly related to the production of the product (compare Wimmer and Züst 2001).[12]

This PSS can have an additional bonus. In general, the user will now have to pay the integrated costs for each time he or she uses the product, unlike in the case of the former PSS types. Also, access to the product is a bit more complicated. This implies that in this system the use of the product in general will be discouraged a little. This might have additional positive environmental effects if it leads to a less-use situation or to a more frequent use of more environmental friendly alternatives (e.g. public transport as a complement to car renting or sharing).

Product pooling

The analysis for product pooling is similar to that for renting and sharing, with one major difference. Product pooling implies that the same product is used at the same time by more users (e.g. car pooling). This can have even more impact reductions as in

12   The benefits in this type of PSS also depend on whether new products are designed or available that fit better to the sharing system than to individual uses. For example, in car-sharing systems the providers have to take existing cars that might be less well designed for shared uses but, in the German bike sharing system Call a Bike, a special new bike was developed that fits very well with the system, is robust, ergonomic, vandalism-proof and has an electronic lock.

the case of sharing and renting, particularly if the life-cycle impacts are related to the use of the product.

Pay-per-unit use

Two aspects concerning the PSS 'pay-per-unit use' are of relevance:

- The provider is responsible for all life-cycle costs, which provides a powerful incentive to design a product that is optimised over the life-cycle in terms of costs, and of which elements can be re-used after the product's useful life

- In specific cases (e.g. pay-per-wash) the user will make a more conscious use of the service, though in other cases (e.g. copiers at work) it depends if the pay-per-use system directly charges for every single use (e.g. each copy) or if the costs are accumulated and paid at the end of a month and by a third party (e.g. employer). The direct feedback function is an important factor for changes in users' behaviour

A very important issue is that the provider feels an incentive to continually improve its product with life-cycle performance in mind. In sum, though there is no total shift in technical production system, there is an important redefinition of the relation with the user. The net effect is a reasonable potential for sustainability gains.

Activity management/outsourcing

Activity management or outsourcing usually does not imply a radical change in applied technology, organisation or even behaviour of the user. Yet companies providing activity management (financially) have to be more efficient and be more knowledgeable than the company that outsourced the activity to stay in business. This can be realised by a more efficient use of capital goods and materials and other marginal improvements. This includes improvements since the activity management supplier is able to perform the task more professionally, also in terms of preventing environmental and social impacts. Since in essence the way of doing things does not change radically, it seems unlikely that the sustainability gains are more than several dozen per cent. On top of that, in many cases the (financial efficiency) gains are realised on personnel costs rather than material costs, which is less relevant for impact reduction.

Functional result

Offering a functional result can imply a radical change in technology and also a radical change in behaviour of the user. In principle this has the highest potential for impact reduction. At a high level of abstraction, a result is promised and the provider in principle can decide on the approach to deliver the result. This provider will hence try to do so in the most cost-effective way, which in principle bears the promise of a search for radical innovations. In theory, hence also the most radical environmental improvements could be realised.

The results of this discussion are plotted in Figure 4.4. The figure suggests a clear pattern. Product-related services (1 and 2) score in general on mechanisms that normally do not lead to radical sustainability improvements. For product lease, it is even uncertain whether any sustainability gains are made, since the user feels no incentive to use the product carefully. Product rental, sharing and pooling will give average to high impact reductions, mainly because the product is much more intensively used. Activity management usually does not lead to a radical shift in approach to the activity, but provides many incentives to find cumulative (marginal) improvements. The same applies for pay-per-unit use. And particularly the PSS type functional results can lead to very high impact reductions, if the provider succeeds in shifting to a much more efficient technical system. Of course, this is a generic assessment. Occasionally, one may find a case where product-related advice and consultancy lead to radical (say a Factor 4) sustainability improvement, and there will also be cases of functional PSS that give no sustainability improvement. The case analysis in the next section can shed more light on this issue.

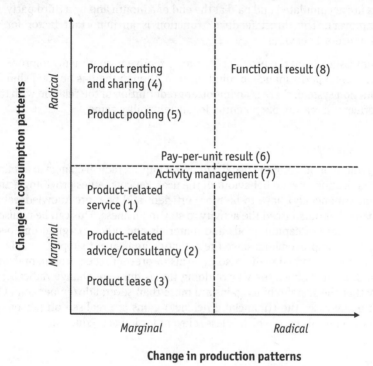

Change in production patterns

FIGURE 4.4 Influence of different PSS types on production and consumption patterns

4.3.2 Sustainability per type of PSS: cases

Within SusProNet, a relational database has been created that contains some 200 PSS cases. For all these cases, issues have been inventoried such as the relevant need area or consumption domain, maximum expected market penetration, drivers and barriers to implementation, and so on.

This database also contains information about the type of PSS and a qualitative evaluation of the environmental performance in comparison with the most relevant competing product system. Two types of (cradle-to-grave) environmental impact were analysed: energy use and material use within the product or product-service system. The analysis was based on expert judgement, performed by a small group (three persons) out of the SusProNet team. Scores were given on a five-point scale: radical (Factor X), intermediate (Factor 2) or marginal improvement, or marginal and intermediate (Factor 2) deterioration. To some extent, this analysis is of course crude and results have to be used carefully. At the same time, the persons doing the scoring had a considerable knowledge in product evaluations. In several cases the scores could be based on well-founded underlying studies (e.g. the environmental evaluation of Meijkamp 2000 on car-sharing services). In most other cases the score of the PSS compared with the product system was obvious. In cases of doubt, no score was given.[13]

Materials

No	Type	Radical improvement (Factor 4–10)	Inter-mediate improvement (Factor 2)	Incre-mental improvement (0–20%)	Limited nega-tive (−20%)	Quite negative (minus Factor 2)
1	Product-related service		26	41	1	
2	Product-related consultancy			12		
3	Product lease		4	10		
4	Product renting or sharing	2	14	6		
5	Product pooling		2	1		
6	Pay-per-service unit		1	3	1	
7	Activity management/outsourcing	1	12	6	3	
8	Functional result	4	2	14		

TABLE 4.4 Number of PSS per category (out of 200) and its sustainability improvement compared with a competing product (theme: material use)

13 This exercise was executed with the help of Dynamo, a structured, relational database that now contains a few thousand technical and non-technical developments normally used for foresight and strategic sector analyses. We used it to develop the above cross-analyses between PSS types and environmental potential. The 200+ individual cases we used can be viewed via www.dynamo.tno.nl, but outside parties unfortunately cannot perform the analysis on their own.

No	Type	Radical improve-ment (Factor 4–10)	Inter-mediate improve-ment (Factor 2)	Incre-mental improve-ment (0–20%)	Limited nega-tive (–20%)	Quite negative (minus Factor 2)
1	Product-related service		13	47	2	
2	Product-related consultancy			11		
3	Product lease		3	11		
4	Product renting or sharing	2	11	8		
5	Product pooling		1	1	1	
6	Pay-per-service unit			4	1	
7	Activity management/outsourcing		7	12	2	
8	Functional result	5	3	11	2	

TABLE 4.5 Number of PSS per category (out of 200) and its sustainability improvement compared with a competing product (theme: energy use)

At first sight, the tables give some results that are at odds with the hypotheses formulated in Section 4.3.1. Some of the product-related services can have intermediate improvements, two PSS in the category 'product renting and sharing' have a radical potential, and two PSS in the category 'functional result' have limited negative environmental consequences. At a closer look, though, the scores can be explained very well:

● The 26 and 13 (Tables 4.4 and 4.5, respectively) product-related services giving intermediate improvements are for a very large part services aimed at taking back the product for recycling after its use. Only if this particular service is offered, and then only in countries where recycling and energy recovery after collection via 'regular' waste channels is limited, are high environmental gains likely

● The radical improvements in the category 'renting and sharing' are ski rental and the 'Call a bike' system as developed in Munich, which is very successful in providing 'after-transport' after train journeys. The ski example indicates that under specific conditions rental and sharing systems can lead to high improvements. This is the case when:
  – The impacts during use are negligible and hence only the impacts of production and waste management are relevant (valid for skis, but not for e.g. cars)
  – The product, when in private ownership, is used with a very low intensity. In such cases, rental and sharing systems can lead to a more intense use of several factors, implying that, for the same number of users, a reduction of products by several factors can result—and hence an environmental sustainability improvement of several factors can be expected

In the bike rental case, the positive score is caused not just by the rental business model as such: there is little difference in impact if a journey is made on an owned or a rented bike. However, in this case we acknowledged that the rental business model helped to make bikes—in conjunction with the public transport system—a stronger competitor for cars. It is this potential shift from car to bike and public transport that led to the high score

● The negative scores for 'Functional result' concern food services brought at the home, notably a breakfast delivery service and a delivery service for *à la carte* food. We assumed here that such services would replace own cooking at home. Under this assumption the service generates more impacts owing to the dedicated and extra transport for delivery. If these services replace a visit to a restaurant, however, then probably a neutral score or even a small improvement should have been indicated in Tables 4.4 and 4.5

The other results are well in line with the hypotheses formulated in Section 4.3.1. Product renting and sharing often intensified the use of material artefacts, leading to a Factor 2 improvement (compare Meijkamp 2000). Some functional results made a totally new solution possible compared with the product concept. Many examples leading to radical improvements were ICT-based solutions for traditional activities, such as distance-learning courses replacing teaching in a school context.

4.3.3 Review and discussion

On the basis of the former sections, we can formulate now a set of working hypotheses on the environmental sustainability potential of the different types of PSS. They are summarised in Figure 4.5. In sum, the conclusions are:

● Product-related service (1), advice and consultancy (2), and product lease (3) have probably marginal environmental benefits, since one can expect at best mainly incremental change such as better maintenance. Product lease can be even worse if the users have incentives to use the product with less care than when they own it. Only if the product-related service concerns a take-back and recycling service are higher impact reductions possible

● Product renting, sharing or pooling (4, 5) can have major environmental benefits if the burden is related to the production of the artefact, since the same product is shared and used more intensively. Particularly for products that, when owned, are used with a very low intensity, improvements can be high. However, if in the case of product renting or sharing the use phase dominates and the arrangement does not lead to a low-use behaviour, it is of little help. The total use time of all users together does not diminish. For such products with a high impact in the use stage, product pooling has major (extra) environmental benefits: there will be lower impacts since more people make use of the product at the same time

● Pay-per-unit use (6) overcomes the split incentive between production costs of a product and costs made in the use phase. It is likely that at least incremental gains will be realised, but since the technological system in principle does not change radically, no radical improvements can be expected

PSS type	Environmental impacts compared with a reference situation (product)				
	Worse	Equal	Incremental reduction (<20%)	Considerable reduction (<50%)	Radical reduction (<90%)
1 Product-related service			←——————→		
2 Product-related consultancy			←————→		
3 Product lease		←——————→			
4 Product renting and sharing			←—————————→		
5 Product pooling			←—————————→		
6 Pay-per unit use			←————————→		
7 Activity management			←—————————→		
8 Functional result				←——————————————→	

- Renting, sharing: considerably to radically better if impacts are related to product production and the product—when traditionally owned—is used with very low intensity
- Pooling: additional reductions compared with sharing/renting if there are important impacts related to the use phase
- Renting, sharing, pooling: even higher if the system leads to no-use behaviour
- All PSS: if the new business model enhances the competitive position of environmentally friendly technologies (e.g. Call a bike) higher improvements can be at stake (not usual and case-specific)

FIGURE 4.5 Tentative (environmental) sustainability characteristics of different PSS types

- Activity management/outsourcing (7) will lead to lower environmental impacts if (monetary) efficiency gains are particularly related to materials and artefacts, and not time input of humans

- Functional result (8) has in theory the highest potential since the provider offers a result closer to a final client need and hence has more degrees of freedom to design a low-impact system

Overall, most PSS seem to lead to some environmental improvements, or at least no worse environmental performance. Leasing may be an exception, since it can make users less responsible for the careful use of the product. A potential of up to around Factor 2 is probably available for renting and sharing, pooling, pay-per-unit use and for product-related services (if this focuses on waste recycling). And in some cases a PSS business model can be a facilitator and encourage the use of products with lower impacts (as the Call a bike example illustrates). However, most PSS types seem not to be the inherent avenues to the Factor X world as they are sometimes presented. Real Factor X potential is only inherently embedded in the PSS type 'Functional results'. And for all the PSS types the individual case will determine whether the potential is realised. After all, it will be companies deciding about implementing PSS, and they will decide to do so mainly on economic considerations. In product systems where human resources rather than materials form a major cost factor, it may well be that a PSS (such as activity management) will be mainly implemented to reap the benefit of a more efficient use of labour, and not to reduce material flows or emissions.

4.4 Conclusions

On the basis of the former sections, the following conclusions can be drawn.

1. The need for decoupling in terms of a 'one size fits all' Factor X reduction goal of material use per unit of wealth is not generally accepted. Emission reduction targets of such order of magnitude find better support. However, seen from both perspectives, for some types of impact and some types of resource use, population and wealth growth will make the need for a radical absolute decoupling inevitable

2. The scientific jury is still out with regard to whether there is a kind of 'natural' tendency that when the wealth level rises (absolute) decoupling will occur (other than for a period of some decades, and for relatively small mass flows and emissions). It seems plausible that active and targeted interventions are needed if one wants to reach Factor X goals

3. Factors that can contribute to a decoupling of environmental impact and enhancement of quality of life are:
   - Improving emission factors (potential: several factors for small mass flows; most, if not all, historical successes with regard to decoupling have been reached via this approach)
   - Enhancing efficiency of production of product functions (potential: Factor X in case of radical changes in socio-technical systems)
   - Intensifying use of product functions (potential: Factor 2, depending on intensity enhancement)
   - Switching expenditure to 'intangible' value (potential: Factor 2; many expenditures on apparently 'intangible' services demand input of underlying 'hardware' and appear to have still relatively high life-cycle impacts per euro spent)
   - Improving 'non-market quality of life' (potential: large; for most Western economies 'life satisfaction' or 'happiness' has not risen significantly in the last 50 years despite a Factor 3–6 increase in real economic growth)

4. The rebound effect works via the same mechanisms as indicated above, but in the opposite direction. The larger the intervention in the system, and the longer the time horizon, the more difficult rebounds can be predicted

5. Product-services have a potential to realise decoupling. However, as conclusion 3 shows, this is not a law set in stone. First, the sweeping claims that a shift to product-services automatically leads to a Factor X world find no ground in reality. Many services offered are just an envelope around a system

filled with products and materials and on a life-cycle basis do not score much better than products. Second, it is paramount to acknowledge the difference between types of product-service:

- Product-oriented services leave the existing system largely as it is. Normally, sustainability improvements of a few dozen per cent due to issues such as better maintenance can be expected at best—or maybe a Factor 2 improvement, if the service boosts product or material recycling.
- Use-oriented services (and particularly product renting, sharing and pooling) intensify the use of the products. This can give intermediate (Factor 2) improvements.
- Result-oriented services are in fact the only ones with a real 'Factor X' potential—under the condition that the supplier of the service develops a fully novel way of function fulfilment.

The conclusion is that the debate on sustainability of product-services has been utterly confused. Yes, there is a Factor X potential. And in exceptional cases product- or use-oriented PSS may stimulate the introduction of Factor X technologies and structures. But real Factor X potential can in general only be attributed to *one specific type of PSS*: functional result. Other PSS have a clear potential to contribute to sustainability, but this must not be exaggerated to the mythical 'Factor X' proportions as is sometimes done. So our somewhat trivial conclusion is also that the more radical the system changes, the higher the potential of moving it to greater sustainability. Furthermore, whether the available potential is realised depends on a focused effort to *design* PSS to be as sustainable as possible, preferably stimulated by the right framework conditions and suitable tools (cf. Chapter 5).

This is not to say that the concept of PSS has only limited value for decoupling: on the contrary. PSS thinking moves away from existing product concepts, and inherently focuses on the final *consumption function* that needs to be fulfilled. This enormously enhances the degrees of freedom to find improvement options. It allows for designing a system that fulfils the final customer/consumer need, which can consist of as little material product as possible and more non-material services. Without a change in framework conditions, the concept of PSS may not bring sustainability on its own. But designing need fulfilment systems making use of a (particularly a result-oriented) PSS mind-set indicates how systems have to be organised to reach the Factor X.

The toolbox for
product-service development

Part III
**Product-service
development**

5
The toolbox for product-service development

Martijn Verkuijl and Ursula Tischner
econcept, Germany

Arnold Tukker
TNO, The Netherlands

This chapter gives an overview of methods and tools used in PSS development and design processes. As PSS consist of products and services, it is logical to start with a discussion on methodologies and tools for product and service design, because different experts suggest their use also for PSS design. The chapter is hence divided into three research areas: product design, service design and product-service systems design.

In the following we discuss first approaches to product design, service design and then the extension of a product design method to PSS design. Then we describe the most important methods developed especially for PSS design, present PSS models/methodology for specific need areas, and finally introduce PSS design tools. The extended description of tools can be found in Annex 2, in alphabetical order.

5.1 Product and service design

5.1.1 Product design

Product design/industrial design is an activity to create and realise products (and sometimes also services). It is a field that has been practised professionally since the industrial revolution, i.e. for more than a hundred years. Thus it is not necessary to describe in detail the best practice of product design because it is well known. What is interesting for the focus of this book is the state of the art of integration of environmental and social aspects (sustainability) into the routines of product development and design.

Integrating environmental aspects is also a field which has been researched for some decades, and with the ISO technical report 14062 on *Integrating Environmental Aspects into Product Design and Development,* published in 2002, and with many national ecodesign guides, knowledge about best practice is available on the market (ISO 2002).

ISO technical report 14062 describes the integration of environmental aspects into product development and design in six process steps and suggests tools to use in each of the steps (see Fig. 5.1).

Although knowledge and practice in product design and ecodesign are quite advanced there are still gaps:

Phase in product design process	Tools
1. Planning, product, project specification Define the problem. Describe as clearly as possible the service unit/functional unit of the new product. Plan the project steps, budget, time-frame, etc. Analyse reference product if appropriate, set priorities, formulate rough product specifications	● Marketing tools ● LCA, MIPS or CED analyses, checklists for environmental strengths/weaknesses analysis
2. Concept design Search for environmentally friendly solutions. How can the customer demands and product specifications be fulfilled with the lowest environmental impact? Also think about designing services instead of a product. Select best ideas. Formulate more detailed product specifications	● Creativity techniques, eco-innovation methods ● Decision matrix, portfolio or spider diagrams for comparison and selection of ideas
3. Detailed design Detail the solutions selected. Integrate all environmentally relevant aspects into whole product life-cycle and the previously defined product specification together with normal design criteria	● Design guides and handbooks, checklists, rules of thumb, LIDS wheel, House of (Environmental) Quality, cost assessment tools
4. Testing/final evaluation before market launch Test prototypes and concepts. Evaluate if all criteria, including environmental ones, have been met. Change design if necessary	● Normal testing tools, environmental strengths/weaknesses analysis (see Phase 1)
5. Market launch Production and marketing of final product. Prior to market launch, communication and marketing strategies are developed that include environmental aspects	● Eco-(marketing tools) ● Green communication tools, eco-labelling
6. Product review/process review Review success of product on the market. Give feedback on redesign process of product or design of similar new products. Review success of planning method and tools; change and adapt if appropriate	● Marketing tools, checklists and spider diagrams as controlling tools

Feedback loops

FIGURE 5.1 Ecodesign process scheme and tools

Sources: Tischner *et al.* 2000; ISO 2002

- Integration of social aspects is still very difficult. Practicable indicators and tools covering social and ethical aspects and the routines for integration into design and development are missing

- Dissemination in small and medium-sized companies. Most of the ecodesign tools and methods are for large companies and they do most of the ecodesign activities. It is necessary to translate the methods and tools and adapt them to the specific needs of medium-sized and small enterprises, which make up almost 90% of business

- Attention to the soft factors of sustainable design and ecodesign such as aesthetics, product semantics, cultural aspects, consumer behaviour and preferences

Interestingly, many of the methods and tools of the two areas service design and product-service system design are adopted and borrowed from the field of product development and design.

5.1.2 Service design

Many methods and tools from the service engineering field are variations on product design methods and tools. These paragraphs give an overview and examples of such methods and tools. Then tools especially developed for service design are discussed.

To guarantee service quality and success and for problem-solving in the different steps of development and design of services, specific methods and approaches exist but they are often not adapted to the specific needs and co-operative operations in this area. In general, service design methods discern three main steps: analysis, creation and realisation. Tools that play a role in these major design steps in service design are: blueprinting for visualising the structure of a service, gap analyses for detecting possible problems, and quality function deployment (QFD) for minimising those gaps. More and more scenario development methods are opening their doors for integrating service design.

Process innovation methods are available for service design as for product design. The aims of the transfer of product development and assessment methods to the development of services are in general to develop services more systematically and with a quality orientation. In more detail, the aims are to systemise processes and to create guidelines and operation sequences, and to develop widespread and accompanying methods, which can be constantly adapted and improved (TÜV 2002). An example of such a systematic innovation management system for services is the matrix structure (TÜV 2002). It suggests the following common steps: idea generation, concretion, assessment, decision and realisation. In every step tasks and responsibilities are identified and have to be completed before entering the next step. The tools used within the method are very similar to those used in product design methods. The complexity or time expense is also similar to the product development version.

Another example of a systematic innovation management system for services is the 'service engineering management' method (TÜV 2002). This method is an example of a method with common process steps but with tools customised to service development and service marketing. The process is based on three main steps: service creation, service development and service management. The method is designed to connect with other business processes such as planning, market research and marketing. Examples of the 'servicised' tools are:

- FMEA (failure mode and effect analysis) and QFD (quality function deployment)

- Assessment tool for checking and guideline for realisation of the service development process

In designing the service system, customer input will need to be interpreted in a manner that ensures the minimisation of the gaps identified in the gap analyses. A key tool for this is quality function deployment (QFD). QFD is a structured approach to defining customer needs or requirements and translating them into specific plans to produce products to meet those needs. An adaptation of QFD for the development of services is described in Maylor 2000 and in TÜV 2002.

Another 'servicised' method is the 'integration reference model for service engineering' of Siemens (CT SE 3), which is a method for describing the decisive factors of success of services and for an integral assessment and improvement of the service development process (TÜV 2002). This method is based on a software tool and helps in recognising potentials for improvements in order to optimise processes. It includes four steps: analysis, definition of new processes, pilot application with feedback and the roll-out. In this method common tools are used, such as interviews, and tools from software development, such as the software CMM (capability maturity model) for increasing the maturity of software processes (Paulk *et al.* 1995).

For the assessment of the functionality and quality of the service development and design process, specific service design tools are available. These are adaptations of existing product development assessment tools (TÜV 2002). The assessment tools vary from auditing and certification models to models for process improvement.

Idea generation and assessment tools for service development form another group of specific tools. The tools also have their background in product development. Some examples are checklists, portfolio diagrams and idea assessment by value–benefit analysis.

Figure 5.2 gives an overview of the 'servicised' methods and tools mentioned in this section. The figure shows the purposes of these methods and tools and indicates their complexity. Extensive descriptions of the tools can be found in Annex 2.

Besides these methods and tools from the service engineering field, which are mainly variations of product design tools, there are tools especially developed for service development and design. These are presented below.

Systematically describing a service: service blueprint

Blueprinting is a tool specifically designed for service development. A service blueprint is the main tool for translating the desired design qualities into a system that delivers these. A blueprint is a model of the service system describing the progress of a customer through the service system in terms of activities and time (Zeithaml 1996; Maylor 2000). The activities that constitute the service are chronologically ordered and the interaction with the customer is the central theme. To produce a blueprint, Zeithaml recommends eight steps, which are summarised below:

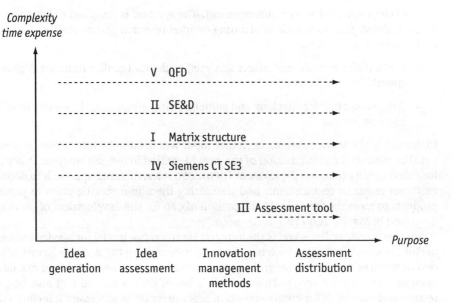

**FIGURE 5.2 Overview of 'servicised' methods and tools, their use in service
development and their time expense/complexity**

Source: TÜV 2002

1. Identify the service process to be blueprinted

2. Map the service process from the customer's point of view

3. Draw the line of interaction

4. Draw the line of visibility

5. Map contact employee actions, both onstage and backstage

6. Draw the line of internal interaction

7. Map internal support activities

8. Add evidence of service at each customer action step

Reijnhoudt (2000) adds an extra step to these eight steps, especially designed for product-oriented companies trying to go into the service business:

9. Add non-physical evidence of service at each customer action step

Gap analyses for services

Services are normally produced by people. And because they are much harder to control and regulate than machines, special tools for detecting service quality have been developed. Service quality can be measured as an input process involving the functional deployment of resources and activities. The output is the delivered service benefits. Consequently, a QFD type input–output framework can be used to study services. Such a service quality framework is presented in Figure 5.3.

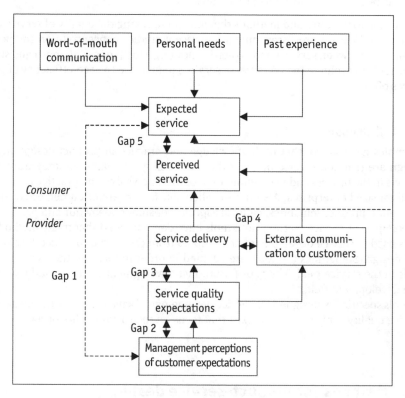

FIGURE 5.3 Service quality framework

Source: Dickson 1994

Gap analysis has very close parallels with the positioning of the service and QFD. The task is for the service provider to identify and reduce the following gaps, which have been identified by researchers as significant barriers to delivering a quality service (Dickson 1994):

- **Gap 1.** Management beliefs about consumer expectations are wrong. Management's benefit segmentation analyses is flawed

- **Gap 2.** Management operational specifications of the desired service do not match management perceptions of the target consumer's desired benefits and expectations. Management's QFD service specification matrix is wrong

- **Gap 3**. The delivered service does not meet management operational specifications. The implementation and control of service production script is basically flawed

- **Gap 4**. Promises do not match performance. The promoted positioning does not match the delivered service

- **Gap 5**. Consumer perceptions of the delivered service do not meet consumer expectations. Consumers are dissatisfied

In addition to the tools and methods that aim at improving the quality of service development and design processes, only a few recent studies concentrate on the possible connection between services and eco-efficiency (e.g. Goedkoop *et al.* 1999) and suggest some tools to evaluate the potential of services to increase the eco-efficiency of a company's offers.

5.1.3 Discussion

Examples have shown that both knowledge and practice in product design and eco-design are rich and diverse but that there are still gaps, mainly in integrating social aspects in the process and in dissemination of this knowledge and practice in small and medium-sized enterprises. Also the so-called soft factors are often neglected, such as aesthetics, product semantics, cultural aspects, consumer behaviour and preferences.

Examples of service methods and tools have demonstrated that many methods and tools used in service development are adopted from the field of product development and design. Sometimes the tools are adapted in order to increase the usability of the tools in the service field. The gaps for product development are also valid for the service development field.

Tools specifically designed for service development focus on improving the delivered service quality. Only a few tools exist that focus on the sustainability of services.

5.2 Methods for product-service design

Many methodologies exist for product development. One was presented in Section 5.1 on product design; another is the product development process of Roozenburg and Eekels as shown in Figure 5.4 (Roozenburg and Eekels 1991).

Some PSS studies argue that methodologies for product and service development are quite comparable (Brezet *et al.* 2001). In Figure 5.5 the product development process of Roozenburg is compared with a service development methodology based on BMBF 1998, Müller 1995 and Brügemann 2000. Although comparable, the two development processes are not automatically combinable in order to create a product-service methodology. For that, the two processes show too much dissimilarity, such as (Brezet *et al.* 2001):

- Different lead times
- Different executors

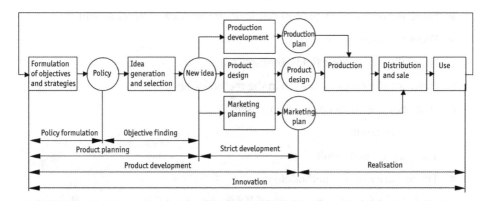

FIGURE 5.4 The product development process of Roozenburg and Eekels 1991

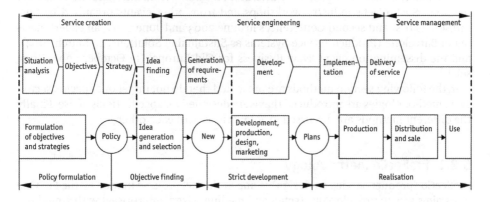

FIGURE 5.5 The product development process compared with the service development process

Source: Brezet *et al.* 2001

- Variable flexibility of the process
- Different variables in the process (e.g. material, time, place)
- Different levels of experience with integrating environmental aspects in the process

The following paragraphs present a collection of different PSS methodologies that were developed to combine the two development processes. These methodologies have different backgrounds and characteristics. They differ in several aspects, such as:

- Similarity to regular product development process and the use of existing or new tools
- Complexity and time intensity
- Providing a strict guideline or just a support structure

- Emphasis on a certain process phase or on the integral development
- Focus on sustainability
- Suitability for specific fields/business areas
- Different steps and tools used in the methodology
- How they deal with cross-cutting issues
- The target group
- The purpose and result
- The maturity of the methodology

The goal of this section is not to give full descriptions of the methods or the projects that developed these methods but to allow comparison and to locate gaps in the existing methodologies. The collection of methodologies in this section has been compiled throughout the SusProNet project by information coming from internal state-of-the-art research, SusProNet's industry workshops and from other events organised by SusProNet: its first and second Conferences in June 2003 and June 2004, an expert meeting in Barcelona (Product-Service Systems as Sustainable Solutions, 26 March 2004), and the dissemination event 'New Business for Old Europe' (13 October 2004, Brussels).[1]

In the following section methods are presented that do not target one specific sector. Then methodologies are introduced that were designed for specific fields of use. Finally the different methods are discussed in comparison with each other.

5.2.1 ProSecCo methodology

ProSecCo (product-service co-design) is one of the PSS projects funded by the EU. One of its aims was to provide SMEs (small and medium-sized enterprises) with a methodology and with tools to manage the development of PSS. The methodology is aimed at SME managers who want to detect opportunities for innovation by creating PSS offerings or implement a PSS development process in their company. This last option includes the proper organisation, infrastructures and resources necessary for PSS development. ProSecCo is not focused on environmental or social aspects of sustainability.

ProSecCo distinguishes several steps in the development of product-service co-designs. These are presented in Figure 5.6.

The developed methodology is an 'opportunity recognising methodology'. This means that it is a generic methodology for the development of products, services and PSS. The end result of the development process can be solely a product or a service but the methodology directs the user towards PSS by focusing on 'innovation' and therefore on opening the door to PSS for companies. The methodology is meant for the development of short-term solutions and not for concepts that lie far ahead.

---

1   Sources, besides those mentioned in this chapter, are the presentations and (abstract) papers from these activities. The presentations and papers from the conferences, and the reports of the industry workshops, can be downloaded from www.suspronet.org.

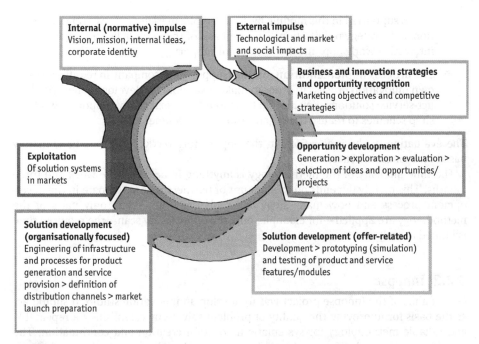

FIGURE 5.6 Generic product-service co-design process

The tools used in the methodology are similar to those of product design processes but are extended to PSS development.

The methodology is software-based. With the aid of an online platform companies can execute the development process by themselves. This platform provides development managers with a work approach, project status information, training and databases with case studies of product-service developments, methods/tools and experts. This online guide became active from the beginning of 2005 accessible via the project homepage (www.prosecco-village.com). However, external consultants can also support the process. If a company opts for external support of consultants, ProSecCo provides access to a database with consultants. These consultants are related to the ProSecCo project and are located in Italy, Germany, Switzerland and Spain.

The methodology is based on three main modules: the diagnosis modules, the opportunity recognition module and the process implementation module. These three modules are supported by a set of tools, methods, glossaries, contacts, links and instruments that help the user in the development process. This support is provided by the online platform mentioned above.

- The **diagnosis modules** are meant to accompany the other two modules during the whole development process in assessing needs for support

- The aim of the **opportunity recognition module** is to generate, identify and evaluate innovative product-service concepts. It consists of a knowledge-based section and an operative section with methodologies and tools. The user is supported in this module by, for example, market analysis, trend detection and strategy redefinition. The emphasis of the module lies on organising interactive workshops involving external support

● The **process implementation module** supports the company in redefining its own innovation process in order to make it suitable for developing new product-service solutions. Key tools in this module are externally supported workshop schemes to realise the organisational development

The evaluation of the innovations in the opportunity recognition module is mainly based on economic issues.

The time intensity of the methodology is anything in between one week and three months. This mainly depends on the amount of partners that participate in the development process and how many steps and tools are used. When only parts of the methodology are applied—for example, only the opportunity scan—the required time is limited as well.

5.2.2 Innopse

One of aims of the Innopse project was to develop an innovation studio. It should act as the basis for improving the quality of problem solving by establishing a repeatable and reliable methodology for systematic innovation creation and continuation. The project targets SMEs because, unlike big companies, they do not have the capability to establish their own specialised department that manages innovation and creativity on a large scale. The supporting methodology used for this innovation studio is the so-called 4Ts concept (see Fig. 5.7). The 4Ts is a comprehensive concept that can be fitted to organisations that offer products and/or services and can be applicable for incremental and radical innovations (emphasis is, however, on incremental innovation).

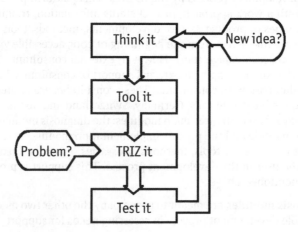

FIGURE 5.7 **The 4Ts innovation concept**

Source: Abdalla 2003

It consists of four steps:

1. **Think it:** scrutinising the idea, benchmarking against company vision and strategies. The following tools are suggested for this phase: balanced score-cards (BSC), brainstorming and mind mapping

2. **Tool it:** integration of the new idea into the process of the organisation while bringing along the viewpoint of the customers. The following tools are suggested for this phase: the affinity diagram, the analytical hierarchy process and quality function deployment (QFD)

3. **TRIZ it.** This stage is a problem-solving stage. Problems might become clear during the 'Tool it' stage or might arise during any stage. TRIZ is a methodology for solving both classical and inventive problems. It is composed of many methods and tools: for example, contradiction table, the 40 inventive principle, ARIZ, 76 standard solutions, separation principles, patterns of evolution and substance field analysis. A general introduction on TRIZ can be found at www.mazur.net/triz/index.html

4. **Test it.** This is the stage where the full implementation of the balanced score-card is performed. The partial use of the BSC in the 'Think it' stage was meant to see whether the new idea fits under any of the organisation's strategic goals and or can be aligned to any of the current initiatives. As the new idea is being developed, it is physically structured in this phase using a scorecard with objectives, measures, targets and initiatives. As it is under test and measurement, practical steps for execution should be put in place and implemented. Measure factors of control can be defined and watched throughout the product life-cycle

The innovation concept that utilises the methods and tools aims to be (fairly) self-explanatory. But mastering the methods and tools requires training and commitment (Abdalla 2003). The innovation studio approach does not have any specific focus on PSS or on sustainability but is an innovation supporting method.

5.2.3 PSS methodology and tools: School of Architecture and Design, Aalborg University

The centre of attention of this methodology, used to develop PSS at the school of Architecture and Design in Aalborg, Denmark, is on catalysing factors that generate cohesion in the system (Morelli 2004). The focal points of the methodology are:

1. Identifying the actors in the network, on the basis of defined analytical frameworks

2. Envisioning possible PSS scenarios, verifying use cases, sequences of actions and actors' roles

3. Working on possible representation and management tools to represent a PSS in all its components: that is, physical elements, logical links and temporal sequences

Suitable tools are proposed for each focal point. For the identification of the actors (step 1) system maps and analytical frameworks are used, providing a set of criteria for the analysis of relevant social groups. Such a framework considers, for each group, a series of parameters according to which the group will tend to shape a product or a system.

For envisioning the PSS (step 2) scenarios and use cases are used. Each scenario is composed of a number of descriptions of events (use cases) that describe the details of the sequence of action for each function included in a scenario. Use cases may be described in a diagrammatic way, which shows the flow of events, actors involved, pre- and post-condition for each use case and alternative paths. The graphical description may also include further information such as the space in which each action takes place and other actions beyond the line of visibility of the service.

Examples of tools for representing the structure of PSS (step 3) are IDEF0 (integration definition for function modelling), use case scenarios and representation techniques. IDEF0 is used in order to model the functions (activities, actions, processes, operations) required by a system or enterprise, and the functional relationships and data (information or objects) that support the integration of those functions.

These tools and methods are not new; they are commonly used in other disciplines. But those methods and tools are or still need to be adequately adapted to PSS development. The contribution of the approach of Aalborg University consists of the application of such tools in design education, with the aim of verifying them and generating a methodology for the design process of a PSS.

5.2.4　BISS methodology

This methodology was developed within TNO STB, the Netherlands. The point of origin of the Business Models for Inherently Sustainable Systems (BISS) methodology is that it is possible to construct business models in such a way that the created PSS inherently induce sustainability (van der Horst in Manzini et al. 2004). According to the methodology's authors, best practice and practical experiences prove that it is possible to create such sustainable business models. The methodology should move companies and organisations towards solutions that generate attractive economic activities, which inherently stimulate ecological and social sustainability (decoupling). This win–win thinking is based on the idea that unsustainable aspects of a current situation, such as waste of material, energy or labour, offer the opportunity to raise profitability. In order to set all the incentives of the actors involved in the system in line with sustainability, a clear understanding of all the incentives of these actors and the mechanisms that can create the decoupling effects are important. The methodology focuses on enabling such understanding.

The methodology is based on the following steps:

- Definition of the current business model
- Mapping out the interests of all the involved actors
- Making a chart of the economic and ecological inefficiencies
- Generation of the new PSS that points towards sustainable business models

● Definition of the new business model and the key contracts; testing is also included here

Examples of recent projects that worked with the BISS methodology are XB networks (teleworking facilities), Essent (energy supply) and HiCS (La Fiambrera, CDN). A lesson learned from using the methodology is that business models for inherently sustainable systems already exist but that they exist implicitly and are not recognised as sustainable business models. These models also are not widespread and have a relatively low impact on society.

5.2.5 The Kathalys method for sustainable product-service innovation

This methodology, developed within TNO, in co-operation with TU Delft in an organisation called Kathalys, can be seen as a predecessor of the BISS methodology. In the course of four years a method for sustainable product-service innovation has been created based on practice at Kathalys (Kathalys 2001).

The method suggests five product-service development phases: exploratory research and definition, design, product/service specification, elaboration and practical experimentation, and implementation. Throughout this development process five tracks are integrated: development of PSS, sustainability, organisation, user, and economic feasibility.

In the five steps of the development process the following activities are carried out:

1. Exploratory research and definition. Information about pressure on the environment is combined with consumer needs, trends and potential technological possibilities. This results in a future vision. Scenarios are often developed in order to examine the various possibilities and to develop sustainable concepts. The result of this phase consists of one or more ideas for possible sustainable innovation

2. Design. In this phase, the constraints of the system that is to be developed (consisting of products and services) are further explored and defined. In this phase, it is extremely important to have co-operation and to create support. The result is a project plan that is borne by a consortium

3. Product/service specification. This is the development phase, resulting in a prototype and a description of the product-service combination

4. Elaboration and practical experimentation. The products and services are worked out further, with the aim of carrying out a practical experiment. The innovations are often so new that a practical test in a real user environment, over a long period, is necessary to determine the added value for the consumer and the environment. The test leads to refinement of the product-service combination

5. Implementation. The product-service combination's development is completed; it is made ready for production and marketed. The new business is up and running

The five tracks are lines of consideration and activity that accompany the development process. They include:

- The development of the product-service combination

- Sustainability. Throughout the course of development, tests of sustainability are completed and adjustments made accordingly

- The organisation. The interests, roles and tasks of the partners in the venture are always an important consideration. At the end of the project, there is a new business for a company or consortium of companies

- The user. The user is involved as much as possible from the first phase of the project onward. At the start, the emphasis is on research into the requirements, wishes and needs of the target group(s). In the course of the project, this emphasis shifts to consumer acceptance and user behaviour

- Economic feasibility. Throughout the entire project, economic feasibility is used as a criterion

The targeted outcomes of the Kathalys approach are summarised in Table 5.1. There the five process phases are combined with the five tracks, creating an overview of all results that should be achieved.

Tracks: Phases:	Product-service combination	Sustainability	Organisation	User	Economic feasibility
1. Exploratory research and definition	Innovation vision	Environmental obstacle(s) and opportunities	Overview of actors	Field of requirements	Economic opportunity
2. Design	System definition	Quantitative environmental objective	Project plan borne by actors	User profile(s)	Turnover of objective
3. Product-service specification	Specified product/service combination	(Hypothetical) environmental assessment	Partner agreement	Evaluation of acceptance	Economic assessment
4. Effect and practice of experiment	Tested product/service combination	Environmental assessment (with practical substantiation)	Business agreement	Practical test	Investment and operations budget
5. Implementation	Fully developed product/service combination	Environmental benefit	Company (with shareholders)	Sustainably fulfilled need	Profit

TABLE 5.1 Overview of the different phases, tracks and results in the Kathalys method

Source: Kathalys 2001

5.2.6 TNO/PricewaterhouseCoopers (PwC) PSS innovation scan for industry

The purpose of the PSS innovation scan is to guide a company in running such a scan in a structured way. This means taking the first steps in the development of a PSS that has 'shareholder value through customer value'. The aim of this scan is to formulate a first business case for PSS that gains management commitment for a feasibility study. The scan works with tools and checklists for the technical contents and with process management tools.

The scan was commissioned by the Dutch Ministry of Housing, Spatial Planning and the Environment and was developed by TNO and PwC. The scan is also available in English.

The scan has been written for professionals working in R&D departments or business developers of industries and for consultants. It does not cover all steps in PSS development, but its aim is to build, within a few days, an impression of whether developing a PSS is a profitable option for the firm with an acceptable business fit. If the analysis is promising, the result should be convincing enough for the firm's management to commit itself to a true PSS business development process that includes resource-intensive steps such as strict development and realisation. Environmental gains are not quantified in this method.

The innovation scan consists of five steps and a preparation phase (step 0). The five steps are presented in Figure 5.8. Depending on the experience of the user it is possible to skip some steps. This is tested with a questionnaire.

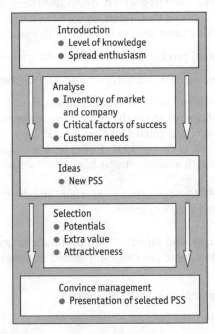

FIGURE 5.8 Steps of the TNO/PwC PSS innovation scan

Source: Tukker and van Halen 2003

The goals of the five steps are the following:

Step 0 is called 'Preparation of the PSS innovation scan'. The goals of this phase are:

- To create general support for running the innovation scan within the company
- To select the project team members and motivate them
- To make an agenda for the scan
- To send invitations and organise the necessary meeting rooms

The members of the project team should have different backgrounds and expertise, such as marketing and communication, product development and design, environment and management.

Step 1 is the 'Introduction of PSS'. Here the goal is to motivate team members and to equalise the common level of knowledge. The team members should be able to answer the following questions:

- What is a PSS?
- What benefits do PSS have for the organisation?
- Which steps are most important for the innovation scan?
- What is the purpose of this project?

Step 2 is the Analysis phase and its goal is to determine the current and future needs (values/wishes) of customers and their relations with the current and future function of the product. The following steps need to be taken in this phase:

- Choosing a (cluster of) product(s) for which the PSS innovation scan is made
- Analysing customer, product, market, company and surrounding actors

Step 3 covers 'Idea generation', where PSS possibilities should be invented. The result will consist of PSS possibilities related to the client perspective and PSS option.

In **step 4**, 'Selection', the generated ideas are checked for 'success' in numerous areas. Several tools are used in this process. Examples are ecodesign portfolio, pragmatic differential, cost–benefit analysis, simple life-cycle assessment (LCA) and Porter's market-actors tool.

The final **step 5** is called 'Management presentation' and directs the presentation of the new PSS innovation to the management.

Many existing tools are suggested for the PSS innovation scan; most of them are general development tools. But some are especially aimed at integrating environmental issues:

- Ecodesign portfolio (selection tool; see Annex 2)
- Pragmatic differential tool (selection tool; see Annex 2)
- Progressive abstraction tool (creativity tool; see Annex 2)

One newly developed tool is the PSS innovation matrix, which can be used either as a kind of creativity tool to develop PSS ideas or to check the completeness of the collected PSS ideas. At least three workshops are necessary to complete the scan. Depending on the size and experience of the participating companies, the estimated time expense for a rough scan is 1.5–3 working days and for a thorough scan 3–20 working days.

5.2.7 DES methodology: design of eco-efficient services

This methodology for developing eco-efficient product-service systems is an outcome of the research project 'Designing Eco-efficient Services' (DES project), which was a collaboration between Delft University of Technology and the Dutch Ministry of Environmental Affairs. The methodology should be regarded as a draft methodology that will be further developed in follow-up projects of the DES project.

The developed methodology is based on the assumption that the structure of regular innovation processes is applicable for the design of PSS. This assumption led to the expectation that, for the development of a PSS methodology, much of the existing product design basics and environmental tools were applicable, but needed to be adapted (Brezet *et al.* 2001). The methodology is not meant as a strict guideline on how eco-efficient PSS should be developed but to assist decision-makers with a structure, suggested actions and tools. In that way the methodology is suitable for a broad variety of PSS. Special attention is paid to the expected complex initiation phase of PSS development compared with conventional innovation processes.

The development process suggested by Brezet *et al.*, shown in Figure 5.9, consists of five steps with suggested activities, tools and results on every process step. Much of these activities and tools still need to be filled in. The authors are aware of the fact that the real development process is never linear as is shown in the figure. Sometimes it is necessary to jump back and forth between stages or to repeat stages. Nevertheless, the suggested process can be used as a framework to structure and communicate the different activities that in the end should lead to a successful eco-efficient service. The DES method separates service design from product design, but shows the step where both design processes come together to form a PSS. The suggested methodology concentrates more on service design with an emphasis on environmental aspects.

The goals of the first step 'Exploration' are to:

● Form a business coalition or set up a new business

● Create a team with a mission

● Produce a project plan

● Describe the system within which the innovation should take place

The second step, 'Policy formulation', must ensure that a policy is created that at least contains the statement that the outcome of the project will be an eco-efficient service. In this phase the time schedule is also defined.

The result of the 'Idea finding' phase is a design brief. Here first ideas are generated and selected. In the design assignment the most important requirements are specified and the decision takes place on which products and services should be part of the eco-efficient service. In the case of a product-service system the design brief need not necessarily go to one person or department. It could, for example, be possible that the ser-

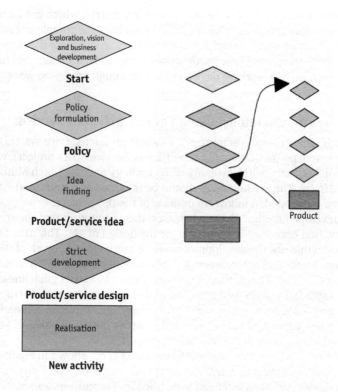

FIGURE 5.9 DES methodology; the right-hand side of the figure shows the possibility of integrating an external product design project into the general service design methodology

Source: Brezet *et al.* 2001

vice part is developed within the company, but products are purchased elsewhere, or vice versa, depending on the present know-how of the company. In the case of a network of companies this is the point at which each company will start to go through its own sub-development process.

In the fourth step, 'Strict development', the actual eco-efficient service is designed. The result should be a detailed and feasible design of the new eco-efficient service.

In the 'Realisation' phase the eco-efficient service is developed further and should result in a market introduction.

The final phase, 'Evaluation', should guarantee a process of continuous improvement. In this phase a final report is made including the environmental and economic effects.

The methodology was tested in several case studies. One of the conclusions was that development of additional tools is necessary, especially to assess the environmental impact of PSS and to find improvement strategies. An example of such an adapted tool is the META matrix, which is included in Annex 2.

5.2.8 MEPSS methodology

The EU funded MEPSS project (Methodology development and Evaluation of PSS), which is also carried out in the growth programme, aims to provide a toolkit that enables industry to successfully implement new PSS that will be in line with their business goals, offer optimal customer satisfaction and will minimise negative environmental and social impacts. The toolkit was developed by researchers in the field of PSS methodology and in close co-operation with industry partners who provided input in the form of business cases (best practice) and participated in testing and refinement workshops for the developed methodologies and tools (van Halen *et al.* 2005).

The MEPSS toolkit allows industry to develop PSS using a formalised framework for innovation that should increase the chances of success and make sure that no core issues are disregarded in the innovation process.

In MEPSS a modular structure for PSS development and design has been developed that allows for different actors, sectors and starting points to find an individual way through the modules. Nevertheless, even in a modular structure there is a sensible order of modules: for example, going from a rough idea and assessment of opportunities to more concrete design and evaluation of the system to market introduction and monitoring of success.

The modular structure is developed by three concept lines within the MEPSS research team: one line dealing with the design methodology, one line dealing with assessment of environmental, economic and social/ethical aspects (people, planet, profit), and another concentrating on success and failure factors and customer acceptance. Figure 5.10 shows the modular MEPSS methodology in an early stage of the process together with the three concept lines.

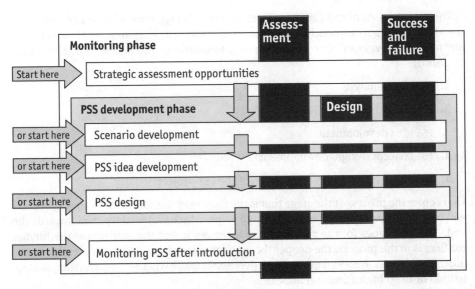

FIGURE 5.10 **The early MEPSS methodology**

Sources: Goedkoop *et al.* 2002 and www.mepss.com

Combined with the modular scheme, a set of tools is suggested by MEPSS that can be used in the different modules. The inventory of tools available for the PSS development process carried out in MEPSS shows that there is already a wealth of tools available for PSS development. However, most of them are currently used in other context (e.g. product development). The MEPSS team chose the most appropriate existing tools and filled the gaps in methodology and tools by developing their own new and suitable tools: for example, for evaluating the sustainability of PSS and for integration of sustainability aspects as guidelines in the PSS development process.

Towards the end of the MEPSS project and after integration of the review process with companies, the MEPSS methodology was refined in the form of a five-step gate-stage procedure, as shown in Figure 5.11.

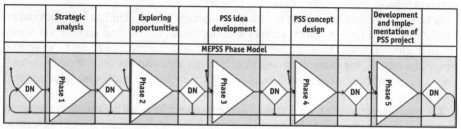

DN = decision node

FIGURE 5.11 The refined MEPSS methodology

Source: www.mepss.nl

The main phases of the (modular) MEPSS methodology have a lot in common with the aforementioned approaches of Brezet *et al.* (2001), Tukker and van Halen (2003), and methods developed for (eco)design (e.g. Roozenburg and Eekels 1991; Tischner *et al.* 2000):

1. Strategic analysis

2. Exploring opportunities

3. PSS idea development

4. PSS concept design/development

5. Development and implementation of the PSS project

Users enter the process at the stage that is the most relevant for them. In all stages users will be guided through the required design steps, which will be deepened towards the end. The same goes for the sustainability assessment and the guidelines: the further the user is in the process, the deeper the assessments will be, and the more elaborated are the guidelines. Between every step a decision is made whether to go further, to stop, to hold or to go back (decision nodes).

At each stage common elements guide the user to develop the PSS:

- A clear objective to be reached is formulated with the aid of a list of questions that the user has to address

- The modular programme of activities provides process descriptions, a decision tree to select the appropriate tools and a tool worksheet to assist execution

- A clear decision process for entering the next phase

An overview of the key questions that the user has to address in the first four stages is given below:

Questions for **Strategic analysis**:

- What are the core competences of my company (in chain perspective, adding real value)?

- Who are our key stakeholders?

- What are the main strengths and weaknesses of my business model?

- What value do we deliver to our clients?

- What do my clients expect of me (today and tomorrow)?

- What are the main technological trends that I should be connected to?

- Where should we improve today's system (people, planet, profit)?

- What are the other strategic issues at stake?

Questions for **Exploring opportunities**:

- What are the main PSS scenarios to guide me into the future?

- Where are the untapped opportunities?

- What are the PSS ideas that could be developed?

- Which set of evaluation criteria for PSS should be used according to the company's priorities?

- Do the ideas generated bring about an improvement in environmental/social impacts and how?

Questions for **PSS idea development**:

- What does each PSS solution generated really offer (functionality, perceived value)?

- What are the main actors involved and how should the PSS interact with the client for each solution?

- What are the platform boundaries and what should the PSS system look like for each solution?

- What PSS solution is the best (to start working on)?

- What are the investment requirements for each solution?

- How do the ideas generated bring about an improvement in environmental/social impacts?

Questions for PSS **design**:

- What should the PSS system look like and what are the platform boundaries?
- What is the set of primary and secondary functionalities offered?
- What is the quality level needed?
- What are the roles, the interactions and the business models of each player in the system (interact with the client and with each other in detail)?
- What is the perceived value of the offer and estimated appreciation of the client and at which maximum costs?
- What are the expected improvements (people, planet, profit)?
- What are the investment requirements?

The MEPSS methodology is accessible by using two main tools: a handbook and a web tool. The handbook gives an introduction, explains the design phases and guides users towards relevant tools. The tool descriptions can be found in the Annex of the MEPSS handbook. The web tool provides content on all layers of the methodology. Its navigation guides the user through the methodology. The web tool also functions as a download platform.

The MEPSS handbook and web tool are available via the website: www.mepss.nl.

5.2.9 Highly Customerised Solutions (HiCS)

The Highly Customerised Solutions (HiCS) project was funded under the GROWTH programme of the 5th Framework Programme of the EU and deals with methodology and case studies for developing sustainable innovations within partnerships of different actors. It does so by generating industrialised, context-specific and sustainable solutions, co-created in a partnership framework with customers and other stakeholders, including industrial partners and NGOs (non-governmental organisations). The area of research is food delivery and shopping, preparation and consumption for people with reduced access to food in Europe. So the goal of HiCS is: co-creating industrialised sustainable solutions for food and people with reduced mobility.

The project partners are located in Spain, Italy, UK, Belgium and the Netherlands. Two examples of the resulting solutions are described below.

PuntoX (Italy)

This solution provides a system of products, services and expert knowledge for delivering individual and healthy food. Target groups of this PSS are customers who want to have healthy food (e.g. athletes), who need a special diet (e.g. diabetics and allergic persons), but also people with a temporary need for a special diet (e.g. pregnant women, patients). These target groups can, for example, compile their menus, which vary in preparation complexity, online. The food is produced using organic agricultural products and for delivery a bicycle delivery service and special dining corners are offered.

In the development of this PSS environmental aspects (increasing the use of organic agriculture) and social aspects (individual, healthy food provision for patients or the elderly, for example) have been tackled.

La Fiambrera (Spain)

The project 'La Fiambrera' focuses primarily on the elderly and people with reduced mobility, who cannot or do not want to cater for themselves any more. Here also a delivery service for menus is offered, which at the same time provides the opportunity for a certain social control. Customers can collect their meals by picking them up at so-called food stations. When this does not happen, it is a signal for the service provider to react and check why the elderly person was not able to collect the food.

At the same time the PSS can service small and medium-sized enterprises with meals. The third component of the PSS is a shopping service for fresh food products, which can be delivered together with the meals. The focus of this PSS is on social sustainability.

In order to develop these partnerships for delivering sustainable innovation, HiCS generated and improved methods to create system-level innovation with PSS (Manzini *et al.* 2004): the so-called **Solution Oriented Partnership Methodology Framework** (SOPMF).

Examples of the methods and tools used in the solution development are 'context of use' analysis, co-operation/partnership methods, innovation scanning, solution design and architecture, benefit planning and assessment/evaluation tools. These tools are part of the integrating solution-oriented partnership methodology framework (see Fig. 5.12). Descriptions of the tools can be found in Annex 2.

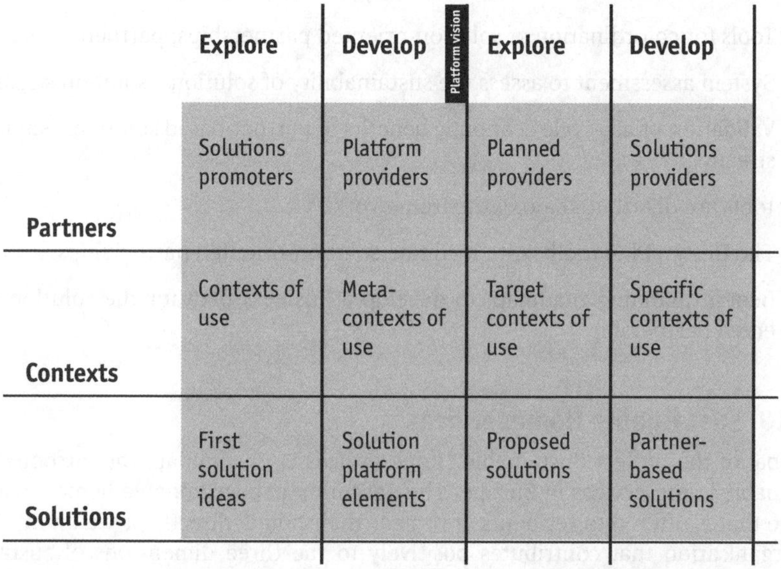

	Explore	Develop	Platform vision	Explore	Develop
Partners	Solutions promoters	Platform providers		Planned providers	Solutions providers
Contexts	Contexts of use	Meta-contexts of use		Target contexts of use	Specific contexts of use
Solutions	First solution ideas	Solution platform elements		Proposed solutions	Partner-based solutions

FIGURE 5.12 Main structure of solution-oriented partnership methodology

Source: Manzini *et al.* 2004

In the course of the project the research partners proposed specific tools to fit the framework and industrial partners used the tools they found most helpful to move towards a partner-based solution. The research partners supported the implementation of the developed new solutions and all partners reflected on progress, tools and the solution-oriented partnership process. In this way research and practice were interconnected and a joint learning process could be organised.

The SOPMF was used to integrate many concepts and tools in one framework and is the main problem-solving tool for setting up a system innovation project within the HiCS project. The progress of the partners, contexts and solutions is visualised in the matrix from left to right.

The basic principle of the SOPMF is to integrate in the process actions that aim to establish alliances between partners and that bring together partners and context. The result is the matrix derived by crossing three streams (partners, contexts and solutions) with four stages of activity, which are exploration and development carried out twice in each stream, before and after developing a common platform vision. The 12 resulting cells suggest key actions in the development process. Horizontal movement in the matrix means that progress has been made in terms of completion of the solution and supporting partnership. Vertical movement means progress has been made in aligning the three themes.

The SOPMF is meant as an interdisciplinary base that facilitators and integrators with different expertise are able to use for creating partnerships among diverse stakeholders. It is not a step-by-step methodology but an open framework that proposes not a linear path but offers different pathways to progress.

Some of the sub-methodologies or toolboxes are bound to a single stream:

- Context-of-use co-research methodology: context stream

- Tools for co-ordination of solution-oriented partnerships: partners stream

- System assessment to assess the sustainability of solutions: solution stream

- Validation of life-cycle economic benefits of partner-based solutions: solution stream

Other tools are distributed along the framework:

- The Design Plan toolbox, to facilitate solution-oriented partnerships

- Benefit planning roadmap, to develop a business plan for the solution-oriented partnership

5.2.10 Sustainable Homeservices

The goal of the project Sustainable Homeservices is to stimulate the introduction of sustainable homeservices in Europe. The definition of a sustainable homeservice is 'a service that is offered to residents at or near their home, directly or via an intermediary organisation that contributes positively to the three dimensions of sustainable development' (www.sustainable-homeservices.com). The hypothesis is that replacing products with services that fulfil the same need of the consumer can reduce the environmental burden. The principle target groups of the project are residents, intermediaries, such as housing organisations, and the service providers. The project recognises that not every product can be replaced by a homeservice. Residents' demands, organisational and economic aspects of the suppliers and intermediaries need to be taken into account.

The project developed a methodology to locate market niches in which the right conditions exist for homeservices. Opportunities for homeservices were analysed in six European countries: Austria, Finland, Germany, The Netherlands, Portugal and Spain. This research was conducted in seven service areas: information and communication, mobility and delivery, care and supervision, recreation, supply and disposal, maintenance and repairs, and safety and security. The basic steps in the methodology are:

- Analysis of the housing situation—looking for framework conditions

- Visualising/categorising the universe of homeservices—answering the questions: Who provides which homeservice? What are the features and demands?

- Questionnaires to the residents to explore which homeservices are mostly used, what features the new/improved homeservices should have and what demands there are for sustainable homeservices

- Questionnaires to external service providers and housing organisations to find out how existing homeservices are organised, to plot a sustainability profile, to locate obstacles and promoting factors, and find trends for the future

- Applying a sustainability evaluation tool to find out whether the homeservice is more sustainable than the reference situation

- Workshop/networking to locate opportunities for new homeservices and define the possible roles of the actors

The methodology seems to be applicable to other need areas as well although the content of its tools needed to be adapted. The Sustainable Homeservice sustainability evaluation tool is included in Annex 2.

5.2.11 Austrian 'Eco-efficient PSS' project

This PSS methodology-related project was carried out within the Austrian research programme 'Factory of Tomorrow' developed by the Austrian Federal Ministry of Transport, Innovation, and Technology (BMVIT).

The 'Eco-efficient PSS' project ran from 2001 to 2003. Its aim was to develop a step-by-step workshop methodology for the development of future markets by the introduction of eco-efficient PSS. During the project a series of five workshops was held with the goal of developing such a methodology for initiating, designing and implementing eco-efficient PSS (cf. www.serviceinnovation.at).[2] The structure of the workshop series was the basis of a practical guideline (manual) for sustainable PSS. The project had a cross-sectoral approach: 13 companies coming from different industry sectors (food

---

2   The publication of the Eco-efficient PSS project is only available in German.

industry, metal, plastics, building and construction, furniture, repair networks, environmental consultants) participated in the workshops.

The sequence of the workshops reflects the process structure applied in the manual. First workshop: A new perspective. The agenda points of this workshop are:

- Introduction to sustainability, ecodesign, the new way of thinking (PSS)
- What are PSS? Emphasis on product-accompanying and product-substituting services
- Successful examples and PSS case studies
- Group work: exploring the existing system versus a user-oriented system

Second workshop: Creativity and innovation for my product:

- Preconditions of innovations
- Creativity techniques for the development of new business ideas
- Practical work: brainstorming

Third workshop: The evaluation of PSS (sustainability performance):

- How to evaluate the sustainability performance of PSS
- Presentation of the sustainability evaluation tool (Improving New Services: INES tool)
- Practical work: using the INES tool

Fourth workshop: Marketing and more—marketing roadmap for the new PSS ideas:

- The marketing of services and of solutions
- Cross-cutting issues for the implementation stage
- Which tools and instruments ease the implementation process?
- Practical work

Fifth workshop: An implementation example from A to Z:

- Description of the PSS
- Presentation of its origins
- Presentation of a practical example (case study)

Sixth workshop: Process evaluation:

- Introduction to evaluation processes (goals, content)
- Presentation of process evaluation checklists

The tools used in the workshops were mainly existing tools: for example, best-practice case studies, brainstorming/-writing, TRIZ, mind mapping, portfolio analysis, checklist for cross-cutting issues and process evaluation checklists. One interesting new tool developed in the project is the INES tool (Improving New Services), described in Annex 2.

Problems and challenges encountered in the workshops that are related to possible gaps in available tools are:

- Finding business partners (communicating the benefits of PSS for industry and finding the same language)

- Identifying new market opportunities

- PSS ideas stay focused on product-oriented solutions

- Each PSS is individual

A lesson learned was that tools should not be too sophisticated. Furthermore, PSS methods and tools may vary by sector.

5.2.12 The PSS innovation workbook by James *et al.*

The focus of this methodology study is on moderating a creation and selection process of possible PSS solutions for companies and giving input to the brainstorming done by companies. The study focused especially on the electronics and ICT sector.

The PSS innovation method is described in *Sustainable Services: An Innovation Workbook* by James *et al.* (2001), which was developed in the context of a European 4th Framework research project (cf. Zaring *et al.* 2001).

The aim of the method is to condense the broad insights generated in the development process into a specific list of possible options from which the most promising can be selected for more detailed consideration during the final stages of the development process. Thus James *et al.* do not suggest a new process step logic but give support to asking the right questions and thinking about the right issues during product-service development. It is suggested that this can be achieved by answering three sequential questions:

- What could you potentially offer as eco-efficient services?

- What eco-efficient services might customers pay for?

- What specific eco-efficient services could you actually offer?

The following is a summary of the input the workbook gives to the companies for answering the three questions above.

Related to the first question 'What could you potentially offer as eco-efficient services?', James *et al.* indicate that there are three generic opportunities available for companies, either singly or in combination:

- A new service concept

- A new client interface

- A new service delivery system

The first and the third option are regarded to be especially relevant to eco-efficiency. Within these categories there are four main service concepts that are seen as supporting eco-efficiency. These are presented to companies as promising areas.

Service concept 1: offering services in association with specific products (product +). One possibility here is to provide add-on services to a product, which extends its utility to customers. Many opportunities occur when products:

- Are difficult to handle

- Require regular maintenance and/or repair, such as industrial cleaning and office equipment

- Require a supporting infrastructure—which can be supplied and maintained by the vendor—to work effectively, e.g. networks for computers

- Require high levels of technical expertise to work effectively

Another class of 'product +' services are those that guarantee specified performance criteria. These are common in the areas of energy and water supply. A third promising area is a move from selling products to hiring or leasing them.

Service concept 2: providing activity management services (also known as facility management), which take responsibility for providing a particular activity on a customer's behalf. This is a situation where a provider provides a complete solution to an ongoing need for a customer. This typically involves:

- Long-term contracts, based on performance of a specified need

- Legal responsibility for achieving the specified performance

- Use of a wide range of products and materials (this is one factor distinguishing it from product-related services, which are still closely linked to a single product)

- A detailed understanding of the customer's business and its needs (often achieved through stationing of the service provider's staff on the customer's premises)

- Involvement in the customer's internal management processes

Service concept 3: providing paid-for advice and information to customers. Examples of this include:

- Customer activities: information about the operations, processes and other activities of the purchaser of the service

- Product and market information: for example, about availability of recycled materials and parts

- System conditions: information about the contextual factors that influence the eco-efficiency of a customer's activities, or those of downstream partners

Service concept 4: providing intermediation services which link buyers and sellers of products. All economies are suboptimal in the sense that there are always some under-utilised capacity, potentially re-usable wastes, etc. This may be because it is not available at the right time, in the right place. However, another barrier to more optimal use has been lack of information about opportunities, primarily because it has been difficult and expensive to collect and collate. The internet and other electronic media overcome this barrier by allowing online markets and brokerage services which make it easier for suppliers to identify potential customers and vice versa.

Eco-efficiency can also be achieved by providing an electronic service which substitutes for a product or a physical activity. This means replacing a materials-intensive means of delivering utility to customers with an information-intensive one.

In answering the second question 'What eco-efficient services might customers pay for?', James *et al.* indicate that there are a number of service-induced customer effects—which again are not mutually exclusive—that contribute to eco-efficiency. They are:

- Behavioural change
- Capacity utilisation
- Dematerialisation/service substitution
- Impact management
- Life extension
- Product redesign
- Resource utilisation
- Revalorisation
- System optimisation

For the third question 'What specific eco-efficient services could you actually offer?', the aim is to identify the specific opportunities of the company and then to select the most promising ideas for further development. A suggested tool to do this is brainstorming. Each suggestion should, in very simple terms, satisfy the criteria of both positive environmental benefit and apparent commercial attractiveness.

5.2.13 Sustainable Product and Service Development: approach for industry

This Sustainable Product and Service Development (SPSD) approach and guide for industry was developed by EPMG, Imperial College London, UK, and Enterprise Ireland, Environmentally Superior Products. The guide provides support for developing more sustainable offerings in the triple-bottom-line context (covering environmental, social and economic aspects). The SPSD approach aims at developing 'innovative offerings' (e.g. services, products, PSS) that are sustainable, achieve the required functionality, meet human needs (or end-user requirements) and are cost-effective (www.enterprise-ireland.com).

The development of the SPSD approach and guide builds on existing support and industry experiences and should be integrated within existing industry sustainability focused approaches such as EMS (environmental management system), Sustainability Management System (SIGMA) and CSR (corporate social responsibility). The guide covers the complete life-cycle of a product and/or service and the associated supply chain.

The guide format presents recommended steps for developing a more sustainable offering. These steps are backed by additional support such as information, training and tools (qualitative and quantitative). The format is open so that the process can be customised to offering, sector, company culture and business systems. The guide has a web-based version: www.sustainableproductsandservices.com.

The steps in the SPSD guide are based on ISO technical report 14062 (ISO 2002). Ongoing/online supporting information and tools guide the process.

- Planning
- Offering development:
  - Concept development
  - Detailed design
  - Testing/prototype
  - Offering launch and marketing
  - Offering review

Planning phase

The core issues of the planning phase are:

- Guidance for initial and ongoing organisation, management and communications, both internally and across the supply chain. The emphasis is on wide stakeholder involvement such as all internal business functions (purchasing, environment, product/service development, finance, marketing, quality management), as well as external partners (e.g. supply/value chain stakeholders, customers (B2B) and experts from SPSD, industry).

- Shifting the focus from the individual company level to the offering supply chain

- Provision of introductory and ongoing information

Offering development phase

To determine the offering in the concept development phase the focus is on the required functionality of the system to meet the end-user need(s). Also, the most sustainable way to provide the required functionality is determined. The central theme in this phase is to widen the view of the companies.

For the sustainability assessment of the offerings the SPSD framework offers some checklists, such as strategies checklist (environmental and social), simplified LCA and environmental product declarations.

The SPSD approach was tested by industry. Within 59 companies nine different, commercially viable offerings were developed, of which three were PSS. These offerings scored predominantly positively on sustainability (compared with the old, reference situation).

5.2.14 PSS models/methodology for specific need areas

The following approaches are not really methodologies for PSS development but are either models of how to structure PSS in a specific business area or how to approach and structure PSS thinking.

PSS model for utilities

This model (see Fig. 5.13) is essentially based on current energy-efficiency services, such as demand-side management (DSM) and least-cost planning (LCP). These services have been used by energy utility companies and are successfully working mostly in business-to-business operations (Mont 2001b). An example is the provision of a constant temperature instead of selling energy.

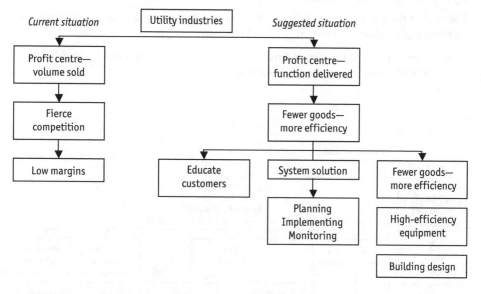

FIGURE 5.13 PSS model for utilities

Source: Mont 2001b

PSS model for companies producing and/or managing chemicals

The starting point of this model is also the potential to decouple the volume of products sold from profitability. This model is based on existing schemes of chemical management services (CMS), which are employed primarily in business-to-business operations. In this model, a CMS provider assumes the responsibility for managing chemicals over some or all stages of the material cycle. The model rests on three premises (Mont 2001b):

● The service provider has the necessary expertise and skills to reduce the absolute use of chemicals and the inefficiencies associated with their management

- The service provider will pursue such improvements, if the proper incentives are in place

- The clients are ready to provide the access for service providers to their facilities and processes and share necessary information with them

The models for utilities and chemical-related businesses are mostly directed towards business-to-business relations. Particular problems arise if these models are applied to private consumers. The difference would be in the complexity of the marketing systems, as well as systems for managing the use phase and/or reverse logistics.

PSS model for durable customer products

The goal of the PSS model for this group (see Fig. 5.14) is to minimise the environmental impact of products in the consumption stage by:

- Improving their efficiency through lower resource consumption and lower consumption of maintenance consumables

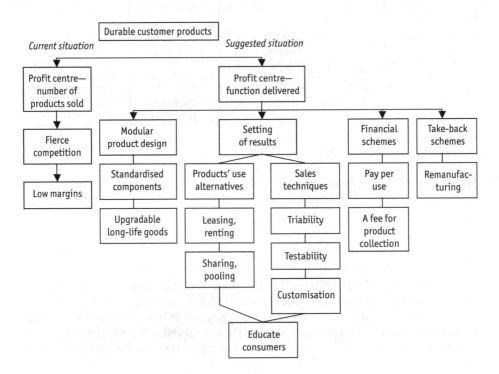

FIGURE 5.14 PSS model for durable consumer products

Source: Mont 2001b

- Improving the efficiency of the function extraction by educating customers on how to use the products in the most efficient, and less environmentally damaging way

- Minimising material throughput by increasing intensity of products' use through shared ownership of the product

- Slowing down material throughput by increasing product lifetime

5.2.15 Overview of the methodologies

Table 5.2 gives an overview of all the PSS methodologies described above, which are not need area-specific. The table allows comparison regarding the following aspects:

- The steps taken in the methodologies

- How the methodology deals with cross-cutting issues of the PSS development process

- The audience or target group

- The purpose and results

- The tools used; PSS-specific tools in bold

Looking at the table the following conclusions can be drawn. The methods organise the process of PSS development. And, although the steps in the methods differ somewhat, they can clearly be grouped into three main blocks:

- Analysis (assessment of strengths and weaknesses, decision-making in prioritisation)

- Idea generation and selection (finding ideas, selecting the most promising ones and detailed design)

- Implementation

Except for the PSS methodology of the Aalborg University, which was developed for students, all methods are targeted at companies that run through the process mostly with the aid of a facilitator (e.g. an external consultant). The intensity of the facilitation varies by methodology and depending on aspects such as size of the company and the experience and knowledge of its employees. The company-oriented methodologies are all developed to be suitable for SMEs. Many also include larger companies or organisations as their potential target group.

The number of methodologies that take sustainability into account is relatively high. As can be seen in Figure 5.15, 10 out of 13 methodologies steer the PSS development process actively towards (environmental) sustainability. ProSecCo, Innopse and the PSS methodology of Aalborg University do not include this specifically in their process.

Of the others, the BISS, Kathalys method and the PSS Innovation Scan for Industry put more emphasis on environmental and economic than on social aspects. That leaves the following methodologies that strive towards sustainability according to the triple bottom line: MEPSS, HiCS, Eco-efficient PSS, DES methodology (covering few social

Methodology	Steps in methodology	How they deal with cross-cutting issues	Audience	Purpose/result	Tools (PSS-specific in bold)
ProSecCo (www.prosecco-village.com)	● Initial phase: strategy development, external input ● Idea generation ● Opportunity development/decide in economic terms ● Solution development: offer/organisational infrastructure ● Go–Decision Gate, Market launch, Exploitation	Decision cluster: check organisational capability, then suggest planning routine	First aiming at SMEs, but now for the informed interested company internal person. If this person is missing, external consultant/process promoter is needed. To support with expertise or knowledge sources (cases, databases) that are not there internally. Depending on starting point of the company. Plus external support	● Improved capability of companies for PSS development ● Concrete result a new solution ● And/or identification of knowledge and skills gap	● Workshop schemes, measuring corporate problems with specific steps, assessment methodology, **online co-operation tools**, software or consulting tool, customising approach ● **Linking area of expertise with decision of problem areas in the process**
INNOPSE innovation studio methodology (Abdalla *et al.* 2003)	● Think it: scrutinising idea, benchmarking against company vision and strategies ● Tool it: integration of new idea into organisation and customers ● TRIZ it: problem-solving stage ● Test it: testing and measurement. Practical steps for execution should be put in place and implemented	This general innovation method is based on a comprehensive methodology that can be fitted to support organisations that offer products and/or services and is more suitable for incremental innovation projects	Targets small and medium-sized enterprises (that want incremental innovation assistance)	Idea development up to 'idea execution and implementation/testing phase'	Balanced scorecards (BSC), brainstorming and mind mapping ● Affinity diagram, the analytical hierarchy process and quality function deployment (QFD) ● TRIZ methodology (i.e. contradiction table, the 40 inventive principle, ARIZ, 76 standard solutions, separation principles, patterns of evolution, substance field analysis)

TABLE 5.2 Overview of the PSS methodologies (continued opposite)

Methodology	Steps in methodology	How they deal with cross-cutting issues	Audience	Purpose/result	Tools (PSS-specific in bold)
PSS methodology, Aalborg University (Morelli 2004)	● Identifying the actors in the network ● Envisioning possible PSS scenarios ● Representing the structure of PSS	The methodology is developed for educational purposes. The format follows the existing design methodology but is largely extended for PSS development	Architecture and design education; students	PSS development methodology for design education	**System maps,** analytical frameworks, scenarios and use cases, IDEF0, **use case scenarios** and **representation techniques.** These tools and methods are not new but are adapted to PSS development
BISS methodology (van der Horst in Manzini *et al.* 2004)	● Definition of current business model ● Mapping out interests of all involved actors ● Making a chart of economical and ecological inefficiencies ● Generation of new PSS ● Definition of the new business model and the key contracts. Also testing	The point of origin is that it is possible to construct business models in such a way that the created PSS inherently induce sustainability. Methodology is open for P, S and PSS solutions	Small, medium-sized and large companies/networks	The methodology focuses on de-linking mechanisms. The end result should be definition and testing of a sustainable business model	**System map,** inefficiencies charts
Kathalys method (Kathalys 2001)	● Exploratory research and definition ● Design ● Product/service specification ● Elaboration and practical experimentation ● Implementation	This fixed methodology is based on existing process steps that guide the user through flexible PSS, sustainability, organisation, user and economical design tracks	Small, medium-sized and large companies/networks	An up-and-running product/service: a fully developed PSS with environmental/economic benefits.	Problem analysis, interviews, Shell scenario method, workshops, ViP method, Delphi, SWOT, roadmaps, LCA, Eco-indicator

TABLE 5.2 (from previous page; continued over)

Methodology	Steps in methodology	How they deal with cross-cutting issues	Audience	Purpose/result	Tools (PSS-specific in bold)
PSS Innovation Scan for Industry (TNO/PwC; Tukker and van Halen 2003)	● Preparation of the PSS ● Innovation Scan ● Introduction of PSS ● Analysis phase ● Idea generation ● Selection ● Management presentation	Flexible system; via questions at the start of each phase the need for further work in this phase is assessed. This allows for doing the scan very quickly if much in-house knowledge is readily available	Small, medium-sized and large companies/networks. The scan has been written for experts working in the R&D departments or business developers of industries and for consultants	The aim of this scan is to formulate a first business case for PSS that gains management commitment for a feasibility study	Most of the tools are general development tools. Some are especially aimed at integrating environmental issues, e.g. Ecodesign portfolio, pragmatic differential tool, progressive abstraction tool
DES methodology (Brezet et al. 2001)	● Exploration, vision and business development ● Policy formulation ● Idea finding ● Strict PSS development ● Realisation	The methodology is not meant as a strict guideline on how eco-efficient PSS should be developed but to assist decision-makers with a structure, suggested actions and tools. In that way the methodology is suitable for the broad variety of PSS	Small, medium-sized and large companies/networks	A detailed and feasible design of the new eco-efficient service that should result in a market introduction. The final phase 'evaluation' should guarantee a process of continuous improvement	Market research tools, SWOT analysis, ViP scenario approach, benchmarking, backcasting, **adapted ecodesign tools** (e.g. **META matrix, adapted LiDS wheel**), Stakeholder analysis, 'Blueprinting', Ecocosts/value approach, Eco-purchase, LCA scenarios, 'Green' communication and financial tools
MEPSS (van Halen et al. 2005)	● Analysis of company and market ● Idea generation identifying opportunities ● Detailed Design ● Implementation	● Matrix, which allows many different ways through the methodology ● Evaluation is cross-cutting issue from simple to advanced (three-tier)	● Designers and external consultants, and/or internal experts in companies. Needs facilitator and process promoter/expert ● Designer can take the role of external facilitator ● Multidisciplinary teams + external	Sustainable solution to deliver satisfaction to the customer	Analysis: **three-tier approach, sustainability**/cost **assessment**, market assessment, **sustainability guidelines**, scenarios, **design plan** (including many steps), **consumer acceptance analysis, system analysis and system maps**

TABLE 5.2 (from previous page; continued opposite)

Methodology	Steps in methodology	How they deal with cross-cutting issues	Audience	Purpose/result	Tools (PSS-specific in bold)
HiCS (Manzini *et al.* 2004)	• Context of use/analysis • Partnership network • Development of solutions/Design	• Flexible system, learning-by-doing approach • Matrix for positioning of starting point and then plan a process	• Large and small companies. With small companies the facilitator was very important; with large companies the facilitator could be the initiator but the process can run on its own with a little external support • Always needs a facilitator/consultant • Multidisciplinary teams + external	• Business plan, pilot case and final assessment • Prepare market launch	• **Context of use analysis, co-ordinating partnership, design plan** (scenarios, user perspective, organisational perspective) • **Benefit plan and validation at system level**, sustainability assessment • **Solution Scan** (scan a company if it is capable of doing PSS), **system map**, interaction storyboard, **solution element brief**, stakeholder motivation matrix
Sustainable Homeservices (Halme *et al.* 2005)	• Analysis of the housing situation • Visualising/categorising the universe of homeservices • Questionnaires to the residents • Questionnaires to external service providers and housing organisations • Applying a sustainability evaluation tool • Locate opportunities for new homeservices and define the possible roles of the actors	The project recognises that not every product can be replaced by a homeservice. Residents' demands, organisational and economical aspects of the suppliers and intermediaries need to be taken into account	The principal target groups of the project are residents, intermediaries, such as the housing organisations, and the service providers	Stimulate the introduction of sustainable homeservices in Europe	Questionnaires, **sustainability evaluation tool**, workshops

TABLE 5.2 (from previous page; continued over)

Methodology	Steps in methodology	How they deal with cross-cutting issues	Audience	Purpose/result	Tools (PSS-specific in bold)
Eco-efficient PSS—Factory of tomorrow (www.serviceinnovation.at)	● Analysis/vision development ● Idea generation ● Evaluation and selection ● Marketing roadmap for PSS ● Implementation step leading to market launch ● Process evaluation	Many complex cross-cutting issues. Evaluation is a cross-cutting issue	● Companies with facilitators ● Especially SMEs (very small: 10–50 people) ● Integrate many stakeholders not just designers ● Multidisciplinary teams + external	Business plan for new PSS offer, prepare market launch	**Workshop concept, case studies,** scenario, customer conferences, **need analysis,** creativity techniques, TRIZ, **INES evaluation,** portfolios, **detailed checklist for implementation issues** including cross-cutting issues, facilitation. **Design manual**
The PSS Innovation Workbook (James et al. 2001)	No process steps but focusing on answering these questions: ● What could you potentially offer as eco-efficient services? ● What eco-efficient services might customers pay for? ● What specific eco-efficient services could you actually offer?	James et al. do not suggest a new process step logic but give support in asking the right questions and thinking about the right issues during product-service development	The study focused especially on the electronics and IT sector	The aim is to condense the broad insights generated in the development process into a specific list of possible options from which the most promising ones can be selected for more detailed consideration during the final stages of the development process	Workshops, brainstorming
Sustainable Product and Service Development (SPSD) approach (Maxwell et al. 2005)	The steps in the guide are based on ISO 14062: ● Planning ● Offering development ● Concept development ● Detailed design ● Testing/prototype ● Offering launch and marketing ● Offering review	The format is open so that the process can be customised to offering, sector, company(ies) culture and business systems. The SPSD approach aims at developing 'innovative offerings'; that can be services, products and PSS	SMEs and others. The SPSD approach was tested with 59 companies	Aims at developing 'innovative offerings' (e.g. services, products, PSS) that are sustainable, achieve the required functionality, meet human needs (or end-user requirements) and are cost-effective	Strategies checklist (environmental and social), simplified LCA and environmental product declarations

TABLE 5.2   (from previous page)

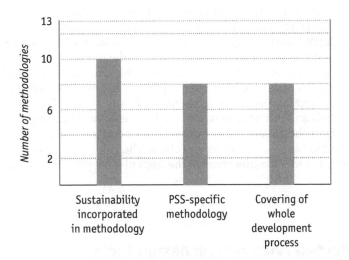

FIGURE 5.15 General characteristics of all the PSS methodologies

aspects), PSS Innovation Handbook, Sustainable Homeservices, and Sustainable Product and Service Development (SPSD).

Eight out of 13 methodologies are specifically aimed at PSS development: MEPSS, Eco-efficient PSS, DES methodology, Kathalys method, PSS Innovation Scan for Industry, PSS Innovation Handbook, Sustainable Homeservices and PSS methodology of Aalborg University. The other five are focused on innovation development in general and do not exclusively direct towards PSS but can also be used to develop products, services or partnerships. These are: ProSecCo, HiCS, Innopse, BISS methodology and Sustainable Product and Service Development (SPSD).

Five methodologies concentrate on specific process phases of the development process:

● Innopse concentrates on the idea development process

● The PSS Innovation Scan for Industry prepares the development team for a management presentation

● The PSS Innovation Handbook is developed to enhance the idea generation and selection phase

● Sustainable Homeservices is focused on locating opportunities and defining the roles of actors in the system

● The PSS methodology (Aalborg University) is focused on idea development and on representation of the developed PSS

The other eight cover the complete development process up to market launch: MEPSS, ProSecCo, HiCS, Eco-efficient PSS, DES methodology, BISS methodology, Kathalys method, Sustainable Product and Service Development (SPSD). So, the methodologies that focus on *sustainability* (covering economic, environmental and social issues), on *PSS development only*, and cover the *complete* development process are MEPSS, Eco-efficient PSS and the DES methodology (the latter with little attention to social aspects).

In Table 5.2 the PSS specific tools that are used in the methodologies are listed (in bold). Following all the research into best practice in (sustainable) PSS methodology and tools the authors of this book have developed an easy and accessible guide to running a first PSS project for companies. It is a compilation and synthesis of the researched methods and tools and enables companies (and students) to run a first PSS project in order to investigate the subject and find out whether it is of interest and useful for them to develop new PSS business strategies and offers. The guide is based on a PowerPoint presentation that guides the user through the steps of a PSS project. It can be found in Annex 1.

5.3 Product-service system design tools

Most of the PSS development and design methodologies presented above suggest working with certain tools at different steps in the process and for different purposes. Such (PSS-specific) tools are indicated in bold in Table 5.2. Below some of the most interesting tools are presented together with a general overview. More tools descriptions can be found in Annex 2 in alphabetical order.

5.3.1 Tools overview

In the overview presented in Figure 5.16 the different tools that are used in PSS design methods are ordered according to their complexity and to six fields of application which more or less explicitly exist in every PSS process:

- General process management
- Analysis/assessment of strengths and weaknesses
- Decision-making, selecting and setting priorities
- Creativity/finding ideas
- Combination of multiple criteria and detailing design
- Implementation

There are also some gaps visible in the overview diagram of PSS tools marked by shaded boxes. In the past some gaps have been identified by research and some of the developed methodologies presented in the previous section have tried to close these gaps; but there are still some left. The approaches to close the gaps are included in the diagram. Similar tools are displayed as a group.

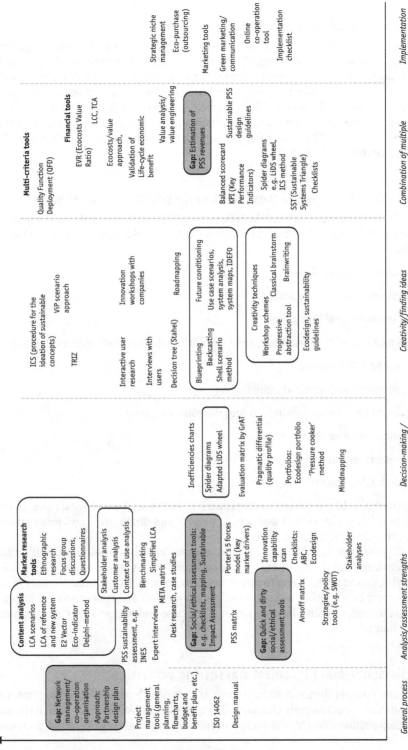

FIGURE 5.16 Tools overview; ordered by complexity and by purpose within the development of PSS

Complexity/time expense

| General process management | Analysis/assessment strengths weaknesses | Decision-making / selecting / setting priorities | Creativity/finding ideas | Combination of multiple criteria, detailing design | Implementation |

Content analysis
LCA scenarios
LCA of reference and new system
E2 Vector
Eco-indicator
Delphi-method

Market research tools
Ethnographic research
Focus group discussions, Questionnaires

Stakeholder analysis
Customer analysis
Context of use analysis

PSS sustainability assessment, e.g. INES
Expert interviews   META matrix
Benchmarking
Simplified LCA

Desk research, case studies

Gap: Network management/ co-operation organisation
Approach: Partnership design plan

Project management tools (general planning, flowcharts, budget and benefit plan, etc.)

ISO 14062

Design manual

Gap: Social/ethical assessment tools: e.g. checklists, mapping, Sustainable Impact Assessment

Innovation capability scan

Checklists:
ABC, Ecodesign

Gap: Quick and dirty social/ethical assessment tools

Porter's 5 forces model (key market drivers)

PSS matrix

Ansoff matrix

Strategies/policy tools (e.g. SWOT)

Stakeholder analyses

Inefficiencies charts

Spider diagrams
Adapted LiDS wheel

Evaluation matrix by GrAT

Pragmatic differential (quality profile)

Portfolios:
Ecodesign portfolio
'Pressure cooker' method

Mindmapping

ICS (procedure for the ideation of sustainable concepts)

TRIZ

ViP scenario approach

Interactive user research

Interviews with users

Decision tree (Stahel)

Innovation workshops with companies

Roadmapping

Blueprinting
Backcasting
Shell scenario method

Future conditioning
Use case scenarios, system analysis, system maps, IDEF0

Creativity techniques   Classical brainstorm

Workshop schemes   Brainwriting
Progressive abstraction tool

Ecodesign, sustainability guidelines

Multi-criteria tools
Quality Function Deployment (QFD)

Financial tools
EVR (Ecocosts Value Ratio)   LCC, TCA

Ecocosts/value approach,

Validation of Life-cycle economic benefit

Value analysis/ value engineering

Gap: Estimation of PSS revenues

Balanced scorecard
KPI (Key Performance Indicators)

Sustainable PSS design guidelines

Spider diagrams e.g. LiDS wheel, ICS method

SST (Sustainable Systems Triangle)

Checklists

Strategic niche management
Eco-purchase (outsourcing)

Marketing tools

Green marketing/ communication

Online co-operation tool

Implementation checklist

5.3.2 Tools for general process management

Tools that can be used for PSS process management have their background in general project management (e.g. planning, flowcharts). A general ecodesign scheme can be found in ISO 14062 as mentioned in Section 5.1.1 on Product design. Visible from the research is a gap in process management tools that deal with multi-stakeholder aspects of PSS. As PSS often involve more stakeholders than pure product or service design, adequate tools for network management, organisation of co-operation and involvement of customers are needed. The 'partnership design plan', developed in the HiCS project is a promising approach (see Annex 2).

5.3.3 Tools for analysis/assessment of strengths and weaknesses

In this field many existing tools are being used (e.g. from the classical marketing side). They vary from simple checklists to complete LCA scenario research tools. Table 5.2 mentions:

- Context of use analysis
- Consumer acceptance analysis
- Innovation capability scans
- PSS sustainability assessment, sustainability evaluation tool, INES evaluation
- Adapted META matrix
- Economical validation at system level

Such tools can be roughly subdivided into the following types:

- Content analysis tools
- Market research tools
- Stakeholder analysis

The gaps in this field are related to assessment of both social and ethical issues; there is a lack of quick social/ethical assessment tools (more qualitative) and more quantitative social/ethical assessment tools.

A weak point, too, is the environmental assessment of systems, because the tools used for environmental assessment of products such as LCA create a heavy burden for the assessing expert when trying to assess a system, for which the boundaries are much wider. It would be desirable to develop an environmental assessment tool for systems that allows for more qualitative evaluation when time and budget in the development project is limited.

5.3.4 Decision-making/selecting/setting priorities

In this field common decision-making tools are used such as portfolio diagrams and decision matrices, qualitatively checking the value of possible solutions. When the aim is to develop sustainable PSS, the tools with an environmental background dominate (for instance, the adapted LiDS [Lifecycle Design Strategies] wheel identified in Fig. 5.16). One group within this field is variations of spider diagrams, which can partly also be used for multi-criteria assessment of solutions.

5.3.5 Creativity/finding ideas

Two main groups of tools can be identified in this field of application:

- Scenario building tools

- Creativity techniques, sometimes enhanced by system analysis and system maps or sustainability guidelines (compare Table 5.2)

In general the tools here vary from simple, yet effective tools for the generation of a number of ideas to more complex tools that guide the user through the creativity process and are almost complete design methods.

5.3.6 Combination of multiple criteria, detailing design

In this field three types of tool can be found:

- Multi-criteria tools

- Financial tools

- Design guidelines

The multi-criteria tools range from lower complexity (checklists) to highly complex tools such as adapted QFD. They always consider a larger number of criteria that a solution must fulfil for it to be chosen for realisation. Financial tools evaluate the cost effects of solutions—some in relation to other factors while some are purely cost assessment tools. In this area a gap can be identified in tools for the specific estimation of PSS cost and revenues, and this is even more so for multi-stakeholder solutions. HiCS developed a tool to fill this gap: the 'Validation of Life-cycle Economic Benefits of Partner-Based Solutions' (see Annex 2). In MEPSS the sustainability assessment tool is cost-based: that is, it translates the environmental and social impacts of solutions into cost factors; thus it becomes a financial tool.

The most elaborate design guidelines covering the sustainability aspects of PSS solutions have been developed in the MEPSS project. They cover all three dimensions of sustainability and offer a simpler (for idea generation) and a more elaborate (for detailed design) level of guidelines (see Annex 2).

5.3.7 Implementation

In the implementation phase of a PSS conventional marketing and business tools are used. The methods reviewed in Table 5.2 use a variety of checklist approaches (e.g. implementation plan, business plan, communication plan). When a focus on sustainability is needed, green marketing and eco-purchasing tools are useful. One interesting specific PSS tool here is strategic niche management, which realises a new solution first in a protected market niche (similar to a pilot project) to learn from these experiences before going to real market launch.

5.4 PSS development experience of SusProNet partner companies

Most of the companies participating in SusProNet have their background in product development and to a lesser extent in service development, rather than development of PSS.

The companies with a background in product development see the service development process as an extension. The result is that service models are frequently left out and that product development models are being used and adapted to the development of PSS. Most companies today already offer some service element in addition to their products. This supports their perception that a further shift into PSS can be based on the 'normal' existing product development models.

Those companies that have a high service element in their products use customer benefits-based design models, which have a holistic approach that maximises value through an understanding of possible commercial drivers, of people, processes, technology and possible partners. But currently, such a holistic approach, integrating these aspects and integrating the two development processes—namely, product and service development—is not widespread.

The experiences of the SusProNet partner companies confirm the statement made above that the integration of sustainability considerations in product and service development is still limited. It is picked up by some leading companies but even then it is not always developed very far, just focused on environmental rather than the social aspects of sustainability, or just included in the later stages of the product(-service) development process (rather than the strategic planning, idea generation and concept development phases).

The experience of the SusProNet companies confirmed that (product or service) business development generally follows the following phases: analysis, creation and realisation. However, opinions differed on how this 'normal' business development process can be converted into a PSS development process. The following sections summarise the experiences and opinions of the companies by phase, preceded by a general section on management.

5.4.1 Management of the PSS development process

There appears to be a large difference in formalisation of the management of the (product and service) business development process among SusProNet partner companies. There are examples of a very formal approach to the innovation process, with well-defined steps and go/no-go decision moments (a so-called 'gate-stage' process. But there are also examples of a more informal approach. Large companies tend to have more formalised processes, whereas small companies do not. In such formalised processes, a programme or project manager normally leads the design and launch of new business propositions. Nowadays more and more of the project manager's work needs some form of support from other business units. Members of the project team are typically from finance, sales, materials sourcing, engineering and other specialised departments. Team members are either dedicated to a single programme or shared between different ones. Programme managers are often responsible for both business and product development. Companies do not expect major differences for a PSS development process.

Many companies use their own tools and procedures for the development process. These tools are related to their current innovation or development processes. Companies feel that these could be adjusted for use in PSS development processes.

5.4.2 Analysis phase

Although the companies use roughly the same general phased approach, they show much dissimilarity in the specific elaboration of the PSS analysis phase. The specific aspects to be analysed do not differ that much between companies (such as market trends, environmental, economic and technological aspects) but the starting point of the process is different. Both a company internal push and a competitor, market or customer pull can act as initiators.

In the analysis phase regular tools are used, such as SWOT analysis, desktop analysis, quality function deployment, value engineering, target costing and market analysis tools. However, the use of these tools and the frequency of use differ between companies.

5.4.3 Idea generation and selection phase

The common business for most of the SusProNet companies is product development. This is also reflected in the modest experience of the participants with PSS-specific tools and methodologies for the idea generation and selection phase. Also, here mainly tools are used that have a background in product development.

Even in companies with formal processes it is not common practice to use specific tools to generate ideas. Either teams or individuals continuously develop ideas. The starting points of ideas also show great diversity, such as originating from a wide range of structured and ongoing activities or from individual promoters. Most companies, however, rely on multiple inputs for this process.

Larger companies tend to have research groups that have the task of generating new technologies and business ideas based on their own or the company's strategic vision; but they also have the task of elaborating new ideas or basic concepts coming from other sources.

When at a certain moment an idea needs more time and money to be elaborated, a more formal decision moment is built in and all relevant departments are involved (e.g. R&D, service, marketing, production, sales). Depending on the size of the company, the preparation of the project proposal is done by a few persons or a larger team with more specific knowledge. The new idea will usually be compared with other options and already running projects, normally by a management team with cross-departmental backgrounds. Selection of ideas is mainly done on the basis of expected (short-term) financial benefits. Examples of important considerations are: revenue, strategic added value, profitability, judgement of project portfolio (balance between short-term and long-term projects, balance between low-risk and high-risk projects), available personnel and investment money, and sometimes opportunities for grants or subsidies.

Most of the companies focus on economic benefits in the idea generation and selection phase, so sustainability as a driver is still in its infancy. PSS have therefore more difficulties in this phase because, for example, revenue is much harder to predict compared with products. One important conclusion of SusProNet for this phase is that for PSS the go/no-go decision criteria should not only include value in monetary terms (cost/revenues) but also cover the immaterial value that can be created by PSS (image, convenience, risk reduction, better customer relations, etc.).

5.4.4 Implementation phase

As most companies in SusProNet have experience with tools from traditional product development, the majority of the companies use or intend to use traditional marketing tools in the implementation phase of a PSS project. PSS implementation is not regarded as being so different from launching other innovations on the market and therefore the expectation is that applying conventional marketing tools is not a problem.

However, some companies expected a difference in testing the PSS idea, since now service elements have to be included in the prototyping and testing phase.

Those companies that include sustainability in the PSS development tend to use green marketing and eco-purchasing tools in the implementation phase.

5.5 Conclusions

5.5.1 PSS methodology

Thirteen PSS methodologies, gathered during the SusProNet project, have been presented in this chapter. These methodologies have been chosen out of the wealth of different available methodologies and tools for product and/or service development and innovation throughout the SusProNet project, because they seemed most interesting and promising for the combination of product and service system design and the inclusion of sustainability. All methods see SMEs as their primary target group, though most of them can also be used by larger companies or organisations. All methodologies rely on some kind of external support, varying from a facilitator of workshops to a full-time external consultant. This facilitation by a highly experienced and somewhat neutral person or actor is seen as extremely important in the PSS design process and in PSS projects because the multi-actor development requires stringent facilitation.

Ten of the methodologies go further than just (economic) PSS business development. They also include environmental aspects and, on top of this, some also include social aspects (following the triple-bottom-line philosophy). The experience of these methods is that the evaluation of environmental and/or social aspects of sustainability is seen as the most complicated element.

This was the reason for the SusProNet partners to develop their own simple PSS sustainability screening tool that was applied in the SusProNet industry workshops. It is included in Annex I of this volume as the SusProNet PSS guide.

Not all the methodologies cover the entire development process or are specifically designed for PSS development. Some methods merely aim to develop a business plan for a PSS rather than the PSS itself. Others focus on development of innovations in general. The methodologies that focus on sustainability (covering economic, environmental and social issues), that are developed for PSS development only, and cover the complete development process are MEPSS, Eco-efficient PSS and the DES methodology (James *et al.* 2001; Brezet *et al.* 2001; van Halen *et al.* 2005). The other methods are, of course, not without value. For instance, methods that focus only on developing a business plan give a quick insight into whether PSS is a promising business model for a firm (e.g. Tukker and van Halen 2003).

Despite the inevitable differences, one can see a clear and converging pattern in all methods reviewed. The methodologies tend to see three main phases in PSS development, roughly split up as follows:

Step 1: analysing

- The current situation

- The reference product/service

- The customer needs and expectations

- The internal situation of companies and their external (potential) partners and thus exploring and identifying new business opportunities in the PSS area

Step 2: creating and detailing new ideas

- Based on the findings or the knowledge available about business opportunities, new ideas for PSS are generated

- The most promising are selected

- The selected idea is detailed

- Evaluation shows whether the detailed concept is good enough to be realised

Step 3: realising the detailed concept

- Preparation of market launch, developing marketing strategy

- Production of the material and immaterial parts of the PSS

- Market testing

- Market launch

- Evaluation of success of concept

- Review of the PSS development process

As with product development, the PSS development process should involve a review of every step and a review of the success of the whole process to organise a continuous improvement as suggested in quality management processes (e.g. ISO 9000ff., ISO 14062).

Furthermore, all the reviewed reports on method development show a clear desire to move away from the conceptual drawing boards and to start application in practice. Most of the methods have been developed in some kind of research context and were partly applied in practice in pilot projects. Now they need broad testing in practice to refine the methodologies. This will also allow for a more elaborated development of methods, and, from a broader perspective, will allow a merging of best methodology practice. The lack of broad PSS methodology application in practice and in a market context can be seen as the main gap in the move towards more successful PSS in the marketplace.

5.5.2 PSS tools

The tools that are used for PSS development can be split up according to their function. The analysed PSS methodologies show that, for all three steps mentioned above (analysis, creation and detailing new ideas, realising the detailed concept), tools have been developed. Tools generally were taken from normal innovation or business development methodologies, but amended with specific PSS content.

From this chapter and Chapter 3, one can deduce that there are the following gaps in availability of tools:

- A PSS is usually put on the market by a network of firms. But tools and methods to find the right partners and organise the new co-operative arrangements efficiently are still largely missing. Only the HiCS project paid some attention to this, and there still seems to be room for improvement (Manzini *et al.* 2004)

- Since PSS is put on the market in networks, the many firm–firm interaction points may create significant transaction costs. PSS development could be facilitated by the development of standard agreements and revenue models for specific PSS types

- In general, the question of how to assess the environmental and social benefits and drawbacks of PSS has not yet been solved in a satisfactory way in the methods reviewed. A main problem is that PSS often delivers a different functionality from a traditional product (e.g. enhanced, or reduced consumer satisfaction; think of a car pooling system versus owing a car, or eating in a restaurant versus dining at home). Furthermore, where environmental assessments (e.g. LCA) are fairly well developed, this is not the case for the assessment of social sustainability

- Since PSS in general include activities formerly performed by the user beyond the (former) point of sales, assessment of costs of the offering become even more complicated than usual. Rigid cost assessment methods are hence essential. This is even more relevant for result-oriented PSS (activity management and functional result), since here the provider has to take responsibility for the use stage. Risks, liabilities, financial uncertainties and ambiguities can be reduced if methods become available for the following points:

- Standardised, meaningful ways of defining specific results
- Development of checklists for the most common use phase risks and liabilities
- Standardised, meaningful ways of dividing the responsibilities for use phase risks and liabilities between user and provider
- Rigid scenario approaches for analysing potential costs for the provider in case of uncertainties with regard to user behaviour or events in the context influencing the use phase

Some of the research projects to design PSS methodologies created their own PSS design and assessment tools (e.g. HiCS and MEPSS project) in order to close these gaps. Examples of new PSS tools are the 'Partnership design plan', the sustainability assessment tools, the 'PSS Sustainability Guidelines', and the 'Validation of Life-cycle Economic Benefits of Partner-Based Solutions'. These tools are included in Annex 2.

For the creation of more strategic and successful (and sustainable) PSS in practice it seems unnecessary to develop more new PSS tools but rather to make the existing tools available to the public, e.g. by offering them via an internet platform, and encourage the use of the existing methodologies and tools. As these are quite diverse and more or less suitable for different types of audience, market situation, sector, etc., one sensible activity could be to offer a 'pathfinder' for companies to select the most suitable PSS methodology and tools for their purposes. After application in practice an evaluation of the success of the methodologies should take place to draw conclusions and recommendations for refinement of the PSS methodologies and further PSS development. Another support is the cases listed in the SusProNet need area reports.

Finally, since different people use tools in different ways and contexts, it seems not absolutely crucial for a successful PSS project what kinds of tool are used, but more how the process is facilitated and which questions and motivations lead the process: 'a fool with a tool is still a fool'.

5.5.3 Best practice of SusProNet partner companies

A review of the experience of the company partners in SusProNet showed that in their new business development processes they in general tend to discern the phases indicated above: analysis, creation and realisation. But in carrying out a development process companies do not rely on PSS methods reviewed here, and mostly use their own specific set of tools and procedures.

Most SusProNet partner companies have a background in product development. There are few that focus on service development only. Although all partner companies offer at least some service, the development of services is mostly seen as an add-on. Companies tend to use and adapt their existing methods and tool set to the specific circumstances for the development of PSS, since they do not expect major differences for a PSS development process. The companies in general had little experience with PSS-specific tools and methodologies.

Apart from the differences in the use of methods and tools, the partner companies showed more dissimilarity in their development processes:

- The degree of formalisation varies. Many companies did not have a very formalised approach to new business development, let alone to PSS development. Large companies tend to have more formalised approaches than SMEs

- The starting point of the development process is different: for example, by a competitor/market pull or a company internal push

Aspects that the companies have in common are:

- The development process tends to become more formal when an idea is developed further

- Sustainability as a driving force is still in its infancy. For example, the selection of ideas is mainly done on the basis of expected financial benefits

5.5.4 Synthesis and conclusions

Table 5.3 synthesises the findings in this chapter with regard to the factors that determine successful PSS development (see e.g. Goedkoop *et al.* 1999; Maßelter and Tischner 2000; Brezet *et al.* 2001; Kathalys 2001; Tukker and van Halen 2003; MEPSS project [to be released]). The table summarises for each main phase in PSS development (analysis, creation, implementation) the following elements:

- Critical success or failure factors that determine the outcome of a PSS project are presented also according to their appearance in the development process

- Possible solutions for these factors are presented together with tools to solve the problems

- Gaps within the PSS development process that occur when there are no tools available for solving the occurring problems

	Names of main PSS design phases	Success/failure factors	Possible solutions	Overview tools to use	Gaps in tool development
Analysing	*Business vision development* *Exploration* *Exploratory research and definition* *Strategic assessment of opportunities* *Analysis of company and market* *Analysis/vision development* *Definition of current business model* *Planning*	To innovate on a system level, people and companies need to have a long-term vision	Formulate strategy and policy for the short, medium and long term	• Strategy and policy tools (e.g SWOT) • Scenario writing • Backcasting • Roadmapping • Context of use analysis	
		System-level innovation involves high risks because of high level of uncertainty	Spread risks by joining forces		
		For system innovations business coalitions or new businesses are needed		• Network management • General process management • Pre-diagnose company scan • Solution scan (company capability scan)	
		(Re)design whole production and consumption systems (PSS)	Multi-stakeholder and -actor approach with new forms of co-operation		Gap in development of tools and methods that organise the new co-operations
				Other tools: • Market research tools (mostly qualitative) • META, a qualitative, quick environmental assessment of a product service system • ViP scenario approach • Benchmarking • Workshops with companies • Delphi method • Shell scenario method • Expert interviews • Desk research • Mind mapping • Ethnographic research	

TABLE 5.3 Synthesis of phases, success/failure factors, possible solutions and tools (continued over)

Source: Structure of the synthesis table based on Brezet *et al.* 2001

Names of main PSS design phases		Success/failure factors	Possible solutions	Overview tools to use	Gaps in tool development
	Policy formulation	Goals and strategies need to be formulated in such a way that an eco-efficient combination of products and services is a possible outcome	View from a higher level of abstraction. What kind of functionality or added value do you want to deliver?	● ViP ● Roadmapping ● Progressive abstraction tool	
	Scenario development	An environmental goal should be formulated	First the current situation needs to be analysed on environmental impact. Then goals for the new PSS can be formulated	● Current ecodesign tools ● LCA scenarios ● Adapted MET matrix (META tool)	
Analysing	*Context of use analysis* *Think it* *Mapping out interests of all involved actors*	Social/ethical goals should be formulated	Analyse present situation, then set goals		Gap in social/ethical assessment tools development
		When a network of companies is involved, a joint goal needs to be formulated	Project management, stakeholder analysis	● Project management tools (planning, flowcharts, budget, etc.) ● Stakeholder motivation matrix	
		A network of companies needs to be managed	Central management	● Network management ● Partnership co-ordination tools	Gap in development of tools and methods

TABLE 5.3 (from previous page; continued opposite)

Names of main PSS design phases	Success/failure factors	Possible solutions	Overview tools to use	Gaps in tool development
Analysing			Other tools: • External analysis (customer need, external opportunities and threats) • Internal analysis (strengths, weaknesses of the company or companies) • Stakeholder analysis • Benchmarking • Workshops with companies and consumers • Expert interviews • Desk research • Interviews with users • Enquiries • Interactive user research • Future conditioning • Eco-indicator • Porter's 5 forces model (key market drivers) • Balanced Scorecard and KPI (key performance indicators) • Spider diagrams (by econcept) • ICS (procedure for the ideation of sustainable concept) • Case studies	that organise the new co-operations

TABLE 5.3 (from previous page; continued over)

Names of main PSS design phases	Success/failure factors	Possible solutions	Overview tools to use	Gaps in tool development
Creation — *Idea finding* / *System design* / *PSS idea development*	• Customer need should be translated in functions, not in products • Customising offers or the delivery of the offer to clients • Creating value for clients, by adding quality and comfort	Function-based market research	• Quality function deployment (QFD) • Workshop schemes • Linking area of expertise with decision of problem areas in the process • Design plan (scenarios, user perspective, organisational perspective) • Interaction storyboard • Use case scenarios	
Idea generation identifying opportunities / *Partnership network* / *Tool it*	Products as well as services should be regarded as possible part of the solution	Environmental gain as a starting point	• Blueprinting • Adapted MET matrix (META matrix) • Adapted LiDS wheel • Green options generation • Benchmarking • Ecocosts/value approach • Pragmatic differential tool • System analysis and system maps	
Making a chart of economical and ecological inefficiencies / *Offering development*	The development of different elements of the solutions should be planned in advance	Project management	• Project management tools • Linking area of expertise with decision of problem areas in the process	
	Commitment of possible consortium is essential	Develop common project agenda/plan	'Pressure cooker' method	
	Creating new functions (new functionality can create new market demand and thus commercial success); making smart or unique combinations		• Creativity techniques to generate ideas • ViP approach • Classical brainstorm • Brainwriting • Progressive abstraction tool • Inefficiencies charts	

TABLE 5.3 (from previous page; continued opposite)

Names of main PSS design phases	Success/failure factors	Possible solutions	Overview tools to use	Gaps in tool development
			Other tools: ● More expanded external analysis, especially among future users ● Second internal analysis ● Ansoff matrix ● PSS matrix (TNO/PwC; see Annex 1) ● Value analysis/value engineering	
Strict development (design) *System design* *PSS design*	The development is split up into several parallel sub-processes	Outsourcing or purchasing	● Eco-purchase ● Blueprinting ● System maps ● Solution element brief ● IDEF0 tool	
Detailed design *Solution development* *Development of solutions/design*	An indication is needed of the environmental gain of designed concepts	Quick and dirty environmental analysis	● LCA scenarios ● EVR (Ecocosts Value Ratio) ● The Sustainable Systems Triangle ● Sustainability/cost assessment ● Sustainability guidelines ● INES evaluation	
Evaluation and selection *TRIZ it*	Indication of the social/ethical impact of designed concepts		● Sustainability/cost assessment ● INES evaluation	Gap in 'quick and dirty' social/ethical assessment tools
Generation of new PSS	The final total solution should result in environmental gain	Special ES strategies and rules of thumb	● Adapted LiDS ● The sustainable systems triangle ● Sustainability/cost assessment	

*(Left margin label spanning rows: **Creation**)*

TABLE 5.3 (from previous page; continued over)

Names of main PSS design phases		Success/failure factors	Possible solutions	Overview tools to use	Gaps in tool development
Creation				Other tools: • Focus group discussions • In-depth customer interviews • Consumer acceptance analysis • Ecodesign portfolio • Pragmatic differential (quality profile) • Simple LCA (e.g. Ecoscan software) • Porter's 5 forces model (key market drivers) • Benefit plan and validation • TRIZ	
Realisation	*Realisation*	All components should be completely developed and tested before the final PSS can be marketed	Thorough planning and management	• Online co-operation tools • Detailed checklist for implementation	
	Elaboration and practical experiment	The solution will often be relatively new for the customer	Good communication: increasing the quality of contacts with clients (e.g. earlier in process, more frequent or personal)	Green communication	
	Implementation				
	Go-Decision Gate	The final version needs to be evaluated on market success and environmental impact	To asses the environmental impact of services, they need to be described as a collection of products	• EVR • LCA scenarios	
	Marketing roadmap for PSS and implementation step				
	Test it	The final version needs to be evaluated for social/ethical aspects	Assessment of social/ethical aspects of e.g. user interface of the PSS design; influence on society, both regional as global factors		Gap in social/ethical assessment tool development
	Definition of new business model and key contracts				

TABLE 5.3 (from previous page; continued opposite)

Names of main PSS design phases		Success/failure factors	Possible solutions	Overview tools to use	Gaps in tool development
Realisation	*(Process) evaluation*	Decreasing the threshold of a large initial or total investment sum for customers, by sharing, leasing or hiring	Use possibility for leasing, sharing or hiring		
	Monitoring PSS after introduction			Tools: ● EVR (Ecocosts Value Ratio) ● Financial tools ● LCA analysis of the new PSS ● E2 Vector	
	Exploitation				

TABLE 5.3 (from previous page)

Part IV
Potential for product-services in five need areas

6
Introduction to the need area-specific chapters

Arnold Tukker
TNO, The Netherlands

As already indicated in Chapter 1, SusProNet consisted of seven lead institutes, some 30 mostly industrial members, and some 20 representatives from other EU-funded PSS (produce-service system) projects. These participants in SusProNet were pragmatically clustered into five groups. Product-services are primarily related to fulfilling an (integrated) final client need. The leading principle for clustering was hence—as far as possible—the final market a participant was interested in, or, in SusProNet terms, the 'need area' his or her organisation served. Each need area group was facilitated by a member (or work package leader) of the SusProNet co-ordination team. The character of the companies involved in SusProNet, and the need to have groups that were more or less of similar sizes determined the need areas chosen:

- Base materials
- Information and communication
- Office workspace
- Food
- Households

The assignment of each need area group was to develop:

- Sector-specific insight into the main areas of opportunities for PSS
- Sector-specific insight into the best approach to develop PSS, and some specific elaborations
- Sector-specific insights in gaps in knowledge, etc.

Furthermore, each group would hopefully be a productive environment for developing PSS ideas. However, since a project such as SusProNet had to focus on networking rather than research in development, PSS development could not be supported in the project.

The following chapters describe the results of this need area work. Below, we briefly describe the common approach that was followed for developing each need area chapter.

6.1 General approach of the need area work

From an initial review of the state of the art in PSS development it had become clear that PSS development normally takes place in three main steps (see Chapter 5). With three workshops (WS) in the project, the logical consequence was that each of them would cover one of the main steps in each main methodology for PSS development, i.e.

- Analysis (of the sector, company strengths and weaknesses, leading to broad ideas about what kind of PSS will have added value)

- Creation (idea generation for practical, concrete PSS, and evaluating the feasibility and added value of these PSS)

- Realisation (how to implement the PSS ideas within companies or clusters of companies)

The first SusProNet conference had the function of validating the outcome of WS1 and disseminating ideas about the areas within sectors where PSS can have added value. The second conference had the function of validating all lessons learned with a much broader audience and disseminating the whole package.

In general, the WP (work package) leader was responsible for doing preparatory inventories and analyses, facilitating workshops and producing results in writing. The members were asked for targeted contributions based on their in-house practice, to provide case material where relevant, and to comment on draft texts. The need area work roughly followed the following tracks:

- Inventory track. Before each workshop/conference the WP leader made an inventory of methods and tools that can be used in this step of PSS development, and made where relevant a need area-specific elaboration. As part of this inventory the SusProNet companies in these need area groups sent information about how they deal with this step in PSS development, what bottlenecks they experienced, etc.

- Active track. Companies were invited to check each step in the PSS development process 'at home' on the basis of their regular business development experiences, and present ideas and bottlenecks inventoried during the workshop

- Learning/reflection track. The results from the inventory and active tracks allowed for learning and reflection. In part this took place during the discussions on the workshops and conferences, and in part it was the task of the WP leader to accumulate the lessons in a final document

6.2 Structure of the need area chapters

During SusProNet, for each need area an extensive report (typically 80–100 pages) was produced containing the following chapters:[1]

1. Introduction
2. Product-services in the need area
3. Analysis (in part based on the results of Workshop 1, January 2003)
4. Idea generation (in part based on the results of Workshop 2, October 2004)
5. Implementation (in part based on the results of Workshop 3, January 2004)
6. Conclusions (written between May and October 2004)

The following chapters contain those sections of Chapters 2–6 of the need area documents that provide insight into the market opportunities, and the need area-specific development problems of PSS. Each chapter deals with the following issues:

● An introduction to the need area, and the experiences with PSS (based on Chapter 2 in the above list)

● An analysis of societal and economic trends and sustainability demand, which allows for a first translation into areas of opportunity for PSS (based on Chapter 3 in the above list)

● An overview of promising PSS ideas (based on Chapter 4 in the above list)

● An overview of the main implementation challenges and approaches to overcome these challenges (based on Chapter 5 in the above list)

---

1   The full need area reports (Frazão and Rocha 2004; Charter *et al.* 2004; Verkuijl *et al.* 2004; Tempelman *et al.* 2004; Vercalsteren and Geerken 2004) are available from the SusProNet co-ordination team and at www.suspronet.org.

7
Need area 1: base materials

Rui Frazão and Cristina Rocha

INETI, Portugal

7.1 Product-service systems for need area 'base materials': an overview

The main aim of this section is to generate a 'bird's eye' view of the state of the art of PSS (product-service systems) in the base materials need area. In-depth analysis of the state of the art, opportunities, best practice and research needs will take place in the following sections. The working definition for base materials, adopted in the context of this project is: materials (substances or compounds) used to perform a given process, either in a site or in a household.

In order to establish a categorisation for this need area, the classification used at EUROSTAT (EC 2001a) for material flow accounts in Europe applies:

- Raw materials
  - Fossil fuels
  - Minerals
  - Biomass
  - Secondary raw materials
- Semi-manufactured products
  - From fossil fuels
  - From minerals
  - From metallic minerals
  - From non-metallic minerals
  - From biomass

Considering the interests of the SusProNet members participating in this group work, and in order to avoid an approach to the subject that is too wide and therefore worthless, this report focuses on two 'sectors' within the need area, which is described in the next section:

- Construction materials
- Chemicals

7.1.1 Description of the sector

The European Union's construction industry

According to the European Construction Industry Federation (FIEC 2003a), the construction activity within the then 15 Member States was worth a total of around €900,000 million (9.9% of the EU's GDP; 49.6% of the EU's gross fixed capital formation). The sector is the largest employer in Europe: more than 11 million people (7.2% of the total employment, 28.1% of industrial employment). However, employment dropped by 10% in 2002.

The EU construction industry comprises over 2.3 million firms, 97% of which are SMEs (small and medium-sized enterprises) with fewer than 20 employees, and 93% with fewer than ten operatives.

The construction industry covers several activities grouped into four sub-sectors:

- Housebuilding sector: includes individual dwellings, apartment blocks and social housing schemes (24% of production)

- Non-residential sector: covers the construction of offices, hospitals, hotels, industrial buildings and educational establishments (33% of production)

- Civil engineering sector: covers the construction of roads, railways, bridges, tunnels and hydraulic structures (18% of production)

- Rehabilitation and maintenance sector: covers the activities of repair, extension and maintenance of dwellings, non-residential buildings, etc. (25% of production)

The growth rate was 0.6% in 2002, ranging from 8.1% in the United Kingdom, due to the contribution from the public sector, and 4.6% in Spain, mainly due to investments in infrastructures, to a growth rate of –5.5% in Germany.

As far as the sub-sectors are concerned, the slowdown (1.4% in 2002; 2.5% in 2001) recorded in the civil engineering sector, which largely depends on public investments, and in the private non-residential sector (–0.7% in 2002; 2.3% in 2001), was partially compensated by a slight recovery in the residential sector (0.5% in 2002).

In 2003, industry expects to see another slowdown in building (0.0% in 2003; 0.4% in 2002), in new housing (–0.8% in 2003; 0.6% in 2002), and in the private non-residential sector (–1.5% in 2003; –0.7% in 2002). On the other hand, industry is expecting improvements in the public non-residential sector (2.8% in 2003; 2.6% in 2002) and in the civil engineering sector (3.1% in 2003; 1.4% in 2002), due to intervention from the public sector in a number of countries.

Therefore, the growth of the sector is mainly being sustained by the public sector.

The European Union's chemicals industry

According to the European Chemical Industry Council (CEFIC 2003a), the EU's chemicals production was estimated at €527 billion; the EU is the leading chemicals producing area in the world (28.6%), followed by the USA (26.3%) and Asia (12.7%, excluding Japan and China). The chemical industry's contribution to the EU gross domestic product amounts to 2.4%.

The output of the chemical industry covers four wide ranges of products:

- Base chemicals cover petrochemicals and derivatives and basic inorganic substances. They are sold to the chemical industry itself or to other industries (38.2% of sales)

- Speciality chemicals cover the auxiliaries for industry, dyes and pigments, oleo-chemicals, crop protection, and paints and inks. Fine chemicals represent pharmaceutical intermediates, agro-intermediates and chemical intermediates (27.8% of sales)

- Pharmaceuticals represent both basic pharmaceutical products and pharmaceutical preparations (23.4 % of sales)

- Consumer chemicals cover soaps and detergents, perfumes and cosmetics, and are sold to final consumers (10.6% of sales)

Over the period 1997–2002, chemicals production grew more strongly in the EU (3.1% per annum) than in either the USA (1%) or Japan (−0.1%). Over ten years (1992–2002), the EU chemicals industry grew by 3.3% per annum, while growth in the US and Japan was 2% and 1.4%, respectively. However, the proportion of EU chemical industry sales (excluding pharmaceuticals) devoted to research and development decreased in 2000 to 2.1%, which is lower than both the USA (2.6%) and Japan (3.5%).

Pharmaceuticals represented the biggest growth of the EU chemical industry over the period 1997–2002 (6.2%). In contrast, consumer chemicals and basic chemicals grew at much more modest rates (2.0% and 0.2%, respectively).

The chemical industry supplies all sectors of the economy. However, the major share (30%) of chemical products is further processed within the sector itself. In many cases, it is only after several processing stages that the products go to outside customers.

The EU chemical industry comprises over 25,000 firms, 98% of which are SMEs. These account for 45% of added value and 46% of employment. Only 2% of the EU firms employ more than 499 employees but generate 55% of the total added value.

7.1.2 Approaches to PSS development

Many examples of PSS for the chemical sector are related to the management of the chemical products, in a varied range of situations: in the most integrated approach the PSS provider is responsible for all activities, from procurement of the chemical (including the search for alternatives) to its end-of-life management. The client is interested in a given *result*, say a chemical reaction, in a specified chemical process, or pest control, and not in the product (the chemical); therefore these are **result-oriented** PSS. Here we find chemical management services[1] or integrated pest management. In other examples of PSS for chemicals, the ownership of the chemical remains with the client but additional services are offered, such as recycling of the chemicals (one well-known example is for solvents) or return of the packaging (**product-oriented** PSS). Fewer examples of **use-oriented** PSS were found, yet there are chemical manufacturers that rent chemicals. The producer owns the substance and rents it to the user, remaining responsible for the end-of-life management.

The same thinking applies for construction materials. Examples are found in the literature where again the client pays for a given *result* (co-development systems in the building industry[2]) or services are added to a *product* (renewing of buildings or reversed logistics of building materials).

Both in the construction materials business and in the chemicals business, the majority of PSS situations fall in the category of **business-to-business** (B2B).

7.1.3 Some examples of current PSS

Table 7.1 describes examples of the above-mentioned PSS relating to construction materials and chemicals. The business relationship (business-to-business [B2B] or business-to-consumer [B2C]) is indicated.

7.2 Analysis: PSS opportunities in the need area 'base materials'

This section aims at analysing trends and developments in the base materials need area. The main aim is to develop foresight for the need area, including the main sustainability boundary conditions, and on this basis to identify broad areas where PSS development could be a useful business model. The analysis presented in this section is focused on the sectors selected earlier:

● Construction materials

● Chemicals

---

1   Chemical management services: the PSS provider manages the procurement, delivery, inspection, inventory, storage, labelling and disposal of chemicals for industrial customers (White *et al.* 1999).
2   Co-development systems in building industries: in this PSS concept a service precedes the delivery of a customised product (or service). 'Co-' means in this case the involvement of the customer in the product, service or PSS development process. Co-development means a substantial change in the role of the client, who becomes active as a co-designer/developer. This requires new methods of communication between the providing companies and their actual and potential clients (Price-waterhouseCoopers, informal communication).

7.2.1 Trends and developments relevant for PSS development

By analysing the main trends for both construction and chemicals sectors, including the regulatory trends, opportunities and threats can be foreseen.

General trends and developments

Construction materials

Owens Corning, the corporation that invented glass fibre, has recently identified basic consumer and industry trends shaping the building materials markets around the world[3] and which provide an interesting overview of developments:

Consumer trends

- **Technology is moving in.** On the one hand, consumers want 'smarter' homes. They have more things to plug in and they want more things to be built in and function automatically. At the same time, the home building industry has been slow to adopt new technology. New software and internet services are making it possible for builders to use technology to design their homes, review plans with consumers, order materials and schedule subcontractors

- **I want it my way.** Consumers are demanding more and more options, leading to a proliferation of products, materials and colours. Today's supermarket is an example of this, where consumers have 30,000 items to choose from. Thirty years ago, grocery stores offered about 900 items. The abundance of options has its benefits, but it also causes confusion and makes for a very competitive environment. This, in turn, leads to escalating expectations regarding service and product quality. When consumers are overwhelmed as they try to navigate through the available options, they tend to choose the comfortable, the classical, the well-known brand. Furthermore, there is the desire to personalise or individualise the home, requirements for the acoustics of living rooms (insulation, 'fine-tuning') and increasing concerns about personal safety

- **I want help.** Pressed for time, consumers are asking suppliers to simplify things and make things easy for them. This interest covers all aspects of a project, from scoping and materials selection through buying, installation services and warranties. Once again, the value of a trusted brand is enhanced. And consumers will increasingly be using the internet for information and education. Colour matching systems and designer style collections will also make buying easier for time-pressed consumers

- **Doing my part—an environmental paradox.** The environment is a paradox because it is a favoured cause of consumers, yet they have a hard time recon-

---

3   Source: Owens Corning, 'Trends Shape Building Materials Market', pressroom.owenscorning. com/trends.html, accessed February 2003.

Example	Reference
Category A: Product-oriented PSS	
Reversed logistics of building materials (B2B) Stybenex Construction, an organisation of five expanded polystyrene (EPS) producers, takes back EPS from construction sites. The EPS parts are cut-offs and spare parts	Goedkoop *et al.* 1999 www.stybenexverp akkingen.nl
Renewing of office buildings (B2B) In order to prevent the huge amount of waste caused by the demolition of old office buildings, the National Audubon Society (New York) renovates old buildings in an efficient (energy- and materials-wise) manner	Goedkoop *et al.* 1999 www.audubon.org
Customised building elements on demand (B2B) Unidek Bouwelementen BV, the Netherlands, delivers complete and customised roof and other elements needed on the building site, for houses as well as for large buildings. Waste materials are taken back to be re-used	Goedkoop *et al.* 1999 www.unidek.com/ nl/index.htm
Packaging returning system for detergents (B2C) Allegrini S.p.A.(Italian producer of detergents and cosmetics) offers Casa Quick, a service of delivery of detergents that are taken to the homes of the clients in a van. Each family draws down the quantity and quality of detergents needed, using special containers which can be filled up even if not completely empty. The environmental benefits are obtained primarily through the optimisation of the distribution, in terms of packaging and transportation and are maximised in highly populated areas, where the transportation component can be optimised when the system is compared with individual travelling to the shops.	Manzini and Vezzoli 2002 www.allegrini.com/ home.htm
Category B: Use-oriented PSS	
Rent-a-chemical (B2B) In collaboration with wholesalers Dow Europe SA is currently developing a rent-a-chemical approach, which will also allow small-scale enterprises (VOC [volatile organic compound] procurement < 1.5 t) to profit from the levy refund. The wholesaler retains ownership of the substance and rents out the substance to user	Jakl *et al.* 2004 www.dow.com/ Homepage/index. html
Category C: Result-oriented PSS/system optimisation	
Chemical management service (B2B) The PSS here described is the chemical management programme Castrol+Plus®, offered by Castrol's Metalworking Division. Extending beyond lubricants, the programme offers the in-plant monitoring and control of industrial clients' chemical systems and the costs associated with the purchase, handling, use and disposal of chemicals. Services include precise product selection, procurement, materials and maintenance management, process engineering, waste minimisation, environmental compliance assistance, health and safety training, laboratory services and identification of opportunities for continuous improvement. Aimed at reducing customers' net total operating costs, more than half of the cost savings for clients comes from improvements in processes. As for Castrol's profit, it comes from fees and, in some cases, from gain sharing derived from cost reductions. For example, the Castrol+Plus® programme with the Navistar International Engine Plant (USA) has led to the reduction in coolant use of over 50%, and in coolant waste of over 90%	White *et al.* 1999; Oldham 2003 www. castroladvantage. com/eng/ Castrolhomepage. shtml www.navistar.com/ site_layout/index. asp

TABLE 7.1 **Examples of PSS in the base materials need area** (continued opposite)

Example	Reference
Chemical management service (B2B) Ashland Inc. is a chemical company that is a supplier of both speciality chemicals and the distribution processes for those chemicals. Ashland has developed an entire management service programme around procurement, use training, regulatory compliance, waste management, disposal/recycling and energy services. This service package helps the customer in reducing operating costs, as well as better managing risk. Contractual arrangements with customers allow for unit pricing structures, reducing chemical use and keeping the management of materials with the supplier	CfSD 2003 www.ashland.com
Integrated pest management (B2B) Koppert Biological Systems' mission is to be the most preferred partner in developing and marketing pollination systems and integrated pest management for protected and high-value crops, by being a reliable provider of innovative, effective and top-quality solutions. The ongoing research and continuous production of beneficials and pollinators contribute to the development of sustainable agriculture and horticulture worldwide. Koppert has a results-oriented research and development department, and worldwide network of contacts. This ecological product innovation not only replaces toxic chemicals; it is also a service–product combination as it is sold per protected square metre	Goedkoop *et al.* 1999 www.koppert.nl/ n003.shtml

TABLE 7.1 (from previous page)

ciling this with their love for larger homes and things to plug in. The company's expectation is that consumers will continue to try to have it both ways. They will increasingly do their part for the environment, even if it means driving bottles and cans to the recycling centre in their new sport utility vehicle. This audience is expected to want their larger home to be resource-efficient

Industry trends

- **Consolidation**. The building materials industry has been experiencing consolidation for several years as large retail chains replace traditional outlets, and large contractors acquire smaller contractor firms or groups of businesses

- **Shortage of skilled labour** in the construction industry. According to Owens Corning, this is a constraint on growth. Builders and manufacturers of all types will be limited by the scarcity of skilled labour. This is expected to drive acceptance of subassemblies, modules and manufactured homes. The trend to subassemblies probably started with kitchen cabinets and has spread to such things as bathroom components and ceiling trusses

- **Emerging markets**. The infrastructure which is taken for granted in North America and Western Europe does not exist in many parts of the world. To sell products, one has to make sure that local codes and specifications will permit their use

These trends made the case for Owens Corning to find new solutions for its customers worldwide, in a model it calls System Thinking: 'Consumers and the industry alike will increasingly appreciate a company that can help them solve problems quickly and efficiently.' The idea for System Thinking was born from the realisation that Owens Corning could offer expertise that extended beyond individual products, and that consumers were looking for complete project solutions. This is in line with PSS thinking and is concurrent with the discussion among the participants in the first SusProNet workshop, which allowed the identification of the following need area specific trends:

- In general, the end-user is not concerned with the selection of base materials to achieve a given result; the main concern is the result itself. Identification of the most effective and efficient material/combination of materials to be used is often seen as an expert's task

- Clients/consumers of base materials are more and more demanding in terms of quality; the manufacturers are considered accountable for what happens to the product. Moreover, service providers' concerns in terms of costs need to meet end-user requirements of quality, effectiveness and efficiency

- Clients don't want to waste time choosing material, which leads to a move towards products that include services such as technical support and efficiency information. Also, the value of time is increasing, the fractioning of capital costs is leading people to leasing schemes, for instance, and control of quality is given more and more importance. These trends lead to a need for more technology-oriented services

- Supply of base materials needs more and more technical support and follow-up for more efficient use. Also, the increasing complexity of materials and products (e.g. higher-performance materials) requires more expertise. An increase in the use of recycled materials that need to meet quality requirements was also identified

Chemicals

Chemical suppliers are transforming into chemical service providers; they are rewarded by their customers for improving chemicals management and environmental performance, not for selling more chemicals (Whaley and Johnson 2001). As a matter of fact, in the chemical industry servicising is a recognised trend, which has been particularly successful in the United States, and interest is growing in Europe (Oldham 2003). Chemicals are particularly amenable to the development of PSS for two key reasons (Reiskin et al. 1999; White et al. 1999):

- Manufacturers' chemicals management costs may exceed their chemical purchase costs by a factor of 5–10; these costs are often not appreciated by the manufacturer and provide opportunities for cost savings and efficiency improvements when addressed by a specialist chemical services provider

- The specialised nature of chemicals and the regulatory requirements attendant to their use and disposal demand attention and expertise throughout their life-cycle—including procurement, delivery, inspection, inventory, storage, labelling, safety, training, tracking, legal liabilities and disposal. These are often more efficiently addressed by a specialist

The chemical management service business model will be discussed in more detail in Sections 7.3 and 7.4.

Regulatory trends in Europe

Construction industry

The so-called 'legislative package' constitutes the result so far of the revision process of the legal framework for the sector started by the European Commission (EC 2000), aiming at simplifying, restructuring and clarifying the existing legislation. The goal is to bring together the three current directives on procedures for the award of public service contracts (92/50/CEE), public supply contracts (93/36/CEE) and public works contracts (93/37/CEE). The 'legislative package' introduces a number of important new elements, including: electronic procurement mechanisms, a new procedure aimed at particularly complex markets ('competitive dialogue'), a reinforcement of the provisions relating to award criteria and to the selection of candidates.

Industry, represented by the European Construction Industry Federation (FIEC 2003b), is mainly concerned with the changes expected for the public works contracts. Industry's reaction can be summarised into three main issues:

- The principle of confidentiality throughout and after the procedures. In the case of public works contracts, the innovative capacity of the operators is reflected in the tenders they submit to the contracting authorities. If the confidentiality of their tenders is not safeguarded, innovation will not be encouraged

- The exclusion of public works contracts from the scope of electronic auctions and dynamic purchasing systems. The proposed electronic auction process is considered to be unsuited to the nature of public works contracts, which aim to achieve a unique performance to meet the specific needs of the contracting authorities and therefore the real costs are only known when the work is finished

- The extension to public works contracts of the provisions concerning contracts awarded to public entities. These provisions are considered to be an obstacle to the fair participation of private construction companies, once public entities are being treated in a preferential way. Any public 'cross-subsidisation' is demanded to be ruled out of the provisions

Another important landmark is the recently published European Commission's proposal for a directive on services in the internal market (COM [2004] 002, dated 13 January 2004). While this directive is relevant to all SusProNet need areas, the position expressed by FIEC in its initial position paper (FIEC 2004) is of importance to the present analysis. The main objectives of the proposal are to achieve a well-functioning internal market in the EU for high-quality, competitive services, by removing legal and administrative barriers to the development of services between Member States. It covers services provided to both consumers and businesses.

FIEC's concerns relate to:

- The 'comprehensive approach' of the proposed directive, as opposed to dealing with one sector at a time, due to the specificities of the working method in the construction sector

- The risk, as identified by FIEC, of contradicting the principles of preventing unfair competition, social dumping and undeclared work as expressed by the so-called 'posting Directive' 96/71/EC (16 December 1996). FIEC states in its initial position paper: 'effective implementation of the posting Directive calls for a significant level of efficient control mechanisms and procedures in the host country [of workers providing the service]'

Hopefully, the potential conflicts with existing labour regulations and principles will be solved in such a manner that the above-mentioned proposal for a directive on services will fulfil its overall goals of a sound promotion of a services-based economy, where product-service systems will have an increasing role. Their potential for sustainability and the adequate features and framework conditions for success are then more and more pertinent in the political and business agendas.

Chemicals industry

In 2001, the EU Commission adopted the 'White Paper on the Strategy for a Future Chemicals Policy' (EC 2001b), in which the need for a new strategy is defended because the existing legislation is considered not to be capable of responding adequately to public and political concern in Europe about the potential impact of chemicals on health and environment. The Commission proposes that existing and new substances should in the future be subject to the same procedure under a single system. The current new substances system should be revised to become more effective and efficient and the revised obligations should be extended to existing substances.

The proposed REACH system (**R**egistration, **E**valuation, and **A**uthorisation of **Chemi**cals) provides for the stepwise collection of information on the estimated 30,000 chemical substances above 1 tonne/year/manufacturer or importer in the EU, in order to provide for appropriate risk management measures:

- **Registration** will place the information submitted by industry in a central database. It is estimated that around 80% of these substances would require only registration

- **Evaluation** will be required for all substances exceeding a production volume of 100 tonne per year per manufacturer or importer in the EU, or at lower tonnage in case of concern. Evaluation will include testing for long-term and chronic effects

- **Authorisation** will be required for substances of very high concern: namely, those with CMR (carcinogenic, mutagenic, repro-toxic) or POP (persistent organic pollutants) characteristics, whenever identified and whatever their tonnage. It is expected that not more than 5% of all substances will be proposed for authorisation, and industry will have to provide the evidence for safe use

A comparison between the present system and REACH is summarised in Table 7.2.

According to the European Chemical Industry Council (CEFIC 2003b), the chemical industry is following the process and welcomes the desire to produce a more transparent and workable chemicals policy. However, industry is concerned with the impact of bureaucracy in the risk-assessment process, believing that more testing on more chem-

Present system	REACH
There are gaps in our knowledge about many of the chemicals on the European market	REACH will close the knowledge gap by providing safety information about all chemicals produced or imported in volumes higher than 1 tonne/year per manufacturer/importer
The 'burden of proof' is on the authorities: they need to prove that a use of a chemical substance is unsafe before they may impose restrictions	The 'burden of proof' is on the industry. It has to be able to prove that the way it intends to use a chemical substance is safe. All actors in the supply chain will be obliged to assess and implement measures to ensure the safety of the chemical substances they handle
Registration requirements start at a production level of 10 kg. At 1 tonne, a series of tests, including animal tests, have to be undertaken	Registration is required only when production/import reaches 1 tonne. As far as possible, animal testing will be minimised
It is relatively costly to introduce a new substance on the market. Cheaper and maybe untested, existing chemicals are often used rather than developing new substances	Innovation of safer substances should be encouraged under REACH
Public authorities are obliged to perform comprehensive risk assessments which are slow and cumbersome	Industry has the responsibility to assess the safety of the intended uses, prior to production and marketing. Authorities will focus on issues of serious concern

TABLE 7.2 Comparison between the current regulatory system for chemicals and the REACH system

Source: Memo/03/99 (EC 2003)

icals will slow down the process. In order not to inhibit innovation, industry urges a faster registration procedure for new substances, and believes that downstream users should be more involved in the management of chemicals.

Sustainability demands

The relationship between material use indicators and GDP gives us a measure for material intensity. Figure 7.1 shows the evolution of per capita material consumption and per capita GDP across the EU Member States, from 1980 to 2000.

Figure 7.1 shows that all countries with a domestic material consumption per capita above the EU-15 average in 1980 remained at an above-average position in 2000. However, the low-income countries Spain, Greece and Portugal worsened their relative position (upward angle) while high-income countries such as the UK, Italy, Netherlands and France improved their relative position (downward angle) (Eurostat 2002).

Overall, the EU economy grew by 56% whereas material use as measured by DMC grew by only 2.7% over a 20-year period. The individual countries show quite diverse performances in their dematerialisation. A group of countries including Germany, the Netherlands, Sweden, France and the UK had absolute decreases in their DMC of between 1.0% and 8.9% while the economy grew by around 50%. Relative dematerialisation can be observed in Belgium/Luxembourg, Austria, Italy, Finland, Ireland, Den-

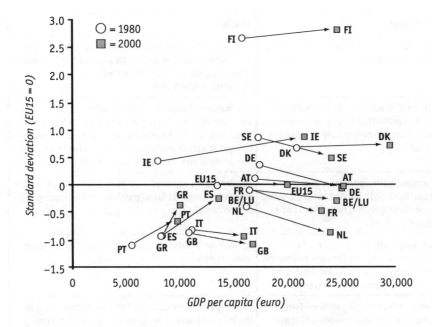

FIGURE 7.1 Material consumption per capita and GDP per capita

Source: Eurostat 2002

mark, Portugal, Spain and the EU as a whole. Minor increases in DMC, between 0.6% and 7.7%, can be observed for Belgium/Luxembourg, Austria, Italy, Denmark and Finland. Ireland was the fastest-growing economy, almost tripling its GDP while its DMC grew by (only) 25% relative to 1980. Portugal and Spain had substantial growth rates for DMC, amounting to about half and two-thirds, respectively, of their GDP growth rates. The only EU Member State to increase its DMC by a larger rate than its GDP was Greece (Eurostat 2002).

The report *The Weight of Nations: Material Outflows from Industrial Economies*, published by the World Resources Institute (Matthews *et al.* 2000), documents and analyses the material output flows for five major OECD countries: Germany, Japan, the Netherlands, the United States and Austria. In 1997, the material requirements of these countries (except Austria) had been studied and it was shown that the total material requirement of those four countries was between 45 and 80 tonnes per capita annually. Except for the relatively modest quantities of materials recycled or added each year to stock in use (largely in the form of infrastructure and durable goods), physical inputs are quickly returned to the environment as pollution or waste, with potential for environmental harm. The key findings from the study are:

1. Industrial economies are becoming more efficient in their use of materials, but waste generation continues to increase. Despite strong economic growth in all countries studied, resource inputs and waste outputs between 1975 and

1996 raised relatively little, on a per capita basis, and fell dramatically when measured against units of economic output. Even as decoupling between economic growth and resource throughput occurred on a per capita and per unit GDP basis, however, overall resource use and waste flows into the environment continued to grow

2. One-half to three-quarters of annual resource inputs to industrial economies are returned to the environment as waste within a year:
    −   Material outputs to the environment from economic activity in the five study countries range from 11 tonnes per person per year in Japan to 25 tonnes per person per year in the United States
    −   When 'hidden flows' are included—flows that do not enter the economy, such as soil erosion, mining overburden, and earth moved during construction—total annual material outputs to the environment range from 21 tonnes per person in Japan to 86 tonnes per person in the United States

3. Outputs of some hazardous materials have been regulated and successfully reduced or stabilised but outputs of many potentially harmful materials continue to increase:
    −   Examples of successes include the reduction or stabilisation of emissions to air of sulphur compounds and lead from gasoline, phosphorus in detergents, and some heavy metals. Quantities of municipal solid wastes sent to landfills have also stabilised or declined in all countries studied
    −   Many other hazardous, or potentially hazardous, material flows are poorly controlled because they occur at the extraction phase or the use and disposal phases of the material cycle, which are outside the traditional area of regulatory scrutiny. Our estimates indicate that many potentially hazardous flows in the United States increased by 25 to 100% between 1975 and 1996

4. The extraction and use of fossil energy resources dominate output flows in all industrial countries. Modern industrial economies are carbon-based. Fossil energy consumption is still rising. Carbon dioxide accounts, on average, for more than 80% by weight of material outflows from economic activity in the five study countries. The atmosphere is by far the biggest dumping ground for industrial wastes.

Other need area-specific issues

Success and failure factors related to the base materials need area include:

●   **Regulation.** Current regulation can work either as a success factor or a failure factor. Waste regulation, for instance, may hinder the development of circular business schemes due to increased bureaucracy associated with a material when considered as waste. On the other hand, waste treatment and disposal requirements imply costs, which are then drivers for recycling and/or re-use schemes

- **Stimulation policies**. Governments can play a very important role in the success of PSS, through the creation of stimulation policies including, for example, tax incentives for PSS developers and green public purchasing policies

- **Economic feasibility**. A successful PSS must have economic feasibility. Sometimes the low cost of virgin materials is a strong obstacle to the implementation of PSS, thus becoming an important failure factor

- **End customer**. Participation of end customers in the definition of companies' business strategies enables the development of PSS. Dialogue with customers as well as their acceptance are considered very important success factors in order to better understand what the market needs are. However, it cannot be underestimated that customers value low costs

- **Transport needs**. Decreased needs for transportation are often a success factor for PSS. The involvement of local and regional suppliers, and/or the adoption of information and communication technologies, are among the most used strategies to reduce transportation needs

- **Appropriate teams**. Cross-functional teams strongly linked with decision-makers and the marketing team are a success factor for PSS

- **Expertise**. Trained staff, both in PSS approaches and in the core business, are needed. The need for expertise potentially enables co-operation between R&D institutions and companies

- **New partnerships**. Willingness to create new partnerships is considered to be a success factor for PSS development and implementation. Several examples show that partners that usually do not co-operate can create innovate schemes once together

- **Uncertainty**. Uncertainty and increased risk are general obstacles to PSS development and implementation, which is a remark applicable to any new business area

7.3 Idea generation and selection

Within the SusProNet project, for each need area, specific PSS ideas were developed. As explained in Chapter 6 this took place in a workshop (held in Lisbon on 25–26 September 2003) facilitated by the authors of this chapter and the member companies of the SusProNet base materials group. The workshop brief was to generate a long list of PSS ideas via a creativity session, and to select the most interesting ones for further elaboration on the basis of an economic, social and environmental assessment and the interest of the participating companies (see Annex 1, Practical Guidelines to PSS Development) This section gives the results of this process.

7.3.1 Need area-specific PSS ideas (long list)

The initial creativity session led to 20 ideas that were afterwards associated, further developed and grouped into three clusters: chemicals, construction materials and a third field which happened to be of interest to several participants: energy/water consumption-related services. The 20 ideas were then briefly analysed and in some cases grouped and enriched. The concepts are briefly described below.

Ideas for PSS related to construction materials

Building and managing infrastructures

- **Idea description**. Result-oriented PSS in which the client is offered an established amount of infrastructure (roads, water pipes, among others) with the guarantee of a given result (safety/resistance) in a period of time, thus leading to the more efficient management of the materials used in these infrastructures

- **Key product elements**. Materials for the roads (not necessarily asphalt); materials for the pipes (also open); supportive equipment for construction/inspection

- **Key service elements**. Construction maintenance/inspection; repairs; contracting; research and development (new materials, new inspection techniques)

Insulation system

- **Idea description**: PSS provided by construction materials suppliers aiming at the optimisation of the use of insulation materials in the construction of new buildings. A focus on renewable materials is expected in this case

- **Key product elements**. Environmentally sound insulation materials

- **Key service elements**. Building co-design

Dry environment

- **Idea description**. Result-oriented PSS offered by suppliers of construction materials. The supplier provides a dry environment within the house, instead of selling roof materials

- **Key product elements**. Roof materials

- **Key service elements**. Roof design

Building restoring services

- **Idea description**. PSS provided by construction companies where a further usage for the building is considered for another reason, aiming at saving building materials. For example, a large industry building from the 19th century could be turned into flats, lofts, theatres, clubs or even a stadium (fill-in with soil would make it green)

- **Key product elements**. Recycling machines; waste management systems (asbestos treatment); construction machines

- **Key service elements**. Delivery of social elements (recreation, sports); decoration advice; infrastructure advice

Recovery of materials from demolition

- **Idea description**. Potential new business area for construction materials suppliers. Demolition materials are no longer seen as waste but as potentially valuable materials. The management of these materials includes their separation and collection for re-use, recycling and energy recovery

- **Key product elements**. Raw materials (concrete aggregates and clinker); wood/paper (re-use/biomass for energy recovery); metals (recycling); glass (recycling); plastics (recycling); platform for separation; trucks

- **Key service elements**. Waste management; supply of secondary materials

Ideas for PSS related to chemicals

Chemical management services

- **Idea description**. The chemical manufacturer manages the use of direct/indirect chemicals on the customer's site. Services offered can include inventory, transportation, testing, recycling and waste management related to chemicals use

- **Key product elements**. Chemicals; IT system; transportation vehicles

- **Key service elements**. Testing, delivery, inventory, process management, recovery/recycling, hazardous chemicals substitution, waste management; cost reduction; reporting; training; safety; quality improvement; expertise

Painting services

- **Idea description**. Result-oriented PSS in which the paint company sells a painting service to meet the customer's requirement, instead of selling pots of paint

- **Key product elements**. Paint; painting materials

- **Key service elements**. Decoration advice; advice on suitable colours/type

Refilling system at the supermarket for cosmetics and cleaners

- **Idea description**. PSS to be provided by supermarkets and/or by cosmetics and cleaners suppliers at supermarkets. Clients can choose to buy the amounts they need using a refilling system instead of buying the existing packages

- **Key product elements**. Cosmetic products; cleaning products; re-usable packaging

- **Key service elements**. Refilling system at the supermarket; provision of re-usable packaging

Take-back of unused medicines

- **Idea description**. PSS provider arranges collection of unused medicines and redistribution. (1) The pharmaceutical company could take back the medicines and sell them again, or (2) the same company or other company or a non-profit organisation could distribute the medicines to people who cannot afford them

- **Key product elements**. Medicines; packaging; trucks/vehicles

- **Key service elements**. Transportation; sorting; repackaging; distribution

Ideas for PSS related to energy and water management

Home energy audit

- **Idea description**. The provider (a construction company, for example) offers an energy audit to save energy costs for homeowners

- **Key product elements**. Building materials; energy

- **Key service elements**. Metering; expertise; home inspection/audit; household upgrades recommendations

Energy conservation services for existing homes

- **Idea description**. The provider (a construction company, for example) pays the monthly energy bills of homeowners

- **Key product elements**. Energy-saving building materials

- **Key service elements**. Home energy balance; energy bill payment; energy saving upgrades; shared energy savings

Energy management services

- **Idea description**. Energy supplier offers customer energy efficiency and management services based on fixed fee or shared gain contract

- **Key product elements**. Electricity/gas; insulation; energy efficiency products; lighting; energy efficient machinery

- **Key service elements**. Energy audit; metering; energy efficiency advice; expertise/personnel

Facility management of energy and water for hotels

- **Idea description**. PSS provider takes care of the delivery of a quantity of energy and the quality of water that is necessary. Hotel owners might concentrate on their core business (tourism)

- **Key product elements**. Remote control consumption system (for energy usage and water usage)

- **Key service elements**. System maintenance; monitoring of usage; delivery of materials/energy needed

7.3.2 Need area-specific PSS ideas (short list)

A further selection process (based on the interest of the participating companies and a quick, economic, social and environmental assessment) resulted in five PSS ideas that the participants were willing to further develop and consider for practical implementation. Implementation issues were briefly discussed, taking into account potential obstacles and drivers related to the following issues:

- Alignment of the idea with the company's strategy, experience and culture

- Building the value network, technological architecture and revenue model

- Framework conditions, namely related to government support

A description of the five ideas and the main implementation issues identified for each of them is presented below.

Idea 1: Chemical management service

Description

The chemical manufacturer (or an independent company) manages the use of direct/indirect chemicals on the customer's site. Services offered can include inventory, transportation, testing, recycling and waste management related to chemicals use.

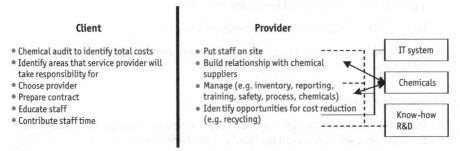

Value network/actors and roles

- CMS manager: deal with sub-suppliers; main point of contact
- CMS staff on-site: operate integrated system; local knowledge; hazardous materials expertise

- Site team: chemical users (e.g. process manager, maintenance, procurement)
- Finance manager: manage contract

Technological architecture

- IT system (link to customer)
- Transportation
- Data reporting system
- New process technology (e.g. recycling technologies)

Revenue model

- Provider profits not aligned with increased production
- Provider compensation tied to quantity and quality of service, not chemical volume
- Customer and provider aligned incentives: benefit from material, labour and waste management costs
- Shared gain contract

Main implementation issues (preliminary)

- The shift from selling chemical products (traditional core business) to providing services raises difficulties in understanding the business
- A trust relationship between all the actors must be created
- The often observed lack of understanding of the cost structure from the client's side makes the business case sometimes difficult
- Book-keeping of chemicals losses is important to make a business case for this PSS
- The economic incentive for outsourcing chemicals management depends on the amount of chemicals use and on the size of the business
- The increasing costs of hazardous waste disposal are an incentive for this PSS, since it is a waste prevention-oriented system
- Conflicts between different businesses units are expected (e.g. service provider and chemicals suppliers)
- Clients do not see it as a need, so a good marketing strategy must be developed
- According to existing similar experiences, only big companies are expected to afford schemes of this kind
- If the service provider is also a chemical supplier, it will manage its own products and its competitors' products as well
- The expected development of the sector-related legislation (TRI regulation in the United States, REACH and ROHS in the European Union) is favourable to this kind of PSS

Idea 2: From insulation to insulation coat 'Isomantel'

Description

The product-service system aims at improving both the quality and the environmental profile of insulation systems for housing, through the use of a new environmentally sound material,

'Isomantel', in prefabricated elements. The company provides the material and co-operates with architects and builders in the design of the new building, providing the know-how to apply the material in the most efficient way.

Client	Provider
• Home buyer: asks for high-quality housing • Contractor: builds the house	• Producer: activates services concept—assembled 'prefab' elements • Subcontractor material: design tailor-made solution • Institutions support

Value network/actors and roles

- PSS provider: selling materials; translating added values (double thermal resistance, fire resistance, moisture control); promotion of concept 'Isomantel'
- Institutions: external reports (LCA, marketing)
- Architects: tailor-made solutions
- Contractor: materialising the project

Technological architecture

- Meetings with end-user
- Listing technical values (internal research and development), environmental values (external input LCA), and economic benefits (external input marketing study)
- Meeting the architect
- Contractor

Revenue model

- PSS provokes market impact growing up (economic profit)
- Multi-functional (non toxic) approach (environmental profit)
- Healthy housing (clients' revenue)

Main implementation issues (preliminary)

- Alignment of PSS idea with the company strategy: Ecobouw is committed to promote sustainable building
- The PSS represents an enlargement of the range of product offers
- This PSS targets a new market for Ecobouw
- A credible label is needed to create a niche market, promoting the new material as a concept, in order to justify price differences with competitors
- Institutional support on environmental and health and safety information and assessments is needed to support the label
- There is a lack of legislation supporting energy savings
- Besides legislation, there is the need for fiscal incentives for energy-saving investments made by house owners or builders

Idea 3: Energy efficiency services (existing homes)

Description

The company offers energy efficiency services and pays customers' energy bills. The company is responsible for making the home energy balance and developing energy-saving upgrades. Profits will come from shared energy savings.

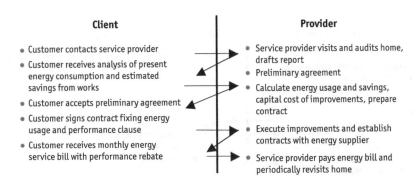

Client	Provider
• Customer contacts service provider	• Service provider visits and audits home, drafts report
• Customer receives analysis of present energy consumption and estimated savings from works	• Preliminary agreement
	• Calculate energy usage and savings, capital cost of improvements, prepare contract
• Customer accepts preliminary agreement	
• Customer signs contract fixing energy usage and performance clause	• Execute improvements and establish contracts with energy supplier
• Customer receives monthly energy service bill with performance rebate	• Service provider pays energy bill and periodically revisits home

Value network/actors and roles

Manufacturer:

- Provide best available technologies materials and equipment for upgrade
- Establish networks of qualified auditors, installers and maintenance
- Protect investment in home of third party (insurance and mortgage letter)
- Identify new opportunities for energy savings
- Technological architecture
- Provide most efficient energy use reduction system for the total building envelope in the most cost-efficient long-term approach

Revenue model

- Service provider gets monthly Δ (bonus)
- Negotiate lowest energy costs as bulk energy buyer

Main implementation issues (preliminary)

- The company's strategy is inconsistent with the service model
- The integration of the PSS with building materials is easy
- A trust relationship between service provider and customer must be created
- Existing legislation is an obstacle for long-term contracts
- The system presents a long payback period for the provider
- Marketing strategy can be based on the concept of a 'new way of buying'; but the question 'how to market the PSS?' is still the key question
- Low cost of energy is not an incentive for this kind of system

Idea 4: Facility management product-service system

Description

The target groups for this PSS are hotel owners or companies running a hotel chain. The service provider takes care of the delivery of energy and water (quantity and quality) that is necessary, allowing the hotel manager to concentrate on the core business (tourism).

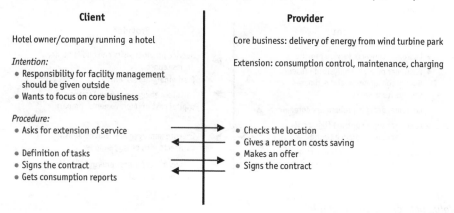

Client	Provider
Hotel owner/company running a hotel	Core business: delivery of energy from wind turbine park
Intention: • Responsibility for facility management should be given outside • Wants to focus on core business	Extension: consumption control, maintenance, charging
Procedure: • Asks for extension of service	• Checks the location • Gives a report on costs saving
• Definition of tasks • Signs the contract • Gets consumption reports	• Makes an offer • Signs the contract

Value network/actors and roles

- Provider's management: offer; accounting
- Maintenance staff: maintenance; keeps track of usage
- Monitoring staff: monitoring and steering role; controls peak consumption
- Technicians: responsible for wind turbine park

Technological architecture

- Installation of the counter (by the provider) on the client side
- Cable
- Wind turbine park; power station; transformer
- Remote control consumption system (hardware, software)
- Maintenance
- Measuring instruments, steering mechanisms
- Monitoring devices

Revenue model

- Business model: renting the service: interest in keep the things working properly
- Low investment on client side, low financial risk, cost control, payment per usage/consumption
- Impact on the market grows up: outstanding service feature
- First-mover effect

Main implementation issues (preliminary)

- It is a renting service, which means it needs low investment on the customer's side
- The energy market is risky, not transparent
- The revenue for the client results from optimised energy sources, energy savings (shared between the provider and the client) and reduced maintenance costs

Idea 5: Recovery of materials from building demolition

Description

This product-service system aims to manage waste from the demolition of buildings, including separation and collection of materials for re-use, recycling and energy recovery.

Client	Provider	
• Client demands service	• Site work database contracting	Logistics: truck routes optimisation
• Several containers for waste separation installed on-site	• Delivery containers	Platform separation:
• Client deposits separated waste in containers		• Metals: to steel foundries
• Client informs containers are full	• Trucks are sent to the site work	• Wood: to wood industries or energy recovery (biomass)
• Containers are collected by truck		• Concrete aggregates: to concrete plants
		• Ceramics: to concrete plants

Interaction | Visibility

Value network/actors and roles

- PSS provider: waste management, logistics optimisation, delivery of containers
- Transport companies: materials transportation
- Recycling companies: materials re-use optimisation

Technological architecture

- Logistics optimisation
- Separation techniques
- Research and development on recycling technologies is needed

Revenue model

Very marginal profit, compared with core business:

- Low investment from provider's side
- No investment from client's side

- High commercial risk: lack of supportive legislation

Sources of revenue:

- From the client
- Saving energy and raw materials for the core business (cement and concrete production

Intangible: image

Main implementation issues (preliminary)

- The company has a sustainability-oriented strategy, therefore this PSS idea is in good alignment with it
- Considering the lack of sector-specific legislation to stimulate this kind of activity, the prices have to be low in the beginning in order to attract clients, which is the main implementation problem
- Clients are the same, either supplying the product or the product-service system
- Research and development initiatives on recycling techniques for these materials are needed
- Wood waste can be used as fuel for cement furnaces
- Economic gains come from savings on energy and raw materials
- A better image is an intangible benefit for the company
- The company is committed to implementing the system
- The main difficulty related to this PSS is the high transportation costs (an optimised logistic is a key factor for the feasibility of the idea)
- Trucks delivering cement are different from the trucks collecting the materials from building demolition

7.4 Implementation

After analysis and idea generation and selection, the next step is the implementation of the developed system. In this section the implementation phase is discussed with a focus on the most important implementation issues for the base materials need area. This section relies on the findings and discussions that took place in SusProNet Workshop 3 (base materials need area).

7.4.1 Need area-specific implementation challenges and policy support

Practical experiences identified by the members of the working group on base materials are described below under the following headings: company internal; value chain; partnership/co-operation; technical feasibility; and institutional.

Idea 1: chemical management service

A chemical manufacturer (or an independent company) supplies and manages use of indirect and/or direct chemicals on the customer's site. Services offered can include inventory, delivery, process management, recovery/recycling, reporting, H&S and waste management. Therefore it is not just an outsourcing model; it adds resources rather than switching resources. Chemical management services focus on innovation of process, not product, through a transformation of the supply chain. It has the potential to result in environmental gains such as reduced chemical use and a decrease in

Headings	Implementation issues	Solutions
Company-internal	• Shift of business strategy • New profit model requires new understanding and training • Higher business risk for supplier • Union opposition	• Separate product/service divisions • Clear relationships with customers; reward better management • Long-term service contract • Communication to promote better understanding
Value chain	• User has lack of cost awareness • High perceived transaction costs • Scale effect/large companies • New revenue model	• Full life-cycle cost audit • Awareness, tools, better planning • Cluster SMEs • Link baseline chemicals use to production levels
Partnership/ co-operation	• Creation of trust relationship between all actors • Supplier-driven chemical management • Complexity in transferring chemical management responsibilities to suppliers • Lack of confidence in supplier capability • Limited finance or venture capital available	• Effective change management/openness of information • CMS programme designed with flexibility to customer requirements • Upper management support, sound communication plan, thoughtful implementation programme • Longer-term, continuous and multi-faceted interaction with suppliers • Raise the level of awareness in the financial community
Institutional	• Lack of understanding of potential benefits of CMS • CMS is small in Europe • European regulatory framework does not adequately support this model • Waste management regulation • REACH legislation • Barriers to recovery and recycling of waste	• Government research to highlight the potential of CMS • European body to serve as catalyst • Economic instruments (incineration tax would stimulate CMS) and regulatory framework (IPPC as an opportunity) • CMS providers help their customers • Communicate potential benefits • Legal definitions of waste should not impede the increased re-use or recycling of chemicals

TABLE 7.3 Summary of implementation issues for idea 1

hazardous waste produced. The implementation issues summarised in Table 7.3 resulted from learning by Green Alliance from the experience of British companies that implemented chemical management services schemes.

Idea 2: from insulation to insulation coat: Isomantel

The product-service system aims at improving both the quality and the environmental profile of insulation systems for housing, through the use of a new environmentally sound material, 'Isomantel', in prefabricated elements. The company provides the material and co-operates with architects and constructers in the design of the new building, providing the know-how to apply the material in the most efficient way. The implementation issues summarised in Table 7.4 resulted from the experience of Ecobouw in the real implementation of the idea being worked out by the company during the SusProNet work.

Headings	Implementation issues	Solutions
Company-internal	• Company expertise in materials with higher potential value • Need for start-up capital	• Company committed to promote sustainable building • Raise the level of awareness in the financial community
Value chain	• Enlargement of the range of product offers	
Partnership/ co-operation	• External support on environment and health and safety information • Need for promotion	• Partnership with research institutes/co-operation with architects • Integration in NGO promoting sustainable building
Technical feasibility	• Quality control for product and concept	• Harmonisation of standards
Institutional	• Credible labelling system • Need for fiscal incentives for energy saving investments	

TABLE 7.4 Summary of implementation issues for idea 2

Idea 3: energy efficiency services (existing homes)

This service starts with a company providing an in-home (or in-business) energy audit followed by energy-using equipment and building upgrades that are paid for by the service provider. The service provider acts as an energy broker for their customers and charges a fixed fee for energy use. The service provider gets the financial value of the energy savings from home and business upgrades and the cost savings from being a high-volume energy purchaser. The implementation issues summarised in Table 7.5 resulted from the experience of Johns Manville in the real implementation of the idea being worked out by the company during SusProNet.

Headings	Implementation issues	Solutions
Company-internal	• Financial opportunity • Sales channels • Unexpected consequences	• Partnership with energy companies • Create new and feed old • Pilot and beta testing
Value chain	• New partners • Customer fear of change	• Patience • Risk sharing/equipment upgrades
Partnership/ co-operation	• Schedule impacts • Government business pace	• Vertical integration • Delegated authority
Technical feasibility	• Internal expertise with service • Design focus changes	• Hire external experts • Wait for implementation
Institutional	• Risk acceptance • Alignment behind initiative	• Risk sharing (external) • Get business leader support

TABLE 7.5 Summary of implementation issues for idea 3

Idea 4: facility management product-service system

The target groups for this PSS are hotel owners or companies running a hotel chain. The service provider takes care of the delivery of energy and water (quantity and quality) that is necessary, allowing the hotel manager to concentrate on the core business (tourism). The implementation issues summarised in Table 7.6 resulted from the experience of BSW, Bildungswerk der Sächsischen Wirtschafp, in the planning of the idea being worked out by the organisation during SusProNet.

Headings	Implementation issues	Solutions
Company-internal	• Reallocation of staff	• Training
Value chain	• More partners involved • Concentration on core business	• Early stage involvement • Reorganisation of supply chain
Partnership/ co-operation	• Scheduled time-frame considerations	• Exchange of timetables (trust-based)
Technical feasibility	• Equipment and interface	• Building of an expert pool
Institutional	• Responsibility in case of emergency	• Emergency plan • Contractualisation

TABLE 7.6 Summary of implementation issues for idea 4

Idea 5: recovery of materials from building demolition

This product-service system aims to manage waste from the demolition of buildings, including separation and collection of materials for re-use, recycling and energy recovery. The implementation issues summarised in Table 7.7 resulted from the experience of Secil in the planning of the idea being worked out by the organisation during Sus-ProNet.

Headings	Implementation issues	Solutions
Company-internal	● Company's commitment to sustainability (positive)	–
Value chain	● Start with low prices ● Opportunity to reduce production costs (energy efficiency)	● Intangible benefits for company and clients
Partnership/ co-operation	● Clients remain the same	● Increase the relationship with the client
Technical feasibility	● Transport logistics	● Optimisation of logistics ● Partnership with transportation companies
Institutional	● Lack of legislation stimulating waste recovery in the sector	● Government recommendations

TABLE 7.7 Summary of implementation issues for idea 5

Review of implementation issues

Company-internal

The first important implementation issue at the company level is the necessary shift away from a material-based business strategy. The potential of reduced material sales conflicts with the traditional sales model. This barrier is particularly obvious for traditional base materials suppliers who are primarily or in significant part material manufacturers, and whose performance is heavily dependent on volume produced and sold.

PSS on base materials pose another important issue for base materials suppliers, which is the new goal of resource efficiency and dematerialisation. In fact, the profit incentive shifts from the volume produced towards the quality and continuity of the result provided, which means that the company needs to learn how to do more and better with less materials. The new profit model requires new understanding and training.

Contracting of the service provided is another potential barrier, particularly in the cases where the system presents a long payback period for the provider, because the existing legislation is, in general, an obstacle to longer-term guarantees/contracts. In the case of chemical suppliers in particular, companies are required to use resources upfront to identify opportunities for chemical use, risk and cost reductions, and implement changes. If cost savings are realised from such improvements, suppliers receive compensation in the form of shared cost savings. If cost savings are not realised, CMS providers may be at risk, which can be minimised by long-term service contracting.

Value chain
In the first place, the user usually has a lack of cost awareness. PSS on base materials, especially the business-to-business systems, must be based on understanding full life-cycle costs (including material, labour and waste management). The product-based model focuses on material cost, and budgets are often spread across different business units.

Another important issue is the liability related to base materials: namely, concerning the quality of the materials used, materials application, and related impacts on health and environment. Contracts must consider the extended producer responsibility policy principle, which is being adopted by European-related legislation.

Transportation costs of raw materials are a potential obstacle in many cases. Logistics needs to be optimised during the design phase.

In the case of chemical suppliers, one must consider companies' size. In fact, chemical management services have largely taken hold in large companies that have large facilities with greater than US$1 million dollars in chemical spend. Because of the economies of scale involved in CMS, the model has not yet been heavily implemented in small to medium-sized enterprises. SMEs often do not require (or warrant) a full-time person on-site to solely perform chemical management activities simply because there is not enough work to keep that individual busy. In addition, SMEs would be likely to have to increase their costs to obtain such enhanced service because cost savings alone would not cover the CMS provider's costs for providing the service. However, CMS has the potential to overcome many of the typical barriers SMEs face, such as lack of knowledge of environmental issues, and benefit these companies through their supplier's expertise, better information management and regulatory compliance. Some SME facilities that are part of larger companies who have a corporate-wide CMS programme have successfully implemented CMS and have overcome this barrier as the smaller facilities are grouped with larger facilities to make the services economically viable. SMEs clustered in a geographical area could potentially overcome the economy of scale.

Partnership/co-operation
One important issue considering partnership and co-operation along the value chain is that the supply chain management must have an aligned incentive for profit. If some companies rely on the results provided and other companies on the volume produced and sold, they will use different strategies to optimise their profits and the system runs a considerable risk of collapse.

Linked to this issue is the need to shorten the supply chain and reach the final user. Often, the success of the system totally depends on reaching the final user needs and expectations. Thus, the distance between the PSS provider and the final user along the chain can become a critical point.

In many cases, there is a lack of confidence in supplier capability (trust in quality of materials; trust in functionality). PSS on base materials creates increased interdependency between supplier and customer that requires high levels of supplier capability, and customer confidence and trust in these abilities. The establishment of longer-term, continuous and multifaceted interaction with suppliers can create the conditions to overcome this potential obstacle.

The PSS provider needs to understand that supplier-driven material management is a huge change for the customer. The supplier can bring new benefits through a systems approach. A technical review can find the right materials for the intended function (e.g. cleaning, coating, de-greasing). The customer has the ability to focus on the core competences.

Technical feasibility

In general, the most important technical issue in this need area is the usually glacial design of base materials. Material suppliers and, often, material users show some resistance to change in this field. Considering that PSS demands flexibility in terms of achieving results fast, with good quality, and at a lower price, this issue can become a problem. This obstacle can perhaps be surmounted by partnerships between companies and design schools or other research institutions.

Institutional

There is a need to raise the level of awareness of the PSS model in the financial community, because there is limited finance or venture capital available for service approaches. Further work needs to be done to target this sector to raise awareness of the opportunities for investment. Fiscal and regulatory changes will be important in directing investors' attention to PSS. Business schools, MBA courses and training should also be used to promote understanding within the business community.

Also, the prices of raw materials and the costs of waste management have to internalise environmental costs to make a case for PSS. The increasing costs of hazardous waste disposal are an incentive for PSS on base materials, since they are in general waste prevention-oriented systems, such as CMS. CMS providers are in a good position to help their customers make substitution decisions. While regulations and cost increases associated with hazardous waste are already creating a downward trend for the waste management industry, CMS could further drive down waste volumes at individual plants, but offer a waste business increased market share through strategic alliances with CMS providers who have a large customer base.

These findings are aligned with what one can find in the literature. For example, White *et al.* (1999) emphasise the need for governments to review any policies that subsidise virgin materials extraction and use, because 'subsidies that reduce the cost of making new "stuff" are inconsistent with efforts to steer the economy away from goods towards more service-oriented modes of enterprise'. At the other end of the product life-cycle, if disposal costs are subsidised, materials recovery activities are placed at a competitive disadvantage.

7.5 Conclusion

The working definition for base materials, adopted in the context of SusProNet is: materials (substances or compounds) used to perform a given process, either in a site or in a household.

The base materials need area is extremely broad. Base materials are inputs to virtually all kinds of activity, product or service. Therefore, after characterising in a broad manner the use of resources required by economic activities a focus was chosen relevant for the companies that participate in the SusProNet initiatives related to this need area: construction materials and chemicals.

The construction sector represents 10% of the EU's GDP and 7% of its employment. The chemical sector contributes 2.4% of European GDP: Europe is the world leader, followed by the USA. They are also interesting areas from a sustainability point of view. Construction minerals make up 44% of the overall material consumption in Europe, and the chemical industry faces complex challenges in terms of toxicity.

The European economy is becoming progressively more efficient in the use of materials, measured in terms of GDP per unit of material use. But due to economic growth the absolute values of resource use and waste generation continually increase. The question of resource use (and the inequity in its consumption, with significant differences between the industrialised and the developing countries) is hence an important sustainability issue. It can be anticipated that innovative solutions (such as those PSS potentially provide) are required to increase the resource productivity to a level where net improvements in dematerialisation are achieved.

7.5.1 PSS in the need area: opportunities and threats

Drivers and opportunity areas

The analysis of business and regulatory trends in the base materials need area has shown a potential for the development of product-service systems, mainly because clients (either business customers or final consumers) are not interested in the ownership of base materials, nor in all the structure necessary (knowledge, tools, trained staff, etc.) to make the most effective and eco-efficient choice, but in getting a given result. This leads to opportunities to develop innovative business models. The trends and sustainability demands discussed in this chapter point out various opportunities for PSS development in the base materials need area (summarised partially in Table 7.8):

- There is room for co-development schemes because the end-user is more interested in the result than in the choice of materials

- The integration of products and services is stimulated by the need, from the service provider's side, to meet end-user requirements in terms of quality, costs and accountability

- In the field of chemicals, management costs are very high when compared with purchase costs. These costs are often not appreciated by the manufacturer and provide for cost savings and efficiency improvements when addressed by a specialist; this is favourable to the success of chemical management services

- Concurrently, regulatory trends in the chemical sector (inherent in the REACH system) are potentially leading to the spread of chemical management services

- Not only in the field of chemicals, but also in that of construction materials, waste management faces more and more stringent regulation, which is supportive of additional services and of integrated product-service solutions

- The increasing complexity of materials, together with the proliferation of specialised materials, is allowing for the development of systems that provide the most effective and efficient use of materials

- The fractioning of capital costs, enabled by leasing schemes, provides opportunities for the development of technology-based PSS

- Regulatory trends in the construction sector (electronic procurement mechanisms and the new provisions for the selection of candidates to public contracts) open windows of opportunity for new partnerships between private companies and public entities, potentially leading to the development of innovative PSS in the sector

- The adoption of a life-cycle perspective by businesses and the stronger cooperation in the value chain are trends that support the provision of *solutions* rather than products

Potential business ideas

A search of existing PSS examples in the two sectors under analysis showed that the vast majority of the cases can be found in a business-to-business situation. Most of them fit into one of the following categories:

- Business schemes that are *circular*: the producer owns the material and recovers it after use (e.g. solvents management systems)

- Business schemes that sell *results* instead of products (e.g. dry environment instead of a roof); here the potential for totally new solutions is higher and there is room for leapfrog changes into sustainability

- Business schemes that *add services*—often recycling/renewing/recovery—to a product

In the SusProNet project five promising PSS ideas were developed:

- Chemical management services, where the chemical manufacturer (or an independent company) manages the use of direct/indirect chemicals on customer's site

- From insulation to insulation coat: the service component of this PSS is the cooperation between the material provider and the architects and constructers in the design of the new building, as well as providing the know-how to apply the material in the most efficient way

- Energy efficiency services, where the service provider (a construction materials manufacturer) is responsible for making the home energy balance and developing energy saving upgrades. Profits will come from shared energy savings

- Facility management PSS, offering energy and water management to hotels. The revenue for the client results from optimised energy sources, energy savings (shared between the provider and the client) and reduced maintenance costs

- Recovery of materials from building demolition: consisting of the management of waste from the demolition of buildings, including separation and collection of materials for re-use, recycling and energy recovery

Pitfalls and threats

In part based on the PSS ideas, the most important pitfalls and threats for PSS implementation in the need area were analysed. They are summarised partially in Table 7.8 and discussed below.

At the **company level**, internal implementation issues are the necessary shift away from material-based business strategy that PSS providers must understand; and the new goal that material suppliers have of resource efficiency and dematerialisation.

Value chain-related implementation issues are the lack of cost awareness by the user; the need to clarify the liability concerning the quality of materials used, materials application, and related impacts on health and environment; obstacles potentially posed by transportation costs; and the size of companies involved, especially in the case of chemical suppliers.

Implementation issues related to **partnership and co-operation** include the importance of all supply chain partners having the same profit incentive; the need to shorten the supply chain and reach the final user; the lack of confidence from customers in supplier capabilities; and the understanding that supplier-driven management is a huge change for customers.

The most important **technical** implementation issue is the usually glacial design of base materials, considering the flexibility demanded by PSS schemes.

Institutional implementation issues are the need to raise the level of awareness of the PSS model in the financial community; the need to internalise environmental costs in the prices of raw materials and waste management costs; and the difficulties that existing legislation poses for long-term service contracting.

7.5.2 PSS and sustainability

This chapter could not conclude that PSS in the building sector and chemical industry would be sustainable per se. Yet the PSS business ideas show that opportunities are certainly there. Chemical management services can reduce the use of chemicals and provide more professional handling. A materials recovery service can contribute greatly to dematerialisation and reduction of energy use. Energy efficiency services aim at an ecological–economic win–win, by sharing the revenues of energy savings between service provider and client.

It is unclear, however, whether such business models would lead to radical sustainability improvements. CMS, for instance, in most cases leads to a more professional and effective handling of the same material. This leads to a reduction of material use (in some cases reported to be in the order of magnitude of 30%), but not the 'Factor X' that some claim.

7.5.3 Policy support

This chapter makes clear that policy can provide clear and positive incentives for PSS development. Examples include:

- More complex HSE regulations with regard to chemicals and more stringent demands with regard to waste management support CMS
- The desire to reduce voluminous waste flows to landfill such as building and demolition waste supports PSS that include take-back services

More generally, (sustainable) PSS development needs facilitation by internalisation of environmental costs, such as for waste management, in prices of materials and chemicals.

Value element	Drivers and opportunities	Development pitfalls and threats
User value/market risk		
Tangible value	Complex regulations (chemicals: REACH; building materials: waste) create markets for product-oriented services	User is unaware of the integrated costs when using a product
Intangible value	Due to the proliferation and complexity of materials, users have difficulty in selecting the best fit. This creates markets for result-oriented services	User does not have sufficient confidence in PSS supplier capabilities Glacial design of materials prevents customising offering via PSS
System costs/financial risk		
Tangible operational costs	Chemicals: management costs are high compared to material costs; activity management may be more cost-effective PSS may reduce system costs	Higher transportation needs and costs
Risk premium, financing, and transaction costs	Construction: new EU procurement regulations may lead to offers of more efficient PSS-related procurement procedures	Liabilities in the system for material performance may be distributed in a different way Chemicals: transaction costs become too high when PSS user is an SME
Other benefits/capability risk		
Improved power position		
Defence to substitutes/loyalty		
High speed of innovation		
Investment in PSS development	Companies are getting used to chain-oriented co-operation	Alignment of profit incentives when building partnership for the PSS
Other transition costs		Change in strategy and mind-set of material suppliers

TABLE 7.8 Review of need area-specific PSS opportunities and threats

8
Need area 2: information and communication technologies

Martin Charter, Graham Adams and Tom Clark
Centre for Sustainable Design, UK

8.1 Product-service systems for need area ICT: an overview

This section provides a 'bird's eye' view of the information and communication technology (ICT) sector. The sector is defined, the ICT market described, and some of the main technology developments are introduced, together with some of the factors driving or inhibiting technology application. The 'state of the art' of PSS development in the sector is summarised and some examples of PSS are provided. The ICT sector is considered from two perspectives:

- Technologies, products and services (i.e. applications and suppliers)
- Needs satisfaction (i.e. functionality and customers)

Technologies are a primary consideration since they are a dominant driver in product and service development. A focus on needs satisfaction and functionality is also important in the context of this book since meeting needs sustainably is the aim of a sustainable PSS and ultimately of sustainable development.

8.1.1 Description of the ICT sector

There is no simple or standard classification for the ICT sector, which covers a wide range of technologies, products and services. Definition is further complicated by rapidly changing technologies and the diffusion of ICT into all sectors of developed economies. The simplest product-related definition is: 'any product or system that processes, stores or communicates information'. It encompasses all digital, information and telecommunications equipment, software and services.

The sector contributes 7.5% of the GDP for Western Europe but is rapidly growing and is a major supporting technology contributing to efficiency improvements and growth in other sectors. The sector is strongly service-oriented; services account for 69% of sales. Products nevertheless play an important part and all services depend on products and infrastructure.

The sector is dominated by large global players in each of the main product and service sub-sectors, but it also includes many smaller suppliers: for example, component and subsystem suppliers and specialist service providers. In 1999 there were 442,000 ICT companies in the EU (Deiss 2001). Many firms, especially larger ones, cannot be readily classified by product or service sector as they are often involved in a range of activities. Restructuring has also led traditional manufacturing companies to outsource/'contract out' production and instead provide system solution services e.g. 'systems integration'. For example, IBM has moved in this direction and become a major player by acquiring PwC (PricewaterhouseCoopers)'s IT consulting division.

Although many of the main players no longer make or supply physical products, products are nevertheless part of the service delivery of many service companies. Furthermore many players manufacture and/or supply both products and services. The distinction between products and services is often blurred and appears to be especially so in this sector although it is service-oriented at the aggregate level.

This trend towards services has been driven by the greater potential for 'value adding' from services, especially in developed countries where international price competition and higher costs have reduced margins in manufacturing. The sectoral shift towards services also reflects the general increase in the importance of services in developed economies. One economic theory explaining this is that, once basic material and product acquisition needs have been satisfied, customers with increasing time constraints (and resources or disposable incomes) demand services for an expanding range of needs and wants, whether as businesses or consumers.

The sector is strongly technology-driven and there have been continuing developments in all aspects of technology; for example:

- Devices across all sectors are increasingly fitted with constantly improving computing power and communications capability, and integrated into a communications web

- There are more channels of communication and increased communication

The main application so far has been in information processing in business, but there has been a shift towards audio-visual and entertainment applications.

When considering the ICT sector in terms of functionality, ICT provides information processing, storage and communications capability for an immense variety of applications across all sectors of the economy. In providing this capability, ICT can directly or indirectly help to satisfy many needs for businesses and individual consumers.

In general, needs satisfaction is indirectly rather than directly met by ICT. Business has a need to manage information and to communicate, not an inherent need and demand for ICT itself. Individual consumers similarly have a need (or want) for various functions—for example, information and communication—not the ICT itself (unless the ICT product fulfils a status or other need).

While ICT can be specifically developed to satisfy customers' needs, in the business sector in particular it is frequently (but clearly not always) technology-driven rather than needs-driven. The rapid development of new technology and short life of many products, combined with intense competition, means time to market is often short. This leaves little time for assessing needs and demands, especially for innovative products.

8.1.2 Approaches to PSS development

The term 'product-service system' (PSS) is not established in business and there is no reason to suppose that the term is likely to become widely adopted, or even adopted at all. None of the participating organisations in the SusProNet ICT group used the term, and PSS was viewed as an academic concept.

Nevertheless, since most products have a service element and vice versa, it can be said that PSS are commonplace and that, formally or informally, PSS development is something that the ICT business already does. The idea that there is 'added value' from services development is not news: for example, in building better and longer-term customer relations. PSS is therefore a useful way of thinking about the optimum mix of products and services for a specific business or product in order to maximise business value.

In a highly competitive global market, diversified global and niche players alike have sought to expand markets or penetrate new ones by offering new services. Major equipment manufacturers have tended to move in the direction of being service providers. This situation has reflected the higher value-added potential in services and the greater potential for market growth. Equipment (e.g. computers and telephones) and infrastructure (e.g. transmitters and cables) nevertheless form a significant part of the market and total product-service system mix.

Among the ICT-related companies participating in SusProNet there has been a trend towards increasing service provision, but for product producers and suppliers the emphasis remains on selling products and adding services. For example, Nokia has periodically considered alternative PSS models such as leasing, but market conditions have not been judged to be suitable for launch. Lower profitability and market attachment to ownership have been barriers to change. The approaches to PSS development appear to reflect the generic approaches summarised in Chapter 5, but will depend on the product, service and market as well as on specific company approaches, methods and resources. Some specific examples of the participating companies include the following:

- Alcatel supplies and integrates its own and third-party telecoms systems and equipment. It applies a range of standard business methods for delivery of market and customer-oriented solutions. Services are a major aspect of the PSS mix

- Heidelberger Druckmaschinen, which manufactures/supplies printing equipment, can take responsibility for defining finance and strategy processes, the product life-cycle management process, including the quality gate process, and carries out systematic customer surveys and market studies for needs analysis. It also has a customer-centred organisation for solution provision

- Nokia designs, manufactures and sells its own mobile phone products. It has a range of processes for product development and management from idea generation to marketing. It has evaluated but not yet pursued alternative PSS business models for direct involvement in the re-use mobile phone market. Mobile services are expected to be a large new growth area

8.1.3 Some examples of current PSS

In general, examples of direct PSS applications by the ICT sector itself reflect most of the generic categories defined in Chapter 2.

For product-oriented services, the material content or impacts may be the same as for a 'pure' product, but the PSS aims to 'add value' by locking the customer into an ongoing relationship with the supplier. There may be environmental benefits where product life is extended or when the supplier takes back the product and refurbishes it or recycles the materials. For example, it is common for computer suppliers to provide a 'basic box', which can be readily upgraded as processing capability, memory and software are developed.

For use-oriented services, the main applications of PSS appear to be in B2B (business-to-business) transactions. There are a number of obvious reasons why PSS arrangements are commonplace in business:

- Business decisions are (at least in theory) generally made on a rational economic basis and there is generally less likely to be emotional attachment to product ownership

- Rapid developments in new technology, short product lives, needs for equipment servicing and capital constraints all act as disincentives to product ownership. A package of service and support improves access to more efficient new technology upgrades as well as providing operational security

- Leasing or renting may avoid capital costs and can be tax-efficient

Both the IT and telecoms sectors have been especially active in offering diverse services for business customers in which PSS have figured strongly, with both products and services being provided together as part of systems packages. For example, in the case of IT the package provided might include in-house data processing equipment and support services, or it might involve centralised data processing on the service provider's premises.

The product-service mix of copiers and other office equipment tends to be more product-oriented but with a substantial service element as in leasing and support services.

In the consumer and household sector, cultural factors, such as status or the desire to own, besides other factors such as easy access to credit, make customer ownership the dominant model. Product-oriented service extensions are nevertheless common such as financing and service agreements for IT and entertainment equipment. Sometimes equipment may be rented. For example, in the telecoms sector, the supplier owns the infrastructure, and handsets and other devices are often rented. Renting of video cassettes and DVDs is also common. Product ownership may not necessarily be demanded, for instance, in the following circumstances:

- Occasional or one-off use

- High level of availability not required

- High capital or other costs but no attachment, status or cultural benefit from ownership

- Technology changes rapidly

PSS application by ICT product and service suppliers is the first focus for this work especially for influencing the design of ICT-based PSS. However, given the ubiquity of ICT, the main potential for application of ICT to PSS is likely to lie in wider applications in other sectors within the economy as a whole (i.e. in the business, government and household sectors) and in interactions between these sectors. The results for the other working groups illustrate that ICT is a vital supporting technology for all economic sectors.

In such applications the ICT might be incorporated in another product, say a vehicle, and then becomes part of the mobility and other functional need satisfied by vehicle manufacturers and distributors. There are many existing and potential applications in this area: for example, monitoring fuel efficiency and maintenance needs, route planning to avoid congestion, and entertainment.

Apart from the widespread application of microchips in products, examples of communications technology being applied in wider product and service areas are still generally few, new and undeveloped. There has nevertheless been increasing application in some B2B and B2C (business-to-customer) areas: for example, e-commerce, online shopping, travel booking and banking, and government activities such as online taxation and information provision. Generally these are examples of replacing existing services with online services, rather than replacing products with services. Through direct transactions these types of arrangement tend to replace or reduce the need for intermediate warehouse, retail or office premises and staff. Their delivery nevertheless is achieved through PSS and there may be significant benefits in saving energy and transport costs and reducing environmental impacts.

As discussed in Section 8.1.1, there has been a general shift to a service-based economy in most developed countries. This might be expected to increase the development of PSS in B2B transactions.

WPI and other research has identified significant obstacles to implementing PSS in business as well as consumer and other sectors. Where PSS options are potentially beneficial, successful implementation requires an understanding of the specific needs and obstacles on a case-by-case basis as well as at the generic level. In many cases these may only be overcome through policies aimed at changing consumption patterns.

The following are examples of some ICT PSS applications applied to the white goods sector.

Electrolux pay-per-use in the white goods sector

Electrolux completed a pilot scheme based on a pay-per-use system with washing machines during 1999/2000 in Gotland, Sweden. Instead of selling or renting out the appliances, it was paid by consumers according to how much the appliances were used (see Dudda *et al.* 2001). When the project was started, 7,000 smart meters were installed, mainly around the city of Visby. Since the EU has calculated that up to 90% of the environmental impact can be attributed to the use stage of a washing machine, the pay-per-use method would give a financial incentive to do fewer washes. In addition Electrolux chose its most energy-efficient machine for the trial.

The trial was ended because of poor market response. This was in part because users in general want to own their own machines, although the project did identify that there was a niche market for low-income families. Additionally, the pay-per-use scheme did result in a reduction in the number of washes and energy use.

Toshiba pay-per-use in the white goods sector[1]

This PSS targets people living alone for short periods, such as students and sales people, and offers for rental a package of four appliances (4.2 kg automatic washing machine, 120 litre two-door fridge-freezer, 15 inch flat screen television, and a cooking oven-range). Within the rental agreement, Toshiba covers any repairs, delivery, installation and removal, plus the end-of-life recycling fees.

While Toshiba may see this niche market as good business, it may also be part of a much broader strategy. Toshiba has stated that it wishes to move away from dependence on low-margin, highly competitive products to offering solutions based on software/services. Bearing this in mind, it may be Toshiba's long-term strategy to link pay-per-use with a new range of networked home appliances, since these can be programmed to report on energy usage and therefore used as a basis for charging, without the utility companies having to install special meters. This would not only create a much larger market but also be of interest for the international markets.

Toshiba home networked appliances[2]

Toshiba has launched home network units that can receive/send information via the internet: for example, new operation modes such as menus and home management control. Three models of networked home electric appliances are being marketed: a refrigerator, microwave oven and home laundry. The appliances have built-in self-monitoring capabilities that will notify a repair company if a problem arises. By means of Bluetooth, the user is connected via a wireless access point to the Toshiba Web service, which controls home electric appliances.

The system can propose cooking menus, manage the food in the refrigerator and perform other tasks by simple operation of a home terminal. Furthermore, by using the customer's mobile phone the contents of the refrigerator can be checked from the

1 CfSD Research: Toshiba Home Appliances, Pay-Per-Use; www.cfsd.org.uk/PSS/Home_appliances_pay_per_use.htm.

2 CfSD Research: Networked home appliances; www.cfsd.org.uk/PSS/Ex_networked_home_appliances.htm.

supermarket. A recipe can be sent to the refrigerator and microwave oven, and a washing method sent to the washing machine. The home terminal (BHT-1002A), coupled with Bluetooth, serves as an entertainment system, which allows the user to enjoy the internet, email, etc. in a wireless environment everywhere in the house. Toshiba is planning to offer a system that wirelessly monitors the door/window opening/closing information, the lighting, etc. in the house. It can be seen that there is only a small step required to include pay-per-use as part of the product-service.

8.1.4 Conclusions

Although the ICT sector is still not the largest sector in the economies of developed countries, it is already having considerable influence on economic development and human welfare through its ubiquitous contribution to improving the efficiency and communications potential of business and other organisations. Rapid technology developments have potentially profound implications for economies and societies but these are being largely driven by what is technically possible and by commercial demands rather than by consideration of needs.

While the term 'PSS' is not used, it offers a useful approach to optimising the product-service mix. The ICT sector is already service-oriented though significantly supported by products and infrastructure. PSS arrangements are commonplace, especially in B2B transactions, although they are less common in B2C. It is commonly recognised that there are opportunities to 'add value' through services in saturated markets.

Various generic approaches can be used for product and service idea generation, design, development and implementation. However, tools for integrating the process would be useful, especially for integrating the product and service elements. Generation of effective PSS will result from 'user' focus in design management, and the availability of good tools.

While there are increased PSS possibilities for ICT products and services in the future, in ICT sector and customer transactions the main potential for application is likely to lie in the wider economy and all its various sectors. As a result of this the scope became so large that a choice regarding what to cover in this report had to be made. Following discussions with the SusProNet ICT partners it was felt that focusing on the product categories related to the EC Directive on Waste Electrical and Electronic Equipment (WEEE) might prove to be a more fruitful area for exploration of PSS and sustainable product-service systems (SPSS) opportunities.

8.2 Analysis: PSS opportunities in need area ICT

ICT is widely recognised as having the characteristics of a 'threshold technology', one that is likely to have far-reaching and transformational implications for all aspects of societies and economies, and in the way we live and work and even think. ICT therefore has major implications for sustainable development. However, its role and impacts in this direction are still unclear.

In this section we consider how ICT developments might influence or be influenced by trends, and how these might influence opportunities for PSS for those product categories related to the WEEE Directive. We consider what methods or tools or approaches might be applied in sustainable PSS development, the degree to which these are being used by companies, opportunities for PSS and areas for further research and development.

8.2.1 Trends and developments relevant for PSS development

This section describes the general social trends impacting the ICT sector, and the PSS opportunities this presents for the product categories falling under the WEEE Directive.[3] More emphasis as a result is put on sustainable PSS, since the new legislation will be a significant driving force for finding sustainable PSS solutions. The WRI/UNEP/WBCSD study *Tomorrow's Markets* and other sources, including work by the Centre for Sustainable Design (CfSD), have been used in identifying trends (Doering *et al.* 2002).

General trends and developments

There are both general and specific sector trends which will have an impact on ICT. Some of these trends are likely to continue, such as population growth. Others are uncertain and would require more detailed scenario or other analysis to assess their development and impacts. Economic development over the long term has seen growth, but over the past few years there has been a period of recession and patchy growth with uncertainty and instability. There are wide disparities in income and wealth, within most countries and between rich and poor countries. The implications for ICT are as follows:

- ICT demand and application increases, but steadily and with some bursts, rather than spectacularly

- ICT access remains limited among the poor majority (in developed as well as developing countries)

- Corporate and government efforts are being stepped up to increase access to ICT as a way of stimulating market and economic growth

The general trend towards globalisation continues; this is resulting in increased world trade, integration and homogenisation. It also increases the power of corporations, wealthy individuals and nations often at the expense of the erosion of local economies and cultures. This trend also diminishes the power and influence of governments but it could be slowed by recession and backlash against negative impacts. The implications for ICT of this trend are as follows:

- Globalisation is facilitated by and in turn stimulates ICT development

- A slowdown or backlash would slow down global trade and ICT application and a major backlash might drive preference for localisation and community values rather than 'Cybersociety'

---

3 See legislation at: www.cfsd.org.uk/seeba.

There has been an explosion in information and communication channels, but this is increasingly resulting in information overload. Those left out are further disadvantaged. The implications for ICT are:

- Uptake of new technologies but preference by many for books and personal contact may limit customer acceptance in many areas

- New technologies, such as artificial intelligence, to reduce the workload for people

As a result of the above trends and the ICT revolution there has been a rapid increase in global networking for both business and personal use. This trend is likely to increase with globalisation, triggering the need for even more ICT solutions, but may be reduced under backlash and localisation scenarios. Other technology areas are also moving rapidly and this will further increase demands on ICT.

Global population growth is, and will remain, a major issue resulting in mass migration from poverty, and environmental and social degradation. ICT opportunities are denied to many in the world, but in the long term such opportunities may be available for developing countries. The large gap between the wealth of the developed and developing countries means that their needs are substantially different, which will influence the trends.

The developed countries in general have an ageing population, because of the falling birth rate in these countries. This has resulted in selective immigration to augment the workforce. An increasing proportion of the populations are 'singles' either because they never marry or because they are divorcees.

In general there is a major market within the developed countries for communications and entertainment and other ICT application needs such as medical monitoring and home shopping.

The developing countries, in contrast, have rapid population growth increases, problems of poverty, serious environmental issues and social degradation. Because of the population growth and lower life expectancy, the average ages in these countries are considerably lower than in the developed countries.

There are substantial affluent and 'modern' sectors within the economies of these countries. However, corruption is a major problem in parts of the developing world and this allows exploitation of the poor by the rich. The increased tendency of the excluded poor and of some countries to reject Western materialism leads to potential conflict.

Accessibility to ICT for the developing countries remains a major problem. Tailored solutions have and are being developed. In general, there is no reluctance to embrace new technologies when they are accessible. Because of the size of the so far untapped market there are substantial opportunities for producers of products and services. The richer social groups are following the trends of developed countries. For the poorer groups, providing shared facilities such internet/telecommunication access is seen as one way of tapping into this market.

The general business trend over the last few years has been towards globalisation. The intense price competition has resulted in substantial outsourcing and subcontracting, and the emergence of virtual ('hollow') companies.[4] Within some sectors these changes have resulted in social, quality, safety and environmental problems.

---

4   TimesOnLine, 'The Age of the Hollow Company', business.timesonline.co.uk/article/0,,8209-1086449,00.html, accessed November 2004.

The impact of this trend in business is a far higher reliance by international companies on electronic communication, as e-commerce is used to manage supplier and customer relationships. This in turn is resulting in an increase in the use of ICT by SMEs.

Sustainability demands

The trends discussed in the previous section have important implications not only for
ICT but also for global sustainable development, and the possibilities for SPSS. Population growth combined with the rising use of energy and resources to meet the increasing demands of the consumer society is resulting in:

- Increased greenhouse gas emissions

- Increased air and water pollution and waste

- Catastrophic loss of biodiversity and ecosystems

- Unsustainable exploitation of natural resources such as forests and fisheries

- Threats to agricultural production and food supplies: for example, salinisa-
  tion, desertification, weather extremes, loss to urbanisation

In general ICT is technology-driven without regard for sustainability consequences and
accelerates negative sustainable development trends, since efficiencies are often offset
by increased material throughputs in industry and commerce. ICT also facilitates global
purchasing by consumers which can both help developing countries move out of their
poverty traps and lead to exploitation of a low paid workforce.

Presently sustainable development trends are unfavourable and there are few signs
of the necessary shifts or of policies and measures to drive the shifts. Although there is
continuing discussion and progress in a few areas, there are more signs of 'business as
usual' involving continuing globalisation wherever possible and continuing technological and economic development with little or no consideration of sustainability implications. However, events may change this.

To further complicate the issue PSS cannot necessarily be seen as the answer for sustainable development in ICT. Digital Europe has issued a booklet called *Making the Net
Work: Steps towards a Sustainable Networked World* (Forum for the Future 2003). It is a
summary of two years of research on the effects of ICT on sustainable development. The
work clearly showed that ICT result-oriented service systems were not necessarily more
sustainable than the products they replace. A good example of this is the downloading
of music from the web. The environmental impact of just downloading music can be
less than half of the impact of purchasing it from a shop, if the consumer uses a broad-
band connection and does not burn the music to a CD. However, a narrowband user
who does burn the music can have an environmental impact of over three times that
from the shop. This shows how complex the analysis of PSS in ICT can become.

Successfully implementing opportunities for sustainable PSS may require integrated
product policy (IPP) measures to stimulate demand and supply. PSS opportunities are
likely to be most attractive for sustainability (and also most profitable for business)
where, for example:

- Information content is high, and there is significant scope for dematerialisation

- Economic case for ownership is limited (e.g. infrequent use)

- There is the potential to shift large markets (i.e. not just a small niche)

Careful analysis is needed to anticipate and avoid possible 'rebound effects' where reduction of one aspect of consumption frees resources to consume more of another. It certainly should not be assumed that all PSS improve sustainability. In the long term a significant shift in the direction of sustainable development, and the sustainable application of ICT, will depend on values shifts in society.

Other need area-specific issues

Profit is the largest motivator for PSS within the ICT industry, and this often rides on the back of new technology since this opens up new markets. In most cases industry does not differentiate between product and service, but more in finding a profitable market.

PSS in B2B is already very common, and demand is likely to continue to grow. Many companies are outsourcing much of their business, and they look for PSS solutions to ensure the businesses run smoothly. In addition much of this outsourcing is into developing countries, and electronic communication networks are required in these countries to support the systems put in place. A further strong driver within large organisations has been the widespread use of office networks, where software and services have been critical to their successful implementation.

Another driver for PSS in B2B could be the new environmental product legislation being introduced in Europe and other countries, which requires the producer to take responsibility for end-of-life disposal. This is already resulting in some companies such as Xerox and Toshiba moving to provide solutions that include end-of-life management rather than just products.

In the field of B2C, the biggest barrier to PSS development is the cultural need to own products. This has been very difficult to overcome except in niche areas such as for products that are seldom used or are used in communal areas, such as washing machines in blocks of apartments. This reluctance to use a service rather than own a product could, however, begin to change as home/consumer networks start to become commonplace. With these systems they only work as a product-service. The Toshiba home network is a good example of this where, by means of Bluetooth, the user is connected via a wireless access point to the Toshiba Web service, which controls home electric appliances.

8.2.2 Conclusions

ICT has many far-reaching applications and implications. ICT developments are likely to continue under all scenarios for the future, with wide application and influence. The rate of and direction of development will depend on the state of the economy, social values and other factors, as well as the future direction of the trends outlined above. In principle, ICT often offers opportunities to dematerialise systems. However, rebound effects and the more frequent use of what basically is an energy-based access system (e.g. music stored on the internet in contrast to CDs) can nullify any potential sustainability gains.

General opportunities

In spite of the difficulties, opportunities can nevertheless be identified which might be attractive in themselves or assisted by implementation of IPP. It is for business to identify and develop specific opportunities. It is nevertheless possible to identify areas of greatest need and potential demand in the face of sustainability or related problems. One approach to identifying and developing opportunities for SPSS is to focus on the functional needs of customers, business and individuals, and consider how these might be met in a more sustainable way while meeting other business and customer criteria.

Criteria for ICT PSS opportunity attractiveness (assuming they are feasible and 'add value' to business, and rebound or other negative impacts can be offset) would include the following:

- Products, services or customer needs where the information content is relatively high offer the most scope for dematerialisation through ICT (e.g. replacing printed with online information)

- Products, services or customer needs where the information content is high and there is currently a high level of equipment, building and transport infrastructure and impact, have the most potential for savings against these things (e.g. teleworking, teleconferencing)

- Products that are relatively expensive, used only occasionally, and where there is little or no status element in ownership, have the most scope for leasing, rental, shared ownership or other utility arrangements

- Products and services that have wide existing or potential application and markets have the most potential for aggregate environmental and social benefits because of their overall impact. By comparison, niche, small market products, however individually 'sustainable', will not have much aggregate impact

- Approaches that are replicable by other products and services enable still wider application. A product or service that has similarities to others can act as an example and help in learning. A highly specialised product may offer less scope for wider application

- Major PSS initiatives by large players are likely to have most influence on the market as a whole, both directly and indirectly by influencing suppliers and smaller competitors. Such initiatives may have most benefit in terms of positive sustainability impacts

- B2B PSS are likely to present most opportunities, at least in the short term. The economic case is usually clear; the chains of relationships and other service aspects are more manageable

There are so far few examples of extensive application of SPSS: that is, PSS developed with the aim of reducing sustainability impacts. Some PSS have nevertheless been developed which have potential incidental sustainable development benefits, and there are some where sustainability has been a consideration. Some are already increasing in application—for example, online banking and teleconferencing—and some are still at the trial or conceptual stage.

When considering the B2C or consumer markets there may be opportunities for more sustainable PSS, but it is hard to see them succeeding and offsetting 'rebound effects', at least in the short term. Since the main direct impacts of ICT products are often in the use and disposal phases, and 'rebound effects' depend on societal norms and other factors, their impacts generally cannot be influenced at the design stage. In the long term a significant shift in the direction of sustainable development, and the sustainable application of ICT, will depend on values shifts in society.

Specific PSS opportunities

Based on the criteria of attractiveness listed above, opportunity zones for PSS in the ICT sector were identified by the companies that participated in the SusProNet ICT group. The first set of PSS opportunities is related to ICT in general, and is listed in Box 8.1. The second set focuses on the narrower set of products listed in the EU WEEE Directive, and basically analyses whether a product-oriented, use-oriented or result-oriented service could be put on the market in relation to the WEEE product category (see Table 8.1). From this exercise, three opportunities appear to offer future financial and sustainable business potential:

- PCs owned by manufacturers and companies charged on usage

- Replacement of PCs by dumb terminals in office and home environments

- Cellular phone switches to cordless telephone when in range of base station

The first opportunity is starting to happen; Hewlett Packard has such a scheme with servers where the amount charged depends partly on the volume of traffic. There are, however, no significant numbers of PCs in B2B that are charged on usage, although leasing is common. For B2C this is not likely to happen until the networked home becomes a reality.

The application of thin-client computing using dumb terminals is growing rapidly in B2B as this saves considerable amounts of money in IT, while decreasing the environmental impact dramatically. Again, this PSS application is not likely to become popular in B2C until home networking arrives.

The use of a cellular phone that switches to a cordless phone when Bluetooth or WiFi is in range has a potentially huge market in both B2B and B2C, since it will bring dramatic savings to the users, while using fewer resources, since only one phone is needed per person for both land and mobile usage. Trials on this have recently been announced.

8.3 Idea generation and selection

This section covers the idea generation and selection phase within the PSS development process. It is based on the current practice researched by the Centre for Sustainable Design and the outcomes of the 2nd SusProNet workshop, held with companies active in the ICT sector. The process was roughly organised according to the Guideline for PSS Development published as Annex 1 to this book. Section 8.3.1 presents a long list of PSS concepts and a selection of priority ideas, which are further elaborated in Section 8.3.2.

8.3.1 Need area-specific PSS ideas (long list)

During the 2nd SusProNet workshop (Lisbon, 25–26 September 2003), the participants of the ICT group workshop split into two groups. One group had the task of generating eight PSS concepts that had good business potential, while the other group concentrated on developing eight PSS concepts that had good sustainability benefits. Each group was given eight areas under which to develop the concepts. Hence, in total 16 ideas were generated from 16 opportunity zones, eight from a sustainability point of view and eight from a business perspective. The need areas and resulting concepts are outlined below.

Sustainability solutions group

- **50% reduction in CO_2 emissions**. Converged transport: the co-ordination of individual transport needs for maximum efficiency and reduced CO_2 emissions

- **50% reduction in material use**. User-centred utility billing: the user monitors consumption (energy/water/gas) and can query use and pay electronically. Visibility would encourage savings in energy, water and gas

- **50% reduction in material extraction**. WEEE identification system: database combined with rf (radio frequency) tagging/bar codes to identify WEEE material content. This would increase recycling and reduce material extraction

- **50% reduction in toxic materials**. Electronic nose to sniff out toxic materials: providing a cost-effective way of detecting banned substances would ensure that legislation can be enforced

- **50% reduction in air pollution**. Remote nodal system: village-based e-learning facilities aimed at children/adults. It would reduce travelling with its resulting air pollution

- **50% reduction in water pollution**. Land log: database of land records incorporating water, pesticide use and associated pollution

- **50% increase in literacy**. Re-live and write: visual/verbal recognition system to improve literacy

Saving or improving the efficiency of production, warehousing and transport, including sharing of facilities, for example, through:

B2B: e-commerce

- Marketing and trading
- Supply chain re-engineering
- Centralised procurement
- Customer relationship management
- Distribution logistics
- M-commerce: use of mobile communications
- E-delivery: databases of customers are scanned to see what is needed

Business: internal operations

- Centralised data processing services (avoids need for customers to have equipment)
- Decentralised/customised manufacturing (small-scale, as needed, reduced transport)
- Teleworking (e.g. BT has 4,000 teleworkers saving 34,000 tonnes CO_2 per year)
- Teleconferencing
- Online banking and accounting (including e-billing; AT&T estimates savings of 600,000 sheets of paper from this)
- Virtual or shared offices

Business–customer and government–customer

- Intelligent home: home networks, to automate the home, including equipment maintenance and energy monitoring to assist customers in optimising energy use
- Online banking: Barclays Bank has suggested that online banking could have as little as one-tenth of the impact of high-street banking
- Online shopping and home delivery
- Distance learning (the Open University in the UK has estimated a 70–90% reduction in emissions per student than campus-based learning)
- Online communications and information (e.g. marketing, public information)
- Online newspapers, instruction manuals
- Online books (e.g. encyclopedias): a book sold through a conventional bookshop is estimated to require 15 times more energy than one sold through Amazon.com (*Source*: Centre for Energy and Climate Solutions), but this depends on using the optimum distribution system
- Equipment rental

Box 8.1   PSS opportunity zones for the ICT sector

IT and telecommunications equipment	Product-oriented service	Use-oriented service	Result-oriented service (product substitution)	Result-oriented service (vertical integration)
Centralised data processing/mainframes	Common in business-to-business. Added functionality and upgrades common for home PCs	Leasing is common in business-to-business		
Minicomputers				
Printer units		Pay on-demand. Hardware is paid for on usage		
Personal computing:			Dumb terminals to replace personal PCs	Limited market for user to construct own machines
PCs (CPU, mouse, screen and keyboard included)				
Laptop computers (CPU, mouse, screen and keyboard included)				
Notebook computers				
Notepad computers				
Printers			Electronic printing	
Copying equipment				
Electrical and electronic typewriters				
Pocket and desk calculators				
Other products for the collection/storage/ processing/ presentation/ communication of information	Common in business-to-business	Common in business-to-business	Some could be replaced by web-based services via PC	
User terminals and systems				
Facsimile			Emails already replacing them	
Telex				
Telephones			Internet calling via the PC	
Pay telephones			Internet phone centres	
Cordless telephones			Single phone for cordless/mobile	
Cellular telephones				
Answering systems		Common in business-to-business	Virtual answering machine	
Other products transmitting sound, images or other information by telecommunications			Some could be replaced by web-based services via PC	

TABLE 8.1 Matrix of PSS opportunities related to the ICT category of WEEE

Sustainability solutions group						
Opportunity zone		*Description*	Scores			
			Fi	En	So	To
01	50% reduction in CO_2 emissions	Converged transport: co-ordination of individual transport for maximum efficiency	17	17	15	49
02	50% reduction in material use	User-centred utility billing: user monitors consumption and can pay electronically	18	20	12	50
03	50% reduction in material extraction	WEEE identification system: readable chip/numbering system. Internet-based	14	24	19	57
04	50% reduction in toxic materials	Electronic nose: identification/recognition/ diagnosis of toxic materials	5	18	14	37
05	50% reduction in air pollution	Village-based flexible e-learning aimed at children/adults	19	24	18	61
06	50% reduction in water pollution	Land log: database of land records incorporating water and pesticide use	11	18	17	46
07	50% increase in literacy	Re-live and write: visual/verbal recognition system to improve literacy	19	7	23	49
08	'Closing the digital divide'	Mobile audio text: text-to-voice system to enable access by the blind	23	11	24	58

Business solutions group						
Opportunity zone		*Description*	Scores			
			Fi	En	So	To
09	Home networks	Menus available from fridge contents, including healthy menus	11	14	4	29
10	E-shopping	Electronic shopping list: shows cheapest source and location in a supermarket	22	9	6	37
11	Electronic printing	Electronic clothing allowing change of colour/pattern	9	2	2	13
12	Centralised data processing	Service provider directory of local plumbers, electricians, etc.	21	9	12	42
13	Online banking	Fixed assets database to enable loans to be given quickly	25	10	16	51
14	Online entertainment	Watch opera, plays live at home (cable, satellite, web)	22	13	21	56
15	Distance learning	Developing-world open university, which can be customised to a country's needs.	21	19	28	68
16	Integrated communication	Customised supply chain management (SCM); automatic ordering through the supply network	30	26	14	70

Fi = Financial; En = Environmental; So = Social; To = Total

TABLE 8.2 Need area-specific PSS idea score sheet

- **'Closing the digital divide'.** Mobile audio text: mobile 'text to voice' systems to enable access by the blind

Business solutions group

- **Home networks.** Menus from the fridge; enter menu to see if have contents
- **E-shopping.** Shopping list used for information on prices and where located in the store
- **Electronic printing.** Electronic clothing; for example, changes colours and patterns
- **Centralised data processing.** Service provide directory of local plumbers, electricians, etc.
- **Online banking.** Database of fixed assets in order to enable fast loan provisions
- **Online entertainment.** Watch 'live events' such as opera from home using transmission by cable, satellite or internet
- **Distance learning.** Developing worldwide open university which can be customised for country's and pupil's individual requirements
- **Integrated communications.** Customised automatic supply chain management

The different concepts were then scored for financial, environmental and social benefits by each participant of the workshop.

From Table 8.2, three PSS concepts were chosen for further analysis. Each concept was assessed from a financial, environmental and social perspective and then ranked. The highest-rated concepts were then chosen. One of these was a combination of the distance learning and flexible e-learning since these two ideas could easily be combined. This concept was called the 'Glocal Open University' since it is a merger of globalisation and localisation. The other two concepts chosen were the 'customised automated supply chain management' concept and the 'electronic nose' concept. The final concept was again a combination of two complementary ideas. These were the 'electronic nose' and 'WEEE identification system'.

8.3.2 Need area-specific PSS ideas (short list)

The three selected ideas are discussed in more detail below.

Glocal Open University

This concept involves the development of a world open university, which can be customised to meet individual country requirements. A central university provides online teaching material based on inputs from individual country education authorities, and also provides teacher training. Learning centres are set up in countries in schools, internet cafes or mobile classrooms (see Fig. 8.1). The latter is a 'classroom in a box'. It consists of a portacabin that can be shipped on a pallet with furniture, computers and telecoms and can be assembled in remote areas. Local face-to-face teaching complements distance learning with exams taken locally. This concept scored very highly on the social aspect and reasonably highly on both financial and environmental aspects.

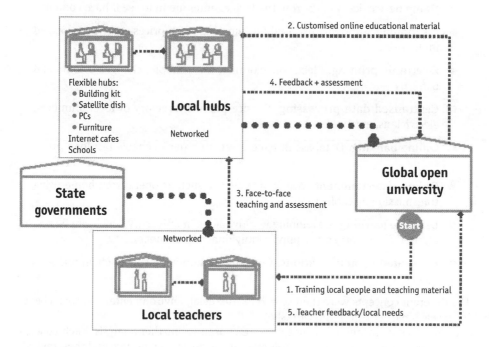

FIGURE 8.1 System map of Glocal Open University

- **Key product elements**: books, CDs and flexible hubs
- **Key service elements**: online electronic teaching material, the training of teachers, networking of pupils and teachers, and examinations
- **Environmental benefits**: reduction of travel for remote locations
- **Financial benefits**: lower operating costs and faster delivery
- **Social benefits**: increases accessibility to education
- **Key stakeholders**: Glocal Open University (merging of global and local education), the local and state government, local teachers, and IT experts
- **Technology infrastructure**: establishing the infrastructure and software
- **Key revenue issues**: state and local governments plus UNESCO (private–public sector funding needed); pupils pay on the basis of what they can afford

Customised automated supply chain management

This is a system to automate the purchasing of parts from a company's supply chain (see Fig. 8.2). When an order is received from a customer the system decides what parts are required and automatically orders them. This concept scored very highly on the financial aspects and reasonably highly on environmental aspects, with an average score for social aspects.

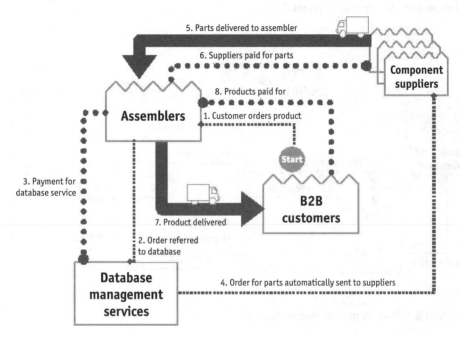

FIGURE 8.2 System map of customised automated supply chain management

- **Key service elements**: central database management
- **Environmental benefits**: reduction of paper (automated system)
- **Financial benefits**: lower operating costs and the faster delivery could result in new business
- **Social benefits**: no major impact
- **Key stakeholders**: customer, the assembler (tier 1 supplier), component manufacturers (tier 2 suppliers), and database management service
- **Technology infrastructure**: establishing the communications infrastructure, and data security
- **Key revenue issues**: payment of database management service

Electronic nose

This uses a sensor that works like a sniffer dog, in order to determine the material content of products, and whether there are any banned materials present (see Fig. 8.3). This is combined with a barcode reader or radio frequency (rf) tag, which can be used to determine the material content from a central database. This concept scored fairly highly on the environmental aspects, had an average score on social aspects and a below-average score for financial aspects.

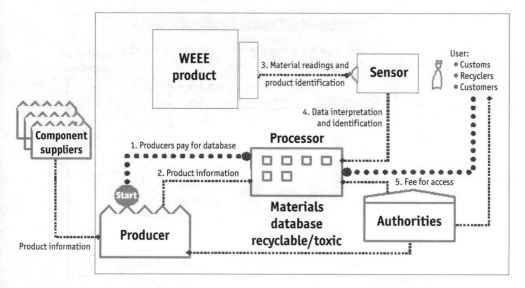

FIGURE 8.3 System map of electronic nose

- **Key product elements**: sensor (nose)

- **Key service elements**: central database management, and software for sensor

- **Environmental benefits**: allows enforcement of environmental requirements on product material content

- **Financial benefits**: considerable cost savings on materials testing

- **Social benefits**: no major impact

- **Key stakeholders**: authorities/trading standards, producer, user (customs, recycler, customer) and the processor

- **Technology infrastructure**: workable sensor, identifying a range of substances, addressing exceptions such as lead in steel, the impact of mixed substances on recyclability, establishing an infrastructure and software/database

- **Key revenue issues**: finance for establishing and running database

8.3.3 Conclusions

The idea generation part of the workshop produced some interesting results, although it did not produce any radical new ideas for PSS. It showed that:

● There are many areas where PSS could be used successfully

● Many of the areas of high PSS interest are dependent on high technology and integrated communications

● Some of the ideas generated from a sustainability perspective were complementary to ideas generated from a business perspective. Two of the three ideas selected for further development were a combination of ideas from both the sustainability and business-focused groups

8.4 Implementation

The implementation of PSS into the ICT sector in B2B is now quite common. It normally results in a closer relationship between producer and customer, and that in turn can result in better customer loyalty. Sometimes producers use a third party to interface with customers, but that does have the downside of losing that closer relationship.

Within B2C PSS is less common, since its growth is constrained by the desire of consumers to own the products.

This section looks at the different elements relevant for the implementation of PSS, how the group participants approach implementation of PSS, and implementation challenges.

8.4.1 Need area-specific implementation challenges and policy support

During WP3 the challenges facing the implementation of the three concepts selected in WP2 were explored in detail from the following aspects:

Company internal characteristics

What are the roadblocks resulting from existing company culture and processes?

● The market size was either too small or too large for the company

● The company does not have in-house core competences for PSS

● Processes have not been put in place to deal with PSS

● There is too much conservatism of the workforce, preventing change

Value chain issues

How do you manage the costs and revenue in a fair way?

- Retaining complete ownership of the PSS allows costs and revenues to be managed effectively

- Getting complementary goals in the value chain will result in all parties pulling in the same direction

- Ensuring that there is a clear agreed and documented payment mechanism for the PSS

- Ensuring that the customer recognises the value of the PSS over owning the product

Partnership and co-operation issues

How do you form and manage a successful partnership?

- Establishing trust between partners

- Ensuring there is a good information exchange between the partners

- Getting government involvement where feasible

Technical feasibility issues

How do you overcome any technical hurdles?

- Ensuring that there are adequate levels of security for information flow

- Forming reliable, cost-effective communications infrastructure

- Developing new technologies to meet the PSS specification

- Addressing any issues of language content for multinational PSS

Institutional issues

What regulatory or economic incentives are required for the PSS to be successful?

- Legislation that results in the need for a PSS: for example, the 'electronic nose' need resulting from the implementation of WEEE

A surprising number of the above issues are specifically PSS-related; issues arising out of partnerships and finance form a large slice of this. However, these issues are not insurmountable and many companies have formed financially successful partnerships to launch a PSS. Care, however, does have to be taken to ensure responsibilities and revenues are fully agreed and documented.

PSS partnerships in industry are now becoming very common. Many ICT companies are being run on a new corporate model, where almost everything is outsourced, and the company just accepts responsibility for the whole supply chain. This has given rise to a new term: 'hollow company'. For example, if you buy a Dell computer you will go through a call centre owned by another company, or if you buy a phone from Sony Ericsson, another company makes it. This is made possible by today's high-speed communications networks. IBM, for instance, has 12,000 suppliers all wired into its system network. These hollow companies have in effect moved heavily into product-service systems, depending on their brand name and services offered to their customers to prosper in the marketplace.

Possibly the biggest roadblock to marketing PSS in the consumer sector is the culture of wanting to own a product, rather than pay for a PSS. More integrated approaches to demand- and supply-side components of product policy (e.g. IPP) may be able to influence this; tax incentives are the most powerful single instrument. These could be tied to encouragement of sustainable PSS. The problem here, though, is determining which PSS is and isn't sustainable. It is an extremely complex area, and often PSS that look sustainable are found not to be when looked at in more detail, since the advantages are more than wiped out by increased demand resulting from their launch.

The most likely way in which consumer resistance to PSS will be overcome is with the introduction of rapid communication systems to the consumer, so high speed automated services can be offered, where the hardware forms a part of the total integrated system. Countries such as Japan already have these fast communication networks in place (ADSL of 8 MB per second costs approximately US$32/month), and as a result one can see the start of the establishment of home networked systems within this country. If Europe does not want to lose out to this emerging market, a similar fast communication system will need to be launched here soon.

8.4.2 Conclusions

The number one key implementation challenge for PSS is customer acceptance of PSS over owning the product. This will take time, and is more likely to be influenced by technology, such as faster communication systems to households, which will allow PSS to be offered that give valuable services and automate the home, rather than by government tax incentives.

Within B2B to be successful a PSS must offer something needed over and above what a customer would get from purchasing just a product. For instance, leasing ICT equipment has the advantage of removing it from capital expenses, and it is often provided as a solution to a company's needs, rather than just leasing computers, printers and so on. Xerox is a good example of how to be successful in this area. Increasingly, Xerox is working with customers to design and redesign their basic business processes. It sells innovative approaches for performing work and for enhancing productivity.

The second major challenge for companies moving into PSS is setting up good partnerships, where the sharing of revenues and responsibilities is agreed and documented. However, with many companies already involved in partnerships through outsourcing of services and products this is less of an issue than it used to be.

8.5 Conclusion

ICT is a diverse, rapidly changing and growing worldwide industry sector. It differs essentially from many regular industry sectors, since ICT is in most cases an enabler for such other industries.

Needs satisfaction is usually indirectly rather than directly met by ICT. Business has a need to manage information and to communicate, not an inherent need and demand for ICT itself. In delivering information and communications solutions there is an increased blurring of the edges between products and services, as many products now include services: for example, software, warranties, free 'take-back', and many services also include products. Product-service systems as a term is hardly used in this industry, although with some 70% of the turnover being service-related, many firms are in effect creating PSS in some form or another.

8.5.1 PSS in the need area: opportunities and threats

Drivers and opportunities

One of the major drivers for ICT has been new technology, which is allowing new PSS solutions to emerge that were not even feasible a few years ago. New network technology, such as ADSL, Bluetooth and WiFi, played a large role in enabling many of the PSS examples discussed. High-speed computing and networks have transformed how businesses are run and organised. It allows global data exchange, so almost any part of the business can be carried out in any part of the world. This promotes the co-design of highly efficient, ICT-enabled business processes. Lower transaction costs made possible by ICT also promotes the organisation of business as networks of individual firms, providing (result-)oriented services to each other. The networked office will also continue the growth of companies offering complete solutions, rather than selling individual pieces of equipment. This trend is likely to slowly trickle down from the multinationals to SMEs.

Concerns about sustainability are now starting to be recognised by governments, and legislation covering end-of-life treatment, dumping waste in the developing world and product material content are starting to appear. This in itself will be a driver for sustainable PSS.

Within the consumer area high-speed computing and networks are slowly moving into the home. This will be a major driver for PSS in B2C since it will spawn opportunities in entertainment, control of household equipment, security, news and communication. When this happens it will be far too complicated in most cases for the householders to buy individual pieces of equipment and join them together into a network. Instead, it is more likely that solutions will be sold, with responsibility for the smooth running of the system retained by the solution provider. Table 8.3 summarises these findings, together with some other generic drivers mentioned in this chapter (such as a move to software due to declining margins in hardware manufacturing or attracting clients by removing upfront capital investment by offering leases).

Potential business ideas

Analysis of trends and issues facing the ICT sector identified eight business-driven and eight sustainability-driven opportunity zones:

Business-driven

- Home networks
- E-shopping
- Electronic printing
- Centralised data processing
- Online banking
- Online entertainment
- Distance learning
- Integrated communications

Sustainability-driven

- Carbon dioxide emissions (opportunity zone: 50% reduction)
- Material use (opportunity zone: 50% reduction)
- Material extraction (opportunity zone: 50% reduction)
- Toxic materials (opportunity zone: 50% reduction)
- Air pollution (opportunity zone: 50% reduction)
- Water pollution (opportunity zone: 50% reduction)
- Literacy (opportunity zone: 50% increase)
- 'Closing the digital divide'

These 16 opportunity zones were used to stimulate idea generation. Each idea generated was evaluated against environmental, social and financial criteria using a simple evaluation and ranking method. From this the five highest rated concepts were chosen, which were then further refined to three concepts. Interestingly, the three concepts were derived from a mix of both business- and sustainability-driven opportunity zones, not just business opportunities:

- Electronic nose: a device for 'sniffing-out' restricted materials in ICT products
- Glocal University: a distance learning approach for the developing world
- Customised supply chain management: an information system for automatic ordering

Development pitfalls and threats

Many of the PSS systems looked at have major hurdles to overcome before they could become commercial successes. Examples are outlined below (see Table 8.3 for a summary of the pitfalls discussed in this chapter):

- Resistance by telecommunications companies could hamper the widespread use of VoIP/WiFi in many countries

- In the B2C context, consumers prefer to own appliances rather than use pay-per-use systems. PSS is likely to remain a niche market until home networks take off. Once this happens the resistance to not owning is likely to fall, as the product becomes a small part of the solution being sold

- Such home networks will also enable other PSS that at present do not yet look attractive on their own. For example:
  - Management of groceries in the home makes much more sense when part of a complete home network
  - Pay-per-use household appliances also make much more sense as a complete home-networked system

In sum, in the short term, the main PSS opportunities are likely to lie in B2B transactions, since it will take time to overcome consumer resistance to not owning the products they use. Another important finding was that the great majority of PSS examples discussed in this chapter were driven by large multinational companies, and by the market. The exception was for the Electrolux pay-per-use washing machine, which was driven by the Environmental Group.

8.5.2 PSS and sustainability

Very little data is available on the environmental and social implications of PSS. One of the most common mistakes is to assume that PSS is always better environmentally and socially. In effect a life-cycle approach has to be taken before any real judgement can be made. The example of downloading music over the internet, which has been discussed in this report, is a classic example of this. Both the repeated download of a piece of music, and the increasing demand can soon negate any initial advantages. It is probably in this area that there is a need for a life-cycle analysis tool directed at PSS systems.

Where PSS can contribute to sustainability, it is usually tied to a technological solution. The use of dumb terminals (thin-client computing) is a case in point. This technology could result in substantive savings in energy and material resources if it replaced the current solution of having an 'all-powerful' computer on each user's desk. The PSS aspect of having centrally installed software that can be supplied on pay-per-use basis, goes hand in hand with this technological solution.

Sustainability does not just mean the environmental impact, but also the social impact. Deciding what a sustainable solution is becomes very difficult when you are trying to decide the importance of social impacts compared with environmental impacts. This becomes even more complicated when PSS solutions are being applied within developing countries. For example, providing central telecommunication and internet facilities in remote towns and villages is extremely good from the social aspect, since it allows businesses within those areas to operate in the global marketplace. However, environmentally it is increasing the global use of energy.

8.5.3 Policy support

There is no specific policy support given to ICT-related PSS. Indirectly, some of the new environmental legislation such as the EU's WEEE, RoHS (Restriction of Hazardous Substances) and EuP (Ecodesign Requirements for Energy-using Products) directives will help to drive some sustainable PSS in the ICT sector.

There are areas where specific EU policies could help to drive PSS. Some of these are:

- Tax incentives and publicity to companies to persuade them to move to thin-client computing: this could result in substantial reductions in energy and resources

- EU policy to move from telephone numbers to IP (internet protocol) addresses to allow the rapid integration of landline, mobile and wireless telecommunications

- EU setting minimum ADSL bandwidth standards to promote PSS solutions within the home

- Incorporation of PSS into the education curriculum of engineering, design and environmental studies

- More research into what makes a sustainable PSS solution

- There is a need to collect better-quality environmental and social information among stakeholders in the life-cycle of ICT PSS

Value element	Drivers and opportunities	Development pitfalls and threats
User value/market risk		
Tangible value	Removing upfront capital expenses (leasing)	User value must exceed the cost of purchasing and using products (B2B)
Intangible value	B2C: penetration of ICT in entertainment, security, news, etc. Since hardware becomes too complex, result-oriented services get opportunities	Customer acceptance of not owing a product (B2C)
System costs/financial risk		
Tangible operational costs	Co-design of new highly efficient ICT-enabled business processes PSS for cost-effective solutions of end-of-life products, driven by legislation such as WEEE Providing customer with different PSS with the same hardware platform to manage costs	
Risk premium, financing and transaction costs	ICT lowers transaction costs, enabling creation of solution-providing networks	Complicated revenue sharing systems and management of responsibilities
Other benefits/capability risk		
Improved power position	Move to software due to low profit margins on manufacturing	
Defence to substitutes/loyalty		
High speed of innovation		
Investment in PSS development	Companies experienced in partnership through outsourcing build PSS easier	Developing the right partnerships
Other transition costs		Resistance of telecom providers may delay introduction of fast B2C communication solutions

TABLE 8.3 Review of need area-specific PSS opportunities and threats

9
Need area 3: offices

Martijn Verkuijl and Ursula Tischner

econcept, Germany

9.1 Product-service systems for need area office: an overview

This chapter gives an overview of the need area office and existing product-service systems (PSS) for the office sector. After a general introduction to the sector the main approaches to PSS development are presented and some examples of PSS that are typical to this sector are described, as researched before the SusProNet PSS idea generation work started. Also the integration of sustainability aspects in the development of PSS for the office is discussed.

9.1.1 Current state of the office sector

The following text summarises facts and figures about the current state of the office sector including:

- The activities of office workers and development of office work
- The European market for office furniture: economic recession
- Cultural differences in the office work in different countries
- Psycho-social aspects in the office environment

The activities of office workers and the development of office work

With the development of industrialised production at the end of the 19th century, engineers managed to split production into simple steps that were completed by workers who operated machines. This needed a new organisational environment to organise, control and administer these steps: hence the office was born as the command bridge of the 'captains of industry'. Around 1900 there were three office workers for every 100 industrial workers. Today over two-thirds of employees in the industrialised countries work in offices. Office work types and the proportion of employees working there can be differentiated into stational (working in individual office/room, 39%), changing (working in several offices in the same building, 38%) and mobile (working at different places and offices, 23%) (see Bullinger *et al.* 2000). Table 9.1 shows the occupational activity of the working population in the former West Germany. It is obvious that the areas of activity, **office work**, **organisation/management** and **education/consultancy/providing information**, have experienced more growth than other activities. Together, these activities make up more than 40% of all occupational activities.

Occupational activity	1973	1980	1991	2010 (forecast)
Production-related activities, including:	41.7%	37.9%	33.4%	29.6%
Extraction, manufacturing, assembly	31.0%	26,9%	18.9%	12.6%
Machine/plant operations, maintenance	5.1%	5.3%	8.2%	10.7%
Repair	5.6%	5.7%	6.3%	6.3%
Primary services, including:	37.1%	37.3%	39.8%	38.9%
Trade, sales	9.7%	9.5%	10.8%	11.1%
Office work, programming, computer screen activities	14.5%	15.5%	17.6%	16.8%
General services: entertainment, cleaning, loading, delivery	12.9%	12.3%	11.4%	11.0%
Secondary services, including:	21.2%	24.8%	26.8%	31.5%
Planning, research, development	5.0%	4.9%	5.0%	5.1%
Organisation/management	3.7%	4.4%	6.1%	9.1%
Assurance, legislation	4.6%	5.0%	3.8%	2.7%
Education, consultancy, information provision	7.9%	10.5%	11.9%	14.6%
Total (million)	**25.9**	**25.5**	**29.7**	**28.0**

TABLE 9.1 Occupational activity of the working population in the former West Germany (1973–2010)

Source: Tessaring 1994

Thus it is obvious that the share of office work in all occupational activities is increasing. But what kinds of activity are carried out in the office? The following types of office work (www.iab.de) and their division (figures from the federal state of Hessen in Germany [ABF aktuell 2002]) can be distinguished (see Table 9.2).

Type of office work	1980	2001
Administrative activities	9.3%	8.3%
Commercial activities	53.5%	56.3%
Management activities	6.6%	5.9%
Technical activities	11.3%	10.1%
Service activities	5.4%	6.7%
Data-processing activities	3.3%	6.8%
Overall infrastructural activities	10.5%	6.1%

TABLE 9.2 Division of office work types

This overview clearly shows that commercial and service activities increased, and that data processing activities experienced a dramatic increase. Other types of office activity decreased.

The European market for office furniture: economic recession

According to a recent study by InterConnection, the total revenue of the European office furniture market in 2002 was €7.8 billion. That means a decline of more than 19.9% in comparison with the year 2001 (€9.7 billion). The prognoses for the following years are slightly more positive: for 2003 a decline of 4.4% is expected; in 2004 and 2005 a growth of 1.3% and 3.8% (respectively) is predicted. The worst market within Europe in 2002 was the Swiss market (−24.8%), followed by the Benelux, Germany, Northern Europe, France and UK/Ireland (−20%).

In the office furniture sector, by far the largest product group is storage. Despite the rumours about the paperless office, storage has a constant market share of 31.6%. At the same time products such as tables have lost 29% of market share. The European office furniture market is still very atomised; the top ten companies generate only 30% of total revenue. In the USA, the five market leaders generate more than 80% of total revenue. There is still no single office furniture market in Europe. Every country has its own distribution system: in Austria (76.1%) and northern Europe (66.7%) direct sale dominates, excluding foreign competitors. Different work cultures in the EU countries (labour conditions, hierarchical factors) also lead to different offices. Thus countries such as Spain and Italy still have a low rate of imported products.

Cultural differences in the office work of different countries

In different countries the office work culture differs. The cultural aspects that are most relevant for the office sector are social behaviour, workspace, communication and openness towards new work methods/models. Because there is more emphasis on cohesiveness in Japanese culture and more emphasis on individual competition in Western culture, Japanese workers differ very much from European and North American workers in their 'analytical structure' regarding demand, control and support (Kawakami and Haratani 1999). Another difference is the preference for certain workspaces such as cellular offices (Germany and Netherlands), group offices (Germany), combi-offices (northern countries) and open-plan offices (Japan).

A very important organisational issue is the need for communication and interaction. Whereas southern European and Japanese workers are used to group work and personal interaction (Collard and DeHerde 1997), in northern countries workers are socially more independent and interaction is mainly functional. Hence teleworking is well accepted there. When it comes to new work methods, the UK is more progressive than many other European countries. Key to successful teleworking are self-confidence and autonomy, qualities that are fostered by the British style of management.[1]

The Finnish self-employed workers are generally highly skilled as managers. That is one reason why Finland is one of the countries with the highest rates of teleworkers. In contrast to that, in France it is still important to go to work as a symbol of status.[2]

Psycho-social factors in the office environment

Experts from sociology and ergonomics are especially interested in researching the new psycho-social conditions that apply to working life, where the demands for flexibility are increasing at a time when many jobs are monotonous and offer little scope for development. To measure psychological and social factors in office work and the health consequences they might have, different models have been proposed: for example, the demand-control model (demands from the job situation related to the degree of control) by Karasek and Theorell (1990) supplemented by the degree of social support from supervisors, work mates (as well as an extended model which could also take into account support from the family) introduced by Johnson and Hall (1988). The demand-control-support model forms the basis of many redesign efforts aimed at improving the work environment. Many researchers have found that work environments designed to enhance the health of workers also enhance productivity. Thus possibilities of redesigning the office environment and organisation so that it makes employees feel more empowered have been discussed, leading to flat hierarchies, more flexibility and participatory approaches.

9.1.2 Approaches to PSS development

PSS as a business concept is not very well known in the office sector; therefore no real PSS methodologies can be found. Out of the large number of tools that are available to help create offices, the most interesting approaches tackle the office as a system of products and services. Some of them are described below.

The **Dutch Ministry of Housing, Spatial planning and the Environment** has produced 'The Office Innovation Guide'. It describes development steps and concepts for office planning: for example, analysis of work processes, workspace planning strategy,

1   news.bbc.co.uk/1/hi/business/930536.stm
2   www.homeworking.com/library/events.htm

responsibilities in the process, workspace and office concepts and profits for responsible actors, such as managers, office workers and facility managers. One essential finding and recommendation in the guide is: do not introduce a new working style/environment only because of cost reasons. The improvement of operational processes should be the focus to reach optimal results.[3]

Another approach by the Management Circle in Eschborn, Germany, is based on a series of seminars 'Office Workplace Design: The Newest Insights for an Holistic Office Optimisation'. Topics exemplified with cases include analysis of buildings, interior and workplace; lighting concepts, acoustic, sound; materials and building materials; IT integration; telework; flexible forms of work and preventative health techniques for employees. The activities address responsible persons for office interiors and workspace and suggest five steps for a holistic design of the office.

Approaches of sustainable PSS to offices

When it comes to the integration of sustainability into workplace design and PSS to offices, hardly any holistic approaches can be found. Complete analyses of environmental strains caused by the total office system are often available only for specific companies and locations, often introduced within the framework of a company's eco-audit or via introduction of an environmental management system (ISO 14001 or EMAS [Eco-Management and Audit Scheme]). This often covers issues such as paper consumption, use optimisation of office technology, energy consumption or waste production in general. Buildings and equipment are rarely looked at because they are often predetermined. Below we give the most interesting approaches tackling the office as a system of products and services including sustainability aspects.

TCO Development tools

TCO Development (2000) offers knowledge tools for companies and organisations that want to improve their workplaces with respect to environment and health aspects.[4] TCO has a set of different tools for measuring aspects of the work environment, study material, training and educational material. One example is the brochure 'First Aid for a Better Workplace', which deals with problems related to ergonomics.

Sustainable Accommodation for the New Economy

Sustainable Accommodation for the New Economy (SANE) was a two-year EC-funded research project under the fifth framework programme considering the combined impact of the new economy on people, process, place and technology to create new ways for qualified employment exchange. Its focus is on the creation of sustainable, multi-location workplaces for knowledge workers across Europe, encompassing both virtual and physical spaces. The SANE Unified Framework for Workplace Design integrates three perspectives: people, process and place. Steps in the design process are:

● Development of a workspace model that meets the organisations' requirements for virtual, physical, public and private space

3   www.rijksgebouwendienst.nl/kantin/kantin.htm
4   www.tcodevelopment.com

- Analysis of interaction (physical space and virtual communication)

- Specification and development of ICT applications, services and infrastructures to support distributed mobile work

Within the SANE project a workplace model was developed that describes three types of office working space: cafe (informal meetings, chatting), club (individual and collaborative work) and cloister (private, confidential work).

Cornell University International Workplace Studies Program
The Cornell University International Workplace Studies Program (IWSP) was launched in 1989.[5] It focuses on the ecology of new ways of working. Using the framework of organisational ecology, the IWSP examines workplace strategies as a complex ecosystem in which one simultaneously considers the cost–benefit implications of the interplay of work processes, employee demographics, physical design, information technology and organisational culture as they converge in a workplace strategy.

9.1.3 Some examples of current PSS for offices

PSS categorisation

A wide range of PSS already exists in the office sector. As indicated in Chapter 2, the SusProNet network used a common definition and categorisation of product-service systems defining three categories: A, product-oriented PSS; B, use-oriented PSS; and C, result-oriented PSS. Box 9.1 presents a selection of PSS examples typical for the different categories.

PSS found in the first category, product-oriented PSS, mainly provide an extra service on top of an existing product (e.g. furniture maintenance, warranties, end-of-life treatment). This category also includes customisation services (e.g. custom-built computers). In the second category, use-oriented PSS, rental and lease concepts dominate the office area such as rental/leasing of equipment and furnishing. In the third category, result-oriented PSS, both PSS that replace existing products and PSS that offer contracting (e.g. energy supply) can be found in the office field.

9.1.4 Conclusions

A whole range of PSS already exists in the office. The office sector contains PSS that are both business-to-business and business-to-consumer and they cover all three PSS categories. The majority of use-oriented and product-oriented PSS currently found in the office sector is based on leasing/rental systems or provision of an extra service on top of an existing product. Concepts such as outsourcing and improved facility management are emerging and leading towards the third PSS dimension: result-oriented PSS. The presented approaches for office design, even the more holistic approaches, are not focused on the systematic vision of system innovations in the office area, covering

5   iwsp.human.cornell.edu

Project
Category A: Product-oriented PSS

Master Piece, if-Computer: software that makes placing carpets easier, saving material, time and money

Researched case (econcept—BMBF Cases Maßelter and Tischner 2000), www.ifcomputer.de

---

Wilkahn offers a maintenance, refurbishment and end-of-life disposal service for its swivel office chairs. This allows customers to extend the useful life of their chairs, and enables Wilkahn to re-use some components in new products. This means there is less need for new products, with consequent resource savings. The long lifetime of the products is important to this plan, which can be optimised by supplementary services.

Researched case (James *et al.* 2001; Zaring *et al.* 2001), www.wilkhahn.com, environmental report of the company 2000

Renew Inc. restores previously owned Steelcase office furniture systems to their original 'as new' condition, using environmentally responsible refinishing techniques. Renew offers four services programmes that maximise the value of your existing furniture assets. These services programmes can be used to purchase either remanufactured Renew or new Steelcase furniture.

Non-researched case from the Centre for Sustainable Design; www.cfsd.org.uk

---

Used Office Furniture Depot offers a combination of used office furniture and renting. It offers remanufactured Steelcase, Herman Miller, Haworth and Knoll workstations and office furniture.

www.used-office-furniture-depot.com

Project
Category B: Use-oriented PSS

Virtual Station: virtual office service system

Virtual Station supplies a full range of services and infrastructure for a complete office. Clients pay only for the periods in which they use the service. Like other 'virtual offices', Virtual Station spaces are designed to provide efficiency and comfort at a low cost. The offices come equipped with computers, printers, scanners, internet access, etc. Secretarial services such as receptionists, personalised voicemail, answering and remittance of calls and fax, transmission of emails with personal address, creation of business stationery, etc. are generally available. More specialised services are also accessible such as support for advertising campaigns, administrative assistance and bank services. Logistic solutions include lease of rooms for meetings, consultations or interviews with candidates, mini-auditorium lease and coffee-break service.

Researched case (Manzini and Vezzoli 2002), www.virtualstation.com.br

Box 9.1 Selection of PSS cases in offices (continued over)

The company **S.O.L.I.D.** in Austria rents out solar equipment and offers the opportunity to avoid the high investment costs of buying a complete solar installation. Three types of contract are possible: providing solar heating in addition to the regular heating installation; total warm water supply including the extra energy (billing according to m^3 of wastewater); total heating supply including the extra energy including heating (billing according to kWh and/or m^3).

www.solid.at

Project
Category C: Result-oriented PSS/system optimisation

WAM!NET provides a managed electronic data transfer service for media and print industries. This allows electronic transfer of documents and files rather than physical transfer by courier or mail, which is much more expensive. The company is now introducing new value-added services such as archiving digital assets (for example, master copies of product images to ensure that the latest version is always used in promotional material) and checking for errors during transmission. The service reduces energy usage and emissions from transport.

Researched case (James *et al.* 2001; Zaring *et al.* 2001)

The German energy contracting organisations **HEW** and **SEC**, like their counterparts in other countries, take responsibility for managing all of their clients' energy needs. This allows the customers to avoid capital outlays and gain from improved resource utilisation (achieved by installing more efficient plants and matching plants with demand more precisely). The environmental benefits are reduced energy requirements—and the emissions associated with its production and use—for delivery of a given quantity of electricity or heat.

Researched case (James *et al.* 2001; Zaring *et al.* 2001)

The research project **SYSKREIS** developed user-optimised system solutions to promote the recycling industry in areas such as the office. The goal of the project SYSKREIS was to develop new business segments and implementation potentials for the recycling industry by implementing a user-optimised system for a 'recyclable office'. The system is designed so that users obtain an individually tuned office system from one supplier, who is supported by a network of manufacturing, trading, recycling and service companies. Purchase, service and recycling/waste disposal are united into a single service.

Researched case (Econcept—BMBF Cases Maßelter and Tischner 2000)

BOX 9.1 (from previous page)

products and services. The analyses and suggestions for improvements related to single products or areas, by definition, stay concentrated on these areas. The guidelines and concepts that cover several areas give guidance for improvements in these areas but are not yet fully connected with each other. SYSKREIS, the project that took the biggest step towards sustainable product service combinations, which ended in late 2000, did not manage to have real market introduction and no real systemic innovation activities were realised. However, the changing needs due to new types of labour and office worlds ask for flexible and efficient solutions in which PSS can play an important role.

9.2 Analysis: PSS opportunities in need area office

This section describes windows of opportunity for PSS as a useful business model within the need area offices. The development and evaluation of opportunities is based on trends and developments in the office sector. This section is based on current practice researched by econcept and on the outcomes of the first industry workshop of Sus-ProNet, held with companies that are active in the office sector (29–30 January, Eindhoven, the Netherlands).

9.2.1 Trends relevant for PSS development for offices

To understand where the business opportunities in the 'office of the future' lie, state-of-the-art knowledge about the office of the future, trends and developments related to customer needs, office sector development and changes in the way we work have to be taken into account, as well as sustainability demands.

Recent developments: the 'office of the future'

Several concepts for restructuring the way we work are currently being discussed (e.g. www.office21.de; Lippert and Nowak 2001). Buzzwords in this context are: 'new work', 'non-territorial office', 'flexible office', 'flexi-working', 'desk sharing', 'home office', 'satellite office', 'virtual office', 'work on demand', 'plug and work'.

The term 'new work', for example, is characterised by German office furniture forums as 'a methodological approach to strengthen competitiveness'. Companies are better equipped to deal with future demands by employing methods such as adapting the work processes to the new market needs (e.g. globalisation and internationalisation), and involving qualified employees in current decisions, increasing their vitality and reaction speed and enabling them to deal with the tough future markets.

However, there are also experts discussing the 'new work issue' as hype created and misunderstood by the office furniture sector.[6] They point out that the concept goes far beyond the design of mobile office containers, saying:

---

6   E.g. www.thur.de/philo/ina/ina40.htm

> New Work is surely part of our future, but not to the extent the marketing departments of the office furniture industry want us to believe. In the future, we will become more focussed on globalisation and the changing values of our post-industrialised society. Mobiles, internet cafes and rolling designer desks are not the core idea of New Work. They are just symptoms that may be seen as fads tomorrow. New Work is not a question about design or technique; it is primarily one of economical and social structures. New Work is ultimately a change in the mind (Kammerer 2002).

Today several changes in office organisation and working methods form the world of the 'office of the future'. These can be categorised as:

- Where do you work—**place of the office**

- How do you organise the working space—**space of the office**

- How do you use the office space—**use of the office**

Place of the office

Where do you carry out the office work? One important principle in new work concepts is: the 'office' is where the office worker is! This requires optimal ICT equipment, internet connections and an optimal integration of 'home' or any other working place with the central office. Working places outside the central office can be:

- **Telework**. Working structurally at least one day a week outside the central office. Either as **tele-home-work**, use of workplace at home, or **tele-satellite-work**, use of satellite offices (office hotels, business clubs, local neighbourhood offices)

- **At the customer**. The need for support, both technical and non-technical, depends strongly on the sort of work carried out

- **On the road**. The great diversity of communication equipment increases the possibilities of working in cars, public transport or planes

Space of the office

How do you organise the available working space? Organisational clusters can be transformed in workplaces in different ways. Five basic existing and new concepts for office design/composition are presented below:

- **Cellular** or **room office**. This relatively old form of the office is dominated by single rooms big enough for one, accompanied by bigger rooms, which are suited for teamwork and other group activities

- **Group office** (4–20 persons) or **open-plan office** (20–100 persons). In this more recent and open office form there are almost no closed rooms available. Permanent traffic of people takes place and concentrated work can be more difficult to carry out. Nevertheless the atmosphere is often more creative

- The **combi-office** is a synthesis of the former two office space designs. It is characterised by a mix of open-plan office (most often in the centre of the building) and cellular offices (commonly positioned against the walls).

Advantages are that climate and lighting in the cellular offices can be individually controlled by the users. Transparent separation walls are used to reduce noise and at the same time to encourage communication

- The **business club** or **centre**. This very modern form of office space design commonly offers a business centre, a team centre and a lounge. The business club is a further development of the combi-office often used as short-term rental office space.

Use of the office

How do you use the available office environment? Two types of work in particular determine the office of the future:

- **From single work to more teamwork**. Flexible working structures, more project work, a faster change in employees and changing employees' demands require flexible office design

- **From a fixed desk to desk sharing/non-territorial work**. Through more flexible working structures and more work completed out of the central office, desk sharing becomes more popular. This means that there are a number of desks shared by a larger number of office workers who spend a specified time out of the central office. The choice of workplace is related to the projects and is therefore team- and activity-oriented. That also requires optimal ICT equipment for employees and at workplaces (mobile telephone, laptop, internet connection, etc.) and flexible storage systems for individual possessions and data of the employees. This office form also means that hierarchies are disappearing or at least becoming flatter.

General trends and developments relevant for the office sector

Trends in the field of offices and related areas

Analysis of several studies and research projects has identified the main trends that influence the office development of the future. These are summarised in Table 9.3.[9]

These trends show a change in the office world, which leads from stationary work towards mobile work, from individual work towards teamwork, from repetitive work towards creative work, from the material office towards a virtual office.

And indeed reality shows that companies are on their way to new work models. In a German survey (www.office21.de; Lippert and Nowak 2001; Berger 2002) 898 office users were interviewed about the way they used offices. Essential results were:

- 91.8% of the interviewees have a fixed workplace of their own, 4.1% work in non-territorial office concepts and 4.1% share a workplace with colleagues

- Overall, the singular office and the combi-office scored the best on satisfaction and performance of the workforce

---

9 See: www.rijksgebouwendienst.nl/kantin/kantin.htm, www.architectureweek.com/2002/0306/ news_3-4.html, www.acfnewsource.org/science/goodbye_dilbert.html, www.ajplus.co.uk/stirling/ portcullis, www.delmatic.com/portcullis.htm, www.workplaceforum.com; Behrendt *et al.* 1999.

General trends
<ul><li>Economic recession</li><li>Shift towards service economy</li><li>Knowledge workers get more important than blue-collar workers</li><li>Finding and keeping good skilled office workers is important for companies</li><li>Global access to information and communication</li><li>Borders between information, communication and entertainment technology will disappear</li><li>Wireless technologies with wider bandwidth and higher speed</li><li>Ubiquitous miniaturised IT equipment, including voice and handwriting recognition</li><li>Virtual services or robot service</li><li>Improving the work–life balance</li><li>Outsourcing of services, just-in-time and lean solutions</li></ul>
Demographic changes
<ul><li>Shrinking workforce in developed countries—growing workforce in developing countries</li><li>Migration and multicultural workforce</li><li>Ageing society, social insurance problematic, specific needs of the elderly have to be met</li><li>Increasingly more women than men in office work (although in lower positions)</li></ul>
New work models, regarding organisational aspects
<ul><li>Increasing share of office work, more part-time jobs</li><li>More work at home (home office)</li><li>More internet, teleworking</li><li>Increasing working hours and flexibility of working time</li><li>Increasing mobility of working population</li><li>Combination of work and private life</li><li>More self-determination, more responsibility of employees, temporary collaboration with different experts (per day, week, several months)</li><li>Less control, flat hierarchies, problem of motivating 'virtual' employees</li></ul>
New work spaces and equipment
<ul><li>Tele-home-work: the workplace at home</li><li>Tele-satellite-work: the use of satellite offices and facilities</li><li>Work at the customer (temporary office)</li><li>'On the road': in cars, public transport or planes</li><li>Office hotels, business clubs where one can rent office space just for the time needed</li><li>Service provider instead of space provider</li><li>Non-territorial offices, where a large number of employees share a smaller number of desks</li></ul>

TABLE 9.3 General trends and developments relevant for the office sector

- Team-oriented office forms, multi-person office, group and combi-office had the longest lifetimes

- Almost 64% of interviewees are involved with 'new work' concepts, such as non-territorial office concepts, telework and forms of mobile work. Ten per cent of the offices have already implemented a new work concept, 29% have experimented with or have started pilot projects based on such concepts, and another 24.6% are interested or are considering it

- 30% of all the interviewees showed an above-average absence from the office

- The biggest changes in ICT were expected to be in document management systems and in the decreasing use of paper in favour of electronic information storage

- Important factors when deciding where to build an office include the quality of the available services, whether inside the office or in the surrounding area (e.g. cafeteria, copy shop, office material supply), and the travel time to the workplace

Trends identified by SusProNet's need area office partners

Also in the SusProNet workshop trends relevant to the office sector were collected, discussed and ranked by the participants. In order to create a useful platform from which areas of opportunity could be developed for PSS in the office need area, the time-span of the analysis was set to be roughly 5–10 years from 2003. Thus five 'megatrends' were identified in order to define the most important aspects that office PSS should tackle (see Table 9.4).

Overall rating	Trends
1st place	Rate of change is increasing
2nd place	Global access to ICT
2nd place	Portable wireless technology
2nd place	Knowledge management
2nd place	Ageing society

TABLE 9.4 'Megatrends'

Sustainability demands in the office field

Overview of the environmental impacts of offices

Kathalys researched the Dutch office situation (1999) and completed environmental assessments for several future office concepts and for future workplaces (Kathalys 2001). A general conclusion is that the decentralised office concept offers clear advantages, especially where space is scarce, i.e. in densely populated areas.

For the work domain, environmental impact is primarily expressed in energy consumption (in MJp/year: the environmental impact primary energy per annum) and space use (in m^2 of occupied land for one year). The **total energy consumption** of the office is equivalent to 115 pico Jp/year. Electricity use is the biggest single energy consumption, followed by commuting, heating and use of paper. One important development is the continual rise in electricity consumption, particularly for office equipment and climate control. This result is quite different for **land use.** Here the use of paper determines 94% of the land use. Since the advent of the PC, paper consumption in offices has risen at least by a factor of two. Each employee produces 175 kg of waste paper per annum. As the average **energy content of paper** is 37 MJ/kg, each employee throws away almost 6,500 MJ of energy in the form of paper waste. As the energy content of one sheet of A4 is much greater than the energy used in making a copy, it is much more energy efficient to make double-sided copies than to use special energy-efficient printers and photocopiers.

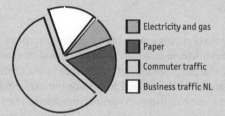

- Electricity and gas
- Paper
- Commuter traffic
- Business traffic NL

Different forms of office have different environmental impacts.
The following four office working methods were compared by Kathalys:

- **Reference office model:** 100–500 people working in one building and commuting every day

- The **mega-office** where several or even tens of thousands of people work in an office complex and commute a maximum of 30 km in each direction every day

- The **decentralised office**: a shared office set up for teleworking for about 30 people at walking distance from their homes

- The **home office.** The employees can telework from home via an online connection with the central network of the company. The working space takes up about 20 m^2 and is not considered part of the regular living space

Box 9.2 Environmental assessment of the office: energy use, land use and paper
(continued opposite)

This comparison produced the following statistics:

Estimate of space used per person in m²

	Reference	Mega-office	Decentralised	Working at home
Gross work space	35	26	23	20
Work surroundings	23	13	0	0
Other work	11	8	5	4
The home	46	46	46	46
Home surroundings	97	97	130	130
Total	212	190	204	200

Annual energy consumption per person over the net office area in kWh or m³ per annum

	Reference	Mega-office	Decentralised	Working at home
Lighting	1,468	1,299	917	1,468
Climate electricity	991	932	548	1,109
Climate gas	915	644	260	1,066
Equipment at home and at the office	622	523	408	684
Total electricity	3,081	2,753	1,874	3,261
Total gas	915	644	260	1,066

Box 9.2 (from previous page)

From this study it can be concluded that the central mega-office is the most efficient in space use; however, by far the most energy-efficient is the decentralised office.

Definitions of a sustainable office

The idea of **sustainable workplaces** was defined on the macro level by the World Commission on Environment and Development in 1988, followed by the Rio conference four years later. In working life this idea implies that not only should industrial injuries and illness be avoided, but also people should be able to use their full potential and creativity in their work. It implies avoiding the negative effects of production and consumption on the environment. Also, other authors state that a sustainable workplace takes into account the ecological and social results of the business as well as the economic results. A sustainable workplace is a place that meets the needs and visions of its occupiers while respecting both the internal and external environment (TCO Development 2000). However, these definitions are too abstract when it comes to a real practical approach. Thus the SusProNet office group and econcept developed its own definition for a sustainable office as one that is:

- Cost-effective, giving optimal conditions for productive work (profit)

- Healthy and allows the user to fulfil his or her needs (physical and psychological), offering a satisfying combination of business and private life

- Eco-efficient in terms of inputs (space, materials, energy) and outputs (waste, emissions) over the whole life-cycle, and reduces the need for transportation (people/goods)

Practical approaches to sustainability in offices

In practice there are initiatives covering single aspects of a sustainable office: architecture/building technology, volume of traffic, electrical and information technology infrastructure, office equipment, light, indoor climate, office interior (furniture, floor coverings), green procurement of office equipment and consumables.

However, more holistic approaches to sustainability of offices are very rare, owing to the complexity of the three dimensions of sustainability: people, planet, profit.

To make the quest for sustainability more operational in practice, the SusProNet office group, supported by econcept's research, formulated the most important sustainability criteria for offices, organised according to the three dimensions of sustainability (Box 9.3).

9.2.2 Conclusions

Important trends in the office sector

During the SusProNet analysis phase many trends were found that have great influence on the office environment. The PSS ideas developed (see Section 9.3) are based on these trends:

- Production leaves industrialised countries to 'low-labour-cost countries', therefore industrialised countries shift towards service economies

Economic criteria

Cost per workplace (as low as possible): e.g. reducing the cost for the office building and infrastructure, increasing the use time, longevity, flexibility and efficiency of office equipment and building, valuing stability and increasing the value of the building and infrastructure, return on investment, amortisation, etc.

Work productivity (as high as possible). This also incorporates work stability, low illness rates, good qualification of employees, productive infrastructure, such as ICT, information and knowledge-management systems

Long-term planning, risk minimisation, risk management: e.g. by multi-functionality of space and infrastructure enabling diverse flexible uses, avoidance of mis-investment and -calculation, proactive consideration of legislative and political conditions, longer-term horizons for planning.

Environmental criteria

Material-efficiency: including building, equipment and consumables, over the whole life-cycle

Energy-efficiency: including heating, light, ICT (excluding transport and mobility)

Space-efficiency: including building, interior, workplace

Hazardous substances and emissions: including indoor climate, noise pollution, electro-smog (excluding transport, mobility)

Re-use, recycling possibilities, waste and disposal: including consumables, building, equipment

Transport and mobility

Social-ethical criteria

Healthy work environment, physical: equipment and infrastructure making work easy and comfortable, ergonomics, safety in the workplace, etc.

Healthy work environment, psychological: workload appropriate to qualification, adequate reward, avoidance of unhealthy stress and mobbing, motivation and satisfaction, self-determination

Fair wages, quality of jobs: accessibility and permeability for different qualifications

Socially responsible corporate culture: equity, barrier-free and respectful of different ages/different cultures, encouraging a participative, innovative and creative environment

Social infrastructure and services: e.g. education and training opportunities, respect for family background of employees (childcare opportunities), respect for employees' combination of job and private life, service offers at workplace (food, shopping, laundry . . .), excellent mobility and transportation opportunities

Box 9.3 Sustainability criteria for offices

- Knowledge workers become more important than blue-collar workers

- Demographic changes: ageing society, more women working in the office than men

- New work models

- Finding and keeping good skilled office workers is more and more difficult and crucial for companies

- ICT influencing all areas of the office

Sustainability in the office sector

Currently the topic of sustainability in offices is discussed in relation to health and productivity issues: sick building syndrome, motivation of employees, cost of illness absence, etc. The quest for eco-efficiency in the inputs (resources) and outputs (waste, emissions) of the office, as well as space use and infrastructure are other common topics. Reduction of transportation and commuter traffic by introducing more flexible forms of work organisation and optimisation of office organisation and environment to increase productivity by increasing motivation and satisfaction of workers are also common today. The discipline of facility management already covers the improved management of buildings, technical infrastructure, office equipment and furniture to decrease (long-term) cost and increase flexibility of work. However, all this does not cover all the dimensions of a sustainable office environment. Thus the SusProNet office group formulated its own definition of a sustainable office and the most important sustainability criteria in the three dimensions, people, planet, profit (see the sections above).

Based on the analysis of the most important trends and developments in the office field and the formulated sustainability criteria, new PSS business ideas were developed in the first SusProNet workshop, which promise to have significant market opportunities.

The most important drivers and obstacles for these ideas were also collected. For a better overview the opportunities were clustered to form windows of opportunity (Table 9.5):

- PSS for office interior

- Software/mobile hardware/connectivity solutions

- Specialised services, outsource solutions, offering to do 'tedious' work for others and increasing efficiency

- PSS based on needs of employees: solutions that focus on specific user needs and specific target groups, such as the elderly; solutions with a health focus

In order to create a sustainable solution for offices we need to look beyond one specific element in the office sector. Integral innovations covering more than one product or field are needed.

PSS idea	Possible drivers	Possible obstacles
PSS for office interior		
Flexible, health-focused and interactive managed interiors	● Health and well-being of employees ● Constant change of interiors ● One interior supplier	● Traditional marketplace ● Many small players ● Cyclical nature of office ● Demand = risky venture to head up
CIRM (corporate infrastructure resource manager)	● The need for flexibility at reasonable costs ● Over its life-cycle, a building will cost four times more to use than it did to build	● Companies owning buildings ● Management structure today
Office building lease that incorporates required communication technologies, flexible premises, flexible lease time, catering, etc. For meeting and leisure. Building owner merges several service providers for optimised level of services	● Profit ● Gathering services that business people need at one place	● High price of learning
Software/mobile hardware/connectivity solutions		
Software application service	● Cost-effective (SMEs) ● Accessibility ● Effective implementation and maintenance ● Flexibility	● Speed of today's telecommunications infrastructure ● Real-time environments need to be emulated if employees are to access applications from any location, and as a result to input or absorb knowledge
ASP solutions (software = commodity)	● Concentration of knowledge and expertise (ASP) → best product and best service ● Company: concentrate on company's business	● Technology is not ready ● Confidential data versus security
Specialised services		
Intelligent agents to facilitate data and knowledge management. They can also extend their services to the field of office assistants. There are advantages in delivering them over the web as a PSS	● Rapidly increasing volume of data and knowledge ● Demand for increased productivity ● Rate of change + numerous carrier changes moves	● Technology is not mature yet ● People, particularly older generations, do not trust the technology ● 'Big brother' effects

TABLE 9.5 **Windows of opportunity: first PSS ideas for offices** (continued over)

PSS idea	Possible drivers	Possible obstacles
Knowledge/experience/skills broker	• Flexible solution provision, lasting from days to life-spans • Life-long learning • Ideas interchange	• Current workplace culture • Individual security • Loss of company's core capabilities, such as control
To offer specific functions (over a limited time), computer performance, 'back office' (call centre . . .)	• Flexibility • No initial investment	• 'Performance contracting' means that an 'additional investor' is needed • If you are not the owner, you will not handle carefully
'Situation-based' services. The system automatically knows where users are and what they need, e.g. office/home office/round-world-office	• Technology is available • Customer need: mobility, flexibility . . . → need for a sustainable environment	• Personal data (security, safety, reliability) • Dependence on a technical system 24h a day • Price
Ultra-light portable computer with permanent (continuous) wireless connection	• Need for info everywhere, every time	• Infrastructure (different standards)
Needs of employees		
Anticipate and meet the office worker's needs before problems arise	• Productivity and efficiency improvements	• Understanding the office worker's situation and needs
Design for elderly, learning while working, adaptation to change	• Ageing + health + learning • Rate of change • Sustainability	• Image (?) • Ego (?)
Enriched simplicity: make systems simpler by extracting essences from complex systems or ideas without losing the richness of the complexity	• Individuality • Self-organising	• Information illiteracy • Gap between connected and not connected increases • Gap between rich and poor increases

TABLE 9.5   (from previous page)

9.3 Idea generation and selection

This section covers the idea generation and selection phase within the PSS development process. It is based on current practice researched by econcept and the outcomes of the second SusProNet workshop, held with companies that are active in the office sector (Lisbon, Portugal, 25 September 2003).

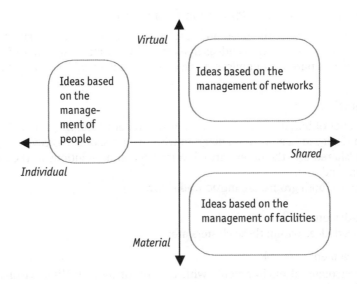

FIGURE 9.1 Cluster of ideas based on the 'profit-driven scenario'

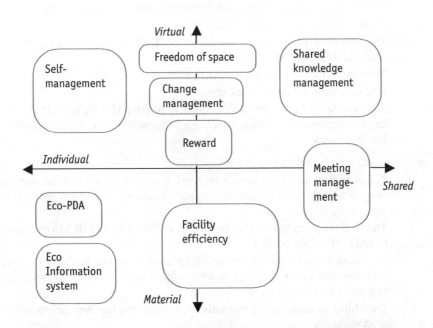

FIGURE 9.2 Cluster of ideas based on the 'environmentally/socially driven scenario'

9.3.1 Need area-specific PSS ideas (long list)

Based on the outcome of the need area analysis (Section 9.2), the SusProNet office group developed product-service ideas in a creativity session using two different scenarios: one with a purely economic and one with a mainly social/environmental focus.

Idea generation

A large number of initial PSS ideas were collected in both scenario groups. They were clustered and placed in a portfolio diagram with two axes, one axis covering 'individual' versus 'shared use' the other 'virtual' versus 'material' solutions as the two poles (see Figs. 9.1 and 9.2).

The results of both groups are introduced below.

The profit-driven scenario

The developed ideas within these clusters are:

- Management of people:
    - Personalised environments with the use of individualised virtual keyboards and virtual decorations
    - Linking telephones and products to a room (e.g. with Bluetooth connections)

- Management of facilities ('ProPark'):
    - Business park management with organised convenience services
    - Business parks that provide childcare
    - Transponders in all office products, as well as the development of transponder software
    - The development of telephones with chip-card access
    - One-stop shop for all service outsourcing
    - The possibility for all small firms to benefit from the facilities that only large companies currently enjoy, e.g. fitness centres, sport facilities, kindergartens

- Management of networks
    - The introduction of the instant network manager, which enables people to work anywhere including services such as information manager or personal work coach
    - The facilitation of knowledge networks, enabling knowledge to be transferred to the right person
    - The move from hierarchies to activities: looking at the business process from the view of activities, e.g. asking 'what do you want to sell?', and cutting away unsuitable steps
    - The ability to earn money not only by transferring but connecting information
    - The possibility of closing all offices and establishing new work environments such as meeting clubhouses; space managed by a planning officer could be rented

The people- and planet-driven scenario
The developed ideas within these clusters are:

- Self-management:
  - Training programmes that encourage teamwork, a new office culture and shared knowledge
  - Adventure games to facilitate life-long personal and professional development and self-assessment
  - Rental agreements for electronics, secretaries, phones, etc.; this could be managed by a personal agent
  - Training, life-long learning, matching employees with other experts
  - Coaching services for managing the 'freedom' of employees
  - Personal assistants, who help to organise employees' careers and social insurance

- Freedom of space (can be combined with meeting management):
  - Assistance with working in decentralised office facilities; e.g. truck, briefcase, cafe
  - The ability to take important decisions outside the office, to a more welcoming place
  - Change management
  - Change management adviser who also gives advice to schools
  - Cluster reward
  - More reward systems: for example, based on the quality of work and not on time

- Shared knowledge management:
  - Electronically shared information and material: for example, in libraries. There should be no 'private' information collection
  - Accessible and up-to-date knowledge management services

- Meeting management:
  - Shared virtual meetings, e.g. videoconferences
  - Efficient meeting scheduling using the intranet
  - The opportunity to avoid trips, although informal trips are necessary, as they motivate workers and create connections with locals
  - Eco-PDA (personal digital assistant)
  - Advanced PDA tools combined with life-cycle tools, giving information on ecological issues and informing about possible alternative decisions

- Eco-information system:
  - Personal energy/resource consumption meters, which can be combined with the Eco-PDA
  - Energy meters for switching lights, computer and heating on and off
  - Automatic energy control units utilising intelligent furniture and other products; with service support

- Facility efficiency:
    - A set of 'tools' for workers to take with them, reducing office space and making it non-territorial and improving the design
    - The eradication of material infrastructure; facilities management and other services are outsourced
    - Shared office infrastructure: the individual rents/owns individual tools and common objects, but the infrastructure is owned/rented by a company
    - Failure-free products, such as printers
    - Printing on demand, projections on office walls, paper-saving computer-based group discussions
    - The projection of a company's logo and corporate image in building interiors
    - The generation of an inspiring atmosphere using projections, creating a virtual environment that addresses all the senses, including the sense of smell

Idea selection

From the ideas generated, the most promising were selected using a combination of two methods. First, group participants ranked the ideas according to their personal/company perspective. Then a simple ranking tool was used to score ideas on the three sustainability axes of profit, planet and people (ranging from -1 = worse than the current situation, to $+1$ = better than the current situation). The PSS screening tool developed within SusProNet is part of the Guideline that can be found in Annex 1 of this book. It was very surprising that, although the two scenario groups had completely different goals (profit versus planet/people), many parallel ideas were developed. Thus at the end the groups decided to combine different ideas from the two scenarios. Finally, three ideas were selected for further specification because they got the highest points in ranking and sustainability evaluation:

- **Eco-PDA**, from the environmentally/socially driven scenario

- **Pro-Park**, from the facility management idea cluster in the profit-driven scenario

- **Self-assessment centre**, based on overlapping ideas from both scenarios

9.3.2 Need area-specific PSS ideas (short list)

Below the three selected PSS ideas for the office of the future as developed in the SusProNet workshops are described in more detail.

Eco-PDA

The Eco-Personal Digital Assistant (Figs. 9.3 and 9.4) provides an instant read-out of the environmental benefit/harm caused by various choices the user can make. It also

FIGURE 9.3 Advertisement for the Eco-PDA

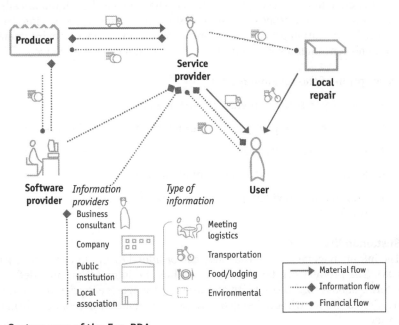

FIGURE 9.4 System map of the Eco-PDA

Actor	Role
Producer	Produces PDA
Software provider	Provides and updates software
Service provider	Sells Eco-PDA and information
Local shop	Takes care of PDA repair if necessary
User	Uses PDA and information
Information provider	Provides info either to service provider or directly to PDA

TABLE 9.6 Description of the value network/actors and roles

offers alternatives for areas such as transport, food and organising meetings. The hand-held PDA has an instant Internet connection and collects the input data to be analysed for environmental and economical impact. The Eco-PDA then automatically ranks the chosen options and proposes a more sustainable option based on information from external information providers such as transportation services, environmental institutions and consumer testing institutes. Information on cost is also given.

Description of the revenue model

- User pays a service provider for PDA and info
- Service provider pays producer for PDA hardware and local repair
- Producer pays software provider
- Software provider pays information providers
- Information providers pay service provider for services such as advertising (optional)

Sustainability effects

The info-management for eco-choices can be added to an (almost) existing product (a PDA). The product can be altered, as well as the information provided. The system informs about eco-choices, motivates users and suggests eco-friendly solutions. It gives freedom of choice without being overly moral, and makes accessing information much easier.

Pro-management

'Multi-space and services for multi-companies': pro-management offers the possibility to re-use space, reorganise organisations and deliver services (Figs. 9.5 and 9.6). PSS such as furniture and convenience services should deliver the means to do so. Central in the system is the space. This 'park centre' accommodates the hardware such as furniture, PDAs, telephones and communication devices. This hardware is equipped with transponders, enabling an intelligent building system. The park centre also accommo-

FIGURE 9.5 Advertisement for pro-management

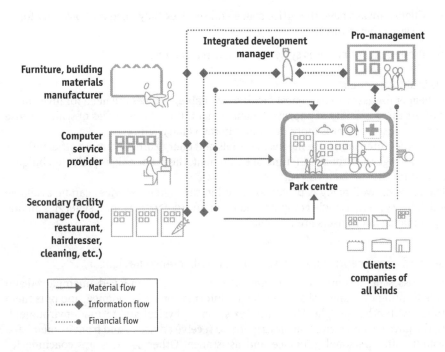

FIGURE 9.6 System map of pro-management

Actor	Role
Furniture manufacturers	Provide furniture, etc.
Computer service provider	Provide software and hardware
Food etc. provider	Catering, cleaning, services, childcare, hairdresser, shops
Pro-management	Overall organiser, customer-oriented
Integrated development manager	Co-ordinator of manufacturing developments
Clients	Require offices and services
Park centre	Deliver service

TABLE 9.7 Description of the value network/actors and roles

dates the services such as rental of furniture, 'one-stop shop', provision of security of software and organisation of convenience services.

Description of revenue model

- Clients always have the office space and services they need and pay only for services they really use

- Pro-manager optimises system and distributes money

Sustainability effects

It is cheaper for users, makes latest facilities available, reduces the need for investment and offers the possibility of improved management. It uses economies of scale because the pro-manager/renter is more dominant in the value chain.

The higher intensity of use means materials and energy are used more efficiently. As there is a danger of a shorter lifetime of equipment, the proper high-quality techniques and products should be involved.

The focus on well-being is professionalised in the system; services can be available (food delivery) that a single company could not afford. Furthermore, synergies among the pro-management users are possible.

Self-assessment centre: personal development science navigator

The self-assessment centre (Figs. 9.7 and 9.8) provides self-employed, unemployed and people wanting to change jobs with relevant information and guidance, and puts them in touch with other people. The centre exists in a physical and virtual environment. Both the physical and virtual facilities give and receive advice to and from its members. Assistants offer personal guidance and assistance. Other services are coaching for inspiration, job centres and technical support. The virtual environment can, for example, be a self-assessment adventure game.

FIGURE 9.7 Advertisement for the self-assessment centre

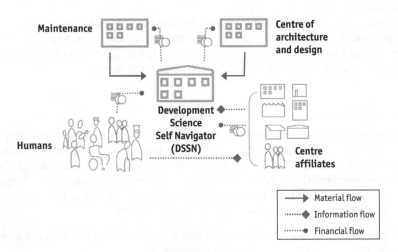

FIGURE 9.8 System map of the self-assessment centre

Actor	Role
Self-navigator centre	Provide structure (formula) and process schemes (living organism)
Centre architecture and design service	Set-up, initialise and update formula Define roles and mandates
Centre affiliates	Present economic realities of supply and demand Provide/represent (sub-)areas of expertise
Human individuals	Give and receive advice on topics such as coaching, job and technical support, both individually and as corporate members
Maintenance	Support infrastructure and maintenance

TABLE 9.8 Description of the value network/actors and roles

Description of revenue model

- Fixed subscription fees

- Additional variable fees: for example, for services used

- A system of bonuses

Sustainability effects

Social sustainability in particular increases; life-long learning and development of people is promoted. Employees, freelancers and the unemployed can enter the network, receive advice and give advice to others. Knowledge in the system is increased and exchanged. Also, material objects can be exchanged and shared.

9.3.3 Conclusions

The ideas developed and elaborated during the workshops cover a broad area of the office. They are both B2B and B2C and include product-oriented, use-oriented and result-oriented PSS. Despite being based on fundamentally different profit and socially/environmentally motivated scenarios, the developed ideas have a large overlap. This overlapping of high business and sustainability potential is linked with the recent developments in the office sector. PSS for offices can:

- Lead to high efficiency (both economically and environmentally): e.g. outsourcing, economics of scale, virtualisation

- Decrease the amount of office building needed

- Support flexibility of work (worker satisfaction)

- Offer a better balance between work and private life

- Improve the working environment (productivity of workers)

- Reduce the need for commuting

- Create more quality time for employees: e.g. shopping service

- Improve educational and training activities (development of employees)

The developed PSS ideas for the office sector show that a natural connection between the three dimensions of sustainability is feasible. In short: when the employees are satisfied they are more productive, when the infrastructure is more environmentally sound it is more cost-efficient, and virtualisation and decentralisation of offices can work positively in all three dimensions.

9.4 Implementation

This section discusses the challenges for implementing PSS ideas in the office field. The implementation issues for the developed PSS ideas, which were discussed in Section 9.3, are presented and dominant issues for the need area office are identified. Then, based on best practice and research, generic solution approaches are presented. Finally (policy) measures that can help in overcoming these implementation challenges are discussed.

9.4.1 Need area-specific implementation challenges and policy support

The implementation challenges in this section are the result of the elaboration of the PSS ideas developed throughout the SusProNet workshops. For every idea implementation issues were listed and the most important selected. PSS-specific and need area-specific issues were identified. Table 9.9 summarises the implementation issues for the PSS concepts for offices as developed in the SusProNet workshops. The issues are divided into PSS-specific and non-PSS-specific issues.

Concerning the **company internal** characteristics, issues related to the change in mentality necessary for developing, producing and selling PSS instead of products or services, dominate. Possible solutions point towards a 'PSS training' of employees.

- **Value chain**-related issues are mainly about the focus on the needs of customers and the need to convince them of the value of a PSS. Furthermore a sound power distribution along the value chain is important

- For **partnership and co-operation** similar issues occur: convincing the partners of the PSS idea, and distribution of power and responsibilities among the partners

- Issues related to the **technical feasibility** of the PSS idea are linked to the complexity and the scope of the project

The PSS specific implementation issues presented above do not include need area-specific issues. However, the lack of technical implementation issues could be office need area-specific, because of the highly advanced and rapid developments in the ICT sector.

Main headings	Implementation issues
A. Company-internal characteristics	**Issues for Pro-management (and real Veldhoen + company hospital case)** ● A Pro-management development team has to be formed ● The PSS idea needs a lot of new partners with new visions → Solution: training for all partners ● Need for management qualities to manage such a huge and complex system **Issues for self-assessment centre** ● Who is the process-starting and promoting/leading company? Game producer, government, training provider, chamber of commerce? E.g. rehabilitation, health insurance **Issues for Eco-PDA (and HP real case experience)** ● Thinking on services is not integrated in innovation of producer/did not see it in connection with environmental issues → Solution: need for paradigm shift ● The service does not fit withstrategic plan → Solution: could be developed and sold to other companies ● Needs training of sales force that is used to sell products *Non-PSS-specific issues* ● *Need a lot of organisational changes* ● *Private or public concept* ● *Need for big projects (HP-related)*
B. Value chain issues	**Issues for Pro-management (and real Veldhoen + company hospital case)** ● It must be a concept for all workers/companies → Solution: needs of customers should be in the focus; e.g. 'patient'-oriented ● Who defines the quality levels in the system? ● Customers must be convinced about the intangible value of the new concept ● The cultural acceptance of sharing space, goods, service, etc. **Issues for self-assessment centre** ● Who pays and who gets revenues? → Solution: give and take system ('can this be commercial?') ● Power distribution in system ● Needs a lot of new partners ● Has to take cultural differences into account **Issues for Eco-PDA (and HP real case experience)** ● Convince customer that the value is better than delivered by a product ● How to avoid copycats/property rights? How to maintain the value? ● How is value created if the idea of PSS is copying, i.e. all people are getting involved → Solutions: divide the market and find own specific niche/customer group *Non-PSS-specific issues* ● *Privacy issues; who is the owner of all information?* ● *Convince about environmental information as benefit*

TABLE 9.9 Implementation issues for each PSS idea; PSS- and non-PSS-specific issues
(continued opposite)

Main headings	Implementation issues
C. Partnership and co-operation issues	**Issues for Pro-management (and real Veldhoen + company hospital case)** ● A lot of new partners with 'old' working style have to be convinced all the time that the new concept is good → Solution: training for all partners ● Responsibility in the system? Who is responsible if something goes wrong? **Issues for self-assessment centre** ● Way of delivering the concept is very unclear: which partners, how revenues are distributed, how quality is controlled **Issues for Eco-PDA (and HP real case experience)** ● Sales channels must be convinced about the new PSS ● Who is handling technical support? Can be very expensive ● Power distribution between product and service provider? Distribution of revenues, etc. ● Difficult if big service provider is already in the market; e.g. large telephone companies ***Non-PSS-specific issues*** ● *Process how to realise that kind of huge system: start from scratch, build on existing things, etc.*
D. Technical feasibility issues	**Issues for Pro-management (and real Veldhoen + company hospital case)** ● Non-PSS information management → Solution: information available everywhere ● (Old) products are not fitting into the new system ● Logistically very advanced concept **Issues for self-assessment centre** ● Scope of project is huge! ● What kind of info is produced? **Issues for Eco-PDA (and HP real case experience)** . . . no PSS-related issues found ***Non-PSS-specific issues*** ● *Non-PSS technology is no problem* ● *How to gather all the information; e.g. LCA of products*
E. Institutional issues	**Issues for Pro-management (and real Veldhoen + company hospital case)** ● New system must adapt to all the different work cultures; must be standardised but at the same time very flexible → Solution: work with government to change regulations **Issues for self-assessment centre** ● Concept is more like a foundation; but who pays? ● Concept as a training centre would require a curriculum ● Needs support by public/government **Issues for Eco-PDA (and HP real case experience)** ● Innovation needs large number of products. PSS concepts often need only small number of products, so who is interested in doing the product innovation? → Solution: give more room for innovation ***Non-PSS-specific issues*** ● *Regulation about work, safety, health, etc. might be hindering* ● *Long discussions necessary; involves a lot of 'societal' groups*

TABLE 9.9 (from previous page)

A: Company-internal characteristics

PSS is not part of normal business strategy

Solutions

- PSS concept could be developed and sold to other companies; start up new company with PSS, develop strategic business development tool and routine to include PSS thinking

B: Value chain issues

Customer acceptance

- Create clear benefits for customers/offer satisfaction
- Specify PSS for specific target groups
- Save them money and time
- Increase their flexibility, offer individualised solutions
- Offer service around the clock
- Enable customers to learn and increase their capacity
- Support their own business
- Offer participation in decisions
- Change financial/payment system, e.g. service-for-service options, decrease initial access cost, e.g. shared ownership (buy-in) concepts
- Communicate clear benefits for customers
- Guarantee quality
- Create a highly attractive brand/image

Revenue distribution: 'who gets the money?'

Solutions

- Economies of scale → cost + organisational benefits
- Excellent organisation and contracts
- Fair distribution of rights and duties
- One partner must be leader and process promoter/moderator (can also be an external, 'neutral' consultant)

C: Partnership and co-operation issues

Find the right partners

Solutions

- PSS quality check of partners, select the right partners carefully, identify roles exactly and openly, take care to achieve excellent communication
- Work with local providers; 'give-and-take', lower prices through economy of scale effects

Box 9.4 **Shortlist of PSS-specific implementation issues** (continued opposite)

- Training for all partners
- Right incentives especially for sales personnel/partners

D: Technical feasibility issues

- Technology was not seen as a big implementation issue

One solution: use intelligent technological infrastructure/system to enable the services

E: Institutional issues

PSS is not seen as innovation; therefore it is hard to find support

Solutions

- Lobby for PSS concepts with governments and other organisations
- Include PSS thinking in national and European policy, research programmes, subsidies, legislation, standardisation, purchasing programmes, label schemes
- Arguments for PSS: they improve environment/neighbourhood, leading to urban renewal; they also fulfil social needs of society
- Design sustainable PSS so that they genuinely contribute value to the social and natural environment and communicate same

Box 9.4 (from previous page)

Dominant PSS-specific implementation issues and generic solutions

From all the implementation issues mentioned above, those selected as the most important ones by the workshop participants are listed in Box 9.4.

Remarkably, no PSS-specific implementation issues under the main heading 'technical feasibility issues' were selected by the workshop participants. Out of the long list of implementation issues, no need area-specific issues were found. This has a direct link with the diversified character of the need area office: it contains both B2B as well as B2C PSS and covers PSS of all kinds (product-oriented, use-oriented and result-oriented) and in almost all fields of need, from information, communication, education and entertainment to food and health, from activities normally done in households (cleaning clothes, shopping) to providing basic utilities, such as power, water, heat and all the office equipment and consumables.

Research issues

Further research should be carried out on the implementation issue of consumer/customer acceptance. It would be very helpful to answer the question: which PSS are successful for which target groups (B2B/B2C and different consumer groups) in which cultures, as there are also many regional differences in office use and company cultures.

Furthermore, the integration of PSS thinking into strategic business development as well as policy decisions and programmes is a field for further investigation and research.

Policy support

The lack of PSS support by government and policy was clearly identified as one of the important implementation problems. Therefore the policy of national government and the EC should be changed so that developing new product-service systems is seen as an equally important innovation activity as development of new technologies, thus deserving the same funding opportunities and support. That would mean expanding the term 'innovation' from technological innovation to organisational and social innovation. Regarding legislation it cannot clearly be stated whether legislation is supporting or hindering PSS development. Some laws support PSS (e.g. increasing producer responsibility), some are counterproductive (e.g. some guarantees and liability standards, legislation ruling the transportation of waste [old products]). Therefore governmental organisations should bring PSS into focus when analysing what kinds of consequence their regulations and legislation have. One direct PSS support created by governments can be achieved by integration of PSS concepts in public purchasing activities and guidelines, i.e. by preferring sustainable PSS to buying products. In the office area especially municipalities and public administrations could set excellent examples by choosing sustainable PSS in their own offices. Support from government for new sustainable PSS ideas can also take place in the form of communication campaigns—for example, a general campaign for sustainable PSS for end consumers, thus trying to educate and convince consumers that owning products is not always necessary.

Finally, inclusion of PSS in education (e.g. design, engineering and business schools) and professional training is another way in which PSS support can be driven by government.

9.4.2 Conclusions

No real need area-specific PSS implementation issues could be found in the office field. This is due to the diversified character of the need area office and the PSS therein.

The **change in mentality** necessary for selling or buying a PSS instead of selling or buying products affects both the company internal characteristics and the complete value chain including the customer. For this reason it is recommended to have a strong and clear communication for a PSS offer internally and externally. A company has to focus on the needs of customers and has to convince them of the value of a PSS. 'PSS training' for both partners and employees is also highly recommended. In addition, the retail structure can act as a bottleneck, which means that if the sales personnel do not have enough incentives to promote PSS (instead of products) the PSS will not be successful.

For a **solid partnership** trust and a good distribution of risks, power and responsibilities as well as revenues between the partners is important. For companies it can be difficult to convince possible partners of the PSS idea and therefore they have difficulties finding new partners and co-operative arrangements.

The **current political support** and subsidy structure and research focus do not support the concept of PSS. New PSS ideas, which are often organisational and social innovations, are not seen as innovations and therefore not funded.

Issues related to the **technical feasibility** of the PSS concept are not seen as a major burden. Technological implementation issues are linked to the complex nature and the scope of such PSS projects and the use of the latest ICT, because PSS projects are very often based on exchange and management of complex information and involve complex organisational structures due to a larger number of partners.

Financially it was discussed that PSS often need investment at the beginning and the return on investment is gained over a longer period of time, compared with product sales. However, that was not seen as such a big difference from other innovation projects, which generally need investment. On the other hand, PSS can be simpler and quicker to implement, as they are often not based on technological innovation, which takes a lot of time, but on changing the organisational structure in a system.

The two most important **policy measures** to support PSS are to include sustainable PSS in public purchasing guidelines, giving them a higher priority than product sales, and to include PSS (i.e. social and organisational innovation) in research programmes, subsidy and support structures on an equal footing to technological innovation.

9.5 Conclusion

This section summarises the practical opportunities for PSS in the need area office. Both the business and the sustainability potential are discussed, and the main pitfalls in PSS development and policy options for supporting PSS business and sustainability potential in the need area office are described. Although PSS for the office are nothing new and also not necessarily sustainable, they offer high potentials on the level of market success *and* sustainability. Unfortunately, at the moment there is no systematic method established and widely used in practice to achieve such success.

9.5.1 PSS in the need area: opportunities and threats

Drivers and opportunities

The reason for attributing high business and sustainability potential to PSS for offices is that they are in line with all of the recent and anticipated developments in the office sector and new work organisation. PSS for offices can:

- Lead to high efficiency economically and environmentally, by improved facility management outsourcing, using economy-of-scale effects, virtualisation, etc.

- Decrease the number of office buildings needed by enabling decentralised work

- Support more flexibility of work, more freedom of the workers and thus increase their satisfaction

- Offer better combination of work and private life

- Improve the working environment and therefore the productivity of the workers and their well-being at the same time reducing illness hours

- Reduce the need for commuting, save time and reduce environmental impact

- Make use of all the new IC and other intelligent technologies for moving towards greater sustainability

- Offer better healthcare, leisure activities and wellness services for the workers and create more quality time by eliminating many inconvenient activities

- Improve educational and training activities, taking care of life-long learning and personal development of the employees

Thus the biggest driver for sustainable PSS in the field of offices is that all the three dimensions of sustainability (environment, economic and social) are very naturally connected in the office: when the workers are happy, they are more productive; when the building and infrastructure is more environmentally efficient, they are also cost-efficient; virtualisation and decentralisation of offices is positive in all three dimensions, and PSS are very much in line with the trends and developments of the office of the future. Table 9.10 summarises these and other drivers mentioned in this chapter.

Potential business ideas

Based on the analysis of market trends and sustainability aspects relevant for the office sector, new PSS ideas for the office were developed. They come from four windows of opportunity: PSS for office interiors, software/mobile hardware/connectivity solutions, specialised services/outsource solutions and PSS based on the needs of employees.

The elaborated PSS for the office cover a broad area. They are both B2B and B2C and include product-oriented, use-oriented and result-oriented PSS. The diversity of the developed PSS is also demonstrated by Figure 9.9, which ranks the developed PSS ideas according to the question of whether the material product or the non-material service is more dominant in the system.

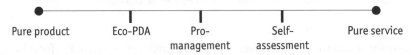

FIGURE 9.9 **The developed PSS ranked on the PSS categorisation scale**

Both research and best practice showed that PSS can be and are already a highly interesting and successful model for developing new business ideas in the need area office. Obvious drivers for this are the changes in the office work organisation and that PSS for offices target mainly companies as customers. Therefore the financial and tax system is often supportive of PSS (e.g. leasing, renting and result-oriented systems), which are variable cost factors and do not need a huge initial investment of customers.

Development pitfalls and threats

No pitfalls were found that are uniquely related to the need area office. The diversified character of the need area does not allow a very specific focus. This wide variety of PSS found in the office sector is illustrated by the available PSS examples: both B2B as well as B2C PSS, and PSS of all kinds (product-oriented, use-oriented and result-oriented), as well as covering many other need areas. However, some generic pitfalls also play a crucial role in the office sector (see Table 9.10). One is the required change in mentality within companies and throughout the whole value chain in order to sell or buy a PSS instead of selling or buying products. Also crucial is a solid partnership, which needs trust and a fair distribution of risks, power and responsibilities as well as revenues. If these pitfalls are not overcome, then PSS developers will find it difficult to:

- Focus on the needs of customers and to convince them of the value of a PSS

- Convince possible partners of the PSS idea

- Find new partners and co-operative arrangements

'PSS training' for both partners and employees is therefore recommended as well as an excellent internal and external communication strategy.

9.5.2 PSS and sustainability

In the need area office the topic of sustainability is currently related to health, productivity and eco-efficiency issues. However, this does not cover all the dimensions of a sustainable office environment. In order to create a sustainable solution we need to look beyond one specific element in the office sector. Integral innovations covering more than one product or field give the opportunity to create a sustainable solution. Rough sustainability analyses using the sustainability criteria identified for the office area showed that the PSS ideas developed by the SusProNet office group are in principle leading towards more sustainability. A surprising outcome of the office working groups was that, despite being based on fundamentally different profit and socially/environmentally motivated scenarios, the developed ideas had a large overlap, which shows that PSS can create so called 'win–win–win situations' in the office sector (people, planet, profit). It occurs that the sustainability aspects of the developed ideas, besides giving inspiration to idea generation, play a crucial role in the realisation phase (detailing the concept and evaluation). The decisions made in this final phase have great influence on the final degree of sustainability.

9.5.3 Policy support

The current political support and subsidy structure and research focus do not support the concept of sustainable PSS. New PSS ideas, which are often organisational and social innovations, are not seen as innovations and therefore lack support. Political actors should integrate PSS thinking into the formulation of legislation, regulation and research programmes and they should include sustainable PSS in their activities as market actors, e.g. in purchasing programmes. A very important initiative would be to integrate PSS thinking into current educational programmes (e.g. of design, engineering and business schools) as well as training programmes for professionals.

Value element	Drivers and opportunities	Development pitfalls and threats
User value/market risk		
Tangible value	● Less office space needed due to decentralisation of work ● More efficient business processes and learning	
Intangible value	● Improved worker conditions and efficiency, e.g. by reduction of commuting	● Change in mentality and strategy of the user
System costs/financial risk		
Tangible operational costs	● Efficiency enhancement due to improved outsourcing, scale effects, virtualisation ● Tax system-friendly for PSS/leasing	
Risk premium, financing and transaction costs		● PSS often needs investment in hardware which is not sold; payback hence takes place over a longer time
Other benefits/capability risk		
Improved power position		
Defence to substitutes/loyalty		
High speed of innovation	● PSS can be developed quickly; the main system changes are organisational	
Investment in PSS development		● Developing the right partnerships ● PSS is development is complex ● PSS is not seen as innovation and hence often not in innovation stimulation programmes
Other transition costs		● Change in mentality and strategy of suppliers, e.g. its sales force

TABLE 9.10 Review of need area-specific PSS opportunities and threats

10
Need area 4: food

Erik Tempelman, Peter Joore, Tom van der Horst and Helma Luiten

TNO, The Netherlands

With contributions from Erwin Lindeijer and Michiel van Schie (TNO, The Netherlands)
and Lucia Rampino (Politecnico di Milano, Italy)

10.1 PSS for need area food: an overview

This section gives an overview of product-service systems (PSS) for the need area food. A sketch of the sector is presented, plus a description of the main approaches to PSS development as practised in this sector. Numerous examples of food PSS are also included. The chapter ends with some tentative conclusions.

10.1.1 Description of the need area food

Physical production and delivery chains

Food is a highly diverse group of more or less solid nourishing items; beverage is equally diverse but more fluid. The sources of food may be comparable for food and beverages, although in the latter water is a much more important resource. The routes to produce and deliver food and beverage differ slightly; the route typical for food is depicted in Figure 10.1. SusProNet focuses on the consumer and on the distribution to the removing phase.

In the early days, the food chain was short. Farmers sold their wares (meats, dairy products and vegetables) via public auction to the local greengrocers. Customers went to the greengrocers, bought the raw ingredients and prepared these themselves. Nowadays, the food chain is often much longer. Vegetables can still be bought as raw ingredients, but they are also part of ready-to-eat meals or pre-prepared meal components

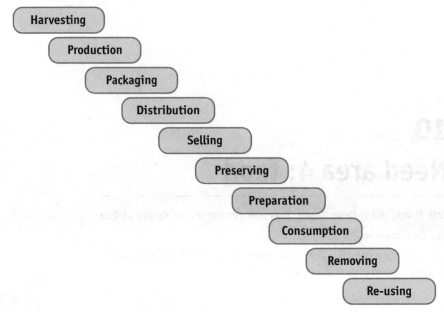

FIGURE 10.1 Links in the food chain

(such as pre-cleaned and diced vegetables), can be bought deep-frozen, canned, etc. There is a host of new links in the chain: processing companies and traders, but also producers of equipment and additives, for instance. All these extra links have increased the freedom of choice for the customer, but they also have serious consequences for food safety and particularly 'traceability', i.e. keeping track of where food has been and what has happened to it. Of course, this is most critical for meat products, because the bacteria that can live off meat often breed enthusiastically in the human digestive tract as well.

Key data for the need area[1]

With an annual production of €626 billion, the food and drink industry is the largest manufacturing sector in the EU, accounting for 13% of the total manufacturing sector (this and the following figures are for 2003, i.e. from before the recent EU expansion, unless mentioned otherwise). Five countries dominate the union, jointly representing some 80% of total EU production: France, Germany, Italy, the UK and Spain. The food and drink industry provides work for some 3.6 million employees, which accounts for 13% of the total amount of people working in the manufacturing industry. Some 62% of these people work in SMEs (small and medium-sized enterprises); the remaining 38% are employed by large companies. When the number of companies is considered,

---

1   The data under this heading all come from the Confederation of the Food and Drink Industries of the EU (CIAA 2003a).

this seemingly well-balanced situation falls apart completely: more than 99% of all food and drink industry companies are SMEs, many of them very small. It can be concluded that the need area is dominated by SMEs in terms of people and number of companies.

Food and drink is the most important consumption item. In 2000, food and non-alcoholic beverages took up 12.8% of the total EU household expenditure. This should not come as a surprise to those who realise that there really is no alternative to food. In this, it is essentially different from, for example, cars or electronics. Such consumables may make life pleasant and interesting, but food is what makes life possible in the first place. Of course, people often strive to combine what is necessary with what is enjoyable. Adding such 'experience food and drink' (e.g. alcoholic beverages, but also catering services, tobacco, etc.) to the total, we arrive at the significantly higher number of 18% (EC 1997). Note that, in relatively poor Member States, household expenditure on food and drink is significantly higher than in those that are relatively rich: compare 18.5% for Portugal against 11.9% for Germany (against the first average of 12.8%). So, as people get richer, they spend relatively less on food and drink, excluding the 'experience economy'. With the average EU citizen getting a little wealthier every year, it is no surprise that, percentage-wise, household expenditure on food and drink is steadily declining. The industry responds to this threat by being unusually active in the field of marketing and new product development. As an illustration: German consumers see no less than 2,000 new food products every year. Dairy products, pre-prepared meals, cheeses and frozen products are at the forefront of this innovation (CIAA 2003b).

Table 10.1 presents the European (*not* EU) top ten agri-food companies. Their combined sales represent 26% of the total volume of €626 billion. The European number one, Nestlé, is also the world's leading food and drink company; Unilever is the world's number five.

Name	Sales	Country	Products
Nestlé	60.4	Switzerland	Cereal, dairy, beverages, confectionery
Unilever	27.4	NL/UK	Dairy, beverages, dressings, frozen goods, cooking products
Diageo	15.0	UK	Alcoholic beverages
Danone	13.5	France	Dairy, beverages, biscuits, cereals
Heineken	10.3	NL	Alcoholic beverages
Cadbury Schweppes	8.4	UK	Beverages, confectionery
Parmalat	7.6	Italy	Dairy, gourmet, biscuits, beverages
Interbrew	6.9	Belgium	Alcoholic beverages
Scottish & Newcastle	6.7	UK	Alcoholic beverages
Associated British Foods	6.7	UK	Sugar, starches, baking products, meat, dairy

TABLE 10.1 Top ten of European food and drink companies by sales (€ billions)

Organisation within the need area

Figure 10.2 presents the main actors in the food chain. The first actor is the farmer who harvests the ingredients. Next, the auctioneer sells these ingredients to the wholesaler. The wholesaler is the supplier for the hotel and restaurant, retail and catering actors. They make up the interface to the customer. Note that all actors, except for the end consumer, have to comply with food safety regulations that are maintained by food control organisations. Note also that the complexity of the chain is such that it makes more sense to talk of a 'food web' instead.

Apart from these 'direct food actors' there are more parties involved in the total need area food, such as manufacturers of professional food equipment. But there are even more actors involved that are not directly related to food, but still interact with the customer: kitchen equipment manufacturers, kitchen sellers, food delivery service providers, internet providers—the list is virtually endless. Then there are the branch organisations: it can safely be said that each product category, such as meat, cheese, vegetables and fruits, has its own lobby group, usually operating on a national level. The sector is too large and diverse to discuss the main players in Europe in more detail, also because with such a widening of the system boundaries it is difficult to keep track of the functional unit (i.e. food consumed by people) and prevent problems of allocation.

10.1.2   Approaches to PSS development in the need area food

In the need area food, product, service and product-service system development all take place next to each other (see Table 10.2 for examples). In general, new food developments are generated along the paths and for the reasons described in Chapters 3 and 5 of this book. Still, these developments have certain unique features, including:

- For food itself, the classical division of product-, use- and result-oriented PSS is not relevant: you cannot lease or rent food, because 'to use' implies 'to digest'. **All PSS involving food itself is, by definition, product-oriented**. Of course, this does not apply to food equipment

- People buy food every day and their tastes can change rapidly. Therefore, new products have to be put on the market just as quickly to succeed. Food equipment, however, has a much longer life-span. Here, innovation and marketing can therefore take much longer

- Food consumption, perhaps more than any other product, varies strongly with the calendar: ice cream and rosé wine in summer, eggs at Easter, turkey at Christmas, etc. Furthermore, there are strong food traditions in each country, as a brief comparison of, for example, English and Italian breakfasts shows

- All major religions include spice laws, which control the kinds of food that believers can or cannot eat, the kinds of food that can or cannot be freely combined and/or the time when certain foods are to be eaten, or when people should fast. Spice laws can even define how food is to be produced and can easily lead to conflicts with the actual legal system that is in place

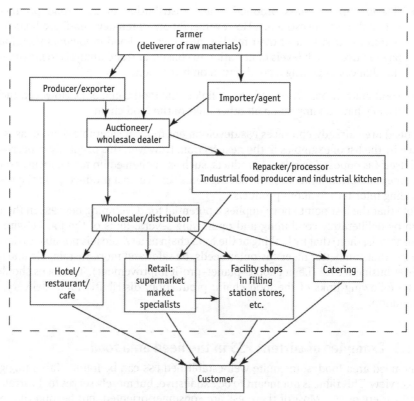

FIGURE 10.2 Primary actors in the need area food

Production	Distribution and delivery	Preparation
Deep-frozen products	Retail distribution	Hotel/restaurant/snack-bar
Canned and sealed products	Hotel/restaurant/bar delivery	Institutional preparation (hospitals, etc.)
Fresh compound food	Hospital/home for aged or disabled delivery	On-street preparation
Professional food preparation ingredients	Home delivery service (groceries, pizzas, Chinese take-away food, etc.)	Innovations in home cooking devices (for fresh or pre-prepared meals)
Novel protein food production (as a substitute for meat)	Private home delivery (by car, bike)	Home warming of prepared meals (microwave) (decrease of preparation time)

TABLE 10.2 Examples of food PSS development

- Gearing up for mass production and distribution of new food products demands huge investments. However, eight out of ten new retail products fail within the first year of their market introduction. Food innovators therefore pay relatively high levels of attention to consumer trend analysis to maximise the chances of getting a good return on investment

- Food innovations are aimed at one link of the food chain only. However, they usually have an impact on all other links of the food chain

The need area already embraces PSS development to a considerable degree, as is also shown by the list of examples in the next section. However, this primarily concerns the food itself (as opposed to related products, such as kitchen equipment), focuses on the consumer and often limits itself to 'adding some service' to a product, as in the case of providing information about products.

Note that the last point above implies a potential for developing new PSS in the food chain by deliberately combining and optimising several links of the food chain. The hypothesis is, then, that by looking at the food chain as a whole it is possible to develop new PSS that can better meet customer needs, be safer and more sustainable and offer a better business case (i.e. a people–planet–profit improvement). The focus should be on the following links of the food chain: production, distribution and delivery, and preparation.

10.1.3 Examples of current PSS in the need area food

In the need area food, some quite well-established PSS can be found. Table 10.3 gives an overview. This table is not meant to be exhaustive, but merely serves to illustrate the broad variety of PSS. Most of these PSS are consumer-oriented, but beyond that point they are not easily classified. Several of them imply short cuts in the food chain, eliminating one or more links (e.g. the Odin vegetable bag). Others imply expanding markets beyond food (e.g. Albert Heijn i-mode). Services that specifically focus on ecological sustainability issues, such as material and energy efficiency, are scarce, although many of them can conceivably contribute to this through a greater degree of professionalism and through industrialisation of food production. Likewise, social sustainability aspects are rarely addressed specifically by food PSS.

10.1.4 Conclusions

The need area food is continuously changing. Over the years, food chains have developed from simple and short to long and complex, with a multitude of actors all trying to get a piece of the immense market. This has increased consumer choice and value, but has also given rise to concerns regarding health, safety, environment and ethics.

In all links in the food chain, from production through distribution and delivery to preparation, we have seen and we will continue to see many significant innovations. These innovations usually affect most links in the chain, even though they are normally intended for a single link only. There seems to be a potential for innovations that are deliberately aimed at the food chain as a whole. PSS can be among these innovations, especially when they involve partnerships of different actors.

PSS name	Description	Provider added value	Customer added value	Eco-effect	Reference
Food production phases: harvesting, production, packaging					
Koppert pest management	Crop protocols, side-effect monitoring over the internet	Farmer convenience, improved pest control	–	Less use of pesticides	www.koppert.nl
Odin vegetable bag	Weekly vegetable package plus producer support	Links producers to consumers, assures outlet, promotes locally grown food	Convenience, lower price, discover new ingredients and recipes	>50% less environmental burden	www.odin.nl
BOEUF	Organic meat package	As above	As above	As above	Goedkoop *et al.* 1999
Food acquisition phases: distribution, selling, preserving					
Online product ordering	E-commerce: ordering food over the internet	Customer bonding, build up database	Time savings, possibly also discounts	Depends on amount of avoided transport	www.albert.nl or www.maxfoodmarket.nl
Cold chain manager	Optimised storage through use of IT and sensors	Lower cost, lower losses, more control	–	Reduction of energy use, reduction of losses	www.ipo1.com
Supermarket hand scanner	Payment facility	Saves staff, no cash required, build up database	Time savings, no cash required	–	www.ind.tno.nl
Bottled tap water	Service provided by water company	Retain market share	Assured quality	–	Goedkoop *et al.* 1999
Meals out-of-the-wall	Supermarkets selling food outside office hours	Enter new market	Convenience	–	Goedkoop *et al.* 1999

Note: any reduction in eco-effect is difficult to determine without specific contextual information

TABLE 10.3 **Examples of current food PSS by phase (refer also to Fig. 10.1)** (continued over)

PSS name	Description	Provider added value	Customer added value	Eco-effect	Reference
Meal delivery service (home)	Delivery of pizza, Chinese food etc.	Higher profit margins	Convenience, experience (for exotic foods)	Depends on amount of avoided transport	–
Meal delivery service (work)	As above	Higher profit margins, employee bonding, B2B opportunities	Convenience	As above	www.intrastore.nl, www.max@work or www.swinxx.com
Siemens HomeDeliveryBox	Refrigerator and storage next to front door, accessible by delivery staff	New market	Agenda freedom: get food delivered without having to be at home	TBD	www.siemens.com
Tafeltje dekje, II Laboratorio	(Voluntary) food delivery service for the elderly and less mobile	–	Food security, social contacts, safety	Possible benefits when professional production is more efficient than home cooking	Goedkoop et al. 1999
Food preparation and consumption phases					
Deep-frozen meals with preparation guide	Meals 'tuned' for easy heating in specially prepared microwaves	Customer bonding	Convenience, higher quality	Possibly lower eco-impact because of lower food losses	www.apetito.de and www.sharp.com
Eating out—cheap	Full meal service	Standard service, high turnover	Convenience	Slightly lower eco-effect	–
Eating out—expensive	Full meal service	Standard service, high profit margins, prestige	Convenience plus experience and status	Higher eco-effect	–

TABLE 10.3 (from previous page; continued opposite)

PSS name	Description	Provider added value	Customer added value	Eco-effect	Reference
Ready-to-heat meals	Convenience foods	Higher profit margins	Convenience	Possibly lower eco-impact because of efficient production	–
Food heating in shop	Food preparation by customer in shop	Entering fast-food market	Convenience	TBD	www.ah.nl
Upgrading programme for kitchen equipment	Offering (functional) changes and maintenance	Customer bonding	Increased durability	Lifetime extension of equipment (~10% less eco-effect)	Brezet *et al.* 2001; www.atagpartners.nl
Home cook	Professional cook prepares your meal for you in your own home	New market opportunities	Higher quality, experience, status	–	www.homecooking.nl or www.freeks.nl
Other					
AH i-mode	Internet service	Customer bonding, build up database	Convenience, additional services	–	www.ah.nl

TABLE 10.3 (from previous page)

Many PSS have already been developed and introduced in the market. Some of these are characterised by a strong product component (e.g. Siemens HomeDeliveryBox), others have both a product and a service component (e.g. Odin vegetable bag) that are of comparable importance and a third class is predominantly based on the service component (e.g. eating out). As such, the need area shows no preference. Note that the food itself in any food PSS is there to be consumed and digested; in this regard, PSS can only be product-oriented. Finally, there seems to be considerable PSS development in food itself, but relatively little in food-related products, such as kitchen equipment. This hints at a window of opportunity for innovative partnerships.

PSS holds promise, but what are the business opportunities for the need area food, and how can sustainability (environmental and social sustainability) be taken along as the key boundary condition that it should be? Those are the first two questions for the next section. Trend analysis will turn out to be a key tool in finding answers.

The sector is so large that a focus for this chapter had to be chosen. We decided to focus on those links of the food chain that directly involve the consumer: from 'selling' to 'removing' (see Fig. 10.1).

10.2 Analysis: PSS opportunities in the need area food

This section aims at identifying broad areas where PSS is a promising business opportunity within the need area food. This identification is based on trends and developments in the area. Also, social and ecological sustainability is presented as a key boundary condition for these opportunities. These topics can be found in Section 10.2.1. The section ends with the main conclusions, synthesising the trends and sustainability issues into opportunities for sustainable PSS in the need area.

10.2.1 Trends and developments relevant for PSS development

Trends and developments can be categorised in many different ways. For this section, we have selected the three categories of (1) consumer trends, (2) economic developments and (3) technological trends and developments, including innovations in food itself. This distinction is somewhat arbitrary, and there is quite some overlap between the trends, but it is a useful distinction nevertheless.

Consumer trends

Ageing population
In Europe today, seniors represent 130 million people, i.e. about one-third of the population. Today, life expectancy in Europe is 79.2 years for women and 73.2 for men, while it was only 63 in 1960. Although an ageing population occurs virtually everywhere in the world, Europe will be the continent with the highest proportion of seniors: 45% in 2020 and 50% in 2040. Between 1990 and 2050, the European 60+ will double, the 75+ will triple and the 85+ will increase fivefold.

Within such a large group, it makes sense to make a further distinction. Senioragency divides the group 'elderly' into three sub-groups on the basis of their personal value systems (Trend Conference 2002): the pre-war generation (born 1915–1929), the silent generation (1930–1945) and the protest generation (1946–1955). Senioragency advises us to follow this division because people tend to adhere to their values for their whole life. Note that, in some respects, the protest generation is the generation of the now, the generation to keep in mind. They have a lot of money and also the tendency to spend it.

Smaller households

Apart from ageing, the most general demographic development in Europe is the smaller household size (FDF 2002) related to increased individualisation: from 3.2 in 1970 to 2.1 in 2020. Families get smaller as fewer children are being born. To ensure demographic renewal, any country needs a birth rate of 2.1 children per woman. In Europe, it is now only 1.45. The highest is Ireland with 1.86 and the lowest Spain with 1.11. All of these rates are obviously too low to ensure renewal and even maintenance of the population. Also, it ultimately affects ageing too. Note that immigration mitigates this effect considerably. Specifically for the food branch, the range and nature of products provided by the food and drink industry is a reflection of the changes in demographics towards smaller households and what consumers want to buy.

Health and obesity

OECD countries share a trend towards higher consumption of meat (except Poland), cheese, fruits, vegetables and bottled drinks. Total caloric content is also increasing in several countries despite its already high intake. Only a negligible minority of the world population consumes the recommended average of 400 grams of fruit and vegetables per day (WHO/FAO 2002), although average European consumption comes close with 372 grams (WHO 1998). This situation has improved markedly since 1990 due to extensive information on appropriate eating habits, but there is still quite a way to go before diets are optimal (Valota *et al.* 2002).

There is a distinct and important trend towards obesity. Higher incomes have increased the consumption of fats and meat, which drive up weight. The OECD foresees a 7% increase (compared with 1996) of per capita meat consumption for the European region as a whole (OECD 2001). Per capita consumption of cereals (mostly in refined form) and vegetable oils is also likely to increase. Furthermore, meat consumption is expected to grow until 2020, most explosively in the developing world and by 16% in the developed world (Rosegrant 2001). Obesity is currently considered a major health threat.

Declining confidence in food safety

'Food has never been as safe as it is today'. This opinion is shared by several institutions and companies, including LTO, TNO Voeding, EU LNV and Campina (Slob *et al.* 2002). In the UK, food quality and safety has never been so high, and is the core strength of the food industry (FDF 2002). On the other hand, the same actors note that there are bottlenecks. These relate to the lack of transparency of the complex food chain, the practicalities of adequate food safety control and irrational consumer behaviour, which cannot be controlled effectively (for example, buying chicken breast in the morning and then spending all day in a hot city market before putting it in the refrigerator).

Consumer confidence in food safety is high, but the levels are declining owing to the numerous food scares in the meat industry (BSE, foot-and-mouth disease, pork plague, chicken plague). Note that there is no one-to-one relation between confidence and consumption (apparently and astonishingly, people buy food even though they think it is not safe), nor is there a perfect match between actual and perceived food safety.

Appropriately enough for the information age, many of today's consumers want to be able to find out what they are eating: for instance, whether food contains genetically modified soybeans or if it is compatible with their personal allergies. This explains why so many of today's packaging mentions a telephone number or even a website. EU laws are now being made that make it compulsory for manufacturers to inform the public of the presence, if any, of genetically modified food components in their products (CIAA 2003b). Similarly, information about allergens must now be provided by law.

Multi-activity lifestyle

Because of the smaller households and individualisation, one person now has to perform many different tasks, whereas in the old days one person in a family had to perform only one type of task. Time management therefore becomes more important and, increasingly, consumers are willing to trade time for money: for example, by buying relatively expensive, but quickly prepared convenience food instead of buying the various ingredients separately, which would be cheaper but would take more time. Also, family sit-down meals are on the decline: instead, the various members of the family often take their meals separately, in their own time. More and more, the family house is becoming a hotel, its various 'guests' coming and going, and eating, as they please.

Economic trends

Stagnating economic growth

On average, Europeans are still seeing an increase in wealth (FDF 2002). However, economic growth is stagnating for the moment. The downturn started in 2001. The attacks of 11 September and business scandals such as that related to Enron further accelerated it. Also, the introduction of the euro has effectively been a source of inflation, causing the prices of many consumer products to rise. All this has made people more cautious about spending money. Consumer confidence has decreased.

As Edelkoort formulated (Trend Conference 2002):

> All of a sudden, the order of the world is disturbed, the good and quiet times are over, we live in a stormy moment where crusades come alive again, in which good and evil stand diametrically opposed to one another, in which forces of the right and of the left fight and kill each other and in which the East–West dialogue is miserably stranded in an isolationist impulse that divides and rules the world. People are beleaguered by violence, are threatened by food, are killed by bacteria and are humiliated by the fact that they have no voice. People feel very small and fear the worst.

Complementary to these sentiments, the RIVM expects a growing difference in income per capita, the continuing rise of the 24-hour economy, an increasing number of one-and-a-half and double-income households and stronger reliance on market forces through increased privatisation (RIVM 2000).

Global–local

In the past decade, globalisation has been the major economic trend. The promise of economies of scale has been one of the driving forces behind this trend, along with the development of new, cheap production facilities and the opening of new markets. IT has been the most important enabling technology. Now, after some years of experience, we can see that globalisation is not over yet, but the first cracks can already be seen. The recent scandal at Ahold (February 2003) is an example of such a crack.[2]

Both Edelkoort and Rohde spoke at a recent trend conference (Trend Conference 2002) about this new trend of localisation. Edelkoort: 'Globalisation as an important trend is over. Europe does not speak the same language as America anymore. Things have to be unique again. People now are universal but with a local touch.' Rohde: 'Your neighbourhood is important. And also international cosmopolite quality standards [matter], but with a local flavour. The local and regional aspects are cool again.'

Italy, Spain and France developed, as a contra-trend to globalisation, certificates for original food and drink products. In Italy, for example, there is the DOP standard (from Denominazione di Origine Protetta) that protects typical food products. These products sometimes have difficulties in respecting the EU hygiene rules, because these rules do not take into account traditional and artisan productive methods still followed by small and local farmers.

New agricultural regulation[3]

In the coming years it is very likely that the economic landscape with regard to the primary sector in the EU will undergo significant changes. Currently, in the EU, a very important part of the EU budget is channelled into subsidising agricultural products, to an extent that this practice is from many expert sources criticised as an irrational, unethical and essentially wasteful policy. Whatever the political background of this conflict, even the staunchest subsidy supporters (and, not accidentally, its most important stakeholders, such as France) are considering a reshuffling of the subsidy practices, and a relaxation of protectionism and other barriers that the EU uses to protect its farmers.

In any case it is very reasonable to expect that in the near future these trade barriers will be removed to some significant extent. This will lead to an increase in the imports of agricultural products to the EU, from areas of the developing world especially, now prevented from exporting their products to the EU because of the policies in place. Although it cannot be certain to what extent this process will develop, it is very likely that this different sourcing of agricultural products to the EU markets will have impacts on the food sector, such as those sketched below:

- A change to consumer preferences and to culinary practices, as new products increasingly enter EU markets

---

2   Royal Ahold is one of the world's largest international retail grocery and food service companies, headquartered in the Netherlands. The company's ambitious global expansion was halted by fraud at the chain's American subsidiary US Foodservice and by a board-level accounting scandal. In February 2003, the CEO and CFO resigned following charges of financial irregularities. The scandal left the company in disarray, selling off many of its foreign subsidiaries at unfavourable prices.

3   This trend description was kindly delivered by N. Sakkas of ApInTech, January 2003.

● A more intense food security problem, as a result of the fact that the source of these products will now be remote, producers may often be unaware of the best practice in agricultural products harvesting and early processing, and products may not be as easily controlled and standardised in terms of quality

Food trends and technologies

Convenience food
Consumer spending on food as a percentage of total household expenditure has steadily declined in most countries, sharpening competition in the food processing and retail sectors and leading to an explosion in the number of food products and services offered to the consumer (OECD 2001). Most of these new food products indicate a clear trend towards convenience food that is of excellent quality, certainly not the 'junk food' of days long gone. The following quotes come from an article in a Dutch newspaper (*Volkskrant*, 19 October 2002) and give a rough impression of the visions of companies relating to this trend:

> P. Havinga, the director of Albert, the home delivery service of the Ahold's Dutch supermarket chain Albert Heijn, expects that within a couple of years, 40% of the Dutch households will not be able to cook anymore. Some new houses now lack a serious kitchen.

> J.W. Grievink, food expert of Cap Gemini Ernst & Young consulting, expects that within 15 years consumers will spend as much money on outdoor eating or ready-to-eat products as on products to prepare your own meal, primarily to save time. Before World War II, people spent over two hours in the kitchen preparing a meal. Now it is only 20 minutes and this will even decrease to 18 minutes.

> Van Trijp, University of Wageningen and the Unilever Corporation, claims that this transition to spending more on food outdoors will even go faster: 'We do not want to make our own soup or peel potatoes. Nowadays people only use two to five ingredients to cook a complete meal'.

> The selling of raw ingredients for cooking decreased from 65% of the total shopping in 1996 to 55% in 2001. It is foreseen that this will only be 37% in 2006.[4] On the other hand, the selling of ready-to-cook ingredients will increase from 24% in 1996 to 31% in 2006. And the market share for ready-to-heat meals has increased by 50% since 1997. Albert Heijn expects in 2002 an increase of 33% on the turnover from ready-meals, compared to 2000. This will lead to 20 million ready-to-eat meals.

So-called finger food is an interesting new sub-trend of convenience food. Finger food is not tied to a fixed moment of the day, but can be eaten at any time desired. For example, at work, it is not eaten during the fixed canteen hours but at anytime during the full working day. Food that can be eaten behind the steering wheel of a car is another noteworthy sub-trend. On the other hand, food is not all about convenience now. We do see people spending a lot of time cooking at weekends. Apparently, when people have the time, they still want to experiment and prepare 'nouvelle cuisine' meals.

4   See the website of the Dutch Central Bureau for Food, www.cbl.nl.

Health food

Next to the trend towards convenience food there is a rising interest in foods perceived as healthy. The focus on low-fat products of five years ago is now shifting towards nutritionally fortified foods: iodised salt, fortified fruit juices, breakfast cereals, calcium-enhanced milk. These are called functional foods and meet specific needs, fight disease or (the ultimate promise) promote longevity. Also, there is a greater demand for animal product alternatives such as vegetarian burgers, soy and rice milk, cheese alternatives and non-dairy desserts (OECD 2001).

In past years, functional foods were expected to become very successful but, so far, this expectation has not become a reality. Reasons for the continued absence of success are unclear claims, high prices and bad taste (Eye 2003). Some companies have already sold their functional food business sectors. Others, such as Unilever, still believe in this trend. The company has recently launched Becel proactive, a low-fat margarine claimed to reduce LDL-cholesterol levels if consumed in the proper doses. Within other product groups, such as sandwich spreads and sweets, Unilever is developing more functional foods. Still, the message around such products may be too difficult for most consumers.

Organic food

Of the total annual turnover of food, 1.5% originates from organic cultivation. This includes vegetables, fruit, dairy products, eggs and processed ingredients. Forty per cent of these products are bought in specialised organic food shops, 40% in supermarkets, 10% via food packages such as the Odin vegetable bag and the remaining 10% directly from the farm. The supermarket share is growing slightly. In Holland, the turnover of organic food (in general) is growing by 15% annually. In other European countries, the number is higher, about 30% annually. This low growth rate of organic food in Holland is due to the no-nonsense, efficiency-only focus of most Dutch farmers, the price-conscious behaviour of Dutch shoppers and the fact that retailers have adopted a me-too rather than a me-first attitude.

Kitchen ICT

Technical developments by producers have already strongly shaped developments in the kitchen, with tools such as the microwave oven, electric kitchen utensils and innovative packaging. Recent developments related to the internet and intelligent homes (known as domotica) have just started to support further changes. ICT developments in general will boost novel technological convenience systems for consumers (EU 1997).

A possible near-future innovation is the introduction of intelligent[5] refrigerators. These can autonomously keep track of their contents and can automatically order new supplies should this be necessary. Refer to the Brainfridge project from Solinet (www.solinet-research.com/brainfridge) or the Screenfridge from Electrolux. At the moment, this technological trend raises more questions than it answers. For example, it is still unclear to what extent consumers will want to stay in control. However, it seems certain that a lot of new developments will be realised as technology push and subsequently sold as 'package deals', leaving the consumer no real choice.

---

5   It is all relative: don't expect your 2010 fridge to perform anything that would require real (human) intelligence.

Online shopping

The growth in online food shopping is a third technological trend worth watching. In 2004, more than 60 million Europeans shopped online, an increase of 50% from early 2003. In the same year, some 53% of Europeans had access to the internet (Forrester 2004). In 2001, more than 100,000 households already used this shopping method. Albert, the internet shop of Dutch retailer Albert Heijn, claims to gain a hundred new customers every week, mainly from double-income households. The choice offered by these web shops is also increasing: Albert Heijn now claims to offer 9,200 products. However, Max Foodmarket, the main competitor of Albert in Holland, stopped its online shopping services in December 2002 because it could not realise the required return on investment. The director of Albert admits that, when talking about online shopping, it is better to speak of market development instead of market share. Note that online shopping has to compete with other channels for groceries, such as large supermarkets, station shops and local shops.

Tracking and tracing

Developments in IT make it possible to track the origin of food ingredients and to trace them on their way through the food chain. As sensors get ever cheaper, this development becomes more relevant. It offers lots of possibilities for food safety control. In 2004, the EU government made it compulsory by law to label genetically modified animal feed (CIAA 2003b), which is a clear application of tracking and tracing.

Ecological sustainability

One particularly relevant and informative set of scenarios has been made by WWF (Loh 2002). It has developed two main indices: the Living Planet Index (based on trends since 1970 in forest, freshwater and marine populations of 2–300 species each) and the Ecological Footprint (based on land requirement for crops, grazing, forest products and CO_2 absorption to compensate CO_2 emissions from energy production). Both indices present a gloomy picture. The Living Planet Index has been decreasing to below 70% since 1970, and the world Ecological Footprint has increased by 80% since 1960 (surpassing the Earth's carrying capacity before 1980). According to UN growth scenarios used in Loh 2002, meat, fish and seafood consumption will be the quickest to increase, doubling before the middle of this century. Natural limitations have not been considered in these scenarios. This would lead to a world Ecological Footprint of about two planets: 1.8–2.2 times the Earth's natural biomass productivity would be required.

Environmental life-cycle assessments (LCAs) provide a complementary picture to these scenarios. From such analyses, it can be concluded that the main environmental impacts related to food are caused in the primary production stage (growing crops and cattle). Only for energy use are there relevant contributions from other stages of the life-cycle, such as production, storage (cooling) and transportation. Packaging, the source of considerable public debate where it concerns food and the environment, generally contributes less than 5% to the total energy consumption, although very small and complex packaging units may contribute more than 10% (Krutwagen and Lindeijer 2001). More important are food losses, which occur in every link of the food chain and which represent significant energy impacts considering the functional unit of, for example, one meal consumed. Refining the unit to 'food effectively digested' brings to light the impact of over-consumption: especially in industrialised countries, people eat too much protein from meat (Krutwagen and Lindeijer 2001). Fat is also over-consumed, with obesity as a result.

To summarise: although most of the environmental burden is caused in the agricultural stage (except for energy use), all links in the food chain contribute to the high total impact due to food losses and over-consumption. After all, the relevant functional unit of analysis such as that discussed here is the food that is actually consumed by the customer. Preventing food losses is therefore a sensible and promising way of improving the ecological sustainability of food. Promoting organic food is another.

Food security

Next to ecological sustainability there is the issue of food security, addressed at the International Conference on Sustainable Food Security for All by 2020 (Eid 2001). Important quantitative inputs for this conference were the global food scenarios to 2020 prepared by the International Food Policy Research Institute (Rosegrant *et al.* 2001). These scenarios are driven by a model that mainly uses population growth, income/price changes and policy measures to assess impacts on food security. Note that, in this context, 'security' relates to 'having enough food for all', as opposed to food safety, which is described under 'Consumer trends' above, i.e. food that is safe to eat.

Food security will demand area and yield expansions that are not easily achievable. Water will be the major constraint in many developing countries, and the most productive cereal areas in North America, India and China will soon be approaching biophysical limits. Impacts of climate change are not incorporated in these models (Rosegrant *et al.* 2001), nor are any other impacts on the Earth's carrying capacity. Similarly, shifts in consumer preference are not accounted for. The explosive demand for meat in developing countries will require an exponential growth in land use. The plain reason for this is that the number of people that can be fed from rice and potatoes is 19 and 22 per ha, as opposed to 1 or 2 per ha from beef and lamb, respectively (WHO/FAO 2002). Also, worldwide, the food diversity promoted by the WHO cannot be guaranteed. This can be illustrated by the fourfold increase of fruit and vegetable imports to the United Kingdom over the past decade, at the expense of local availability in developing countries (WHO/FAO 2002; Valota *et al.* 2002). Accessibility to food is largely an economic issue; food security itself is not sufficient to allow everyone to have access to food of sufficient quality and variety (Argenti 2002).

From the above it may be concluded that food security in the coming decades largely depends on food production and distribution issues. Depending on the extent to which these issues are given due consideration, global lifestyles could develop in different directions (see e.g. Wilkinson 1998). This depends not only on political choices. The future will also be shaped by consumer preferences and producers' initiatives. For instance, the effect of consumer demand for sustainable food products should not be underestimated, and sustainable development should be considered at all parts of the food chain (FDF 2002). Communication is an important tool that can be used by governmental institutions, producers and consumers alike. But a fairer and more open market is equally important, if not more important.

Reflections on socially sustainable food PSS

Compared with the research on ecological sustainability described above, systematic research on social sustainability is still in its infancy. Still, this subject also merits attention. At the SusProNet events, it became clear that preserving cultural diversity should be high on the agenda if a PSS is to be socially sustainable, as opposed to the cultural erosion caused by today's massive, one-dimensional global food industry. It should be noted, however, that this issue is surrounded by personal politics and preferences, and that, despite good journalism (Naomi Klein's best-selling book *No Logo* comes to mind), an objective assessment is still lacking.

Beyond cultural diversity there is the more fundamental problem of feedback, or rather, the lack of it. In today's world, the complexity of the food chain makes it almost impossible for consumers to take responsibility for their actions and choices. This ultimately leads, for instance, to unsustainable conditions for animals in livestock farms that no one would accept for their pets, but also to, for example, the exploitation of developing-world farmers. It can be argued that giving consumers more information about what happens to their food and to the people involved will remind them of their responsibilities. This process of stakeholder involvement should therefore also be a priority for socially sustainable food PSS.

Two additional priorities have already been covered earlier in this report and need only be repeated here briefly. The first is the issue of fair trade; the second is the issue of 'good food for all', both for the developing world, where people basically have too little food and/or unbalanced diets, and for the industrialised world, where obesity has now become a tragic standard. It is comparatively easy to come up with more dimensions of the social sustainability problem (e.g. participation of the elderly, strengthening local economies, etc.), but this report leaves it at four priorities (see also the next section).

10.2.2 Conclusions: opportunities for sustainable food PSS

To characterise present PSS in the need area food, we have cross-referenced the existing PSS as listed in Table 10.3 with the trends described in Section 10.2.1 (see Table 10.4). Table 10.4 reflects the fact that the main trends behind PSS are multi-activity lifestyle and an ageing population, both combined with convenience food. IT appears as a major enabler behind many PSS. Other important trends are health, global–local and organic food, as combined in the Odin vegetable bag PSS. Moreover, this particular combination shows major advances towards reducing agricultural impact, whereas the delivery service-type PSS merely raises the questions of energy use and transport intensity: that is, possible negative effects on ecological sustainability.

Chapters 3 and 5 list drivers for PSS as seen from a business perspective. Rather than repeating these here as projected on the various PSS described in Section 10.1.3, we choose the alternative perspective of customer added value. Doing this, we find that the existing food PSS add at least one of six types of customer value (see Fig. 10.3):

● Provide customers with information about products and/or build up trust in them

● Give customers access to new experiences (entertainment, mood)

A Ucon is a visual representation of a researched user context issue, from 'icons for you'.

FIGURE 10.3 Ucons for customer added value

- Get customer result without hassle, doubt or fears[6] ('no worries')

- Save customer time and/or effort

- Enable customers to do something that they normally can't do

- Give 'agenda freedom': give customers not just what they want, but also when and where they want

Note that overall cost reduction of an existing PSS is also a way to increase customer value, because, in this way, the PSS value proposition improves; the customer gets more value for money.

Regarding ecological and social sustainability, the following eight demands can be made from food PSS (refer to Section 10.2.1 for details and explanations), as also shown in Figures 10.4 and 10.5: reduce transport intensity, food losses, energy use and agricultural impact (e.g. by use of organically grown food) for the 'planet' dimension, and respect and preserve cultural diversity, stimulate fair trade, increase stakeholder involvement and transparency, and ensure good food for all for the 'people' dimension.

Table 10.4 reveals areas of opportunity for sustainable food PSS, for example:

- Combining **health, health food** and **good food for all**

- Combining **food safety** and **tracking and tracing**

- Combining **smaller households**, **IT** and **food losses**

Further refinement of the existing PSS with a stronger focus on sustainability demands is of course also a promising option for creating sustainable food PSS.

---

6   Food safety can also be placed under this Ucon.

| Transport intensity | Food losses | Energy use | Agricultural impact |

FIGURE 10.4 Ucons for ecological sustainability ('planet')

| Cultural diversity | Fair trade | Stakeholder involvement | Over-consumption |

FIGURE 10.5 Ucons for social sustainability ('people')

10.3 Idea generation and selection

This section presents some ideas for sustainable food PSS, generated during the Sus-ProNet project. In the process, both the design plan generated by the HiCS project and a new selection tool, the sustainability screen, created by the SusProNet project, have proved useful (see Annex 1 to this book). The design plan is a conceptual design method for visualising a PSS idea, with so-called 'system maps' showing the three flows of information, money and matter, and with 'advertisement posters' showing the PSS in its intended context of use (Jégou and Joore 2004). The sustainability screen is a quick and easy-to-use tool for assessing the potential of a PSS idea with respect to people, planet and profit.

10.3.1 Need area-specific PSS ideas (long list)

During the first Open Conference (Amsterdam, June 2003), the SusProNet Food group organised a workshop on the subject of idea generation. Starting from the main trends and sustainability considerations in the need area described in Section 10.2.1, five groups (food group member companies and conference visitors) came up with possible ideas for PSS. Next, they selected these on the basis of people, planet and profit considerations and detailed the most promising five ideas into a presentable PSS. Below, these five suggestions are briefly described.

	Consumer trends					Economic trends		Food and technology trends							Sustainability demands					
	Ageing	Smaller households	Health and obesity	Food safety	Multi-activity lifestyle	Economic growth	Global–local	Convenience food	Health food	Exotic food	Organic food	IT	Online shopping	Tracking and tracing	Cultural diversity	Energy use and transport	Agricultural impact	Good food for all	Stakeholder involvement	Fair trade
Koppert pest management												+					+			
Odin vegetable bag			+	+			+			+	+						+		+	
BOEUF				+			+				+	+					+		+	
Online product ordering					+			+				+		+		-?				
Supermarket hand scanner												+								
Bottled tap water				+					+							-				
Meals out-of-the-wall					+			+								+?				
Eating out—cheap		+			+			+												
Eating out—expensive								+		+						-	-			
Meal delivery services (home)								+								-?	-			
Meal delivery services (work)								+								-?		+	-	
Siemens home delivery box					+			+				+								
'Tafeltje-dekje'	+																			
Il Laboratorio	+							+							+?	+?		+?		
Apetito/Sharp 'Zeitsprung'	+											+						+		
Ready-to-heat meals	+				+			+												
Food heating in shop					+					+										
ATAG partner						+						+								
Home cook																+				
AH i-mode												+								

TABLE 10.4 Cross-referencing of various food PSS (see Section 10.1.3) against consumer trends, economic trends, food and technology trends, and sustainability demands (Section 10.2.1)

The Taste Exchanger a.k.a. 'Meet & Eat'

The Taste Exchanger a.k.a. 'Meet & Eat' is a PSS aimed at archetype 'Ahmed', who stands for the immigrants that now make up a significant part of many European countries. It is a food marketplace and communal eating house, where people of different cultures can do their groceries, get take-away food, prepare (and share) their meals or have a quiet, sit-down meal in the restaurant section. Rather than throwing them away, food leftovers are saved for 'fusion recipes'. This PSS specifically addresses the needs for (immigrant) people to feel part of a community and to have a wide range of food experiences. Ecological sustainability is improved by throwing away less food (see Fig. 10.6).

FIGURE 10.6 Advertisement poster (impression) of PSS The Taste Exchanger

The Human Vending Machine (HVM)

The Human Vending Machine (HVM) is a PSS aimed at archetype 'Bill', representative of the yuppies who lead such busy lives that they forget to eat, let alone eat healthily. The HVM is a person. He or she makes sure Bill eats well every day by passing by at his office, suggesting a meal and getting it for him from a range of local take-away shops. The food is delivered at Bill's office or—at night—at the fitness club, where all the Bills meet and socialise in a special HVM corner. This PSS addresses the need of people to save as much time as possible, yet still eat healthily and have some social contacts during eating. Carefully organised logistics, use of locally produced food and efficient modes of transport (e.g. electro-assisted recumbent tricycles) are used to improve ecological sustainability.

Still Cooking (and you are invited)

Still Cooking (and you are invited) is a PSS aimed at archetype 'Granny', representative of the growing group of elderly in Europe who have reduced mobility. Still Cooking offers her anything from unprocessed ingredients to a fully catered meal, plus all the facilities for preparing and eating the food. Where possible, the system relies on low-cost delivery through neighbours, family, etc. In contrast to conventional meal-delivery services, the system allows Granny to receive guests and share her culinary experiences with them. It also keeps track of her health, and can adjust diet, portions, etc.

where necessary, even co-delivering medicine. This PSS addresses the need for elderly people to be active, independent and dignified members of the community, as well as their need to stay healthy. Efficient preparation and transport of food, as well as prevention of food losses, is used to improve ecological sustainability (see Fig. 10.7).

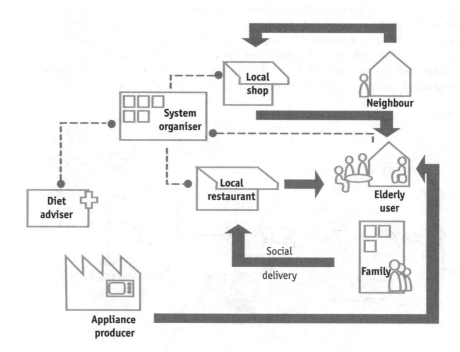

FIGURE 10.7 System map of PSS Still Cooking

Edu-Tainment on FHE

Edu-Tainment on FHE delivers Food, Health and a nice Environment to archetype 'Baby': that is, the schoolchildren of the near future. Baby gets healthy food—as opposed to today's obesity-inducing diets—combined with awareness-raising games and information (*Editor's note:* in this future vision, 'don't play with your food!' will no longer be heard). The food is delivered through a standard catering service; the added products are the interactive games. This PSS is aimed at the need for schoolchildren to have a healthy, fun meal. In raising awareness about environmental issues, it will indirectly improve ecological sustainability.[7]

---

7 Another example of 'convergent evolution', this PSS idea is very similar to 'S'Cool Box' (see page 291).

Bon Belly®

Bon Belly® is a PSS aimed at the employees of 'the Boss', the archetypal manager of an SME with less than 24 workers and, hence, no canteen. It delivers full-service food catering based on locally produced products, combined with a range of other chores. An all-encompassing employee database (the so-called B-3™ system) makes sure that everyone gets what he or she needs for optimal productivity. A special awareness-raising tool, the Bon Belly Barometer™, shows how the system performs from day to day, regarding people, planet and profit. This PSS meets the need of employees to have a healthy meal and the need of the Boss to have a productive workforce. Ecological sustainability is improved as with the previous PSS idea (see Fig. 10.8).

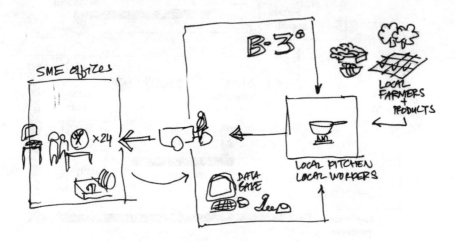

FIGURE 10.8 Rough system map of PSS Bon Belly

Sustainable food PSS ideas: six more

During the second SusProNet workshop, the process of idea generation and selection was repeated, but now with a clear focus on the social sustainability issue of obesity among kids. PSS ideas were put forward to solve this issue in the context of use of schools. The main problems that were identified with such PSS were the facts that healthy eating is considered to be boring, not tasty enough and 'uncool', plus the lack of feedback (kids do not know what they are eating), compounded by the power of marketing that stimulates unhealthy consumption patterns. Next to the kids themselves, the main stakeholders include schools, parents and the media. From there, solution elements were defined. Inspired by this list, six sketches of new PSS were then made, as described below.

- 'The future You': make it a game to get the energy balance right
- 'Customised full day full package': package for different eating moments

- 'My-health.com': trace what you eat by taking photographs with a mobile phone and upload them to a diet centre for feedback

- Pokemon Fruit toys: Eat 'm all! Provide fresh fruit to school kids packaged in toys that are collectable. Extend fruity toys to TV series and computer games

- Health snack: a small package with a card inside that allows access to a specific website, informational portal

- Fast-food company with a focus on healthy food, providing customisable food

10.3.2 Need area-specific PSS ideas (short list)

The ideas were ranked using the simplified PSS sustainability screen included in the Guideline published as Annex I to this book. The best two were then detailed further. These two were the S'Cool Box and the Fun Food PSS. Essentially, both are variations of the second of the six ideas. They are described below.

S'Cool Box

The S'Cool Box contains everything a child needs to eat during a day at school. It's healthy, it's educational, it's personal, it's multicultural but most of all it's cool. A food provider together with a food research institute balances the food health. The S'Cool Box is a designed box that enhances logistics, which are difficult because of the individual needs; it is also an educational instrument in itself. All made to look cool, because the most important person who finally decides whether to use it is the child! (See also Figs. 10.9 and 10.10.)

The S'Cool Box **value network** consists of various actors. The food supplier, equipment supplier, distributor and programme manager (who defines the contents of the box) work at the supply side, with a food health centre as adviser to the programme manager. Parents pay for the box, and schools act as facilitators making time and space available. Supporting agents are the media ('health programmes for kids'), government (who put healthy food on the education agenda and sponsor the concept) and health insurers, who co-finance this preventive approach.

The **technological architecture** follows straightforwardly from the roles of the actors in the value network, whereas the **revenue model** consists of contributions by parents, government and insurance companies, which need to be divided between the actors in the supply chain of the S'Cool Box.

New food PSS: Fun Food

The Fun Food concept provides healthy food to children in school. Supermarkets deliver the Fun Food products directly to the schools, but also have these products on a special display within the supermarket. The Fun Food brand is therefore easily recognisable. The Fun Food is healthy, well balanced and fun for the specific consumer. To achieve this, Fun Food Inc. makes food prescriptions, based on a health advisory institute. The fun part of the food is very important to make the children in school want to eat it (refer to Figs. 10.11 and 10.12).

FIGURE 10.9 Advertisement poster for S'Cool Box

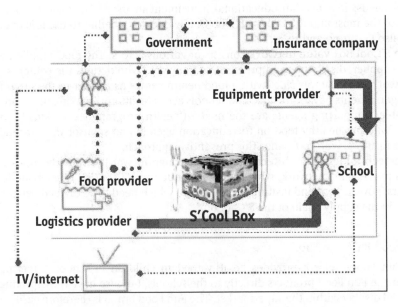

FIGURE 10.10 System map for S'Cool Box

FIGURE 10.11 Advertisement poster for Fun Food

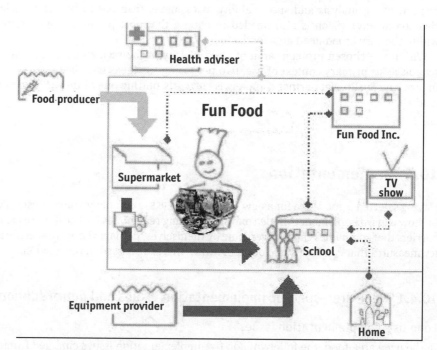

FIGURE 10.12 System map for Fun Food

There are also Fun Food events. The school kids learn to cook and learn about food origin and health in a playful and competitive way. There are even Fun Food finals where the best child cooks from different schools compete against each other. Television plays an important role. Weekly, the new recipes are discussed and tips and backgrounds on the different ingredients are given. This information can be used in the school competition. Of course, the television station covers the Fun Food finals and turns it into a national event (see Fig. 10.12).

The Fun Food **value network** has several actors. The food supplier and the supermarket work on the supply side, with the health adviser coming in for added value and support. The school and the kids act on the demand side, with the TV company coming in as an extra client who at the same time adds value as well. Fun Food Inc. acts as overall co-ordinator.

The Fun Food **technological architecture** consists of a web-ordering and information service, nutritional expertise, special (innovative) food, TV show facilities and rights, a Fun Food corner in shops and the packaging. The **revenue model** consists of profit on food sold, profit on commercials in the TV shows, higher margins through certification, licensing and governmental support for healthier children.

10.3.3 Conclusions

The work on idea generation on food PSS within SusProNet made clear that it is not very efficient to try to find ideas without a clear demarcation of the problem area. Within a well-defined problem area, it is much easier to find promising ideas for PSS. In this respect, trend analysis and sustainability assessments turn out to be not sufficient: clear (company) vision is also needed to choose the most promising opportunities within the very broad need area food.

Within the chosen problem area of child obesity, to be tackled by a PSS that has schools as its primary context of use, two promising PSS ideas have been worked out. In fact, one SusProNet partner company is currently putting one of these ideas on the market.

10.4 Implementation

Having selected a good idea for a new (sustainable) PSS, a company's next question will be 'how can we implement this idea and start making real money?' Also, if there are any barriers that companies cannot overcome by themselves, perhaps there are specific policy measures that can take some of them away. This is discussed in this section.

10.4.1 Need area-specific implementation issues and policy support

Long list of implementation issues

In the need area food, the following top five implementation issues emerged from the desk research discussed in Sections 10.1 and 10.2:

- System complexity

- Unconventional revenue model

- New and unknown risks

- Limited span of control (because of other partners)

- For SPSS: it is still difficult to make money out of social and ecological sustainability

Additionally, the following questions arose: (1) how to improve a PSS when it is running, how make it a self-learning system and how to attract new investors; and (2) how to 'measure' social and ecological sustainability, also accounting for rebound effects.

The elaboration of the PSS ideas S'Cool Box and Fun Food in SusProNet's Food group led to a variety of case-specific implementation issues:

Company internal characteristics

- There is a clear need for proof that sufficient schools are interested

- An existing market player (caterer) is required

- Diversity of experience is necessary (health, nutrition, education)

Value chain issues

- Can insurance companies in fact lower premiums for participating parents?

Partnership and co-operation

- School staff are busy; is it enough compensation that kids are more alert and attentive?

- Parents should be involved to provide feedback and share the experience with kids

Feasibility

- There should be sufficient space at school to eat

- One central player should be responsible for quality

- Trials are essential to build up experience

- Eating food at schools will generate a mess: who will clean this up?

Institutional and societal constraints

- Does society accept philanthropic behaviour from 'non-ethical' multinationals?

- Does society accept branding in schools?

- Are catering companies allowed to operate in schools?

- Company must have HACCP (Hazard Analysis and Critical Control Point) certification (= 'ISO 9000' for food)

- Company must also have certification for the dietary and educational components

- Depending on the EU state there may be a difference between VAT on food ingredients (low) and meals (high), which puts the system at a disadvantage

- Subsidies are necessary to overcome start-up costs and determine feasibility

- Volunteers can be useful in reducing direct costs, but certain ethnic groups may be excluded (e.g. certain Muslim women not allowed outside without company)

Need area-specific implementation issues

On closer inspection, it becomes clear that most of the implementation issues just mentioned are not specific for the need area food. As such, they demand no specific food policy measures. In fact many of them are not specific for PSS either, but are merely part of product or service business as usual. But not all: here are the issues that are clearly need area-specific.

- Hygiene is typical for the need area. It has been noticed before that all links in the food chain except the end consumer have to adhere to strict standards for food safety and hygiene. So, if food preparation, for instance, moves from private to corporate hands, the issue inevitably comes in

- Marketing is by itself not an issue (refer to S'Cool Box: with the right marketing, it turns out to be quite possible to get children to eat healthy snacks), but it may be unacceptable to have too much company interference with the day-to-day, personal activity of eating. Likewise, people will not accept too much meddling of insurance companies in their lives regardless of any reduction in insurance premiums

- VAT rates may be disadvantageous for PSS: food components usually fall into the lowest category, but many services are taxed at a higher rate

- Integration of food and food equipment into one PSS is made more complex because of the mismatch in product life-spans and the resulting differences in companies producing these items

- Eating healthy food now yields a financial benefit only later, because health problems and the ensuing reductions in productivity and costs of healthcare are postponed. So, the business model is 'open in time'. Furthermore, the actors investing in healthy food today are likely to be different from those who reap the benefits: the business model is 'open in space' as well

Policy support

The answer to the question of whether PSS development in the need area food contributes to sustainability is yes, provided that changes at a system level are taken into account. Policy measures must therefore be based on this fact to be effective in the first place.

Changes at a system level are necessary. Innovations on a product level and on a PSS level often end in a deadlock because the incentives of the actors that are involved (the seller, the producer, the client, etc.) are not in line with each other and with sustainability. More elements in the system need to change, besides the introduction of a new product or PSS in order to reach sustainability. Other elements are, for example, the business models (the selling formula, the relationships, contracts and agreements between different actors, etc.), the infrastructure, law and regulation (Luiten *et al.* 2003).

This corresponds to the suggestion of Tukker (2004), who states that PSS on a functional level have the highest potential. PSS on a functional level are also called result-oriented PSS. Instead of offering a product, the provider closely looks at the needs of the client and offers what he or she really needs (so instead of 'a sandwich' he offers you daily a healthy lunch with exactly the variety you wish). The provider promises a result closer to a final client need and hence has more degrees of freedom to design a low-impact delivery system. However, as Tukker states, there are also three problems with this PSS. First, the provider promises a result, which puts all liabilities at his or her side. Second, the provider might not be in control of all elements needed to provide the result. Third, often abstract functional demands are difficult to translate into concrete (quality performance) indicators, essential for sound agreements between provider and user.

The most important thing is that business drivers should be taken as the starting point. To put it simply: often the driver for a salesperson is to sell as many products as possible. That is what he or she is accountable for. This mechanism is in general not in line with sustainability. And, when a service is added to this product in order to add to the fulfilment of the customer but the seller is still accountable for selling as many products as possible, it is obvious that the intended impact of adding the service (namely contributing to sustainability) will not be reached.

A company that earns money on the energy savings of a customer is a potentially inherently sustainable business model. The company sells advice and practical help for the customer to save energy. And from every euro that this customer saves, the company gets—for instance—20%. Now the incentive of this company is to get the customer to save as much energy as possible! The interests of the company (economic gains), the customer (money savings) and the environment (energy saving) are all in line. Therefore, new business models need to be developed in order to get the incentives and interests of all the actors (including sustainability) in line. That is the only way economic, ecological and social sustainability can be reached.

Both the companies and the government have a shared responsibility to develop these models and implement them. The government can play a crucial role. It can:

● Initiate pilot cases in the need area food

● Act as a client in a business case. Think of introducing a flexible and sustainable food delivery system for the employees of the government

- Be one of the financers for specific cases. Think of new business models for organic food (that will reach a broader audience than the people that now know of the Odin vegetable bags), new business models for food supply in school, for elderly care, in hospitals, etc.

- Carry the risks for investors and give a guarantee that investors will get their investments back if an initiative fails

- Set the right conditions for an inherently sustainable business model, such as tax reduction possibilities

- Through education, raise public awareness about healthy eating

- Stimulate organic agriculture and foster fair trade

One interesting point has to be made about the actors that are involved in a pilot case (or in a real-life situation). At SusProNet WS3, one of the companies that were present at WS1 and WS2 could not be present. Before WS3 this company (a provider of frozen meals) played a crucial role in one of the ideas that were generated within the group. In WS3 this concept was redeveloped and, after the transformation, the cool chain had disappeared from the concept. Because the actor was not there the importance of what he or she represented was not there either. Such effects should be taken into account by careful selection of the actors in a partnership. For example, when it is stated (e.g. by the government) that a new solution should be socially sustainable, then specific social representatives should be part of the actors that are involved in the development of the new business. Otherwise, social sustainability aspects will always play a minor role.

10.4.2 Conclusions

The difficulty of successfully implementing the projected food delivery solutions S'Cool Box and Fun Food lies primarily in the system complexity, the facts that these types of PSS have an unconventional revenue model (e.g. this can include selling TV rights), that there are new and unknown risks, and that each partner has a limited span of control. With these implementation issues, it is no surprise that such types of PSS should be designed to be much simpler, with one actor clearly in control. It seems safe to assume that this step will show its value in general: keep it simple and put one actor in charge of your (food) PSS.

Need area-specific implementation issues include hygiene, marketing ethics, VAT differences between food components and service components and the mismatch between product life-spans of food and food equipment. Also, the real benefits of healthy eating today emerge only later, in the form of improved productivity and lower costs of healthcare.

The main roles of the government in overcoming these barriers are to stimulate pilot projects of sustainable food PSS and to help in bearing financial risks. Also, the government has a clear role in education about the benefits of healthy food. Finally, it should stimulate organic agriculture and foster fair trade.

10.5 Conclusions

PSS for the need area food is by itself a very large theme. Therefore, this chapter has zoomed in on the smaller, more manageable subject of 'food delivery solutions for children at school'. This enabled a hands-on study of the implementation issues of such types of PSS. At the same time, however, it essentially prevents us now from drawing evidence-based conclusions that have validity over the total need area beyond those conclusions that are more or less obvious. With this caveat, here are the conclusions on the subject of PSS in the need area food.

10.5.1 PSS in the need area: opportunities and threats

Drivers and opportunities

Innovation is a key factor in the need area food, with new products and services being developed continuously. Usually, these innovations are aimed at one link in the food chain, although they affect more than one link. There is a clear potential for multi-link innovations, and PSS can be considered to be a part of such innovations. Many PSS already exist in the need area, but these are predominantly aimed at the food and its delivery itself; PSS related to equipment are less numerous.

The main consumer trends behind PSS development are an ageing population, health and obesity, double-income and single-adult families and multi-activity lifestyle, leading to a continually shrinking available amount of time for food preparation. Important economic trends include the upcoming changes in agricultural subsidies in the EU and a trend designated as 'global–local': a breakaway from globalisation through, for example, the rise of regional speciality foods. Convenience food is the main technological trend, with IT as the enabling technology behind most innovations in the need area. A final issue dominating food today is the declining confidence in food safety.

This chapter showed that the main business opportunities for food PSS exist when the PSS offered one of the following types of customer added value (see Table 10.5):

- Save customer time and/or effort

- Enable customers to do something that they normally can't do

- Give 'agenda freedom': give customers not just what they want, but also when and where they want

- Give customers access to new experiences (entertainment, mood)

- Provide customers with information about products and/or build up trust in them

- Get customer result without hassle, doubt or fears ('no worries')

Potential business ideas

As indicated, due to the breadth of the area food the analysis of business ideas was focused on the social sustainability issue of obesity among children. PSS ideas were put forward to solve this issue in the context of use of schools. The main problems that were identified with such PSS were the facts that healthy eating is considered to be boring, not tasty enough and 'uncool', plus the lack of feedback (kids do not know what they are eating), compounded by the power of marketing that stimulates unhealthy consumption patterns. The idea generation led to six PSS concepts:

- 'The future You': make it a game to get the energy balance right

- 'Customised full day full package': package for different eating moments

- 'My-health.com': trace what you eat by taking photographs with a mobile phone and upload them to a diet centre for feedback

- Pokemon Fruit toys: Eat 'm all! Provide fresh fruit to school kids packaged in toys that are collectable. Extend fruity toys to TV series and computer games

- Health snack: a small package with a card inside that allows access to a specific website, informational portal

- Fast-food company with a focus on healthy food, providing customisable food

Variations of the second and sixth concept were further elaborated as S'Cool Box and the Fun Food PSS. The S'Cool Box contains everything a child needs to eat during a day at school. It's healthy, it's educational, it's personal, it's multicultural but most of all it's cool. A food provider together with a food research institute balances the food health. The Fun Food concept provides healthy food to children in school. Supermarkets deliver the Fun Food products directly to the schools, but also have these products on a special display within the supermarket. The Fun Food brand is therefore easily recognisable. Fun Food is healthy, well balanced and fun for the specific consumer. To achieve this, Fun Food Inc. makes the food 'prescriptions', based on a health advisory institute.

Development pitfalls and threats

A number of generic PSS development pitfalls were identified, such as system complexity, an unconventional revenue model, new and unknown risks, and a limited span of control (because of other partners).The advice here is: keep it simple, don't try to solve everything at once, and put one actor in the partnership firmly in charge. One of the ensuing questions is how to manage intellectual property rights (IPR) in partnerships: for example, by prior agreements, patenting crucial technological components or relying on brand names. Need area-specific problems include (see Table 10.5):

- Hygiene. All links in the food chain except the end consumer have to adhere to strict standards for food safety and hygiene. So, if food preparation, for instance, moves from private to corporate hands, the issue inevitably comes in

- Privacy. It may be unacceptable to have too much company interference with the day-to-day, personal activity of eating. Likewise, people will not accept too much meddling of insurance companies in their lives regardless of any reduction in insurance premiums

- VAT. Rates may be disadvantageous for PSS; food components usually fall into the lowest category, but many services are taxed at a higher rate

- Time gaps. Eating healthy food now yields a financial benefit only later, because health problems and the ensuing reductions in productivity and costs of healthcare are postponed. So, the business model is 'open in time'. Furthermore, the actors investing in healthy food today are likely to be different from those who reap the benefits: the business model is 'open in space' as well

10.5.2 PSS and sustainability

Regarding ecological and social sustainability, the following eight demands can be made from food PSS:

- Reduce food losses

- Reduce energy use

- Reduce agricultural impact (e.g. by use of organically grown food)

- Reduce transport intensity

- Reduce over-consumption and improve consumer health

- Increase stakeholder involvement and transparency ('know what you are eating')

- Stimulate fair trade

- Increase global food security

Today, few PSS exist that are aimed at increasing sustainability, but there are clear opportunities for sustainable PSS:

- Combining **health**, **health food** and **over-consumption**

- Combining **food safety** and **tracking and tracing**

- Combining **smaller households**, IT and **food losses**

At the same time, it is clear that PSS will not automatically lead to sustainability. A meal from fresh, locally supplied ingredients, prepared at home, usually scores better on energy use, transport intensity and maybe agricultural impact than a centrally pre-prepared meal that is distributed via a cooling or freezing chain.

10.5.3 Policy support

Governments have clear responsibilities in stimulating SPSS: for instance, by granting start-up subsidies that enable low-risk pilot projects and learning-by-doing. This can be done at a local level. At an intermediate level, governments should strive towards goals that are difficult to realise by partnerships of (commercial) actors, such as fighting obesity by promoting healthy food. At a global level, governments should foster fair trade and ensure world food security. These sustainability demands are clearly beyond the reach of PSS partnerships.

Value element	Drivers and opportunities	Development pitfalls and threats
User value/market risk		
Tangible value	Save customer time and effort	
Intangible value	Provide new experiences, agenda freedom, trust	• Healthy eating now gives health benefits only later, consumers may not connect this • PSS must not interfere with the privacy of eating
System costs/financial risk		
Tangible operational costs	Reduce system costs	• PSS are often high-VAT; unprocessed food low-VAT • Food processing by consumers needs no compliance with hygiene regulation, processing by PSS suppliers does
Risk premium, financing and transaction costs		• Firms investing in healthy food PSS now will not be the beneficiaries of reduced healthcare costs later
Other benefits/capability risk		
Improved power position		
Defence to substitutes/loyalty		
High speed of innovation		
Investment in PSS development		
Other transition costs		

TABLE 10.5 Review of need area-specific PSS opportunities and threats

11
Need area 5: households

An Vercalsteren and Theo Geerken

VITO, Belgium

11.1 Product-service systems for need area households: an overview

The main aim of this section is to generate a 'bird's eye' view of the state of the art of PSS in the sector households. Based on a generic description of households (composition, evolution) and an overview of household expenditures, the most important needs within households are identified. This section also describes a few examples of existing PSS in the sector.

11.1.1 Description of the sector

In most European countries, the number of households has increased over the past decade while the rise in population has been far lower. As a result, the average size of households has decreased. Another aspect is the increase in the share of single and single-parent households in the total number of private households. The population structure in Europe (see Table 11.1) is clearly in motion, which results in changes in consumption patterns. The supply side must now be targeted more at smaller households, on the one hand because of the falling share of large families, on the other hand because of the rising share of single and single-parent households. A second social phenomenon is the growing increase in the age of the population. In terms of consumption, these seniors will become a more and more important target group. In conclusion, the slowing increase in population and the increase of the age of the population will be of importance in nearly all European countries. Figures for the last five years show an average population growth in Europe of 1% (exceptions are Turkey, 8%, and Ireland, 6%) (van Gool and Vermee 2002).

	Population (x 1,000)	Number of households (x 1,000)	Average number of persons per household	Share of specific age categories	
				0–25 y	+65 y
Belgium	10,239	4,237	2.4	31.1	16.6
Denmark	5,349	2,444	2.2	29.9	14.8
Germany	82,163	37,795	2.2	26.8	16.2
France	59,000	24,400	2.4	31.9	–
United Kingdom	57,171	24,310	2.4	33.3	15.3
Hungary	10,043	3,869	2.6	32.8	19.6
Ireland	3,800	1,259	3.0	41.0	11.4
Italy	57,680	20,684	2.8	29.3	16.4
The Netherlands	15,864	6,828	2.3	28.9	13.6
Norway	4,500	2,000	2.3	32.0	15.0
Austria	8,091	3,192	2.5	28.8	15.5
Portugal			3.0	35.5	14.1

TABLE 11.1 Demographic-economic country profile

Before starting to think about possibilities for PSS in households, the sector needs to be well defined. The diversity of the sector requires a selection of specific needs. In order to cover the major part of the sector with a limited number of needs, the most important (read: financial-economic) needs are selected based on patterns of consumer spending. These consumer spending figures are based on the national index figures for consumption prices and are, for some European countries, clustered in Table 11.2 (Jasch and Hrauda 2000). The index figure is an economic indicator that reflects objectively the evolution of prices in time, for a bundle of products and services that are bought by households, and that is representative for their consumption patterns.

Looking at the household expenditures the following needs are the most important:

- Living (house, water, electricity, heating)
- Food
- Transport and communication
- Entertainment
- Clothing/(home) furnishing

In general, households spend most of their money on housing, water, electricity and heating (fuels). This is understandable, since most of these are basic needs. There are,

Structure of household expenditures (%)	Austria	Germany	The Netherlands	Spain	Belgium
Food and beverage	16.92	21.0	14.39	25.25	22.75
Clothing	10.77	7.7	5.98	8.04	8.20
Living	21.92	25.5	27.17	23.53	14.66
Home furnishing	8.49	8.4	7.07	6.2	8.61
Health	5.79	6.1	4.18	4.60	3.96
Transport and communication	17.47	17.1	11.19	12.99	16.03
Entertainment	12.66	9.8	10.68	7.89	11.72
Hotels, pubs and restaurants	4.01	–	5.99	8.61	6.62
Other goods and services	1.97	4.4	13.35	2.88	7.45

TABLE 11.2 **Structure of household expenditures based on index figures**

however, country-specific differences. The index figures show that Belgian households spend less on living than on food. This is partly a consequence of the typical housing sector in Belgium. The majority of the Belgian population owns a house, while this is not the case in many other countries such as the Netherlands. Also, the costs of electricity depend among other things on the market (free market or not).

11.1.2 Approaches to PSS development

Little is known about the approach and development of the present PSS in households. However, it is evident that most of the PSS that are currently in use in households originated from after-sales services (consumer electronics), shared (public) distribution networks (cable TV, telephone, electricity, water), hiring/leasing (house renting) and contracting people (cleaning service, gardener).

Traditionally a whole range of services already exist in households; however, for the most part, these services are not initiated based on PSS thinking in general but more on practical existing market needs and opportunities.

- After-sales services. These kinds of service started as a necessity because of the low reliability of products. Later on, this developed as a kind of extra service to the consumer

- Shared (public) distribution networks. These systems originated from the public responsibility to develop a common infrastructure and to let individual users pay for the shared use of this infrastructure (high investment level). Nowadays, these services are more and more liberalised and are subject to a free market

- Hiring/leasing. This originated from flexibility wishes of the consumers, lack of investment money and social responsibility from authorities and companies

- Contracting people. The most important reason for the initiation of these services is the lack of time or professionalism of people

Two questions can be posed on the basis of these PSS examples: (i) Is the PSS (product and service component) developed by one company/organisation? (ii) Does the product have to be adjusted to the service or can a standard product be used? After-sales services and shared distribution networks are in most cases developed by one organisation; for hiring and leasing of movable goods more parties are involved. In this case a standard product is used and a service is added to the product. In the case of hiring and leasing non-movable goods (e.g. apartments), the product and service are usually the responsibility of the same organisation. When contracting people, standard products are used.

11.1.3 Some examples of current PSS

Looking at the need area households, one can distinguish already-existing PSS. However, in most cases these services are not acknowledged by consumers as being PSS. Some of the most widely known examples are the following:

- Distribution of drinking water to households through public distribution system

- Electricity networks for transporting electricity to houses

- Telephone service (cable distribution system)

- Cable television (cable distribution system)

- Public transport/taxi

- Dry-cleaning services

- Cleaning services: many households (especially with both partners working outside the home) hire cleaners or window cleaning services

- Libraries

- Video renting

- Video-on-demand

Furthermore, more recently, some developments that are specifically aimed at offering services instead of existing products are appearing on the market such as car-sharing systems and voice mail services offered by telecom operators. These examples of PSS are more or less 'established', which means they have become largely accepted by consumers. Many other examples of PSS exist that are still subject to a niche market. A summary (Goedkoop *et al.* 1999) is given in Table 11.3.

Looking at all the examples of PSS in households, one can distinguish two types of 'tangible product' within the product content: movable and immovable property. The biggest difference between these two is the way these 'products' are brought to consumers: for movable property the 'product' is transported to consumers (either by the consumer or the service provider) (e.g. libraries, car sharing), while in the case of immovable property consumers must transfer themselves to the 'product' (e.g. house renting, time-sharing of holiday accommodation).

11.1.4 Conclusions

Historically many (product-)services already exist for households, with different origins and different paths of introduction. However, households do not acknowledge these as being PSS since these do not replace a former product and have always been offered as services (cable TV, telephone, etc.). The situation with regard to the acceptance of PSS is different when replacing an existing product by a service. Since households attach great importance to the status of owning products, they will not exchange a product with a service that easily. At present, acceptance of PSS is increasing in relation to transportation (car sharing) and ICT-related services (video on demand, telephone services such as voicemail). Only recently have 'product' producers or new service providers begun to try to sell more service-oriented PSS.

Looking at household expenditures, a wide diversity of needs exist within households. Therefore there is a need to clearly define the needs that will be focused on in this study. Based on the list of the most important needs of households, a limited number of needs for further research in the field of PSS were selected. The need for food is partly covered in the need area 'food', so food will not be the subject of this need area. Furthermore, it was decided to focus the research on the 'needs that are consumed within or nearby the house', which implies that transport is also excluded from the research area. The household needs that will be focused on are:

- Living (heating, water, electricity)
- Entertainment
- Communication
- Clothing and furnishing

11.2 Analysis: PSS opportunities in the need area households

This section presents an analysis of trends and developments in households. The main aim is to develop foresight for the sector, including the main sustainability boundary conditions, and on this basis to identify broad areas where PSS development could be a useful business model. The analysis presented in this section is focused on the needs selected earlier: living (heating, water, electricity), entertainment, communication, clothing and furnishing.

PSS	Description	Company(ies)
Support in using medicines	On demand the Organon company (Oss, NL) gives doctors, pharmacies and users of medicines personal information about the use of their products	Organon (NL)
Subscription shaving lotion	Together with Beiersdorff (Nivea), Philips Domestic Appliances introduced a shaving machine for those who were used to wet shaving: Cool skin. The consumer can subscribe to the sachets that need to be used within the machine	Philips Domestic Appliances and Beiersdorff (D)
Return-guarantee plastic garden furniture	Hartman is a producer of plastic garden furniture. 'Hartman Groengarantie' is a return guarantee for their own furniture so these can be re-used in new furniture	Hartman Groep nv (NL)
Customised computer configuration	Dell Computers sells computer configurations completely according to all requirements the customers have (e.g. after an email dialogue)	Dell
Voicemail service	AT&T, producer of professional digital telephone exchange equipment, provides a voicemail service in its equipment, so answering machines are no longer needed	AT&T, Alcatel, others
Gas advice	The Gasunie, supplier of gas in the Netherlands, advises all users about technical aspects of using gas and possibilities for savings in its use	NV Nederlandse Gasunie (NL), other gas suppliers in other countries
Online shopping service	To serve a bigger market Albert Heijn supermarket in the Netherlands created an online shopping service. Customers can order their products by a tele- or internet service. The products are delivered to wherever the customer wants	Albert Heijn (NL), Delhaize (B), others
Electrolux launderette	Shops for washing clothes are a very well known and old product/service combination. Consumers save on the investment of a washing machine, use the probably better method of washing in the shop. The energy use and waste are centralised and diminished in this way. In the case of the Electrolux washing machines the design is optimised for use in launderettes and for being more (eco-)efficient	Electrolux

TABLE 11.3 PSS in households (continued opposite)

PSS	Description	Company(ies)
Cash converters	The Cash Converter concept is based on a cradle-to-cradle philosophy. Once rejected, even defect products can be brought to a Cash Converter shop. In return people receive a small amount of money. The products are repaired, or will be used as 'part-supplier' for other products	Cash Converter
Economy measurement in washing machines	Miele developed a washing machine that notifies the user of the energy that is being used at the moment and advises the user about times when it is possible to do the washing more economically	Miele
Take it @ Leave it	Because many people are so busy working, they don't have time to have their shoes repaired, etc. For these people the service Shop 'Take it @ Leave it' was introduced in train stations. People can order the service or product they want in the morning, go to work, and collect it when they return home	Take it @ Leave it
Nappy service	To reduce the enormous waste problem a company developed a service with old-fashioned, durable cotton nappies. The service takes care of the nappy washing. The clean ones are delivered while the dirty ones are taken away	Culotte luierservice (NL)
Sony 'Exchange and refurbishment' programme	The repair of a defect product can be very complex and time-consuming. That's why it is more efficient to centralise this kind of service. To do something about the long repair time, Sony has a stock of already repaired, second-hand products that can be returned immediately	Sony
Magazine collection and distribution	Many people want to read a lot of magazines. It would be very expensive for them to subscribe to all magazines they are interested in. That's why some companies set up a sharing system of magazines, so that they are bought only once for more readers	De Leesmap (NL)

TABLE 11.3 (from previous page; continued over)

PSS	Description	Company(ies)
Time sharing of luxury leisure-time goods	A group of people can buy luxury leisure time goods such as yachts, second houses, etc. Together they share costs and time of use. The goods are owned by a foundation created by the investors	TMC
Refurbishing of furniture	To be able to refurbish their products after some years of use, furniture producer Gelderland designs its products in such a way as to fit to these demands	Gelderland, Culemborg, Leolux
Sustainable maintenance programme social housing foundation	Social housing corporations have programmes for sustainable housing maintenance. The buildings are not only refurbished in a durable way, they are upgraded as well: for example, with a solar water heater	
Leasing of baby goods	In some places it is possible to lease goods that are needed for babies only. When they are grown up, the lease contract is ended	
Kodak recycle camera	Kodak produces cameras with a film included. The whole camera with film is returned to have the film developed and printed. The cameras can be re-used with new films	Eastman Kodak
Suit in the right size	Buying a new suit can take a lot of time. So Bijenkorf set up a service especially for those customers whose time is at a premium. Once they have communicated their specific wishes and size, Bijenkorf searches the collection and makes a selection. In this way shopping can be done more efficiently	De Bijenkorf (NL)
Library at home	Some people are not able to visit a public library: for example, old or ill people and the disabled. So an extra service is added. With this service library books are delivered at home	Public library Delft (NL)
Sofa lease	As the next step after refurbishment, Leolux is examining the possibilities of sofa lease. Together with a retailer and a consultant it has already been discovered that environmental performance can be drastically improved when customers bring back their sofa after a few years for refurbishment, or for re-use of parts	Leolux, Eijerkamp (NL)

TABLE 11.3 (from previous page; continued opposite)

PSS	Description	Company(ies)
Mobile phone set	Libertel offer a GSM device for free (or at reduced price) to any new client, with a montly subscription fee and bill	Libertel, other providers
Leasing of art	Leasing of works of art instead of buying them	Art Capital Group, Art Lease, Art Rent&Lease
Books	Print-on-demand books customised to user specifications (larger text, etc.), e-books	IBM, others
Carpets	Evergreen lease takes care of all maintenance requirements for user, instead of user buying the carpet	Interface
Leasing of washing machines	Leasing of washing machines and dryers to students	Splash lease (NL)
Photos	Digital processing and storing of photos instead of traditional photographs	Several producers
Renting of toys	A variety of toys, games, etc. can be borrowed in a way that is very similar to a public library	Eureka toy library (South Africa)
Co-housing communities	Combines traditional living with the advantages of community living. Every household has a private residence designed to be self-sufficient (kitchen, etc.), but also shares some facilities (such as dining room, children's playroom, etc.)	Co-housing communities (Denmark)
Homeservices	Inventory of homeservices in European countries (www.sustainable-homeservices.com)	

TABLE 11.3 (from previous page)

11.2.1 Trends and developments relevant for PSS development

By analysing trends in households, opportunities and threats can be foreseen. This section will describe general social trends that will have an impact on households and specific trends with regard to households. The described trends form a mixture of extrapolated trends that are based on the current situation and trends that are forecasted by experts.

General trends and developments

There are general (more global) trends that influence household expenditures (globalisation and technological innovations). Furthermore, some sector-specific trends are evident that also act as driving forces for household consumption patterns.

The most important general trend is the increasing globalisation/liberalisation of the economy. We are moving towards a single unified global system involving a reduction of barriers to allow cross-border flows. Economic liberalisation leads to a process of deregulation that increases mobility of people, capital and information. Another general trend is the economic transition from a traditional manufacturing-based economy to a knowledge-intensive and ICT-based economy. One can raise questions over whether this trend leads to either democratisation or elite formation.

Current and projected household consumption patterns are influenced by a number of specific driving forces. Rising per capita income, demographics (more working women, more single-person households, larger retirement population) and accompanying changes in lifestyles have led to more individualised buying patterns, a shift towards more processed and packaged products, higher levels of appliance ownership, and a wider use of services and recreation. Higher incomes have also increased the number of objects that households purchase. Technology, institutions and infrastructure also play an important role in influencing household consumption and behaviour. They create the prevailing conditions faced by households in their everyday life, and can either expand or constrain the product options available to them.

Trends that influence household consumption patterns can be divided into three categories: social, economic and technological. The most important trends and developments have been gathered from many literature sources and are presented in Table 11.4 (Cooper and Mayers 2000; Littig 2000; OECD 2002).

A discussion with the participants in this need area resulted in a list of the most important trends in households:

● **Smaller households**. As described earlier, an obvious demographic development in Europe is the smaller household size. This is because there are fewer children per family and more single-parent and single-person households

● **More individual lifestyles**. Because of the smaller households and the individualisation in society one person has to perform many different tasks, whereas only a few decades ago each person in a family had to perform only one type of task. This is one of the reasons why people look for convenience products and services

● **Time is scarce/24-hour economy**. More men and women have joined the labour force, which implies that people have less free time available. Most of them want to use this free time as efficiently as possible and expect suppliers (shops, supermarkets, etc.) to be available any time of day. The 24-hour economy provides freedom on the one hand and requires planning on the other

● **Globalisation versus nationalism**. The economy shows a trend towards more globalisation (in industry, but also in households one can find more influences from, for example, the Far East). In opposition to this trend and maybe in reaction to the unification of Europe, people attach more importance to national aspects such as language, culture and employment

● **Ageing population**. Ageing of the population is occurring everywhere in Europe. On the planet, there were 500 million people aged 60+ in 1990. This number rose to 600 million in 2000 and is expected to further increase to 1,100 million in 2020. Europe will be the continent with the highest proportion of seniors: 45% in 2020 and 50% as from 2040. This trend will lead to an increasing demand for convenience, safety and care. These seniors also have significant purchasing power

- **Availability of everything.** Since all kinds of product are widely available, households can find an appropriate product for every specific need. This leads to an overload of products within households

- **ICT is omnipresent.** Communication is ubiquitous: mobile phone, mail, internet, video communication. On the one hand this is a positive evolution since people communicate more easily and are better informed. On the other hand, there are negative effects such as less personal contact

- **Decreasing basic technical knowledge of households.** Since many appliances in households have become 'smarter' and suppliers offer more after-sales services, households have less knowledge about the appliances (error analysis and use)

Key driving factors for any consumption are: economic growth, growing per capita disposable income, lifestyle, cultural tastes for diversity and spontaneity, demographic trend towards more single-person households, participation of women in labour force and longer and healthier lifestyles.

Sustainability demands

Sustainability as considered in this report is judged on three issues: environmental consequences, economic viability and social implications.

Looking at the environmental impacts of households, an OECD study resulted in the following conclusions. Per capita private consumption has increased steadily over the last two decades, and is expected to continue to follow GDP growth in the period to 2020. Product and technological innovations have reduced the energy and material intensity of many consumer goods. However, the increasing volume of goods used and discarded, and the structure of consumer demand have outweighed many of these gains.

Households as a group are not the largest contributor to most environmental pressures, but their impact is significant and will intensify over the next two decades (OECD 2002):

- **Energy.** Energy use in OECD countries grew by 36% from 1973 to 1998 and is expected to grow by another 35% by 2020

- **Transport.** Total motor vehicle stock in OECD countries (550 million vehicles, of which 75% are personal cars) will grow by 32% by 2020, motor vehicle kilometres will increase by 40%

- **Waste.** Municipal waste will grow by 43% from 1995 to 2020 (to 700 million tonnes per year). In 1997, OECD households generated on average 67% of municipal waste loads. Recycling rates have increased. There is a trend towards increased packaging waste (pre-packaged food and food service packaging)

Social trends at the household level	Needs that are influenced
Increasingly sedentary lifestyles	● Food ● Communication ● Clothing ● Entertainment ● Healthcare ● Living ● Furnishing
Evolutions in working conditions: decrease in working hours, rise in number of days of paid leave	● Entertainment ● Healthcare ● Living
Increase of women in labour force → more dual-income households	● Clothing ● Entertainment
Splintering of day: individualisation of time budget within households	● Food ● Living
Longer life expectancy and reduction of retirement age → ageing population	● Food ● Entertainment ● Healthcare ● Living
Products that used to be luxury are now seen as necessities (washing machine, dishwasher, microwave, television)	● Energy use ● Entertainment ● Living (energy use, water use) ● Furnishing
More smaller and single-person households	● Food ● Living (energy use, water use)
Urbanisation: more people move from rural to urban areas	● Living
Decreased differences between gender: increasing number of households run by men and increasing number of women on labour market	● Food
Change of information needs and communication habits	● Communication
Quality time	● Entertainment
More critical consumers (especially 50+)	● Living
Time is scarce: everything must go quicker, faster, on-demand/24 h economy	● Living ● Communication ● Entertainment ● Food
Zap culture → more confusion	● Living
'Big brother' effect—demystification of people	● Living
Importance of safety	● Living
Cocooning	● Furnishing

TABLE 11.4 Social, economic and technological trends at household level
(continued opposite)

Nationalism versus globalisation	• Living • Food
Economical trends at the household level	**Needs that are influenced**
Increase in wealth and income (more buying power [50+])	• Food • Entertainment • Clothing • Healthcare • Furnishing
More home floor space per capita	• Living (energy use for heating)
Higher levels of cooling and heating comfort	• Living (energy use)
Higher expenditure on products per person	
Growth of the tertiary sector (services)	• Communication
Labour becomes less space- and time-dependent	• Food • Communication • Clothing • Living
Availability of everything	• Entertainment • Living • Communication
Production shift towards Far East (developing world)	
Technological trends at the household level	**Needs that are influenced**
More efficient heating technology and building materials (insulation)	• Living (energy use for heating)
Availability of diverse electronic appliances	• Living (energy use, water use) • Entertainment • Communication
Availability of water and energy-efficient appliances	• Living (energy use, water use)
Wireless application and communication	• Entertainment • Communication
Function integration	• Entertainment • Communication
Trend towards digital technology	• Entertainment • Communication
Miniaturisation of technology	• Entertainment • Communication
Increased use of renewable and biodegradable products	
Technology for information on demand (music, books)/ICT is omnipresent	• Entertainment • Communication
Improvement in sorting and recycling technologies	

TABLE 11.4 (from previous page)

- **Water**. Households are relatively small consumers of water and household demand for freshwater has stabilised or declined in nine OECD countries. In many other countries population growth and expanded water use have outweighed the effect of water-saving technology and behaviour. Most water is used for bathing and showering, toilet flushing and washing clothes. The average household consumption in Europe amounts to 150 litre/day (33% personal hygiene, 33% clothes and dishwashing, 20–30% toilet and 5% drinking water)

- **Food**. OECD households are consuming more meat, vegetables, fish, processed, imported and organic food than in the past. The most significant environmental impacts from food occur early in the production chain, but households influence these impacts through their choice of diet and demand for food-related services. Households also directly affect the environment through food-related energy consumption and waste generation

Studies have been performed that look at the main environmental impact per household function. Depending on the methodology (top-down or bottom-up) and the system boundaries, different studies come to somewhat different conclusions. The basic conclusions, however, do not differ.

A study conducted by Institut Wallon and VITO (Nemry *et al.* 2002) shows that in Belgium building occupancy is responsible for over 40% of all energy consumed and transportation for 34% (expressed as percentage contribution to the total pressure related to Belgian consumption). Looking at the consumption of raw materials, 67% of the total consumption can be attributed to the building structure and 17% to the transport sector. Other significant areas are ICT and packaging. Table 11.5 lists all categories and impact indicators that were taken into account for this study and indicates the important contributors.[1]

The same key areas are indicated in a European study; again building occupancy and transportation are the most important (Labouze *et al.* 2003). The conclusions of this study are summarised in Table 11.6.

A Dutch study (Nijdam and Wilting 2003) comes to somewhat different conclusions (because a top-down approach is applied [i/o (input–output) analysis]). In particular the areas of food and leisure contribute the most to environmental impact, as a percentage contribution to the total pressure related to Dutch consumption. The relatively low importance of transport is due to the fact that transportation is divided into

---

1   For each study the following are given:
- The total number of impact indicators considered in the study and in this analysis (limited to common environmental themes over all studies and for which clear, interpretable results were available)
- An overview of the environmental indicators considered in the study
- The total number of commodity categories at sub-levels considered in the study
- An overview of the commodity categories that are considered important for at least one of the environmental themes (the non-relevant categories are not listed). The '80-percentile' share refers to the highest commodity categories that altogether cover 80% of the total for that impact category. The number of times a commodity category is listed in the 80-percentile shares is mentioned in Table 11.5. The same is done for the '60-percentile' shares and '40-percentile' shares

Institut Wallon/VITO			
Total number of impact indicators considered: 12			
Impact indicators considered: primary energy, total material intensity, material intensity metals, material intensity minerals, material intensity organic, material intensity synthetic, water use, resource depletion, acidification, smog, greenhouse gases, waste			
Total number of sub-level commodity categories: 16			
Categories sub-level IW/VITO study	**%80**	**%60**	**%40**
Passenger transport	9	6	6
Total building structure	8	6	3
Industrial packaging	7	5	3
Household packaging	4	1	1
Interior climate	4	2	2
Office machines	3	2	1
Furniture	1	0	0
Hot water	1	0	0
Lighting	1	0	0
Healthcare and detergents	1	0	0
Sanitary equipment	1	1	1
Number of commodity categories relevant in at least one impact category	**11**	**7**	**7**

TABLE 11.5 Results of study by Institut Wallon/VITO

Source: Nemry *et al.* 2002

'labour', 'leisure' and 'food (shopping)', whereas the other studies use 'transport' as a functional area in itself. The researchers have no clear explanation for the low importance of the housing sector. Table 11.7 summarises the conclusions of this study.

Replacing products by product-service systems will not automatically lead to environmental benefits: for example, leasing can be beneficial but also detrimental because it might allow consumers to use products that were otherwise unaffordable. Through services where the property rights of the products are not transferred to the consumer there will be more responsibility on the part of the service provider for the use and end-of-life phase and this might lead to better environmental and economic perspectives through better life-cycle management.

Other need area-specific issues

One of the main challenges to adopting PSS is the cultural shift necessary for consumers and industry to prefer having a need met by a service rather than owning a physical product. Around the world, lifestyles promote personal material accumulation, individualism and luxurious comfort.

BIO/02			
Total number of impact indicators considered: 8			
Indicators considered: primary energy, resource depletion, acidification, eutrophication, smog, greenhouse gases, municipal and industrial waste, inert waste			
Total number of sub-level commodity categories: 34			
Categories sub-level BIO/02 study	**%80**	**%60**	**%40**
Personal cars	5	5	5
Goods transport (road, rail, water)	5	5	2
Building structure (commercial and residential)	4	3	0
Textile—apparel	4	1	0
Vegetables	4	2	2
Space heating—domestic	4	3	3
EEE—domestic appliances	3	2	1
Animal food	3	1	1
Packaging—household	2	1	1
Municipal waste	2	0	0
Cleaning agents	2	1	0
Water heating—domestic	2	0	0
Space heating—commercial	2	2	0
Appliances and lighting—commercial	2	0	0
Civil work (roads and other infrastructures)	1	1	1
Packaging—industrial	1	0	0
Furniture	1	0	0
Gardening	1	1	1
Paper products	1	1	0
Public transport (road, rail, water, air)	1	0	0
Building occupancy—commercial	1	1	0
Appliances and lighting—domestic	1	0	0
Building occupancy—domestic	1	1	1
Number of commodity categories relevant in at least one impact category	**23**	**16**	**10**

TABLE 11.6 Results of the study by BIO Intelligence/02

Source: Labouze *et al.* 2003

RIVM			
Total number of impact indicators considered: 6			
Indicators considered: land use, water use, acidification, eutrophication, smog, climate			
Total number of sub-level commodity categories: 65			
Categories sub-level RIVM study	**%80**	**%60**	**%40**
Clothes	6	4	0
Non-animal food	6	6	6
Animal food	6	6	4
Restaurant, pub, etc.	6	2	0
Holidays	6	4	0
Electricity	5	1	0
Rent and mortgage	5	3	1
Furniture	4	0	0
Commuting, private transport	3	3	2
Kitchen appliances, etc.	3	0	0
Newspapers, periodicals, books	3	0	0
TV, radio ('brown goods'/electronics)	3	0	0
Garden, excluding furniture	3	0	0
Heating	3	2	1
Shoes	2	0	0
Accessories	2	0	0
Energy, hot water	2	0	0
Shelter—other	2	0	0
Personal care—water	1	0	0
Personal care—other	1	0	0
Alcoholic beverages	1	0	0
Smoking	1	0	0
Painting and paper	1	0	0
Flowers and plants (in house)	1	0	0
Taxes	1	0	0
Number of commodity categories relevant in at least one impact category	**25**	**12**	**6**

TABLE 11.7 Results of the study by RIVM

Source: Nijdam and Wilting 2003

Some trends that are discussed above initiate/initiated additional needs for households, which can be/are fulfilled by PSS. One example is the consumer's desire to get information and entertainment on demand. This has already resulted in the development and market acceptance of systems such as video-on-demand, which is made available through the development of set-top boxes. The informatics and electronics sector have anticipated this desire.

Businesses that consider offering PSS for households should start by analysing the needs and desires of these households and try to anticipate what is coming. The above-mentioned trends give an indication of this. There are some distinct trends that trigger households (and thus businesses) to pay for services rather than for products.

- Studies show that consumers are willing to pay for convenience, such as the ability to view programmes at convenient times, but they appear to be less willing to pay for higher quality

- Some products, such as personal computers, are rather expensive and depreciate in value over a very short period. Consequently, consumers might be attracted to the ability to purchase the service supplied by the PC if they feel they have not had good value from purchasing products in the past

- PSS related to leasing/renting of products are of interest to the consumer for financial reasons (it does not pay to buy the product) or the fact that a product is infrequently used (garden equipment, do-it-yourself equipment) or fashionable (carpets, furniture, art)

- PSS have a greater chance of being acknowledged as an alternative to private purchase and ownership if they promise additional utility. This may be a social event, a special type of product (washing machine) or an increase in efficiency of a tool (home and garden)

- The ageing population offers perspectives for new PSS, since these persons have quite a lot of leisure time, greater health needs and disposable income

- The increase of single-person households also shows some PSS opportunities. For example, these people will not easily buy products such as washing machines (little time and little space). They might prefer to use laundry services (note the difference between launderettes and laundry services: the former require the users to wash the laundry themselves, while laundry services collect the laundry and do the washing)

Conclusions

Considering the PSS already in use in households, the trends that are discussed above and the demands of the consumers (product ownership), one can conclude that services that replace pure products are not likely to be accepted in the household sector. Few examples that demonstrate the opposite were found and the examples that do exist have a low market penetration. In most cases, one has to start with a product and think of new possibilities for expanding the features, adding value, the consumer's ease and financial 'benefits' for consumers.

From a sustainability perspective, a focus on building occupancy with specific attention to energy consumption is recommended. Transportation is also a point of interest from the sustainability side; however, this falls outside the scope of this study.

In general PSS have an increasing sustainability potential from product-oriented to use- to result-oriented PSS. Products that have a high impact in the production phase are attractive for sharing. Pooling systems reduce the sustainability impact even more because they have a positive influence on the production and use phase.

Based on a literature study combined with the results of PSS projects, it seems that the most important criteria for consumers to accept services are cost saving, added value, time saving and convenience (to some extent).

PSS are likely to be a success when:

- The PSS results in a substantially decreased level of organisation (from a customer point of view): the service has to increase the user's comfort level, has to be offered near to or at home and preferably different services should be provided by one contact address

- It fulfils a temporary need that makes an own investment less attractive (hiring a holiday house or tent for some weeks is very popular)

- The price level is 'reasonable': studies show that consumers want to pay for care and supervision, for repairs, supply and disposal. The willingness to pay is much less for consulting and information services and leisure-time activities

Businesses thinking about PSS concepts for households should keep in mind the following rules of thumb. Success factors (with regard to the demand side) include:

- Focus on densely populated regions: in big cities and holiday centres there is the best infrastructure and population density to be economically successful

- Focus on expensive products: people will be more willing to pay for a service offering all (and more of) the product's functions if the product requires a large investment cost

- Focus on infrequently used products

- Focus on rapidly evolving products

- Focus on products that require a large storage space

- Focus on products with location-bounded use: e.g. skiing equipment

- Focus on products that require professional maintenance and professional advice/instructions for use

- Offer user flexibility (changing needs): a good example in this context is households with growing children, whose needs change quite frequently

- Offer added value/additional services: PSS offering more quality, flexibility, better price and comfort

- Offer clear savings in cost: PSS systems such as collective use have more potential to succeed wherever they create clear financial advantages

- Advertise and communicate the service intensively: users rarely search actively for services

Failure factors (with regard to the demand side) include:

- Consumer ownership (status, personal relation): the powerful influence of the trend towards individualism and ownership over the past 20 years encourages ownership. Also, the personal relation with the product (e.g. car) favours possession

- Preference for permanent accessibility: people often like the ability to use a product whenever they want

- Organisational complications of services: no permanent accessibility, more and recurring travel time, reservation requirement

Failure factors (with regard to the supply side) include:

- A critical mass is needed in order to successfully (in commercial terms) bring a PSS into the market. Since one should start on a small level (which is economically inefficient), a company often has difficulties in keeping the PSS on the market

- For some products, a change towards PSS cannot be instigated in one country alone due to the global nature of the sector (for example, the electronics industry)

- Services need more organisation and also involve more financial risks for the provider. Selling is easier and quicker money!

- Government policy currently favours the traditional 'transactional economy' model of high economic growth through individual acquisition and ownership

In general one can conclude that new PSS development needs leadership and vision, should satisfy a real need, should offer added value and needs must be based on by stakeholder analysis and communication of benefits.

11.2.2 Conclusions

The literature study showed that PSS concepts that focus on services that create extra possibilities for existing products are the most likely to succeed in the sector of households.

The opportunity areas identified on the basis of the trends, sustainability aspects and success and failure factors are outlined on a graph (Fig. 11.1) to reflect their product or service content and their (expected) influence on sustainability. The sustainability impact of the PSS opportunities on the graph is mainly based on the environmental impact. The assessment of the sustainability impact happened purely intuitively without making use of a sustainability tool.

Opportunity areas for PSS

1. High-quality reading file
2. Mobile house modules (central energy and water)
3. Integration of more appliances in one (e.g. video/DVD/television)
4. No maintenance garden
5. 'Water your plants' system
6. Rent your furniture
7. Video-on-demand
8. Integration of products and services
9. Solar vacuum cleaner
10. Customise your consumer product
11. Home control at a distance
12. Domotica (intelligent homes) for the elderly, safety, children
13. Garden lease
14. Gardening service (design, planting and maintenance)
15. Car maintenance subscription
16. Time management training for households
17. Personalised electronics in smart module
18. Local print shop with expert
19. Smart products
20. Global mobility service (car, train, etc.)
21. Video conference with remote family
22. Reliable porter service
23. Socialising service for 60+
24. ICT support via internet
25. Automatic filling refrigerator and cabinets
26. Maintenance for computers/virus help
27. Product life-cycle care
28. Annual hygienic carpet cleaning
29. Household management + implementation
30. Monitored cleaning

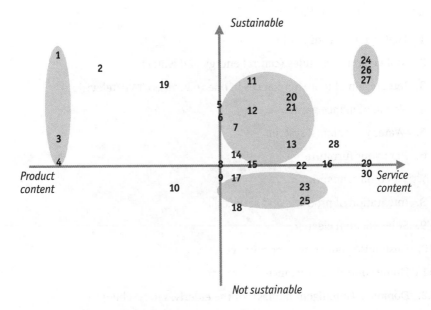

FIGURE 11.1 Opportunity areas for PSS in households

Some of the opportunity areas mentioned above are rather concrete 'PSS cases'. When summarising the broad areas of opportunity, the following areas can be derived:

- Garden maintenance
- Smart products
- House cleaning
- Distant home control
- Socialising services
- Leasing of art/culture/furniture and culture-on-demand
- Household management
- Integration of different appliances

11.3 Idea generation and selection

This section gives an analysis of PSS ideas for households. It is largely based on the work of the companies and facilitators of the household group during SusProNet's 2nd workshop in September 2003.

11.3.1 Need area-specific PSS ideas (long list)

Idea generation

The idea generation stage with the companies was based on two scenarios: one from a purely business perspective (profit-driven scenario) and the other was inspired by sustainability goals (planet-/people-driven scenario). As a starting point, the eight most promising opportunity areas are taken. Finally, ideas were constructed by combining several similar or complementary ideas. The ideas, organised according to the opportunity areas, are shown below:

Area: garden maintenance

- Shared tool shop with neighbours: share garden tools and exchange advice, compost, re-usable waste in a local community

- Fashion garden: flexible and modular build-up garden which requires low maintenance

Area: household management

- Household adviser/consultant: consultant that advises households on possible savings in energy consumption (heating), water consumption, etc.

- Laundry service 'en route': contracted by employees, when going to the office/workplace one can drop off dirty clothes somewhere along the route and pick them up when going home

- Energy feedback meter (water, safety, domotica, etc.): installation of meter in households, according to the principle 'to measure is to know'

Area: smart products

- Smart (safety) agent: installation of devices that check specific aspects in the house such as switching off lights, switching off coffee machine, closing the doors.

- Health meter: personal health meter to monitor specific health problems such as heart problems, asthma or high blood pressure

Area: house cleaning

- Dust source prevention/removal and advice: professional advice on the main sources of dust and consultation on preventative measures and time to do the cleaning activities

Area: distant home control

- Collective energy management: tool to spread peaks in energy consumption, collective purchase of fuel which can give savings in cost

Area: socialising services

- Community eco-teams: socialising service
- Concierge for neighbourhood: offer of standard set of services such as temporary childcare, possibly combined with garden tooling
- Fitness for the elderly: socialising service
- Mixing generations/human capacities: combination of, for example, childcare and care for elderly or lunch for schools and lunch for elderly

Area: integration of different appliances

- Infotainment (ultimate domotica system): integration of different senses in one system such as seeing (vision, lighting), hearing (music), smelling (odours) and feeling (HVAC [heating, ventilation and air conditioning])
- Mobile heating system

Area: leasing of art/culture/. . .

- Rent a whole interior
- Customised 2D images (LCD projector): e.g. changing artwork

Idea selection

Out of the 17 ideas that were generated, the most promising were selected. This selection was based on a simple ranking tool that is designed to score ideas on the three sustainability aspects: profit (economic), planet (environmental) and people (social) (ranking from –1 = worse than existing to 0 = status quo to +1 = better than existing situation). We refer to the sustainability screening tool included as Annex 1 to this book.

For the detailed scoring process we refer to the report underlying this chapter (Vercalsteren and Geerken 2004). Based on the average scores four ideas were selected for further elaboration:

- Household adviser/consultant: energy feedback meter
- Garden tool shed
- Health meter
- Infotainment

11.3.2 Need area-specific PSS ideas (short list)

The shortlisted ideas are discussed in more detail below.

Household adviser/consultant—energy feedback meter
Household adviser/consultant—energy feedback meter (see Fig. 11.2) (expands to water, safety, domotica system) consults on possible savings. The social aspect of this idea is rated poorly, while the environmental and economic aspect is assessed to be quite good.

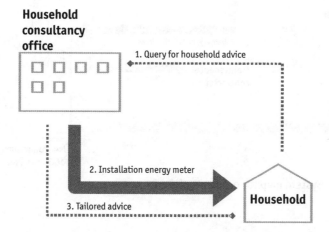

FIGURE 11.2 System map for household adviser/consultant—energy feedback meter

Garden toolshed
Shared garden tools in a local community, exchange of advice, compost, re-usable waste and so on (see Fig. 11.3). This idea scored equally on all three sustainability aspects.

Health meter
Modular mobile heart monitoring device with real-time expert feedback (heartbeat, asthma, CO_2/CO in big cities, UV meter, blood pressure) (see Fig. 11.4). This scored very highly on the profit aspect since people are willing to pay for medical assistance; the other two aspects were rated very low.

Infotainment
The ultimate 'domotica' system (integration of many different appliances). This idea is considered to have no (positive or negative) influence on the environmental aspect of sustainability.

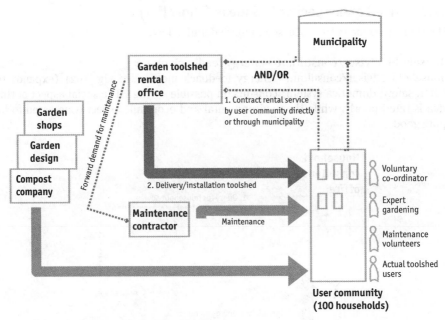

FIGURE 11.3 System map for garden toolshed

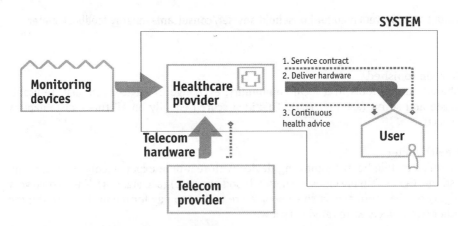

FIGURE 11.4 System map for health meter

11.3.3 Conclusions

The ideas based on the 'profit' perspective come from the possibilities offered by new technologies or from the perceived needs of people that are not fulfilled satisfactorily today. The ideas based on the 'people and planet' perspective are mainly focused on social needs and on greater dematerialisation by increased efficiency, better re-usability and smarter systems. However, there is a considerable amount of overlap between ideas from the 'profit' perspective only and those from the 'people and planet' perspective only. For instance, the many ideas related to domotica do exist in both perspectives and can offer benefits for both. Thinking of profitable ideas also means thinking of market acceptance and that means fulfilment of the real needs of people.

11.4 Implementation

Once specific ideas are selected for further elaboration, actions have to be taken to realise these ideas. During this implementation stage difficulties may arise related to company internal issues, marketing issues and others. In this section the implementation phase is discussed with a focus on need area-specific implementation issues.

11.4.1 Need area-specific implementation challenges and policy support

When elaborating the four PSS ideas defined above, issues that complicate the smooth implementation of the PSS become clear. These implementation issues have been grouped into issues that are related to the company itself, the value chain, partnership and co-operation, technical feasibility and institutions.

Company internal issues

- Limited organisational capacity

- No or limited PSS culture in company or partners (e.g. healthcare experts must adopt a new working style when working with health meters)

- Perceived threat of current business volume (rental and selling), either for lead company or for partners

- Cost per fee

- Limited in-house knowledge and/or experience about PSS

- No availability of mass sales channels

- Requirement of 24-hour service

- Requirement of mass customised service orientation

- End consumers (households) attach importance to their privacy

- Difficulties in guaranteeing continuity (e.g. garden toolshed, which relies on volunteers)

Value chain issues

- Hourly personnel rate increases when adding service component
- Revenue model: who pays for non-use period of rental equipment or for investment costs for end-user equipment, recovery of unavoidable costs, copyright issues?
- Limited experience in lead company with attracting consumer clients
- Offer in products and services is too limited to provide choice to clients
- The product in question is a low-cost issue for consumers (e.g. energy)
- Customers need solutions, not only tools
- Lead company has no direct access and communication with consumers
- Difficulty in offering continuous added value (value declines over time)

Partnership and co-operation issues

- Need for co-operation with the municipality (e.g. garden toolshed for offering free space)
- Risk of becoming the competitor of present customers
- How to deal with issues of confidentiality

Technical feasibility issues

- Service providers must acquire knowledge (which is presently available in the lead company) in difficult and complex subjects (e.g. energy management)
- Labour cost for installing equipment at consumers' homes is relatively high
- Need for technical compatibility

Institutional issues

- Agreement on liability for damage of rental equipment
- Differences between countries in, for example, selection of power generation
- Piracy issues when, for example, the internet is used for the service

A number of these implementation issues are PSS-specific. First, in order to avoid conflict situations between the partners/stakeholders, clear agreements on the business and **revenue model** have to be made. If no common interests exist or can be created among the stakeholders, the chance of commercial success is low. A roundtable (with all relevant partners) can be a means to look for common interests. This should be done as soon as possible and if necessary the agreements can be adjusted over the course of the project when the outline of costs is complete. One should aim to create win–win solutions for all stakeholders, clearly dividing the costs and the benefits of the PSS. The risks should be spread among the partners. Besides the revenue model for the stakeholders on the supply side, the cost (price) for the demand side must also be clearly defined, according to the consumers' needs (e.g. pay for savings, pay-per-use, investments for consumers [equipment]).

Second, **organisational bottlenecks** often relate to a lack of *experience* or *knowledge* on the service component of the PSS, on joining partnerships and so on. A company that is focused on products does not know how to start thinking about and elaborating PSS. One possible means to gain experience in this field is the participation in pilot and demonstration projects. This allows a company to acquire specific experience and knowledge without running too many (financial) risks and enables a screening of the market for the interest in PSS. Another important rule in this context is to keep it simple. A product-oriented company should not concentrate on a complex PSS to start with, but preferably add some service component to existing products. This also allows the company's customers to gradually accept more service-oriented activities.

An organisational bottleneck is often also the *paradigm shift* that is needed to accept that products are partly or entirely replaced by services. This shift in mentality or culture from possession of products to using services that offer the same function is not only of importance for consumers but also for companies. Consumers' attitudes can possibly be influenced by governmental initiatives; however, the cumbersome structure of many companies is difficult to change in a short period.

Third, one of the major obstacles is related to the **value proposition**: how can consumers be persuaded to 'buy' the PSS? The sustainability aspect of PSS is not enough to draw consumers over the line; the PSS must give value for money and should be a logical step forward for the consumer. It could be an advantage if the company offered the benefit for the consumer directly with the acquisition of the PSS in order to convince more consumers.

Fourth, the **regional culture** of consumers is also a point of attention. Between countries big differences exist in the residential sector: in some countries the majority of households rent a house, while in other countries it is common practice to own a house; in some regions apartments are the main means of housing while other regions are focused on single-family dwellings. Another aspect is the regional differences in sharing public goods: in some regions shared goods are taken care of, in others these goods are neglected. The regional culture can be a point of attention for PSS suppliers. One should gear the PSS to the regional culture (regional customisation).

To conclude, it is possible to identify implementation issues that are *specific for the need area households*:

- 24/7 service. A PSS tends to be more successful if the service is offered 24 hours a day and 7 days a week, which demands great flexibility from the PSS provider

- Many consumers (1 million versus 10). The PSS provider does not have a select group of potential clients, thus he or she cannot take into account the requirements of all clients

- Risks in predicting consumer behaviour. Households tend to have a non-predictable behaviour when it concerns ownership of goods. This relates also to the following issue

- Consumers show more emotional behaviour

- Privacy of consumers ('big brother'). Some services imply occasional visits or even continuous follow-up of households, which could be an invasion of privacy

- Legal contracts are too complex for households (small print)

- Consumers are further away in the chain (retail in between). This complicates the organisational component of the PSS, since the service is ideally offered to the consumer via the retailer

- Revenue model is more complicated. More stakeholders are involved because of the longer chain between service provider and consumer, among other things

- In the case of service components using labour: competition with no wages (no labour costs counted when doing it yourself) or lower wages ('tax evasion'/'black economy' in some countries). In B2B the wages for outsourcing labour are much more similar than in B2C

A number of implementation issues can be partly solved by policy initiatives. Governments can initiate and fund demonstration projects in order to disseminate the PSS concept among companies and consumers and to allow companies to acquire knowledge and experience in the field, which is an incentive for further activities in this area. Government money can help companies and consumers over a threshold in the starting period, but eventually the business should be able to live on its own. Besides funding, policy can also include measures to influence the consumer's attitude such as increased taxes for the purchase of certain products (which will stimulate renting/leasing) or positive stimuli such as discounts when households participate in specific service-like activities. An important policy initiative would be to integrate the PSS thinking into current educational programmes: for example, in design, engineering and business schools, as well as training programmes for professionals.

11.4.2 Conclusions

Unlike the case in Chapter 9 on offices, in the need area households PSS-specific and even need area-specific implementation issues can be identified in PSS development. This all has to do with the fact that one deals here with a (private) consumer market. Privacy, 24/7 access to the PSS, unpredictable and relatively emotional behaviour, and the need to keep things (revenue models, technical architecture) simple are all issues to take into account. In addition, a PSS often has to compete with 'do-it-yourself' or even 'black economy' labour wages when households organise product maintenance or servicing themselves. Delivering PSS to households successfully is certainly not impossible, as the examples in Table 11.3 show. But it seems safe to say that a thorough analysis of the implementation issues and potential failure factors is here probably even more important than usual in new business development.

Apart from traditional government support via subsidies for pilot projects, and internalising environmental costs in products, PSS development can be stimulated in an unconventional way as well. The HomeServices project in particular showed that, in order to reach households, alternative (or non-business) PSS providers can play an important role (Halme *et al.* 2004). A significant potential for PSS for households is offered by the housing organisations that reach many potential users. Often an NGO (or local community) fits better as the leader of a PSS than a traditional company because sustainability is not the core business of (most) companies.

11.5 Conclusion

Based on the most important household expenditure areas, this chapter focused on a limited number of needs for further research in the field of PSS. It was decided to focus the research on the 'needs that are consumed within or nearby the house', which implies that transport is not part of this research area. With food already covered in Chapter 10, the household needs that were covered are:

- Living (heating, water, electricity)
- Entertainment
- Communication
- Clothing and furnishing

11.5.1 PSS in the need area: opportunities and threats

Drivers and opportunities

Historically, many services already exist in households, with different origins and different paths of introduction. However, households do not acknowledge these as being PSS since these do not replace a former product and have always been offered as services (such as cable TV, telephone). In a similar vein, some trends may lead to enhancement of the market for household PSS, particularly in the field of information and entertainment on demand. This has already resulted in the development and market acceptance of systems such as video-on-demand, which is made available through the development of set-top boxes.

However, the sense of product ownership and privacy in households is strong. It is unlikely that in households services replacing pure products will be accepted. The few examples that do exist have a low market penetration. Based on a literature study combined with the results of PSS projects, it seems that the most important criteria for consumers to accept services are cost saving, added value, time saving and convenience (to some extent). Hence, in most cases, one has to start with a product and think of new possibilities for expanding the features, adding value, the consumer's ease and financial 'benefits' for consumers.

In this sector the presence of housing organisations in the country is also an important factor in influencing the provision and use of services. Other drivers for providing PSS are the service use culture of the country, the regulatory framework (indirect labour costs, labour market regulations) and the building design.

Potential business ideas

The analysis of trends, sustainability aspects and success and failure factors led to the following broad areas of opportunity for PSS in households:

- Leasing of art/culture/furniture and culture-on-demand
- Integration of different appliances
- Garden maintenance
- House cleaning
- Distant home control
- Personalised consumer products/electronics
- Household management
- Socialising services
- Smart products

The following specific ideas were identified as most promising for further elaboration:

- **Garden toolshed**: shared garden tools in a local community, exchange of advice, compost, re-usable waste, etc.

- **Household advisor/consultant—energy feedback meter** (expand to water, safety, domotica system): consult on possible savings

- **Health meter**: modular mobile heart monitoring device with real-time expert feedback (heartbeat, asthma, CO_2/CO in big cities, UV meter, blood pressure)

- **Infotainment**: ultimate domotica system (integration of different appliances)

Development pitfalls and threats

A number of generic development pitfalls in PSS have already been mentioned in this chapter (such as the higher complexity of the value network and the revenue model). However, there are also a number of household-specific implementation issues. These can be ascribed to the business-to-consumer character of this need area, which creates a completely different situation from a business-to-business area and include (see Table 11.8):

- 24/7 service. A PSS tends to be more successful if the service is offered 24 hours a day and 7 days a week, which demands great flexibility from the PSS provider

- Volume of production. A high volume needs many individual households as customers, and tailoring the offer to individual customer needs becomes relatively difficult

- Risks in predicting consumer behaviour. Households tend to show unpredictable behaviour when it concerns ownership of goods. This relates also to the following issue

- Privacy of consumers ('big brother'). Some services imply occasional visits or even continuous follow-up of households, which could be an invasion of privacy

- Legal contracts are too complex for households (small print)

- In the case of service components using labour: competition with no wages (no labour costs counted when doing it yourself) or lower wages ('tax evasion'/'black economy' in some countries). In B2B the wages for outsourcing labour are much more similar than in B2C

11.5.2 PSS and sustainability

Studies have shown that housing (materials and occupancy), food and transport are the most important household functions contributing to environmental impact. Other significant areas are ICT and packaging (which is normally part of, for example, food and ICT).

Replacing products by product-service systems will not automatically lead to environmental benefits. For instance, leasing can be beneficial but also detrimental because it might allow consumers to use products that were otherwise unaffordable. Through services where the property rights of the products are not transferred to the consumer there will be more responsibility on the part of the service provider for the use and end-of-life phase and this might lead to better environmental and economic perspectives through better life-cycle management.

11.5.3 Policy support

Policy can influence the implementation of PSS on the supply side and on the consumer side. A number of implementation issues that hamper companies in offering PSS can be partly solved by policy initiatives. Governments can initiate and fund demonstration projects in order to disseminate the PSS concept among companies and consumers and to allow companies to acquire knowledge and experience in the field, which is an incentive for further activities in this area. Government money can help companies and consumers over a threshold in the starting period, but eventually the business should be able to live on its own. Besides funding, policy can also include measures to influence the consumer's attitude, such as increased taxes for the purchase of certain products (which will stimulate renting/leasing) or positive stimuli such as discounts when households participate in specific service-like activities.

An important policy initiative would be to integrate the PSS thinking into current educational programmes: for example, in design, engineering and business schools, as well as training programmes for professionals.

Value element	Drivers and opportunities	Development pitfalls and threaths
User value/market risk		
Tangible value		
Intangible value	Penetration of ICT in entertainment etc.; see under ICT	● Strong inherent preference of ownership ● High volume needs many individual customers; tailored offerings become more difficult ● Privacy concerns: 'big brother' fear
System costs/financial risk		
Tangible operational costs		● In B2C PSS competes with DIY ('no wages') and low taxes ('black economy') providers ● A 24 hr, 7 day/week service is required but costly
Risk premium, financing and transaction costs		● Predicting consumer behaviour is difficult ● Complicated revenue sharing systems ● More transactions ● Complicated contracting
Other benefits/capability risk		
Improved power position		
Defence to substitutes/loyalty		
High speed of innovation		
Investment in PSS development	Housing organisations can be 'natural' PSS suppliers	
Other transition costs		

TABLE 11.8 Review of need area-specific PSS opportunities and threats

Part V
Reflections and conclusions

12
Towards an integrated approach to PSS design

Ursula Tischner

econcept, Germany

Arnold Tukker

TNO, The Netherlands

In this chapter we want to pull together the lessons learned from the previous chapters, concentrating on the issue of PSS development. We do so in the following steps:

- A discussion of the main differences between business systems selling PSS and regular products (Section 12.1)

- Implications of becoming a more PSS-oriented firm for the most important business functions (Section 12.2)

- The main differences between regular business development and PSS development, and particularly the pitfalls in PSS development (Sections 12.3 and 12.4)

- The implications for PSS development approaches and guidelines (Section 12.5)

12.1 What are the main differences in PSS versus normal business systems?

Most companies today are either focused on product offerings or service offerings on the market. The strategic development and implementation of holistic PSS value propositions and hence also sustainable PSS value propositions need a different approach from that of offering mainly products or mainly services. But what are the specificities of (sustainable) PSS?

12.1.1 Relation of material product and non-material service

The importance/value of material products including infrastructure in the system versus the importance of non-material service is different. From a sustainability viewpoint, one goal is to increase the importance of non-material service and decrease the importance of material products. Solutions using almost no material inputs would be perfect if energy and transportation intensity are also low.

When material products are needed in the system, then it has to be decided: is the design based on already existing products (which one partner in the system produces) or does it need new product design? A decision has to be taken on whether the product has to be designed to meet the service aspects or the service has to be designed to meet the product characteristics. According to this decision, the specifications for product design or service design have to be formulated.

12.1.2 Co-operation and partnership

In a PSS the actors needed to offer the product-service system in a professional way have to be identified, taking into account which core competences the partners have. Then an organisation is needed so that all partners profit in the system and that it is as cost-efficient as possible. Important aspects are how co-operation will work in practice, what information exchange is necessary, which costs will occur for the partners and how the will the revenues be distributed, which contracts have to be made, etc.

12.1.3 Organisation

In a PSS the product life-cycle and the service life-cycle and how they come together have to be organised in an efficient way. This also means that the actors responsible for product development and design and service development and design, and the timing of the production of product and production of service have to be integrated. Other important aspects are how the system can be organised in a highly professional way offering the product-service system as close and convenient as possible to the customer/consumer, and how to avoid transport of material products or people in the system.

12.1.4　Customer/consumer relation

The starting questions for PSS considerations should be which consumer/customer needs shall be fulfilled and how to create as much value as possible for the customer for as little cost as possible. Furthermore, in a PSS that changes the ownership relations in the system it is very important to identify exactly which target group the PSS is aiming at and what kind of ownership ideas and culture this specific target group has. For example:

- How open is a customer to using services instead of or accompanying products?

- How can the product-service system be communicated to the customer?

- What are the benefits for the customers compared with other existing offers?

- Can any inconveniences (e.g. dealing with waste disposal) and risks (e.g. handling hazardous substances) be reduced for the customer by offering a new PSS?

- Can any opportunities be offered for the customers to be involved in the design of the system (e.g. mass customisation)?

All this is done with the goal of reaching a high level of customer/consumer satisfaction and therefore establishing a close and long-term customer relationship through the new PSS.

12.1.5　User interface

In a PSS with a high value in service the user interface is normally dominated by personnel rather than by the material product. Thus it is very important how this user interface is designed, how the staff in contact with the customer are trained and motivated. As services themselves are mainly non-material, the question is how the brand image and the value is communicated, how the point of sale can be designed in a way that expresses the idea and character of the PSS, increases confidence of the customers, and attracts customers to use the system.

Obstacles here can be, for example, that sales people are paid by the number of product sales. Then they will not embrace a service concept, unless the provider offers them other (financial) incentives to sell the PSS instead of products. Often training of sales personnel and retailers is essential.

12.1.6　Financial structure

In a PSS quite often the payback period (return on investment) for a produced product is longer than in a pure product-selling concept: for example, car sharing, leasing, contracting. That means the PSS provider needs to hold the necessary financial resources or have the right financing partners on board to bridge this period. Furthermore, with co-operative arrangement of different companies the revenue distribution in the system has to be clarified and fixed in contracts. The same is true for the tasks and duties that the co-operating partners have: for example, guarantees, or who is responsible in case of an accident.

When shifting from a product sales-oriented concept to a PSS or developing a new PSS from scratch, these specificities have to be explored and taken into account to increase the likelihood of success.

12.2 What are the changes needed in business functions?

When a company wants to take up and use the PSS concept as a business model systematically, the integration of PSS thinking has to be ensured in every department and along the whole development and innovation process, often even involving external actors. Product-service orientation will benefit from multi-functionality and co-operation and requires user/customer-focused innovation and development activities as well as market research. Experience shows that it is very beneficial if the company establishes a PSS steward (person driving the project) or a PSS department, which connects the marketing, research, development, support/service departments and possibly external partners (supplier, customer, retailer), so that development project and information exchange can be carried out successfully. An alternative is to involve an external adviser/consultant, who is experienced in the field. This person can also have the function of process promoter in PSS projects where a consortium of companies is developing the new PSS together. In such projects a 'neutral' entity can facilitate and moderate the process a bit more easily than one of the companies in the consortium.

The following sections show the new roles of different company departments/functions and their tasks in PSS projects, and illustrate the process by using the example of an internet-based music store.

12.2.1 Corporate functions/strategic management

Strategic management has to understand the potential of PSS business ideas (training), encourage the employees to think in a more PSS-oriented way (top-down process), and check in every case whether the suggested PSS projects are beneficial and promising. However, experience shows that the benefits of a PSS project do not necessarily lie in short-term financial benefits but in a better market position, better customer/consumer relationship, better sustainability of the company and so on. Thus the criteria to decide about a new business idea should include these aspects. In most cases the financial side of the new PSS requires longer-term planning than a pure product sales concept. That has to be acknowledged by strategic management while taking 'go' or 'no go' decisions.

When deciding that the PSS should be developed and implemented, management must be aware that a few accompanying activities are necessary, such as regular PSS training courses for employees and sometimes even customers, or new incentives for retail to sell PSS instead or in addition to products. The fundamental decision of whether a PSS will be realised within the scope of the company or in co-operation with other companies/external partners or as a new start-up also has to be taken by management.

When PSS involves co-operation with external partners it has to be organised so that all partners profit from the system and that the revenue distribution in the system is fair.

A computer software provider decided to set up a new online music download service including the internet site, the software and the MP3 players under its own name and offer this as an additional retail channel for the music industry and independent labels. This was driven by the fact that the customer demand was clearly there but downloads were mainly done illegally.

The price structure was chosen to be competitive with buying real CDs. Every 'album' costs €9.90 but one can also buy single songs for €0.99 each. The gain is disbursed proportionally to the music industry, which pays the musicians, to the infrastructure provider (host) providing the storage and to the online music store.

Sustainability aspects. Production of CDs and booklets, transportation and distribution via real music stores are eliminated as is overproduction and waste. This reduces overall costs and material as well as energy consumption. The whole system is much more flexible and convenient for the users.

Box 12.1 The Internet Music Store

12.2.2 Marketing

The marketing department has to integrate strategic tools such as the SWOT (strengths, weaknesses, opportunities and threats) analysis and system map to analyse the current market situation and take into account possible future developments. The goal is to understand when, where and how PSS can be a promising and sustainable business idea for the company. A shift from 'traditional' market research, based on surveys, warranty returns and service calls, to consumer- and service-oriented marketing is necessary. Competitor-oriented market research or business development based on a benchmarking strategy does not necessarily lead to customer or service orientation.

Then the targets for the PSS projects have to be formulated taking into account sustainability, efficiency and convenience as well as financial aspects. These plans have to be introduced to strategic management.

12.2.3 Product design

The product development and design team should integrate PSS thinking and gain PSS knowledge (training, learning from successful cases) and consult PSS sustainability guidelines, which lead from product orientation to PSS orientation and inclusion of sustainability aspects. They should put the customer/consumer demands in the focus of their development and innovation activities and think in terms of needs and functions

By analysing the market, the marketing department of the company developed the idea of commercialising the so far illegal provision of music files via the internet, because the acceptance of these services was clearly there.

Legislation was about to be established that prohibited peer-to-peer music networks, because the music industry was complaining.

Consumer needs to be tackled were identified as: buy music and listen to music virtually/via the internet. The task was defined as: set up a highly efficient, convenient and attractive online service combined with the necessary software and material device (MP3 player) to listen to the music offline.

This was formulated by marketing/management as the briefing for the product-service development team.

Box 12.2 The Internet Music Store

first, not in terms of products. Depending on the position and power of the product development experts in the company the suggestion to go for PSS solutions can also come from the product developers and designers (bottom-up process). In the course of the development process, product development should search for close co-operation with the service experts and excellent timing of material product development and immaterial service development processes. At specific decision gates in the product-service development process, (life-cycle) cost and potential return on investment have to be calculated for the developed solution as well as the achieved benefits and values for the customers, and a decision has to be made on whether the solution is good enough to be successful on the market.

The product developers of the computer company developed the MP3 player as the material product necessary to complete the service. They made it in close co-operation with the software developers who developed the software, for the MP3 player as well as for the online service. The features on both had to be integrated. The MP3 player can hold over 10,000 songs, and can be attached to headphones, home music systems and car stereo systems.

Box 12.3 The Internet Music Store

12.2.4 Service development

A service development team can be established to co-ordinate the PSS development process, if it does not already exist in the company. In particular, the experts who were involved in customer services should be part of this group. The service team has to transfer the quality of the service through the user interface to the specific target group. As services are mainly intangible, the challenge is to communicate the brand image and value via the user interface, which can also be the personnel dealing with customer contacts. The ultimate goal is to reach customer satisfaction and therefore establish a close customer relationship through the system. The expert(s) responsible for service development have to work closely together with the experts developing the products. Sometimes it can lead to quicker market launch if products can be used in the systems that are already there. If this is not possible, co-ordination between service and product development has to ensure that the products meet the specifications that the service providers need (and vice versa).

The online music store is an application that offers download of customised music choice, administration of the customer's individual music collection, and easy browsing through all titles in the music store. With just one click a song or an album can be purchased and all from the computer at home or elsewhere. Thus it is a very convenient and highly customised way of offering music to customers. The adequate material products (MP3 players) and network requirements (fast internet connections) made this system possible.

Box 12.4 The Internet Music Store

12.2.5 Purchasing/inbound logistics

Value chain management is the task here: find partners and actors to co-operate with. Take into account which core competences the different companies have, which expertise is lacking and which additional competences are needed. Build the right consortium around the new PSS to make it most profitable and successful.

This can be done by the service development team or by the PSS steward or by the purchasing experts (probably involving some training to introduce the PSS concept to them).

For identification of necessary partners and communication of the concept within the consortium of partners the description form of the new PSS as given in Annex 1 can be used.

Successfully developing and launching the online music store needed integration of the music industry and independent labels into the service.

To make the service really accessible for all consumers, different accessories were developed: for example, adapters to access all home stereos in a household or cars. Part of this was done together with other companies, such as a car audio system producer.

Box 12.5 The Internet Music Store

12.2.6 Sales and distribution

The sales or retail departments supported by product/service development and marketing should check how the new PSS has to be offered and priced in order to be more attractive to the customer than just buying a product. When it is launched (maybe in a smaller test market first) retail should check whether the PSS is accepted and how the service could be improved or expanded. Training of retail personnel and external retailers is often necessary and the right incentives should be given to 'sell' the PSS instead of a pure product.

The internet music store is much more comparable to Amazon or other internet retailers than to the normal retail channels for CDs. So for the music industry it is convenient to become part of that new system. The internet host is just the technical enabler of the system. The leader in the project is still the computer/software company, which also gives the system its own brand identity.

Box 12.6 The Internet Music Store

12.2.7 Marketing and communication

Throughout the development process the argument to support the new service should be communicated to the marketing and communication departments so that they can design a communication strategy for the right target group and with the right arguments/style to attract customers to the new PSS. Often PSS are new to customers and different from their normal idea of purchasing and owning a product; this requires careful negotiation in communication campaigns.

The online music store was launched broadly communicating the new possibilities for consumers: services that were impossible before (exclusive tracks or videos, 'recommend to friends' or 'listeners also bought . . .') and for a price that is much cheaper than comparable CDs. Furthermore, it is a legal alternative to illegally downloading music from the internet. By designing the material device and the earphones in a unique and visible way, which differentiates it from all other MP3 players, the product also communicated that its user belongs to the 'new cool crowd' using this specific online service.

Box 12.7 The Internet Music Store

12.3 Where does PSS design differ from normal business development?

One very important step to shift to PSS is to identify (basic) needs of the customers/clients. A basic need for instance would mean 'listening to nice music', but not 'going to a shop to buy a music CD'. So an important question that should be integrated in all market research activities is: what exactly and really do the customers/consumers want from us, what is their real need behind the purchase of a product or a service, and how can we fulfil these needs in a highly efficient, convenient and sustainable way? These kinds of question enable the enterprise to develop a new business strategy or offer, often consisting of a combination of suitable products and services.

When new and promising PSS concepts are developed, there are different strategies in order to become a successful PSS provider:

● Developing a new line of business, which integrates PSS from the beginning (PSS start-up)

● Integrating a service into an existing product line

● Attaching a product to an existing service

Depending on the starting point of the company (product producer/service provider/start-up), the approaches to PSS development are different. Nevertheless, it is (virtually) always necessary to establish, find and involve the complementary expertise: if you start as a product supplier, service expertise is needed and vice versa.

After the initial analysis of the current market and possible PSS opportunities, a PSS development project can be started just as a normal product development project. However, to be successful, the right company departments/experts and partners must be involved and in each phase of the project (idea development, design, implementation) there should be controls to ensure that the initially defined targets can be achieved.

12.4 What are the main pitfalls to deal with and do current methods cover them?

In Chapter 3, Section 3.3 analysed the main attention points in product-service development on the basis of a thorough review of the business literature: the market risk, capability risk and financial risk. The previous sections in this chapter discussed the main characteristics of product-services in comparison with normal business development on the basis of the full findings of this book. The main points of attention in product-service development are not really different from those mentioned in Table 3.3 (the arguments are reproduced in a simpler way as Table 12.1):

1. A rigorous analysis of costs and (tangible and intangible) value created is even more essential than in the case of normal product development, since now

	Drivers	Barriers
Market risk (will customers like it?)	• In saturated, commoditised markets product-services can create extra value and diversification • Market parties focus on core competences and outsource the rest • Consumers try to save time by buying integrated solutions	• It is still an early stage in the industry life-cycle; differentiation can still come from technical product performance • Consumers attribute high intangible value to products • High costs of the new value proposition prevent offering value for money

Capability risk (can we do it?)	• Company leadership endorses
	  – Client-oriented culture, also via incentive systems
	  – Openness to new ideas
	
	• Service-oriented capabilities already available
	
	• Experience in building up new competences and/or leveraging capabilities with new business partners
	
	• Current business partners support and/or have experience with product-service development
	
	• Public support structures and funding for change (e.g. innovation centres for SMEs; business clubs, training centres)
		• Low connection with current unique selling propositions and core competences
		
		• No interest from top management, and/or a product-oriented rather than client-oriented culture
		
		• Current business partners or institutional arrangements in chain oppose change
		
		• New crucial capabilities cannot be developed in-house
		
		• New business partners needed but no suitable are available:
		  – Lack of trust
		  – No complementary size
		  – No quick connection and long mutual learning needed
		  – Network becomes unmanageable
		
		• For result-oriented services: result cannot be specified in operational terms

Financial risk (is it profitable?)	• Customer value/production costs is positive • Builds unique client relationships and hence better customer loyalty* • Direct client information, leading to higher innovation speed • (Sometimes) potential for creating an improved company image	• Liabilities formerly for the user are taken over and the related costs cannot be estimated • Transaction costs, if high (contracting, payment systems, etc.)

* This loyalty can have a negative form, e.g. if a long-term service contract is arranged that 'ties in' the customer so that he or she cannot shop around anymore for a more cost-effective service component

TABLE 12.1 **Drivers and barriers for product-service development**

often difficult-to-control cost categories related to the use phase of a product have to be taken into account

2. Product-service development requires a rigid and thorough client orientation, and opportunities can be found that are relatively incremental (quite closely related to the existing product lines) but also radical ('value innovations' or 'new game' offerings)

3. Owing to the more complex nature of the value proposition and the expanded mix of competences needed to produce it, it has often to be put on the market by a partnership network

4. Analysing to what extent current company assets are suitable to support product-service development is hence crucial

5. In order to become a company that is successful in product-service development, the orientation and culture of most company elements needs to be changed (or, alternatively, this must be organised as a spin-off unit that does not take the burden of existing cultures and procedures with it)

When we compare these findings with the review of methodologies in Chapter 5, we see that most of them do quite well in describing a general gate-stage process for product-service development, including tools for analysing the current situation, developing ideas and overcoming implementation challenges. Yet we may also conclude that the toolbox that existed before SusProNet and some other major EU projects (HiCS, MEPSS, ProSecCo) started, was probably weak on the following points:

1. Analysing company assets. Most methods mention in the analysis stage the word 'SWOT', but do not call for a specific analysis of the strengths and weaknesses of the company's assets, nor its flexibility with regard to innovating or improving them

2. Client orientation. Some of the more sustainability-oriented methods seem to take the *sustainability* problems as a starting point for developing PSS, whereas the success of its implementation ultimately lies in the *client orientation* of the PSS

3. Discerning different levels in product-service development. Some methods still focus very much on improving or expanding the existing product system, leaving radical options largely out of sight. Other methods primarily aim at developing radical innovations, leaving probably many of the more interesting and feasible options for companies untouched

4. Partnering. Most methods hardly mention the issue of partnering as a point of attention in its own right, but list it as one of the 'realisation issues'. As shown particularly in the HiCS project (Manzini *et al.* 2004), this is a topic in its own right. Which activities for 'making' the PSS are relevant, which ones should be outsourced, and how to look for complementary partners is not discussed in detail in most methods

5. Rigorous market, financial and capability checks

6. Culture and structure of the company. This is hardly mentioned as an issue by any of the methods reviewed in Chapter 5, nor is the potential benefit of having the PSS organised as a spin-off or relatively separate entity from the main company

12.5   What does this all imply for PSS development approaches?

The implications of the above are clear: PSS development methods simply should include the aforementioned PSS-specific pitfalls as attention points.

We have produced in Annex 1 a simple PSS development guide that tries to pay specific attention to these pitfalls. The guide has the following characteristics:

● Simple and short. It can be read in 0.5 to 1 hour

● Building on existing methods. We cut and pasted methods developed in other projects, and hence by no means claim it is totally original work

● To be used as a 'light guide' rather than a textbook. Parallel to SusProNet, a variety of projects have been concluded that have produced comprehensive methodological textbooks, notably the MEPSS Handbook (www.mepss.nl) and the HiCS book *Solution Oriented Partnership* (Manzini *et al.* 2004). However, none of these projects produced a 'lightweight' version that tells us 'how to do PSS'

The added value of Annex 1 is hence mainly to provide a quick, accessible insight into how PSS development can be organised. Compared with some relatively simple manuals at national level (e.g. Tukker and van Halen 2003), the advantage is that this Annex includes lessons learned from a broad range of projects and experiences completed in the meantime. Annex 1 is complemented by Annex 2 with an alphabetical overview and description of tools often used in PSS development and that are part of many PSS development methods.

Companies can use these Annexes, particularly Annex 1, to get started with PSS development, and adapt it to their own needs making use of procedures and tools that they already have available in-house, or that they can find elsewhere in the literature. Those interested in more in-depth manuals for PSS development are referred to the results of the aforementioned major PSS methodology development projects (see also the References).

13
Conclusions

Arnold Tukker

TNO, The Netherlands

Ursula Tischner

econcept, Germany

The SusProNet project aimed to analyse the state of the practice and knowledge on product-services. Of particular interest was the question of whether offering product-services rather than products could enhance competitiveness of business, while at the same time being an avenue to (radical) improvements with regard to sustainability.

An odd finding rather soon in the project (and this book) was that the term 'product-services' is not commonly used in business. Nevertheless, we decided to continue using it: the term was central in the EU research programme that supported the production of this book, and in literal terms it covers precisely the subject matter of this book.

Product-services are a specific type of value proposition that a business (network) offers to (or co-produces with) its clients. They can be defined as 'a value proposition that consists of a mix of tangible products and intangible services designed and combined so that they jointly are capable of fulfilling final customer needs'. The terminology from the business literature that comes probably closest to our product-service concept is 'functional sales' (though a bit too narrow) or 'integrated solutions' (which may be a bit too generic). The concept of product-services rests on two pillars:

- Inherently taking the final functionality or satisfaction that the user wants to realise as a starting point of business development (instead of the product fulfilling this functionality)

- Elaborating the (business) system that provides this functionality with a 'greenfield' mind-set (instead of taking existing structures, routines and the position of the own firm therein for granted)

This functional and system approach spans a broad space for innovations, which allow for: (1) radical improvements in the value proposition and the related business model; and (2) searching for radically more sustainable ways of fulfilling human needs.

There are various ways to combine products with services. Each combination results in a specific model of organising and doing business (in terms of the value proposition, the revenue model, the value network and technological architecture). This book discerns:

1. **Product-oriented services.** In this model, product sales still dominate, but extra services are offered that support the use of the product. Sub-categories are:
   - Product-related services
   - Product-related advice and consultancy (i.e. on how to use the product)

2. **Use-oriented services.** In this model, the user buys *access* to the product not the product itself. Sub-categories are:
   - Product lease
   - Product renting and sharing
   - Product pooling
   - Pay-per-unit of use

3. **Result-oriented services.** In this model, the relation with the original product (in principle) is most distant: the provider is paid by its client for the delivery of a specific performance or result. Sub-categories are:
   - Activity management (e.g. outsourcing of catering)
   - Result-oriented services (e.g. providing pest control by promising a farmer a maximum crop loss)

In the next sections the final conclusions of the project are drawn. They focus on:

- The market potential of product-services (particularly in a number of need areas central in SusProNet)

- The sustainability potential of product-services

- How to align sustainability and market potential of PSS

- How to reap the benefits of PSS: an action programme for research, policy and business

13.1 PSS in the market: opportunities and threats

The earlier chapters make clear that a switch from just selling products to a more client-oriented offering of a combination of suitable products and service can create many business advantages. The five need areas covered gave a large number of driving forces and successful examples of PSS. We have no doubt that in other need areas not covered in SusProNet similar success stories can be found. At the same time, there are also barriers and threats to PSS development. We will here review the market opportunities and threats of PSS, making use of:

- The factors determining the competitiveness of PSS, as analysed in Chapter 4

- The experiences per need area, as reflected in Chapters 7–11, complemented with information on some 200 PSS cases from a case database developed in SusProNet

13.1.1 Opportunities and threats per need area

Tables 13.1 and 13.2 review the opportunities and threats with regard to PSS per need area, as discussed in Chapters 7–11. They are aligned with the framework for analysing the competitive advantages and disadvantages of PSS developed in Chapter 4.

The tables show two things. First, they show that the framework from Chapter 4 allows for a fairly complete and useful classification of the opportunities and threats with regard to PSS development. Second, they show that, where there are generic rules of thumb with regard to PSS development valid for more than one sector, they often play out in a specific form in a specific need area.

Table 13.1 shows that innovation of the value proposition by offering a product-service rather than a product can help to:

- Provide superior value for the user since:
  - Tangible efforts and hence costs of the user to operate the product are reduced, and replaced by a much more efficient offering by the provider (e.g. base materials: outsourcing management of chemicals to a chemical management system provider liberates the user from dealing in detail with health and safety regulations in which he or she is not specialised)
  - Intangible value is created (e.g. outsourcing office management to a specialised supplier may improve working conditions)

- Lower the costs in the system since:
  - Products are used more efficiently (product-oriented PSS) or intensively (use-oriented PSS)
  - One actor gets a full overview and responsibility for the total system costs related to fulfilling the final need or satisfaction, so that true cost optimisation becomes possible (result-oriented services, e.g. chemical management services under need area base materials)
  - Activities are distributed in such a way in the system that each actor makes best use of his or her core competences (e.g. outsourcing office work space management by a research organisation to a specialist provider)

- Improve the strategic position of the firm in the value chain, improve its innovation potential, and create defence against substitution since:
  - The company moves (often downstream) to include activities in its offering that have a higher profit margin than traditional manufacturing

(product-oriented, result-oriented and in part use-oriented services; see e.g. in ICT the move to software development by hardware suppliers)

- A more intensive (contractual) relationship with the client is arranged, which leads to higher loyalty, better insight into problems with the current offering, and insight into the true problems the offering has to solve for the client

- In general the speed of innovation is higher, which also improves the dynamic capabilities of a firm (see e.g. under Offices in Table 13.1)

However, it is by no means said that product-services in all cases deliver these attractive bonuses. Table 13.2 shows that in several cases the user value can be lower and/or system costs can be higher than a competing, traditional product system:

- Value for the user can be lower since (particularly in the B2C sector) the sense of ownership, privacy and control can be important

- The system costs may be higher because of issues such as:
  - The PSS has to be produced with higher-priced labour, materials and capital (see e.g. under Households and Food: PSS suppliers in the B2C sector often have to compete with 'do it yourself' or 'black economy' wages for labour)
  - The PSS is usually delivered by a firm network, which gets paid per unit of use or result (use-oriented and product-oriented services) and takes over responsibilities in the use phase (result-oriented services). This may create high transaction costs (mentioned under almost all need areas), costs with regard to pre-financing hardware offered to the client (see under Offices), and create new liabilities (see under Base materials)

Even the speed of innovation related to PSS has its counter-argument. Sometimes focusing on excellence in product manufacturing and design is just the key to uniqueness and hence power in the value network, and then diverting the company focus to a new issue such as PSS development is a recipe to lose rather than win the innovation battle.

And, on top of this, development of a PSS may come at a considerable cost. The PSS may be complicated and require a lot of investment. Usually, totally new competences need to be developed or marshalled. In the latter case, new business partners have to be found. It may also be that the PSS offering cannibalises existing business, or diminishes option value rather than enhancing it.

13.1.2 Opportunities and threats by type of PSS

The opportunities and threats of PSS development can also be analysed by *type* of PSS. This analysis has by and large already been done in Chapter 3 and is reflected in Table 13.3. The table shows basically the following:

- Product-oriented services are the least radical ones. The product still plays a central role and a service is added to it. There are no major changes in the client base, and only minor changes in the value proposition, the revenue

Value element	Base materials	ICT	Offices	Food	Households
User value/market risk					
Tangible value	● Complex regulations (chemicals: REACH; building materials: waste) create markets for product-oriented services	● Removing upfront capital expenses (leasing)	● Less office space needed due to decentralisation of work ● More efficient business processes and learning	● Save customer time and effort	
Intangible value	● Due to the proliferation and complexity of materials, users have difficulty in selecting the best fit. This creates markets for result-oriented services	● B2C: penetration of ICT in entertainment, security, news, etc. Since hardware becomes too complex, result-oriented services get opportunities	● Improved worker conditions and efficiency, e.g. by reduction of commuting	● Provide new experiences, agenda freedom, trust	● Penetration of ICT in entertainment etc.; see under ICT
System costs/financial risk					
Tangible operational costs	● Chemicals: management costs are high compared with material costs; activity management may be more cost-effective ● PSS may reduce system costs	● Co-design of new highly efficient ICT-enabled business processes ● Providing customer with different PSS with the same hardware platform to manage costs	● Efficiency enhancement due to improved outsourcing, scale effects, virtualisation ● Tax system-friendly for PSS/leasing	● Reduce system costs	

TABLE 13.1 Opportunities for PSS as identified per need area (continued opposite)

Value element	Base materials	ICT	Offices	Food	Households
Risk premium, financing and transaction costs	• Construction: new EU procurement regulations may lead to offers of more efficient PSS-related procurement procedures	• ICT lowers transaction costs, enabling creation of solution providing networks			
Other benefits/capability risk					
Improved power position		• Move to software due to low profit margins on manufacturing			
Defence to substitutes/loyalty					
High speed of innovation			• PSS can be developed quickly; the main system changes are organisational		
Investment in PSS development	• Companies are getting used to chain-oriented co-operation	• Companies experienced in partnership through outsourcing build PSS easier			• Housing organisations can be 'natural' PSS suppliers
Other transition costs					

TABLE 13.1 (from previous page)

Value element	Base materials	ICT	Offices	Food	Households
User value/market risk					
Tangible value	• User is unaware of the integrated costs when using a product	• User value must exceed the cost of purchasing and using products (B2B)			
Intangible value	• User has not sufficient confidence in PSS supplier capabilities • Glacial design of materials prevents customising offering via PSS	• Customer acceptance of not owning a product (B2C)	• Change in mentality and strategy of the user	• Healthy eating now gives health benefits only later; consumers may not connect this • PSS must not interfere with the privacy of eating	• Strong inherent preference of ownership • High volume needs many individual customers; tailored offerings become more difficult • Privacy concerns: 'big brother' fear
System costs/financial risk					
Tangible costs	• Higher transportation needs and costs			• PSS are often high-VAT; unprocessed food low-VAT • Food processing by consumers needs no compliance with hygiene regulation, processing by PSS suppliers does	• In B2C PSS competes with DIY ('no wages') and low taxes ('black economy') providers • A 24 hr, 7 day/week service is required but costly

TABLE 13.2 Threats to PSS as identified per need area (continued opposite)

Value element	Base materials	ICT	Offices	Food	Households
Risk premium, financing and transaction costs	• Liabilities in the system for material performance may get distributed in a different way • Chemicals: transaction costs become too high when PSS user is an SME	• Complicated revenue sharing systems and management of responsibilities	• PSS often needs investment in hardware which is not sold; payback hence takes place over a longer time	• Firms investing in healthy-food PSS now will not be the beneficiaries of reduced healthcare costs later	• Predicting consumer behaviour is difficult • Complicated revenue sharing systems • More transactions • Complicated contracting
Other benefits/capability risk					
Improved power position					
Defence to substitutes/loyalty					
High speed of innovation					
Investment in PSS development	• Alignment of profit incentives when building partnership for the PSS	• Developing the right partnerships	• Developing the right partnerships • PSS development is complex • PSS is not seen as innovation and hence often not in innovation stimulation programmes		
Other transition costs	• Change in strategy and mind-set of material suppliers	• Resistance of telecom providers may delay introduction of fast B2C communication solutions	• Change in mentality and strategy of suppliers, e.g. its sales force		

TABLE 13.2 (from previous page)

PSS type	User value/ market risk		System costs/ financial risks		Ability to capture value (now and in the future)			Investment and capability risk	
	Tangible value	Intangible value	Tangible costs	Risk premium finance, transaction cost	Power position (% value captured)	Defence to substitutes Client loyalty	High speed of innovation	Investment in PSS development	Other transition costs
1 Product-related service	0/+	0/+	0	0	0	+	0/+	–/0	0
2 Product-related advice and consultancy	0/+	0/+	0	0	0	+	0/+	–/0	0
3 Product lease	0/+		0/–	0/–	+	+/–	0	–	0
4 Product renting or sharing	!	!	+	–				–	–
5 Product pooling	!	!	+	–				–	–
6 Pay-per-unit use	+		+/0	!	+	+	+	–	0
7 Activity management	+	+	+/0	0/–	+	+	+	–	0
8 Functional result	0	!	+(?)	!			+	!	!

+   In general better than reference
0   In general indifferent
–   In general worse than reference
!   Critical factor for which a case-specific analysis is needed
Blank No judgement

TABLE 13.3 A discussion of the value characteristics of different types of PSS

model, the value network and technical architecture. This makes it an excellent category for product-oriented companies to experiment with PSS

- Use-oriented services form an important change in comparison with regular product sales: the product stays in the ownership of the supplier. However, particularly in the business models where the product is no longer directly accessible by the user (product pooling and sharing/renting), this can result in a negatively affected user value:

  - Access to the product is more complicated. One has to register, reserve and pick the product up, usually at a place other than where the product is used. This creates tangible costs for the user

  - Particularly in a B2C context, obtaining ownership over a product is often contributing highly to intangible value components such as esteem, control and power. Renting, sharing and pooling options hence often diminish intangible value

- Result-oriented services are the most radical shift away from a traditional business model. An integrated activity formerly performed by the user is now provided by a supplier. In this category activity management (catering, integrated office services) now become more and more common. The key problem with these PSS is the ability to agree with the user a set of good performance criteria, and to predict/influence the behaviour of the user within reasonable margins. This risk element is particularly relevant for PSS type 'functional result', since the provider takes over all liabilities that in a product-based system were borne by the user

13.1.3 Conclusions

There is nothing magical about the PSS concept. Its main advantage is that the functional orientation and broad systems view creates a mind-set that enables us to find truly radical innovative business propositions and models. In many cases, a thorough analysis may show that a PSS can form an interesting new way of doing business. But it can also be that traditional product-oriented systems appear to be the most efficient way of delivering the highest value for the user. And in such cases a firm should stick to the old-fashioned sales of products. In sum, a company has to deal with PSS concepts as any other idea for a new value proposition. It has to assess thoroughly the:

- Market risk and opportunity (determined by the tangible and intangible value for the user)

- Financial risk and opportunity (determined by traditional system costs, and PSS-specific cost factors such as higher transaction costs, a premium for risks and ambiguities taken over from the user in the case of result- and use-oriented PSS, and dealing with pre-financing costs caused by a delay in incoming cash flows)

- Other potential benefits (such as improving the power position in the value network—though deterioration is also possible if PSS distracts from critical core competences—increased client loyalty, higher option value and higher speed of innovation

● Required investments and capability risk (determined by the existing competences, complexity of the PSS, etc.)

13.2 PSS and sustainability: the (partially) scattered myth

With regard to PSS and sustainability, Chapter 4 drew the following conclusions:

1. The need for decoupling in terms of a 'one size fits all' Factor X goal reduction of material use per unit of wealth is not generally accepted. Emission reduction targets of such an order of magnitude find better support

2. The scientific jury is still out over whether absolute decoupling (other than for a period of some decades, and for relatively small mass flows and emissions) is possible, and if there is a kind of 'natural' tendency that, when the wealth level rises higher, (absolute) decoupling will occur. It seems plausible that active and targeted interventions are needed if one wants to reach Factor X goals

3. Factors that contribute to a decoupling of environmental impact and enhancement of quality of life are:
   – Improving emission factors (potential: Factor X for small mass flows. Most, if not all, historical successes with regard to decoupling have been reached via this approach)
   – Enhancing efficiency of production of product functions (potential: Factor X in case of radical changes in socio-technical systems)
   – Intensifying use of product functions (potential: Factor 2, depending on intensity enhancement)
   – Switching expenditure to 'intangible' value (potential: Factor 2. Many expenditures on apparently 'intangible' services demand input of underlying 'hardware' and appear to have still relatively high life-cycle impacts per euro spent)
   – Improving 'non-market quality of life' (potential: large. For most Western economies 'life satisfaction' or 'happiness' has not significantly risen in the last 50 years despite a Factor 4–6 real economic growth)

4. The rebound effect works via the same mechanisms as indicated above, but in the opposite direction. The larger the intervention in the system, and the longer the time horizon, the more difficult rebounds can be predicted

5. Product-services have a potential to realise decoupling. However, as conclusion 3 already shows, this is not a law set in stone. First, the sweeping claims that a shift to product-services automatically leads to a Factor X world find no

ground in reality. Many services offered are just an envelope around a system filled with products and materials and on a life-cycle basis do not score much better than products. Second, it is paramount to acknowledge the difference between types of product-service:

- Product-oriented services leave the existing system largely as it is. Normally, sustainability improvements of a few dozen per cent arising from issues such as better maintenance can be expected at best—or maybe a Factor 2, if the service boosts product or material recycling

- Use-oriented services (and particularly product renting, sharing and pooling) intensify the use of the products. This can give intermediate (Factor 2) improvements

- Result-oriented services are in fact the only one with a real 'Factor X' potential—under the condition that the supplier of the service develops a fully novel way of function fulfilment

The need area-oriented chapters showed a variety of examples where PSS led to environmental benefits. But opposing examples can also be given. In the case of base materials (Chapter 7), chemical management services (CMS) may lead to savings of up to 30% as a result of the more professional handling and application of chemicals. But a CMS supplier may also seek to realise the same result more economically by applying another—and maybe more toxic—chemical. The use of ICT (Chapter 8) enables often totally new ways of fulfilling functions, with radically lower use of materials and energy (e.g. ICT-enabled education systems that allow for learning at home). Many PSS in the office field (Chapter 9) save costs by using buildings and office equipment more efficiently and effectively, which in turn forms an environmental benefit in itself. But it is certainly not a given that PSS is environmentally beneficial. In the need area food (Chapter 10) examples of convenience foods were shown that rely on central meal preparations and subsequent transport in cooling chains. This may provide a high value for the user, but has quite negative impacts with regard to energy use. And so on.

On a general level, there are certain trends in (post-industrialised) societies that support a move to services (including PSS) as business solutions, such as time shortage, an ageing society, outsourcing, individualisation or production fleeing the high-labour-cost countries. It may be that this trend may help to make expenditures that have on average a somewhat lower impact per euro or dollar than expenditures on pure products. However, as shown by conclusion 3 above there is absolutely no proof that this shift will be radical, and sweeping claims that a switch to a service economy in itself will contribute to radical 'Factor X' improvements must be rejected.

The conclusion is that the debate on sustainability of product-services has been utterly confused. Yes, PSS can be more sustainable than product-oriented business models. And, yes, PSS have even a Factor X potential. But the latter holds mainly for just *one specific type of PSS*: function-oriented services. Only this type of PSS breaks away from existing product-related structures for need fulfilment and brings radically new systems in sight. And even for such types of PSS one must analyse whether the new system is actually less environmentally friendly than the traditional one (as the CMS example above showed). So, sustainability is not an automatic mechanism built into the PSS concept but depends on many conditions.

Should we then leave it at that? Of course, that is far too negative. In the preceding paragraphs we simply wanted to scatter some simplistic myths about PSS and sustainability—since we believe that actions and strategies based on myths are not a good way to reach a sustainable society. But, if used correctly, the PSS concept can have great value for decoupling economic growth from negative environmental impacts. The strength of PSS thinking is that it moves away from existing product concepts, and inherently focuses on the final *need, demand or function* that needs to be fulfilled. This enhances the degrees of freedom to find sustainable improvement options enormously. It allows the design of a system that fulfils the final customer/consumer need, which can consist of as few material products (including lowest energy consumption and transportation intensity) as possible and more non-material services. But to realise this opportunity it is essential that sustainability considerations are integrated into all the steps of a PSS development and design process,[1] that its market launch is carefully prepared in order to be successful, and finally that the solution on the market is reviewed relating to economic, environmental and social impacts. The lessons learned from every new PSS project should be considered in the following projects to organise a continuous improvement process. Furthermore, market research should include PSS as a business option and be focused on customers' needs and demands on a regular basis. Otherwise it will just be a coincidence whether or not a new PSS leads to more sustainability in the production and consumption system.

To conclude, the concept of PSS may not bring sustainability on its own. But designing need fulfilment or ultimately satisfaction systems making use of a (particularly result-oriented) PSS mind-set indicates how systems have to be organised to reach the Factor X.

13.3 Making the myth work: innovate the system, not just the business model

13.3.1 The alleged PSS win–win: some contradictions

Sections 13.1 and 13.2 in combination show an intriguing contradiction with regard to the environmental and economic potential of PSS, summarised in Table 13.4:

1. Product-oriented services are the least problematic type of PSS to introduce by (in many cases still product-oriented) companies. However, since they only marginally change the way of doing things in the system, this leads at best to some incremental environmental improvements

2. Use-oriented services, particularly product renting, sharing and pooling in principle can lead to high environmental gains: capital goods are used more

---

1   Compare, for instance, the sustainability screening tool in the Guideline to PSS development in Annex 1. This tool was used in the industry workshops during SusProNet, with the result that most of the PSS ideas developed showed an improved environmental and social sustainability compared with the reference situation.

intensively and, in the case of pooling, consumables in the use phase are now beneficial for more persons at the same time. However, these categories, particularly in a B2C context, probably in most cases have a considerably lower market value than the competing product, owing to both tangible and intangible user sacrifices

3. Result-oriented services, particularly the type 'functional result', break radically away from the existing product concept and hence have in theory a Factor X potential. However, particularly for this type of PSS the following issue needs attention. There will be some cases where the 'functional result' cannot be operationalised in sufficiently concrete terms, where the liabilities related to the promised result are too high, or where the provider simply has insufficient control over whether (or for which costs) the result can be reached. These issues can be prohibitive in putting a function-oriented PSS on the market (or otherwise only by demanding a high risk premium)

PSS type	Advantages	Disadvantages
1 Product-oriented services	• Easy to implement • Close to core business	• In general only incremental environmental benefits achievable '
2 Use-oriented services (particularly renting, sharing and pooling)	• Medium environmental benefits (Factor 2) • More conscious use since per-use full costs are charged	• Low tangible added value: getting access takes time and effort • Low intangible added value: product ownership is often valued higher by consumers (less relevant for B2B)
3 Result-oriented services (particularly functional results)	• Imply often radical new ways of function fulfilment (Factor X potential)	• Risks/liabilities for reaching the result are taken over by the provider • Results cannot always be agreed on or measured in operational terms • Customer loses power over means

TABLE 13.4 **Contradiction in the economic–environmental win–win of PSS**

Are such contradictions insurmountable? As the many examples with environmental and economic benefits in this book show, this is certainly not the case. In a number of cases, via a smart design of the business model, such seemingly problematic contradictions may be solved. For instance, car-sharing systems are still confined to a niche market. It is still not easy enough to get access to a car from a sharing system. And neither can such a system for many people match the feeling of satisfaction of owning a private car. But the current systems are already much more user-friendly and professional than the first ones set up in the 1980s. And, who knows, in the next decade a smart business developer may prove to be capable of minimising the access problem and even organise the offering in such a way that the esteem and intangible satisfaction of using a car share will become much higher than owning a vehicle. Why should car-sharing organisations always use rather small and dull cars? Why not have loyalty programmes that, say, after ten normal shares allow you to take out that nice Maserati for an afternoon—giving a much better experience than the neighbours who are confined for years with just one choice, the car they possess themselves? Of course, this example is a rather simplified account of the real problem. But it makes clear in which direction one of the answers to the trade-offs in Table 13.4 can be found. Business developers and strategic designers must use all their creativity to find smart solutions for apparently unsolvable contradictions. But it must be accepted that the contradiction exists. The PSS field has seen enough idealistic conceptual sustainable ideas, often developed by people with no business development experience, and which, at best, ended up on a bookshelf because of the total lack of business sense.[2] And of course many business developers have developed PSS that have provided no contribution to sustainability at all. Neither approach is the way forward. An approach that accepts that difficult contradictions have to be mastered is. Against this background, Box 13.1 translates the lessons learned in this book—particularly in Chapters 3 and 4 and Sections 13.1 and 13.3—into seven keys for successful sustainable PSS development. If these rules are obeyed, the chances are that the result of the PSS development process is a sustainable PSS that makes good business sense.

13.3.2 Making the system too narrow: business and users alone cannot always realise Factor X

There is, however, another problem with the idea of reaching radical sustainability improvements via the implementation of PSS. There is an implicit assumption that an economic and environmental/social win–win *does* exist, and that hence the sustainability problem can be solved (almost) entirely in the existing markets and by relatively simple changes in the interaction between a business (network) and its client. True, the PSS concept focuses on functionality (the final goal) rather than the product (the means) and takes into account the provider system in its broadest sense when searching for the win–win. Since this system is so much larger than when one focuses on improvement of products and production processes, the chances are much higher that a deep-seated, yet untapped, win–win option may be found.

Yet it must be acknowledged that this approach has its limits. A company will innovate its business model only if that makes business sense. And several major, stubborn sustainability problems simply have no clear market-based solutions within the existing context of doing business. This has to do with the following:

1. Understanding radical (sustainable) innovation needs a much wider perspective on a system than is provided by narrow business–client interaction along a value chain, which is so dominant in the PSS concept. In this context, we refer to a number of notions introduced in Chapter 3, Section 3.2.1. Real radical innovations usually start in niches: a 'protected space' that is isolated from

---

2   One of the more laudable attempts to at least investigate this 'reality gap' comes from Thierry Kazazian (2002), who thought out sustainable PSS business models with regard to (among others) food and water provision. His book also describes how major companies reacted when he talked to them about his business ideas; unfortunately, in most cases the companies came up with very clear and convincing reasons why it would not be possible for them to implement the ideas.

1. The PSS should preferably include eco-efficiency improvements through changes in product design, product choice or processes applied in the system

2. The PSS should encourage changes in consumption patterns in the system towards lower consumption and more sufficiency (e.g. reduction of car use through car sharing)

3. The responsibilities in the value network should be divided in such a way that each partner in the system makes the best use of its core competences and does tasks that it can do most efficiently

4. The responsibilities in the value network should be divided in such a way that each partner in the system is responsible for a fairly coherent set of activities. Whereas the way in which these activities are performed can still develop over time, the output of these activities must be fairly stable to minimise transaction costs and the need for learning and adaptation across firm borders

5. The life-cycle costs of the PSS should be controlled by one actor, or the responsibilities in the value network and the revenue model should be organised and divided in such a way that each actor is given an incentive to reduce costs and increase efficiency from a life-cycle perspective

6. The remaining PSS-specific risks related to PSS development should be well managed. Examples include:

   - Ensure, particularly for use- and result-oriented services in a B2C context, that the value/cost ratio is better than for competing product offers (tangible and intangible value is often negatively affected since consumers often demand control over means, value ownership highly, and demand quick access to the use of artefacts)

   - Ensure, particularly for result-oriented PSS, that the costs in the use and waste phase can be predicted with sufficient certainty and that the result can be specified in sufficiently operational terms

7. The system should be designed to be flexible, to learn from mistakes, to react quickly to market developments/changing customer demands and should aim for continuous improvement (e.g. also involve training and build up capacity of staff)

Box 13.1 Seven keys to develop sustainable PSS that make good business sense

the regular market where innovations can be tested and become more mature. But, as in ecosystems, radical novelties more often die out in their niche than become mainstream. The following factors provide important barriers for change (compare Elzen *et al.* 2004):

- The **socio-technical landscape**. This landscape provides a (relatively stable) context in which actors interact, such as infrastructures, normative values, world-views and dominant paradigms (Rotmans 2003)
- The **socio-technical regime** (compare Geels 2002a, b), which consists of dominant practices, rules and interests shared and embedded in institutions by a dominant multi-actor network (financiers, users, suppliers, authorities)

2. These factors—or, simply, the context and the framework conditions—determine the 'space' available for innovation within the market context. Figure 13.1 gives an example with regard to the implementation of sustainable consumption structures (adapted from Inaba 2004). In theory, consumers determine what is consumed and hence what is produced. However, the production side of the economy shapes for an important part the context in which consumption takes place—and hence influences not only the opportunities (availability of means) and abilities (access to means) determining how consumers can fulfil their needs, but also what is actually perceived as a need

3. This, in turn, implies that different levels of innovation have to be discerned, each requiring a more complex governance for changing the system (see Fig. 13.2):

- **System optimisation**. Example: introducing an energy label that supports enhancing the fuel efficiency of a car. The typical sustainability improvement is 20–30%. There is no change in the structure of the production–consumption system. Incentives for change are rather 'soft', such as awareness raising approaches that mainly try to influence the attitude of the user (and indirectly the producer)
- **System redesign**. Example: the offer of an integrated mobility system where people use public transport where feasible, and car-sharing systems as a backup. The typical sustainability gains are 50% or more. The structure of the production–consumption interactions changes. Awareness raising is complemented by the availability of an inherently sustainable solution for the mobility problem (albeit still shaped in an existing context and market framework). Not only the attitude but also the behavioural control of the consumer is addressed
- **System innovation**. Example: spatial planning and incentive systems that result in a context of life where a reduced need for transport is inherent. Awareness raising and the availability of inherently sustainable solutions are complemented by adapting the context of life and incentive systems. Not only the attitude and behavioural control are addressed, but also social pressure is put in place

The above suggests that the boundary conditions set by the regime and landscape allow for incremental improvements, and to some extent system redesign, to be

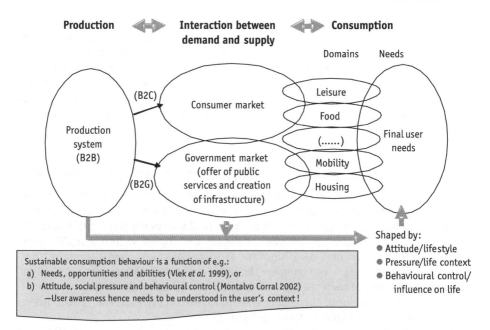

FIGURE 13.1 **The relation between (sustainable) consumption and production**

Source: adapted from the project 'Life-cycle Approaches to Sustainable Consumption', AIST, Japan (Inaba 2004)

What	Sustainability gains	Approaches
1. Optimise systems	Marginal	Awareness raising
2. Redesign systems	Factor 2 (50%)	Awareness raising + offers of (more) sustainable solutions
3. Innovate systems	Substantial (>>50%)	Awareness raising + offers of (inherent) sustainable solutions + adapting context and framework conditions

A system is the combination of:	Context and framework conditions		
	Production structure	Interaction between demand and supply	Consumption structure

FIGURE 13.2 **Levels of change in the production-consumption system and typical sustainability improvements**

realised via traditional market mechanisms. However, a truly radical system innovation will usually encounter a lot of opposition from the existing (and dominant) socio-technical regime. After all, in that case often the factors forming the boundary conditions (existing organisations, institutions and networks that share dominant practices, rules and interests) have to change as well. The conclusion is hence simple. A business model must fit with its specific context. Most radical Factor X changes also require a change of context, and hence cannot be realised by asking a company to change its business model alone.

13.3.3 Innovating systems: the approach of transition management

So how, then, do (radical) system innovations occur? 'Events' that change the landscape can have an important influence (for instance, the discovery of a major gas field in the Netherlands that triggered a shift in the base of energy supply; Correljé and Verbong 2004). Weaknesses and internal pressures developing within a regime form another factor. Niches may also innovate at a quicker pace than the mainstream regime, thereby starting to out compete the latter over time (Christensen 1997).[3] Typically, a combination of such reasons has to occur before the window of opportunity is created that allows the until-then niche systems to take off (Te Riele *et al.* 2000; Tukker and de Bruijn 2002; Kemp and Rotmans 2004).

How the development and direction of system innovations can be actively influenced is still much in debate. Probably the most refined theories on this question of governance have been elaborated by scholars working on the concepts of system innovation and transition management (Geels and Kemp 2000; Rotmans *et al.* 2000; Geels 2002a; Elzen *et al.* 2004). They state that system innovations usually cannot be realised via command-and-control instruments alone, in view of their long time horizon, their co-evolutionary character and multiple causalities. Also, market-based instruments on their own will not work, since regime- and landscape-related market failures are at the root of problems. Such scholars hence tend to favour a combination of the application of market-based instruments, complemented by an indicative planning approach and using a process-oriented philosophy. As formulated by Kemp and Rotmans (2004), key elements of transition management are:

● Long-term thinking as a framework for short-term policy

● Backcasting: setting of short- and longer-term goals based on long-term guiding visions and short-term options

● Thinking in terms of multi-domain and multi-level

● A focus on learning, particularly learning by doing via experimentation

The governance approach further has to be tailored to the different phases of a system innovation. Generally, four phases in system innovations are discerned (compare Table 13.5; adapted from Smits *et al.* 2001; see also Rotmans 2003):

3   For instance, niches can make their way to mainstream applications via processes such as niche accumulation (i.e. several key elements of a new socio-technical regime are applied in several parallel or consecutive niches) or hybridisation (where hybrid forms of old and new technology have a role as intermediates) (compare Geels and Kemp 2000).

	Exploration	Take-off	Acceleration	Stabilisation
Insights from innovation theory in key words	• Creative destruction • Clusters of innovation • Co-evolution of technology and context	• Lock-in • Niches • Strategic niche management • Paradigm shift • Dominant design • Hybrid innovations • Bandwagons	• Momentum • Networks • Alignment • Enrolment • Socio-technical regimes • Learning by doing	• Landscape • Incremental change • Learning by using • Economies of scale • Creative destruction
Key issues	• Awareness • New combinations • Identification of mega-trends	• Mobilisation of relevant actors • Formulation of end-views • Support technology development • Identifying niches • Identifying lock-in	• Standards • Alignment • Enrolment • Direction • Coherence • Creative destruction/ construction	• Reflection on goals • Identification of megatrends • Awareness
Role authorities	• Stimulating participative discussion • Mobilising actors • Development of perspectives	• Keep playing ground broad • Strategic niche management • Put pressure on the old regime	• Adjustment • Stimulating choice of the right options	• Consolidation
Instruments	• Awareness TA • Foresight • Delphi • Scenarios	• Scenario workshops • Subsidies • Niche simulation • Backcasting • Delphi	• Strategic TA • *Constructive TA* • *Strategic workshops* • Cluster policy • Standard setting	

TABLE 13.5 **Phases and instruments for transition management**

Source: taken with adaptations from Smits *et al.* 2001

1. **Exploration.** In the exploration phase the characteristics of a sustainable goal for the system have to be elaborated. This is probably not one single, well-defined point, but rather a direction or a set of goals. Also, likely trends and developments and the characteristics of the system can be inventoried

2. **Take-off.** In this phase, experiments in niches will probably play an important role. Authorities could put pressure on the old system and facilitate the experiments and learning processes

3. An **acceleration** phase, in which the new regime starts to develop. In this phase, the role of the government is likely to change from facilitating to a more determining role (e.g. via standards, legislation, etc.)

4. A **stabilisation** or **saturation** phase, in which the new regime is consolidated

In sum, the role of government varies in each transition phase. Initially, there is a clear need for experimentation and visioning. Later, there is a need for controlling the side-effects of large-scale applications of new technologies. During the whole process monitoring has to take place to ensure that the right adjustments to a sustainable direction are made. Transition management in that sense can be seen as what Hamel and Prahalad (1994)—with regard to individual companies—called 'strategic intent': being clear about the rough direction in which one wants to go, and learning by doing along the way.

13.4 In action: an outline for research, dissemination and policy

In this final section, an agenda with regard to the subject of PSS is given for the main audiences of this book.

The first agenda is targeted at **researchers**. It contains an overview of actions that can be taken up by researchers in the field of business science, sustainable design and sustainable innovation (13.4.1).

The second agenda is targeted at **business** and its **representative organisations**. This agenda reviews actions that can help to make business more efficient and effective by taking up the PSS concept (13.4.2).

The final agenda is targeted at **policy-makers** and **intermediaries**. This agenda lists actions that these actors can carry out to support dissemination of PSS in business, and how innovation towards radically more sustainable systems can be stimulated (13.4.3).

13.4.1 The research agenda

From the analysis of PSS best practice and state of the art in SusProNet, the following guidance for further activities to support (sustainable) PSS development in practice can be derived.

Theory development on PSS

This book has shown that the discussion on the economic and sustainability potential of PSS is surrounded by many myths. Such myths are not necessary if there is a clear theory and insight that can give rules and generic principles on relations such as:

- The type of PSS versus its environmental and social sustainability potential

- The type of PSS versus user value and production costs

- The type of PSS, need area, or even region where the PSS is applied versus the drivers and barriers for implementation that typically play a role

- PSS and rebound effects

This book attempts to develop some theories on these issues, and contains one of the first attempts to check hypotheses with the help of an analysis of some 200 cases. These are not magical or novel approaches in the development of scientific theories, and we are the first to acknowledge that our work was little more than a first, crude attempt to provide some kind of statistical proof of the hypotheses. It is hence rather surprising that, in the ten years since the PSS issue has been on the agenda, this type of rigid theory development has been so scarce. It is of prime importance that the PSS community moves away from developing yet another theoretical concept, or doing yet another individual and unconnected case study, but starts to test existing concepts and ideas against true field data, preferably via statistical approaches. Only via this approach can a true understanding of the value of the PSS concept be developed.

Methodology development on PSS

The methodological toolbox for PSS development is fairly complete. Chapter 5 shows a wealth of—converging—approaches to PSS development. Furthermore, PSS appears to fit well with traditional new business development procedures. We feel that more effort in generic method development is probably superfluous. There are, however, several gaps in existing methods that may need some additional specific attention.

There are gaps in the tools for rapid and robust sustainability evaluation that can give a quick impression especially of the environmental and socio-ethical consequences of a new PSS design. New tools for this were developed in SusProNet and the MEPSS project (see Annex 1). Such tools can benefit from the theory development proposed above.

While PSS development resembles to a fair extent regular business development, there are some idiosyncrasies:

- A PSS is usually put on the market by a network of firms. But tools and methods for finding the right partners and organising the new co-operative arrangements efficiently are still largely missing. Only the HiCS project paid some attention to this, and there seems to be room for improvement (Manzini *et al.* 2004)

- Since PSS is put on the market in networks, the many firm–firm interaction points may create significant transaction costs. PSS development could be facilitated by the development of standard agreements and revenue models for specific PSS types

- Particularly for result-oriented PSS (activity management and functional result) the provider has to take responsibility for the use stage. Risks, liabilities, financial uncertainties and ambiguities can be reduced if methods become available for the following points:
  - Standardised, meaningful ways of defining specific results
  - Development of checklists for the most common use phase risks and liabilities
  - Standardised, meaningful ways of dividing the responsibilities for use phase risks and liabilities between user and provider
  - Rigid scenario approaches for analysing potential costs for the provider in case of uncertainties with regard to user behaviour or events in the context influencing the use phase

Beyond PSS: theory and method development on sustainable system innovation

Finally, having identified the limits of PSS in reaching Factor X sustainability, the question is how radical changes to sustainable consumption and production structures can be realised. This is related to the question of system innovation and transition management put forward in Section 13.3.

A main point here concerns the fact that we are trying to develop a 'management approach' for the unmanageable. After all, the full trajectory of a transition (e.g. the change from a fossil fuel-based energy system to a solar- and hydrogen-based system) is simply too complicated and extended to manage via traditional means–ends approaches (compare the concepts of 'bounded rationality' developed by Simon (1957) and the concept of 'the science of muddling through' of Lindblom [1959]). At the same time, we see that most of the great questions facing the EU (and the world at large) demand a kind of 'management' of complex systems. This is true for problems as different as improving the innovative power of the EU-25, innovating healthcare systems in an ageing society, preventing an 'infarct' in the car transport system in Europe's most densely populated areas, and meeting greenhouse effect reduction targets. Governance of long-term change in complex systems forms a research agenda on its own, which could include (compare KSI 2004):

- Theory development: for instance, on the basis of historical analyses of transitions and system innovations

- The development of new governance approaches suitable for 'management' of transitions and system innovations

- A toolbox for analysing complex systems, the dynamics therein, developing outlines of future desired system constellations, and a related approach for organising the process

- The development of building blocks of alternative systems in niches to use as 'testing grounds'

13.4.2 The business and business support agenda

The agenda for business in principle is easy. Smart business developers simply should analyse what the PSS concept could mean for their firm, and adopt it if it is promising or reject it if in their particular situation it does not work. There is a clear danger in not investigating the broad innovation space created via the system and function concept, and cosily sticking to incremental innovation of the existing product-related business. If there is better value to create or efficiencies to be gained by looking beyond the product concept, there will be a firm that finds it. The only question is whether the lucky finder will be you or your competitor. There are enough examples of firms sticking to product innovation, only to be overwhelmed by a competitor who dealt radically with inefficiencies in the system or created superior value with a PSS concept.

In the ideal case, every firm—if only now and then or via the effort of just a few staff members—should hence give the analysis of working via 'weird' and 'novel' business concepts a structural place in their new business development processes. Unfortunately, as we saw in Chapter 5, this is not always the case. Indeed, many firms do not even have structural routines for searching for innovations and new business models. The practice is that many firms, particularly smaller ones, tend to be conservative and are not eager to even analyse the potential of novelties that at first sight seem a bit risky.

Here, business support functions such as innovation centres, representative organisations and business clubs could support the use of the potential of PSS via:

- Organising the available knowledge on PSS development in an accessible way, possibly including training and educational programmes. As far as possible, this knowledge should be tailored to different application situations (e.g. sectors)

- Developing a transparent case base, by working out the PSS concept for different sectors, different cultures, with different consortia of companies and so on. This creates hands-on insight into the dos and don'ts, and builds an overview of a set of tried and tested success cases. It is particularly such recognisable success stories from other businesses that help to make firms less sceptical about novelties and make them see how the concept could be beneficial for them

13.4.3 The policy agenda

In the EU, the concept of (sustainable) PSS is not explicitly supported by policy. There are no real incentives or regulations driving the implementation of PSS, and there are only very few research and funding programmes that include PSS. One major problem is that mainly technological research and technological innovation is covered by funding and regulation, but social and organisational innovations (new business models, new use patterns, etc.), important elements in PSS development, are not in the focus of policy-makers nor priorities in research funding programmes. Indirectly, some of the new environmental producer responsibility legislation such as the WEEE (Waste Electrical and Electronic Equipment), RoHS (Restrictions on use of Hazardous Substances) and EuP (Energy-using Products) Directives will help drive some sustainable PSS in the wider electrical and electronic industry. The same mechanism is expected for the car industry after implementation of the EoLV (End-of-Life Vehicles Directive).

In this context, we see a number of potential initiatives:

- Integrate PSS thinking into current educational programmes: for example, design, engineering and business schools, as well as training programmes for professionals

- Include PSS (when clearly more sustainable) in public purchasing guidelines and prefer them before product sales

- Include PSS (e.g. social and organisational innovation) in research programmes, subsidy and support structures on an equal footing to technological innovation

- Analyse whether tax structures do not inadvertently hamper (desirable) PSS development (e.g. such as in the case of food, where a 'food PSS' is high-VAT and food ingredients fall under low VAT)

- Analyse whether existing regulations do not hinder the implementation of sensible and sustainable PSS (e.g. the regulations for transportation of waste, which make it very difficult for transnational recycling services to transport waste across borders)

From a sustainability perspective, however, the main policy challenge is of course dealing with the question of how the consumption and production systems in major need areas can make a radical jump in sustainability. In sum, how systems for providing shelter, food, transport, and all the other things mentioned in Figure 13.1 in the next generation will comply with basic sustainability demands. This may not imply that Factor X reductions are needed for all environmental impacts, but in many cases this will be true. In line with the call of government leaders at the World Summit on Sustainable Development (WSSD) in 2002 for all countries to 'Encourage and promote the development of a 10-year framework of programmes in support of regional and national initiatives to accelerate the shift towards sustainable consumption and production', this would imply (a) embarking on a programme of experimenting and testing of the concept of system innovation and (b) where relevant giving the PSS concept a place in it.

Annex 1
A PRACTICAL GUIDE
FOR PSS DEVELOPMENT

Ursula Tischner

econcept, Germany

Arnold Tukker

TNO, The Netherlands

A practical guide to PSS development

Your product-service system (PSS) experience in five steps

This presentation describes a pragmatic stepwise approach to PSS development. It can be used by a team in a company, in workshops, by students and other actors interested in experiencing how PSS development can take place.

It was developed by Arnold Tukker and Ursula Tischner in the framework of the SusProNet project and is based on extensive best-practice research that was undertaken in SusProNet. The guide partly uses tools from other PSS research projects, common tools used in business practice that we adapted to PSS, and some new developments by the authors.

The presentation includes all tools and instructions that you need for a first PSS pilot project. However, it works best if you use it together with the SusProNet book, *New Business for Old Europe* (Tukker and Tischner 2006), where you will find more information about PSS and tools that we refer to but have not included in this guide. More information is also available via the SusProNet website: www.suspronet.org.

How to use this guide

The guide first introduces very briefly the PSS concept and then guides you through five steps of a PSS development process.

1. **Preparation and introduction**
2. **Analysis of PSS opportunities**
3. **PSS idea generation**
4. **PSS design**
5. **Implementation plan**

All the most important tools and tasks are described in this document. Thus it can be copied and directly used in practice. We refer to further helpful tools and information, giving the source to help you find them.

Please read through the document and follow the steps to experience your exciting PSS project and to find out if PSS is an interesting concept for you/your company and can be a valuable business opportunity. Or use the tools and steps described to evaluate, improve and refine your existing product-service concepts. But also be critical and use the go/no-go decision points to find out whether PSS is a way forward for you.

PSS introduction

What are product-service systems (PSS)?

A product-service system is a combination of products and services in a system that are designed to fulfil specific client demands. PSS are already present in the economy; however, they are often called something else, e.g. functional sales.

They can be valuable for companies, because they can offer opportunities for diversification, for improving the market position, for better fulfilling client demands, etc. They are often created because the market is saturated, or the product has become a kind of commodity, so there is not much profit in selling products. Other reasons to go for PSS can be the high risks involved in using a product or fast technological progress, individualisation in the client's demands, etc.

Also with regard to sustainability, PSS can be a promising way of creating win–win solutions:

- That benefit the **customer/consumers** because their demands are better fulfilled
- That benefit the **producers/suppliers** because they secure business in changing markets, improve market position and competitiveness
- And that create benefits for the **natural and social environment**, because the value in the system is created more by non-material services and less by material products; thus material efficiency in the system increases, waste and hazardous substances are avoided, the products are used more efficiently, longer and in closed-loop systems (re-use and recycling), etc.

However, these benefits do not derive automatically by choosing PSS but have to be carefully designed into the concept. The following PSS development method helps to do that.

We will not try to hide the risks that can be involved in moving to PSS: e.g. return on investment might come over a longer period of time than when selling products; liability and risk for the PSS supplier can increase; consumers and retailers are not yet familiar with the PSS concept, so it needs careful communication; PSS can cannibalise product sales; etc.

PSS introduction

PSS categories and examples

Product-service systems are business models or value propositions that aim at the most elegant and efficient combination of products and services to achieve the best customer satisfaction.

There are many different types of PSS; thus it makes sense to distinguish at least three basic PSS categories with eight sub-categories. All of them can be business-to-business (B2B) and business-to-consumer (B2C) offers.

- **Product-oriented PSS**, including services added to products, advice connected to products
- **Use-oriented PSS**, including product lease, renting/sharing, pooling and pay-per-use
- **Result-oriented PSS**, including activity management and functional results

Pure product sales	Product-service system			Pure service offer
	Product-oriented: service added to product; advice related to product	*Use-oriented:* leasing, renting/ sharing, pooling, pay-per-use	*Result-oriented:* activity management; functional result	

From product via use to result-oriented, the importance of the material product decreases in the PSS while the importance of the service increases.

Product-oriented PSS

Where products are still sold but there are services added to the products, e.g. advice on how to use the product, maintenance, take-back and recycling services or customising services, etc.

Use-oriented PSS

Where products are not sold but owned by the service provider and used by the customer, e.g. leasing, sharing and pooling systems. Well-known examples are car-sharing systems or pay-per-use systems such as renting services for photocopiers.

Result-oriented PSS

Where products are not sold and the customer does not care at all how the system works. He or she buys only a specific result that was agreed by customer and provider, e.g. chemical leasing services where the provider organises everything including the application of the chemicals (e.g. in the car industry). The customer pays only for the final result, e.g. that cars are coated.

PSS development: overall approach

PSS development method

Now dive into the subject of PSS development and follow the steps described below and on the following pages.

The process is mainly based on application of tools in workshops with a project team or alone. Thus the following pages describe five steps and tools to be used in the steps.

Text boxes explain how to use the tools and what are the main tasks in the steps.

If you follow this approach, you will very likely end up with one or more interesting PSS for your company/your market/your customers. We guide you through the process up to the implementation plan and the final management presentation. The real implementation of the PSS concept would have to be done after successfully working with this method. And of course you/the management has to check carefully if the PSS idea is interesting for the company and the market and promises market success.

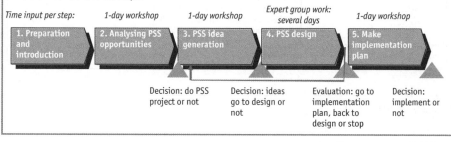

Overall approach

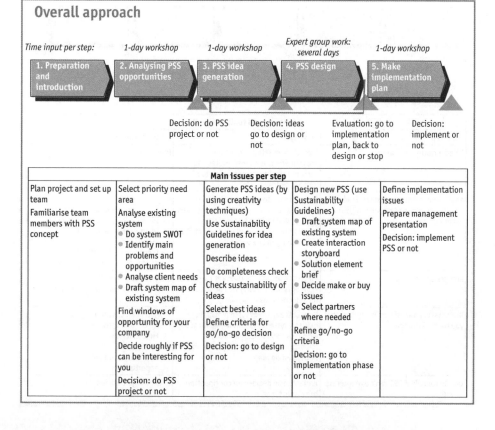

Step 1: preparation and introduction

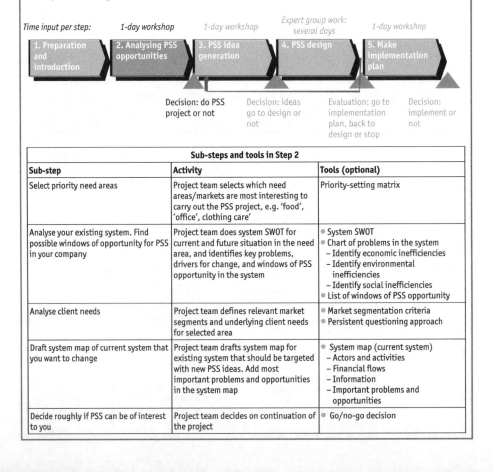

Time input per step: *1-day workshop*   *1-day workshop*   *Expert group work: several days*   *1-day workshop*

1. Preparation and introduction | 2. Analysing PSS opportunities | 3. PSS idea generation | 4. PSS design | 5. Make implementation plan

Decision: do PSS project or not | Decision: ideas go to design or not | Evaluation: go to implementation plan, back to design or stop | Decision: implement or not

Sub-steps and tools in Step 1		
Sub-step	**Activity**	**Tools (suggested)**
Plan project and set up team	Initiator plans the project and sets up the project team, invites the experts (internal from R&D, product design, marketing, EHS and maybe external suppliers, clients, and makes links with management) for a first one-day WS	*Normal project planning tools*
Familiarise team members with PSS concept	Read PSS conclusions and examples in SusProNet	*PSS familiarisation tools*

Step 2: analysis

Time input per step: *1-day workshop*   *1-day workshop*   *Expert group work: several days*   *1-day workshop*

1. Preparation and introduction | 2. Analysing PSS opportunities | 3. PSS idea generation | 4. PSS design | 5. Make implementation plan

Decision: do PSS project or not | Decision: ideas go to design or not | Evaluation: go to implementation plan, back to design or stop | Decision: implement or not

Sub-steps and tools in Step 2		
Sub-step	**Activity**	**Tools (optional)**
Select priority need areas	Project team selects which need areas/markets are most interesting to carry out the PSS project, e.g. 'food', 'office', clothing care'	Priority-setting matrix

Analyse your existing system. Find possible windows of opportunity for PSS in your company	Project team does system SWOT for current and future situation in the need area, and identifies key problems, drivers for change, and windows of PSS opportunity in the system	● System SWOT
		● Chart of problems in the system
		  – Identify economic inefficiencies
		  – Identify environmental inefficiencies
		  – Identify social inefficiencies
		● List of windows of PSS opportunity

Analyse client needs	Project team defines relevant market segments and underlying client needs for selected area	● Market segmentation criteria ● Persistent questioning approach

Draft system map of current system that you want to change	Project team drafts system map for existing system that should be targeted with new PSS ideas. Add most important problems and opportunities in the system map	● System map (current system)
		  – Actors and activities
		  – Financial flows
		  – Information
		  – Important problems and opportunities

Decide roughly if PSS can be of interest to you	Project team decides on continuation of the project	● Go/no-go decision

Step 2a: select priority need area(s)

Questions/factors that support PSS *Answer with yes/no*	Name need area 1	Name need area 2	Name need area 3	Name need area 4
Is an important part of the company's portfolio in the need area? • Turnover and profit • Core competences supported				
Do you face intense price competition in the area?				
Is the market saturation high in the need area?				
Are major changes (technological, cultural, etc.) taking place in the area?				
Do you think there is room to respond better to the needs of the customer in the need area?				
Do you think there are options to stand out from competitors in the area?				
TOTAL yes				

Comments

- Developing PSS around all current value propositions is probably too much work; a pre-selection of a only few need areas is required. Need areas are e.g. nutrition, mobility, cleaning of clothing, equipping an office, etc.
- This matrix facilitates the selection of a need area or areas that are important business fields for the companies and at the same time good areas for PSS development.
- Please name need areas in which you are active or you find interesting, then answer the questions above with 'yes' or 'no' and select the need area or areas that are most promising for you as business fields and show opportunities for new PSS, i.e. the ones with the most 'yes' answers.

Step 2b: do system SWOT/current system

SWOT	Current situation		Future situation	
	Strengths	Weaknesses	Opportunities	Threats
A. Environmental dimension • Materials efficiency (including water) • Energy efficiency • Toxics/environmental risks • Waste minimisation, re-use, recycling • Transport and mobility efficiency • Life-cycle aspects, longevity, cyclic economy (technical/natural cycles) • Bio-compatibility, nature conservation				
B. Socio-cultural dimension • Fulfilment of needs/consumption patterns • Health and safety issues • Living conditions/quality of life • Employment/working conditions • Equity and justice/relation to stakeholders (media, NGOs, etc.) • Respect for cultural diversity				
C. Economic dimension *For the company/ies* • Market position/competitiveness • Profitability/added value for companies • Long-term business development, risk • Partnership/co-operation/chain value captured • Macro-economic effect/market influence *For the customers* • Profitability, affordability, added value for customers (tangible/intangible)				
D. Technology, feasibility				
E. Legislation, regulation, public infrastructure				

Step 2c: from SWOT to PSS opportunities

SWOT results				
Major problems identified in need area				
Customer/consumer needs and demands that are not met or fulfilled satisfactorily				
Major changes in the need area expected in the future				

Major windows of opportunity for PSS solutions in the need area derived from SWOT results				

Step 2d: analyse client needs in selected area(s)

Issue	How to answer	Why it is important
1. Market segmentation What market segment/customers do you serve and where, how and why are your products bought? Do you sell to other companies or direct to the end consumer? Describe your (groups of) customers and, where applicable, your customers' own customers	Apply classical market segmentation techniques	Different customers (segments) have different characteristics and probably different needs. These differences have to be responded to in different ways in developing a PSS
2. Function/value for the customer For each segment, what functions does the product perform for the customer (there may be different ones)?	Use a persistent questioning technique to understand the 'need behind the need' of the client Example: the function of chocolates Q What does the customer want? A A box of chocolates Q What will he do with the box? A Give them to his girlfriend Q Why does he want those chocolates for his girlfriend? A To make up for working overtime the third evening in a row In this way the real function of the chocolates is revealed: a relationship management tool. Competitors are the florist (a bunch of flowers), restaurants (an evening out), or perhaps even a relationship counsellor	The same product can fulfil different functions for different customers and, depending on the situation, even perform different functions for the same customer (for example, chocolates may be bought to make up after an argument, to round off a fine dinner or to satisfy a craving for something sweet). The function that a product performs will be central to the development of a new PSS. It is important to properly understand the conditions under which the product is purchased and what (emotional) value it has for the customer

Step 2e: system map (current system)

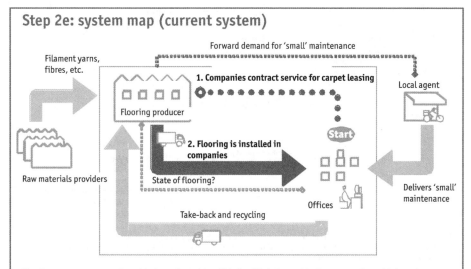

Forward demand for 'small' maintenance

Filament yarns, fibres, etc.

1. Companies contract service for carpet leasing

Local agent

Flooring producer

Start

2. Flooring is installed in companies

Raw materials providers

State of flooring?

Offices

Delivers 'small' maintenance

Take-back and recycling

Sketch a **system map**, starting with the end user(s) and his/her/their demand in the system, then add the main stakeholders and the flows and relationships between them.

- Primary and secondary actors and their roles and tasks in the full delivery of the product/service to fulfil the demand (use icons). Draw system boundary
- Material flows in the system (use full arrows)
- Information flows in the system (use arrows with small dots)
- Financial flows in the system (use arrows with big dots)

For further information, see E. Manzini, L. Collins and S. Evans, *Solution Oriented Partnership* (HiCS project publication, 2004).

Step 2f: identify main problems and opportunities in current system

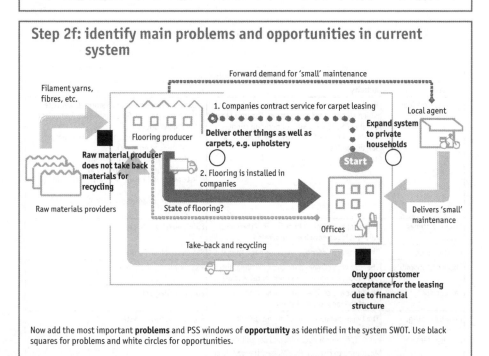

Forward demand for 'small' maintenance

Filament yarns, fibres, etc.

1. Companies contract service for carpet leasing

Local agent

Deliver other things as well as carpets, e.g. upholstery

Flooring producer

Expand system to private households

Raw material producer does not take back materials for recycling

Start

2. Flooring is installed in companies

Raw materials providers

State of flooring?

Offices

Delivers 'small' maintenance

Take-back and recycling

Only poor customer acceptance for the leasing due to financial structure

Now add the most important **problems** and PSS windows of **opportunity** as identified in the system SWOT. Use black squares for problems and white circles for opportunities.

Step 2g: decision: do PSS project or not

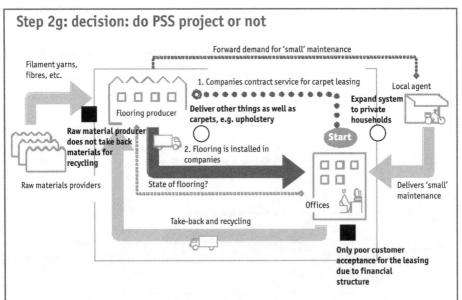

Now **decide** whether the existing **problems** in the system are threatening your company, and whether the PSS windows of **opportunity** are interesting for your company. If so, continue with the PSS project. If not, you might like to tackle another need area or stop the activity.

Step 3: PSS idea generation

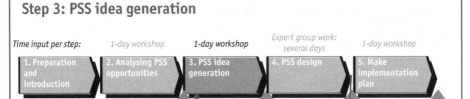

Time input per step:	1-day workshop	1-day workshop	Expert group work: several days	1-day workshop

1. Preparation and introduction
2. Analysing PSS opportunities
3. PSS idea generation
4. PSS design
5. Make implementation plan

Decision: do PSS project or not

Decision: ideas go to design or not

Evaluation: go to implementation plan, back to design or stop

Decision: implement or not

Sub-steps and tools in Step 3		
Sub-step	**Activity**	**Tools**

Generate PSS ideas	The team organises a one-day workshop in which all sub-steps are covered. The idea is to develop PSS ideas taking underlying client needs and the system SWOT from Step 2 as a starting point	● Use creativity tools (brainstorm, brainwrite)
		 ● Use Sustainability Guidelines (see Annex 2 of SusProNet book)
		 ● Use 'archetypical' models for new value creation (see Annex 2)
		   – Expand on the existing offering (consumption cycle analysis)
		   – Look for radical value innovation (strategy canvas)
		   – Look for platform-oriented PSS (see HiCS method)

Do completeness check	The team performs a check to see if the most relevant ideas have been generated	PSS Innovation Matrix
Describe ideas	The ideas are described in a one-page format	PSS Description Format
Check sustainability	The ideas are screened for their sustainability potential (economic, environmental, social)	PSS Sustainability Screen
Select priority ides	The ideas are entered into the portfolio to select the most promising ones	Portfolio Diagram
Define go/no-go criteria and select priority ideas	The team specifies a set of go/no-go criteria. The final PSS ideas are scored on market/financial potential and capability risks According to the quality of ideas, the go/no-go decision is taken	Go/no-go scoring system

Step 3a: creativity tools

Name	Approach
1. Brainstorm	As a rule, brainstorming sessions involve groups of 5–7 people together with a facilitator. The problem, issue or aim is described in a brief introduction. If necessary, participants can ask questions to clarify anything they are unsure about. The group then enters the creative phase, possibly preceded by an exercise designed to get participants to think about something totally different to clear their minds. In the creative phase each participant must come up with as many solutions to the problem as possible: it is almost literally a question of saying the first thing that comes into your head. There are absolutely no inhibitions in this phase.
	Rule 1 Criticism is not permitted
	Rule 2 The more the merrier. Quality is not important yet: ideas will be sifted through later
	Rule 3 Every idea is from everyone. Everyone may (or, rather, must) discuss someone else's idea to turn it into something else. The result is the product of the entire group
	This process, which does not need to last much longer than 15 minutes, often leads to a long list of ideas. After the session, there is a first rough weeding-out of ideas to remove those that are clearly unfeasible and to highlight the ideas that are worth working out in more detail or could at least be considered in a more thorough selection
2. Brainwrite	A brainwriting session starts by forming groups of 4–8 people. The problem or issue is then presented or described. Each participant is given a worksheet containing a table with three columns and as many rows as there are participants. Each participant is asked to write three suggestions on the first row in the three columns. Everyone then gives that worksheet to the person on their left who reads the ideas written down and then writes three ideas in the second row. This goes on until everyone has received each worksheet. The method stimulates the participants to look at the ideas that have already been written and to derive inspiration from them. The result is that a large number of ideas are produced in a very short space of time. The participants evaluate the worksheets again and each participant marks three ideas that they feel are promising. In this way the number of ideas is reduced and only the most interesting ideas are left
For more creativity tools	See www.mindtools.com

Step 3b: PSS sustainability guidelines

Dimension	Categories	Guidelines (examples)
A. Environmental dimension	A.1 system life optimisation A.2 mobility reduction A.3 resources reduction A.4 waste minimisation/valorisation A.5 conservation/bio-compatibility	e.g. Guidelines A.1: ● Can you offer services for shared use of goods? ● Can you add to product/infrastructure offer services for their maintenance, reparability (and substitution)? ● Can you add to product/infrastructure offer services for their technological and/or aesthetic upgradeability? ● Can you add to product/infrastructure offer services for their adaptation to the new context they are introduced in?
B. Socio-cultural dimension	B.1 possibility of customers consuming in a more socially responsible manner *(sufficiency)* B.2 health and safety *(of employees, customers, stakeholders . . .)* B.3 living conditions/quality of life *(customers'/users' perspective)* B.4 employment/working conditions *(employee perspective)* B.5 equity and justice/relation to stakeholders *(society/global perspective)* B.6 Respect cultural diversity *(society/local perspective)*	e.g. Guidelines B.1: ● Can you increase your customers' awareness of sustainability with new PSS? ● Can you offer more individual ways of fulfilling needs in a more sustainable manner with new PSS? ● Can you enhance the transparency of your offer and how it contributes to sustainability? ● Can you avoid possible social rebound effects of your offer? ● Can you create enabling platforms/increase the capacity of your customers through new PSS, e.g. let them participate in the design and production process? ● Can you increase customers' satisfaction, participation/involvement, motivation and awareness?
C. Economic dimension	C.1 market position and competitiveness C.2 profitability/added value for companies C.3 added value for customers C.4 long-term business development/risk *(market risk/implementation issues/return on investment [ROI])* C.5 partnership/co-operation C.6 macro-economic effect	e.g. Guidelines C.1: ● Can you improve/secure your market situation with a new PSS offer? ● Can you develop PSS that are better than the offers of your competitors, e.g. lower prices, better quality, meet customers' demands better? ● Can you fulfil demands of your customers that have not yet been fulfilled?

Use the sustainability guidelines that cover the environmental, social and economic dimension to get inspiration for PSS idea development

For full sustainability guidelines, see Annex 2.

Source: Tischner and Vezoll, MEPSS project; see www.mepss.nl and www.mepss-sdo.polimi.it

Step 3b: completeness check: PSS Innovation Matrix

Potential added value for customer PSS types	Productivity increasing or cost reducing	Comfort increasing	Lower purchasing thresholds	Risk reducing	Better emotional perception and image	Better fit with standards and values
Product-related service						
Advice and consultancy						
Product lease or hire						
Product pooling						
Product sharing						
Pay-per-unit of result						
Activity management/outsourcing						
Functional result						

This **innovation matrix** can be used in two ways:

(a) Generation of ideas
- Select the 2–3 forms of added value that the customer finds most important for the selected market segment/need area (x-axis)
- Think of specific PSS for each of the eight categories of PSS type (y-axis), possibly using the creativity techniques illustrated in the previous slide

(b) Check completeness
- Fill in the ideas that have been generated (for instance, with the tools in the former steps) in the right box
- Decide which boxes stay empty and analyse whether there is any good reason for this (for example, this form of added value is unimportant to the customer or the type of PSS is not feasible for your company in this market)
- If there is no good reason for a box being empty, develop some more PSS ideas that would fit in the blank boxes

Source: Tukker and van Halen 2003

Step 3c: describe ideas

PSS idea no.: Name	
Short description and value proposition:	
Short list of key product elements	Design plan sketch of the system
Short list of key service elements	
Profitable and competitive? ('Profit')	Score:
Environmentally sustainable? ('Planet')	Score:
Social issues solved? ('People')	Score:

Please describe the new PSS ideas by using the form above. The evaluation in the three sustainability dimensions can be carried out with the following rough sustainability check (next three slides).

Step 3d: check sustainability of ideas

PSS idea no.: Name	
Economic/profit aspects **Compare new solution with existing system**	**Score (1 = better; 0 = equal; −1 = worse)**
How profitable/valuable is the solution for the providers (can be a consortium of companies), including cost of production, cost of capital and market value of the solution for the provider(s)? Is it cheaper to produce than the competing product?	
How profitable/valuable is the solution for customers/consumers? Are there concrete, tangible savings in time, material use, etc. for the customer? Does it provide 'priceless' intangible added value such as esteem, experience, etc. for which the customer is willing to pay highly (both in comparison with a traditional product system)?	
How difficult to implement and risky is the solution for the providers? Can a promised result be measured and delivered with a high probability, or has the client a high and uncontrollable influence on the costs? When is the return on investment expected?	
How much does the solution contribute to the ability to sustain value creation in the future? Does it give the consortium that puts the PSS on the market now and in the future a crucial and dominant position in the value chain?	
Total	
Profitable and competitive?	**Score:**

Please score the new PSS ideas compared with the existing reference system as analysed earlier. Score 1 means better; score 0 the same; score −1 worse than the existing system. Add all scores to make up the total, which can be between +4 and −4. Then enter the score in the PSS description form above.

Step 3d: check sustainability of ideas

PSS idea no.: Name	
Environmental/planet aspects **Compare with existing system**	**Score (1 = better; 0 = equal; −1 = worse)**
How good is the solution in terms of material efficiency (including inputs and outputs/waste)?	
How good is the solution in terms of energy efficiency (energy input and recovery of energy without transportation)?	
How good is the solution in terms of toxicity (including input/output of hazardous substances and emissions without transport)?	
How good is the solution in terms of transport efficiency (transportation of goods and people including transport distances, transportation means, volume and packaging)?	
Total	
Environmentally sustainable?	**Score:**

Please score the new PSS ideas compared with the existing reference system as analysed earlier. Score 1 means better; score 0 the same; score −1 worse than the existing system. Add all scores to make up the total, which can be between +4 and −4. Then enter the score in the PSS description form above.

Step 3d: check sustainability of ideas

PSS idea no.: Name	
Social/people aspects **Compare with existing system**	**Score (1 = better; 0 = equal; −1 = worse)**
Does the PSS contribute to quality of work in the production chain (environment, health, safety: enriching the lives of workers by providing learning opportunities, etc.)?	
Does the PSS contribute to the enrichment of the lives of users (by providing learning opportunities, enabling and promoting action rather than passiveness, etc.)?	
Does the PSS contribute to inter- and intra-generational justice (equal wealth and power distribution between societal groups, North–South, not postponing problems to the next generation, etc.)?	
How much does the solution contribute to respect of cultural values and cultural diversity, e.g. customised solutions, contributing to the social well-being of communities, regions, etc. [cultural values])?	
Total	
Social issues solved?	Score:

Please score the new PSS ideas compared with the existing reference system as analysed earlier. Score 1 means better; score 0 the same; score −1 worse than the existing system. Add all scores to make up the total, which can be between +4 and −4. Then enter the score in the PSS description form above.

Step 3e: select priority ideas

		Attractiveness of the PSS (market and financial potential)		
		High	**Low**	
Business fit (low capability risk)	**Strong**	**Interesting: fits in with the core activities** *'Invest to build'* • Develop PSS idea further • Develop a strategy for investing in the development and implementation of the PSS • Create momentum and support • Invest initially in existing market segments and only later expansion into new markets	**Possibly interesting to strengthen the core activities (periphery)** *'Cherry-picking'* • Maximise the synergy with the core activities • Invest only if there are no better strategies available • Use the strengths of the PSS and avoid the pitfalls • Follow a cautious development and implementation path and be prepared to end this process if the prospects of a (permanently) sound business model do not appear good	
	Weak	**Possible new activity alongside existing core activities** *'Grow another branch on the tree'* • Take care, as investing in an entirely new activity is not easy • Concentrate on the most attractive PSS • Investigate whether and how this new business can be taken up	**Little potential;** *'Dead-end business'* • Not interesting at the moment but remain alert to future developments that may improve the prospects	

Now enter all new ideas in the **portfolio diagram** as shown above. Rank them in comparison with each other according to their market and financial potential, i.e. attractiveness and the business fit (i.e. if they involve a low capability risk). At least all ideas that end up in the upper left square should be taken further.

Step 3f: define/apply go/no-go criteria

Elements and importance		
Potential element	Score	Can score be improved, and how?
Market risk: will they buy it? E.g. ● Likely market demand ● Client loyalty	Yes/Medium or unknown/No	

Credibility risk: can we do it? E.g.
● Technological assets (technologies, infrastructure, capacity)
   – Technologies
   – Infrastructure
   – Capacity
● Organisational assets
   – Management style
   – Product and market development capacity
● Available partnerships (e.g. suppliers and distribution channels)
	Yes/Medium or unknown/No	

Financial risk: is it profitable? E.g.
High tangible and intangible value for the client
● Low production costs and high synergetic value
● Improved competitive position
   – More power in value chain
   – Difficult to copy
● Improved potential for innovation (including option value)
	Yes/Medium or unknown/No	

Sustainability risk: are we moving in the right (more sustainable) direction (according to previous evaluation)?	Yes/Medium or unknown/No	

For each 'gate' in the process a set of **go/no-go evaluation criteria** is needed. We propose working with four key questions that can be tailored to the specific situation of the company in question. Please formulate the most important criteria under the headings, then check if the results (the PSS solutions) are good enough to go to the next stage of the process. If not, either redo the step or stop the process.

Step 4: PSS design

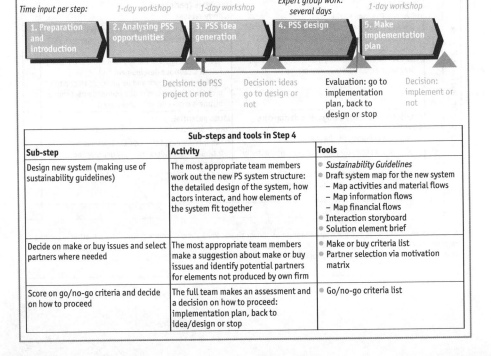

Time input per step: *1-day workshop*   *1-day workshop*   *Expert group work: several days*   *1-day workshop*

1. Preparation and introduction   2. Analysing PSS opportunities   3. PSS idea generation   4. PSS design   5. Make implementation plan

Decision: do PSS project or not   Decision: ideas go to design or not   Evaluation: go to implementation plan, back to design or stop   Decision: implement or not

Sub-steps and tools in Step 4		
Sub-step	Activity	Tools

Design new system (making use of sustainability guidelines)	The most appropriate team members work out the new PS system structure: the detailed design of the system, how actors interact, and how elements of the system fit together	● *Sustainability Guidelines*
		● Draft system map for the new system
		   – Map activities and material flows
		   – Map information flows
		   – Map financial flows
		● Interaction storyboard
		● Solution element brief

Decide on make or buy issues and select partners where needed	The most appropriate team members make a suggestion about make or buy issues and identify potential partners for elements not produced by own firm	● Make or buy criteria list ● Partner selection via motivation matrix
Score on go/no-go criteria and decide on how to proceed	The full team makes an assessment and a decision on how to proceed: implementation plan, back to idea/design or stop	● Go/no-go criteria list

Step 4a: develop system map (new system)

| Platform providers | Integration providers | Intermediate users | Final users |

Food producers

Packaging providers

Public administration

Organic food manager

System organiser

Appliance producer

Dietary management software provider

Dietary adviser

Furniture provider

Family doctor

Local food shop

Assistance provider

Service manager

Home

Office

Your take-away meal

Your all-inclusive meal service

Your dining corner

Your personal meal box

Material flow

Information flow

Now the chosen new PSS ideas have to be detailed further. For this the first step is to develop a system map for the new PS system as was done before for the existing system.

For further information, see E. Manzini, L. Collins and S. Evans, *Solution Oriented Partnership* (HiCS project publication, 2004).

Step 4b: develop interaction storyboard

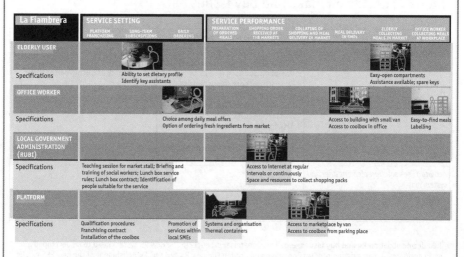

Then develop an **interaction storyboard**, pointing out the steps of interaction between the different actors in the process of providing the PSS.

For further information, see E. Manzini, L. Collins and S. Evans, *Solution Oriented Partnership* (HiCS project publication, 2004).

Step 4c: set up solution element brief

Stake-holders	Tasks for the stakeholders ┼ DESIGN	☐ BUILD/DELIVER	▦ DESIGN AND BUILD/DELIVER

Organic food manager and system organiser

Dietary management software provider

Appliance producer

Assistance provider

Service manager

Others

Next compile a **solution element brief** showing the breakdown of solution elements and their attribution to each of the actors providing the new PSS solution.

For further information, see E. Manzini, L. Collins and S. Evans, *Solution Oriented Partnership* (HiCS project publication, 2004).

Step 4d: decide on make and buy issues

Elements and importance		
Activity needed in system	**Make?** ● Potential for competitive edge is high ● Risk of outsourcing is high ● Close to own core competences ● High synergistic and option value ● Outsourcing generates high transaction costs ● Activity not yet mature or standardised and needs a lot of troubleshooting in interaction with other system elements	**Buy?** ● The reverse of these criteria ● Availability of trusted partnerships
Activity 1: see solution element brief and system map		
Activity 2		
Etc.		

Then decide about **make and buy issues**, e.g. do the material products in the new PS system need to be developed and newly designed, or can existing products be taken and used in the new PS system? Establishment of the new PSS can be quicker when already-existing products and infrastructures can be used. However, often the suitable products are not available, in which case new design has to take place. Related to this decision, the partnership in the PSS system can also change.

Step 4e: select partners with motivation matrix

Gives to...	Organic food manager and system organiser	Dietary management software provider	Appliance producer	Assistance provider	Service manager	Solution centre	Solution-oriented partnership
Organic food manager and system organiser	• To find new perspectives in the organic food industry	• Organic food market expertise to test the validity of the software	• Organic food market expertise to improve the performance of the appliances	• High-quality food products to be offered to customers	• New high-quality convenience meals for vending machines • A new service concept	• Knowledge and expertise from the organic food sector	• Organic brand identity • Expertise in organic supply management
Dietary management software provider	• A way to enhance the real value of the organic food offering	• To enter non-medical markets • To open and finalise research in new areas	• New criteria and dietary tools for the development of appliances for special food needs	• A way to better satisfy customer needs • Potential networking with food specialists	• Adds value to the service portfolio	• Expertise in the dietary industry	• Advice and dietary management through professional software
Appliance producer	• Competences in food processing	• Competences in food processing • Hardware appliances to be integrated with software	• To find applications for advanced food appliances • To enter the service dimension	• A dedicated appliance for customers	• A smart vending machine system	• Expertise and products in the white goods appliances sector	• Smart appliances for food processing • Brand identity
Assistance provider	• Specific knowledge of a very sensitive sector • Inputs and feedback from the reduced access to food context	• Specific knowledge of a very sensitive sector • A new area of business	• Cognitive and physiological feedback to better design the interfaces of new appliances	• To complete the present service offering		• Expertise in assisting people in a specific context	• Social dimension • Access to a specific context
Service manager	• Expertise in a specific market • Expertise in service management	• Feedback from the final users • Statistical databases	• Feedback from the final users • Inputs to integrate service and appliance design		• To expand the service portfolio • To extend the offering to new contexts	• Expertise and entrepreneurship in the vending machine industry	• Service management in specific contexts
Solution centre	• Catalyst in the design and development of ideas • Manage partner development	• To facilitate entry into new businesses • Support in the design and development of ideas	• To facilitate entry into new businesses • Support in the design and development of ideas	• To facilitate entry into new businesses • Support in testing of the solution idea with their customers	• To facilitate entry into new businesses	• To develop expertise in solution design • To obtain visibility as solutions experts	• Tools and expertise to facilitate and manage the partner-based solutions
Solution-oriented partnership	• Expand business and new market opportunities • To become a food solution provider	• Visibility and recognition to the end-user • Feedback from new clients	• New sales channels • Service expertise	• A new idea of service to be used to reach new customers	• A new service to be used to contact new possible context of business	• Opportunity to test a methodological toolbox • Expertise in the food sector	• To provide healthy, convenient meals in different contexts of reduced access to food

Finally, develop a **stakeholder motivation matrix** showing all the partners, their contribution to and benefits from the partnership and potential interactions between them. Thus partner interactions, synergies and potential conflicts can be identified. Once complete, the stakeholder motivation matrix can form the basis of the business plan and the first formal agreement between partners, the memorandum of understanding.

For further information, see E. Manzini, L. Collins and S. Evans, *Solution Oriented Partnership* (HiCS project publication, 2004).

Step 4f: refine/apply go/no-go criteria

Elements and importance		
Potential element	**Score**	**Can score be improved, and how?**
Market risk: will they buy it? • Use criteria developed in Step 3.1	Yes/Medium or unknown/No	
Credibility risk: can we do it? • Use criteria developed in Step 3.1	Yes/Medium or unknown/No	
Financial risk: is it profitable? • Use criteria developed in Step 3.1	Yes/Medium or unknown/No	
Sustainability risk: are we moving in the right (more sustainable) direction (according to sustainability check done for the elaborated PSS solution; see previous slides)?	Yes/Medium or unknown/No	

For each 'gate' in the process a set of **go/no-go evaluation criteria** is needed. We propose working with four key questions that can be tailored to the specific situation of the company in question. Please use the most important criteria under the headings as formulated in the previous phase. Check if they are still the most important criteria and amend if necessary. Then check if the results (the elaborated PSS solutions) are good enough to go to the next stage of the process. If not, either redo the step or stop the process.

Step 5: develop implementation plan

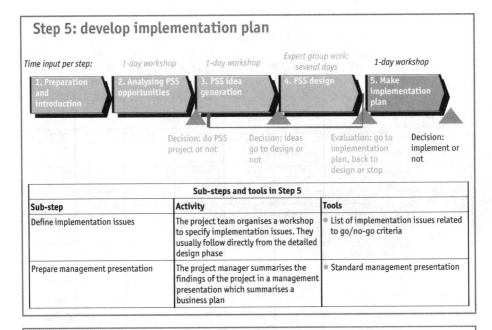

Sub-steps and tools in Step 5		
Sub-step	**Activity**	**Tools**
Define implementation issues	The project team organises a workshop to specify implementation issues. They usually follow directly from the detailed design phase	• List of implementation issues related to go/no-go criteria
Prepare management presentation	The project manager summarises the findings of the project in a management presentation which summarises a business plan	• Standard management presentation

Step 5a: identify implementation issues

		Opportunities	Threats	Controllable by the company?	Proposed solution strategy?
1. The user value (co-)created					
a.	Tangible value				
b.	Intangible value				
2. The (operational) system costs generated					
a.	Tangible costs				
b.	PSS-specific attention points: risk premium, transaction costs, pre-financing costs				
3. Dynamic value creation potential realised					
a.	The power position in the system				
b.	Defence against substitutes				
c.	The speed, ability and flexibility to innovate and shape the future				
4. The investment needed and capability risk to develop the new (business) system					
a.	Investment in PSS development (building the structure, building core and complementary capabilities)				
b.	Other capital losses: cannibalisation, synergies, etc.				

Step 5b: produce a management report

New PSS business opportunity: name of PSS

Use the PSS name from the PSS description form, if it is an original, striking name. If not, reconsider it and find a better one.

Visualisation

Create a draft advertisement if possible to visualise in one image the advantages of the new PSS for the customers.

Brief description of the PSS (take from PSS description form)

Description of the context of the strategy (including the following points to consider):
- What is the purpose (a new PSS meets a need)?
- Which customer segment?
- Why the change? What will it yield? Why is it recommendable?
- Why does it fit in with the company? What policy does it fit in with?

Marketing mix (practical implementation of strategy)

Product-service description: brief description of PSS
Price: what pricing strategy will you adopt to reach the customer segment?
Promotion: how are you going to let customers know what you are supplying?
Place (sales channels): how are you going to sell the PSS (via internet, directly to the customer, call centres)?

Expected result

What do you expect from this strategy in terms of: turnover, profit, market share, value creation, return on investment, customer loyalty, brand awareness, promotion, positioning, etc. (as far as possible give specific and concrete results).

What are the main advantages and risks of the new PSS?

Primary target group: briefly describe the primary target group in the customer segment
Positioning: what unique selling points does the PSS add?
Creative approach: in what creative way will you target the market (what is the key to success)?
Drivers and obstacles: which drivers promote the new PSS? Which risks and difficulties do you have to overcome? What does the success of the strategy depend on? What are the bottlenecks and uncertainties?

Investment

What is needed to implement the strategy and to neutralise uncertainties and bottlenecks in terms of money, people, resources, time, R&D, strategic alliances, etc.? Demonstrate what the new strategy will mean for the company.

Implementation

What are the next steps to implement the PSS? Which actors do you need? What is the suggested timing?

Annex 2
TOOLS, ALPHABETICAL

Martijn Verkuijl and Ursula Tischner
econcept, Germany

Arnold Tukker
TNO, The Netherlands

This annex lists in alphabetical order tools and methods for PSS development. Table A2.1 gives an overview of the tools, plus the phases in PSS development where they are most useful.

Backcasting for exploring PSS

Backcasting is a specific foresight and scenario tool. It tries to specify in a specific field (e.g. energy supply) a normatively desired sustainable future, and then 'backcasts' which steps have to be taken to make this future a reality (e.g Weaver *et al.* 2000; Fig. A2.1). In a way the approach resembles roadmapping, but in general the goal to be reached lies further in the future (typically one generation) which implies that the trajectory for the future cannot be assessed in a deterministic way. For PSS development, backcasting can have a number of advantages, particularly in the PSS analysis phase:

- It enables long-term vision development with regard to major persistent societal problems and connects it to (strategic) actions and choices now at the level of products and services

- It combines design, analysis and participation

Page	Tool/stage in PSS development	Covers full PSS development	Mainly used in PSS development steps below				
			Preparation and introduction	Analysis of PSS opportunities	PSS idea generation	PSS design	Making implementation plan
394	Backcasting for exploring PSS			X			
398	Benchmarking	X					
399	Benefit Planning Roadmap: tool from the HiCS project	X					
401	Blueprinting: systematically describing a (product-)service			X	X	X	
402	Consumption chain analysis for generating new value propositions (MacMillan and McGrath 1997)			X	X		
402	Database(s) of PSS case studies				X		
403	Design Plan: visualisation and communication tool for prospective PSS partnerships from the HiCS project			X	X	X	
404	Eco-efficiency analysis of a product-service			X	X		
405	E2 Vector, quantitative eco-efficiency assessment tool			X	X		
407	Ecodesign: checklist for environmental assessments by econcept			X	X		
408	Eco-design portfolio: selection tool based on environmental performance and feasibility				X		
409	Ethnographic research			X			
409	Gap analyses for services			X			
401	INES tool (Improving New Services): environmental, economic and social assessment tool from the Austrian Eco-efficient PSS project			X			
412	Interaction storyboard: tool from the HiCS project					X	
412	MEPSS toolkit (PSS development method)	X					
414	META matrix for services: environmental and economic assessment tool			X	X		

TABLE A2.1 Overview of tools and methods in Annex 2 (continued over)

Page	Tool/stage in PSS development	Covers full PSS development	Mainly used in PSS development steps below				
			Preparation and introduction	Analysis of PSS opportunities	PSS idea generation	PSS design	Making implementation plan
414	Opportunity Recognition Diagnose: diagnosis modules of ProSecCo						
416	Partnership co-ordinating tools: tools from the HiCS project						X
417	Perceived service quality model, e.g. for car sharing			X	X		
417	Pragmatic Differential tool: generic selection tool			X	X	X	
418	Pre-Diagnose: diagnosis modules of ProSecCo		X				
419	Product-service life-cycle information management and acquisition: getting data for developing PSS			X			
419	Progressive abstraction tool: creativity tool			X	X		
420	Profit pool: analysis of the structure of the value chain (Gadiesh and Gilbert 1998)			X	X		
421	PSS Innovation Matrix: idea generation tool and completeness check				X		
422	Qualitative 4-axes expert panel: assessment of environmental and economic performance, market acceptance and business fit (Goedkoop et al. 1999)			X	X	X	
424	Solution Elements Brief: tool from the HiCS project					X	
425	Solution Scan: tool from the HiCS project			X	X		
426	Spider diagrams: generic visualisation tool for assessments			X	X	X	
427	Stakeholders' Motivation Matrix: tool from the HiCS project					X	
429	Strategy Canvas for generating new value propositions (W. Chan Kim and Renée Mauborgne)			X	X		
429	Sustainability Guidelines for PSS: tool from the MEPSS project				X	X	

TABLE A2.1   (from previous page; continued opposite)

Page	Tool/stage in PSS development	Covers full PSS development	Mainly used in PSS development steps below				
			Preparation and introduction	Analysis of PSS opportunities	PSS idea generation	PSS design	Making implementation plan
435	Sustainability evaluation tool: tool from the Sustainable Homeservices project			X		X	
437	Sustainable Systems Triangle (SST): tool for assessment of the innovation potential of a system			X	X		
438	System Assessment: tool from the HiCS project. Assessment of economic, environmental and social aspects			X	X	X	
440	System organisation map: visualisation and communication tool for prospective PSS partnerships from the HiCS project			X	X	X	
442	Triple Bottom Line Innovation Audit tool	X					
444	Use cases of PSS: graphical representation—tool adapted by School of Architecture and Design, Aalborg University				X		
445	Validation of Life-cycle Economic Benefits of Partner Based Solutions: tool from the HiCS project			X	X	X	
445	Value analysis/value engineering			X		X	
446	ViP approach (Vision in Product development): scenario method	X					

TABLE A2.1 (from previous page)

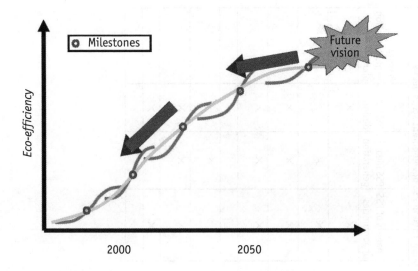

FIGURE A2.1 Backcasting: Looking back from the future

Source: presented by J. Quist, TU Delft, at the Second SusProNet Conference, 3–4 June 2004, Brussels

- It makes normative choices explicit
- It improves focus and thinking, reflexivity, higher-order learning, and strategic relevance

The process steps in the backcasting approach are:

- Problem orientation
- Stakeholder analysis and involvement
- Stakeholder creativity workshop
- Scenario construction
- Scenario assessment
- Backcasting workshop and stakeholder consultation
- Realisation and implementation

Benchmarking

'Benchmarking is the search for industry best practices that lead to superior performance' (Camp 1989, 1995). It differs from a competitor analysis, because it concerns not only the direct competitors but also the best practices in general, which are used as a source of learning and process improvement. Benchmarking is a well-structured process made up of eight steps, and is in fact a full methodology for improving business processes and value propositions (Negro 1992: 213-33):

1. **Definition of the application area.** A definition of the objectives and ambits to be analysed that could be part of the delivery system, the internal processes or the success key factors

2. **Identification of the comparison actors**. A phase that needs a considerable amount of time to collect information from all kinds of sources. Afterwards a selection is made of direct competitors, main competitors, sector leaders, and leading functions or applications, coming from other sectors

3. **Definition of performance targets and evaluation of gaps**. A collection of information after the performance targets (quantitative and qualitative reports) are defined. The results are compared with the internal values, taking into account the differences that come from the diversity of application areas

4. **Planning for change introduction**. A step consisting of an assessment phase based on organisational, economic and technological aspects, consequent planning and resulting in improvements

5. **Realisation of planned actions**

6. **Monitoring of reached targets**. A periodical monitoring of reached targets, to verify the extent of planned improvements, identify differences and define corrective measures

7. **Standardisation of reached improvements and of the benchmarking process**. When successful, the benchmarking process and results should be standardised

8. **Adjusting of objectives**. when the benchmarking process has not been successful or if the external conditions have changed, it is necessary to adjust and redefine the objectives and to control the organisational behaviour

The main results expected are: guaranteed customer satisfaction, in-depth comprehension of success key factors, augmented capacity to define and fulfil important objectives, improvement of competitive position, and keeping up to date in organisational and technological progresses.

Benefit Planning Roadmap: tool from the HiCS project

The Benefit Planning Roadmap is a tool developed for use within the HiCS Solution Oriented Partnership framework (Manzini *et al.* 2004; see also the section on the HiCS method). It was developed by Menno Marien, Laura Vidal, Joanna Lambert, Tommaso Buganza and Alessio Marchesi. The Solution Oriented Partnership Benefits Planning

(SBP) Roadmap describes the methodology to develop a benefit plan for the SBP platform and specific elements. The Solution Oriented Partnership business plan differs from a normal business plan. The Solution Oriented Partnership not only includes profit-oriented companies but could also include other organisations such as governmental and other not-for-profit organisations. Benefits describe a wider aspect of the 'profits' obtained from the solution, including also social and environmental and therefore sustainability benefits. The SBP roadmap starts with an initial company with an innovative idea, and provides ten steps guiding the company in the process of creating a SBP. Furthermore, it provides a 'template' to fill out during the process of developing the solution and the Solution Oriented Partnership. Also it provides a decision-support tool enabling individual companies or organisations to evaluate the benefits and investment impact of joining the partnership.

The ten steps of the SBP roadmap are:

1. **The solution eye-opener**. The eye-opener step could have two possible starts: from the company or from the Solution Centre of HiCS. The results are a first definition of the platform elements and a conversion of individual business ideas into a partnership-oriented business focus

2. **Tentative solution generation**. This step consists of two activities:
   - The generation of the first solution concepts defining elements and possible partners that should be involved
   - The concepts should be illustrated and further explained using the graphical tools and icons as described in the Design Plan

3. **Create the empty SBP**. In this step the first 'benefits-oriented' snapshot will be taken by ordering all the information, ideas and concepts obtained in the previous steps. The snapshot at this level permits the company to reflect on its initial business idea and to get an impression of the business/benefits potential

4. **Search for partners and sell**. The company, supported by the Solution Centre, should search for possible partners that comply with the required partner profiles

5. **The new company-level decision taking**. This step comprises the activities of the organisation at an individual level, to analyse and decide whether the concepts are of interest

6. **The platform vision, definition and solution design development**. This step is where the three development streams are running in parallel in order to design the final solution

7. **Filling the Solution Oriented Partnership Benefits Plan**. In this step a further 'benefits-oriented' snapshot will be taken by ordering all the information, ideas and concepts obtained in the previous step

8. **Search partners and sell (2)**. This step of search and selling is similar to step 4 of the empty level; however, more partners are in the partnership, and the shared interest becomes more complex

9. **The company-level decision-making**. As in step 6, when modifications are made to the concepts, this will lead to changes in expected roles, benefits and investments in the partner-based solution

10. **Freeze**. At this point the SBP should be completely 'filled' and the partnership should sign 'Heads of Agreements'. This means that all partners are aware of their risks, expected benefits, the growth potential, etc. of the proposed solution

Blueprinting: systematically describing a service

Having defined quality from a number of perspectives and, in doing so, discussed many of the design issues, there comes a point when this has to be translated into a system that will deliver these objectives. The main tool for design here is the service blueprint. A blueprint is a model of the service system, covering, in terms of activities and time, the progress of a customer through the service system (Zeithaml 1996; Maylor 2000). With this technique, the activities that constitute the service are chronologically ordered. The interaction with the customer is a central theme. This tool is particularly useful in the analysis stage of PSS development. To make a blueprint Zeithaml gives eight steps that need to be undertaken, which are summarised below (Brezet *et al.* 2001):

● Identify the service process to be blueprinted

● Map the service process from the customer's point of view

● Draw the line of interaction

● Draw the line of visibility

● Map contact employee actions, both onstage and backstage

● Draw the line of internal interaction

● Map internal support activities

● Add evidence of service at each customer action step

Reijnhoudt (2000) adds an extra step to these eight steps, which is especially designed for product-oriented companies trying to go into the service business:

● Add non-physical evidence of service at each customer action step

Consumption chain analysis for generating new value propositions (MacMillan and McGrath)

Some authors, such as MacMillan and McGrath (1997), propose taking the consumption chain as a starting point for finding new value propositions. What a customer does with the product has to be painstakingly mapped. Leading questions in this regard include:

- How is the product installed?

- How is it paid for?

- How is it stored?

- How is it moved?

- What is the customer really using it for?

- What help do they need to use it?

- How is it repaired or serviced?

- What happens if the product is disposed of?

All these steps in the consumption chain in principle provide handles for improvement. To find these improvement options, the customer's experience has to be mapped, via simple 'who', 'where', 'when', 'what' and 'how' questions. A deep understanding of the customer's experience at any step of the consumption chain will identify non-traditional ways for creating new value—probably, in our terms, by offering a product-service. This approach is particularly useful for application in the analysis and idea generation phase of PSS development.

Database(s) of PSS case studies

At www.sustainablePSS.org a database of PSS case studies, including analysis, of innovative PSS that have been implemented in industry is available. The database is structured using the 'case-based reasoning theory'. The data has been analysed to determine trends in areas such as: nature and impact of legislation, senior-management leadership, green consumerism, green marketing and sustainability impacts. This web-based tool should provide information and decision-support for firms interested in developing a PSS project. The database was constructed between 2000 and 2004 and is primarily focused on the UK (Wong 2004). Other databases with PSS cases, although less easily accessible are from the SusProNet project (at www.dynamo.tno.nl) and from the MEPSS project (at www.mepss.nl). Such databases are particularly useful as help in the idea generation step of PSS.

Design Plan: tool from the HiCS project

The **Design Plan** is a design tool to facilitate solution-oriented partnerships (Manzini *et al*. 2004). The tool was developed by François Jégou, Ezio Manzini and Anna Meroni. Its aim is to enhance communication and exchange among partners involved in the development of a Solution Oriented Partnership (PSS). The Design Plan is a strategic design toolbox that works as a series of formats to present, in a synthetic way, a solution involving numerous actors in a complex interaction process. It can play an important role in the analysis phase of PSS design, but also in idea generation, development/design and implementation. The Design Plan formats allow the actors involved to:

- Build a common language
- Support the strategic conversation
- Customise a standard language

The Design Plan works as a mediation tool for collectively building and refining a complex solution:

- Producing synthetic views
- Providing easy-access and flexible formats
- Agreeing a visual contract

The Design Plan is a shared and progressive system for representing and elaborating a solution. It consists of four main formats presenting the solution from different points of view. The common goal is to develop 'generative images' that start particular discussions about the solution. These formats have different contents and correspond to different aims; therefore, they use various levels of abstraction and ways of interpreting the solution. The main Design Plan tools are:

- **System organisation map** (included in this annex). The system organisation map shows the solution from the point of view of the organisation of the partnership providing the solution

- **Interaction storyboard** (included in this annex). The interaction storyboard shows the solution performance along a horizontal time-line. It is the translation of an event, which takes place in space and time, into a sequence of static images and explanatory captions

- **Solution elements brief** (included in this annex). The solution elements brief breaks down the solution into elements that can be recomposed to give different final Partner Based Solutions. It helps to systematise and communicate the complex system

- **Stakeholders' motivation matrix** (included in this annex). The stakeholders' motivation matrix shows the solution from the point of view of the stakeholder's interest in taking part in the partnership. The matrix shows a checklist of motivations, benefits and contributions from each stakeholder's point of view, between individual partners and over the whole partnership

The four main formats of the Design Plan form the input and output for each of the different steps of the Solution Oriented Partnership methodology developed in the HiCS project (presented in Chapter 5, Section 5.3) (see Fig. A2.2).

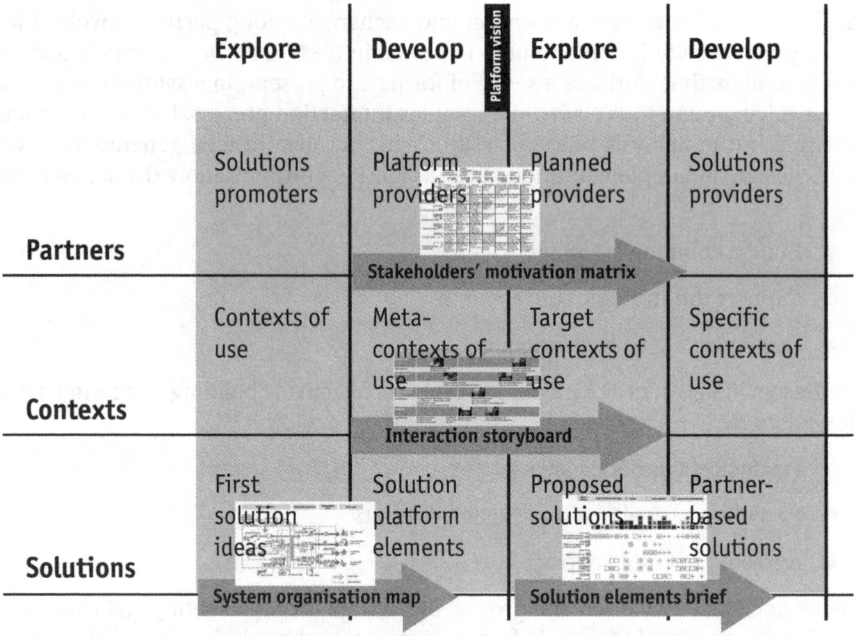

	Explore	**Develop**	Platform vision	**Explore**	**Develop**
Partners	Solutions promoters	Platform providers		Planned providers	Solutions providers
		Stakeholders' motivation matrix			
Contexts	Contexts of use	Meta-contexts of use		Target contexts of use	Specific contexts of use
		Interaction storyboard			
Solutions	First solution ideas	Solution platform elements		Proposed solutions	Partner-based solutions
	System organisation map			Solution elements brief	

FIGURE A2.2   The different formats of the Design Plan distributed along the Solution Oriented Partnership methodological framework

Source: Manzini *et al.* 2004

Eco-efficiency analysis of a product-service

In order to gain a first impression of the eco-efficiency of a service, the scheme to facilitate the identification of eco-efficient producer services (Zaring *et al.* 2001) described in Figure A2.3 can be used. Although this scheme does not provide a complete quantitative analysis (therefore a LCA analysis would be necessary), it gives a first glance of the eco-efficiency potential of a service. The tool is particularly useful for the assessment of environmental and economic aspects in the evaluation stage of the different steps in the PSS development process.

Innovation:											
	What changes?				What are the consequences of the change for:			What are the environmental effects?				
	New service concept	New client interface	Technological options	New service delivery system	Mobility	Behaviour	Efficiency	Energy (less and/ or more durable)	Material flow (less and/or more durable)	Environmentally critical substances	Use of water	Hazardous waste
Providing side												
Consuming side												
Conclusion:												

FIGURE A2.3 Scheme to facilitate the identification of eco-efficient producer services

Source: Zaring *et al.* 2001

E2 Vector: quantitative assessment tool (Goedkoop *et al.* 1999)

The project Product-Service Systems (Goedkoop *et al.* 1999) has resulted in ten case descriptions. Three of these have been worked out quantitatively in terms of economic and ecological characteristics. To get an appealing representation of two core parameters, the economy and ecology axes have been combined. This has resulted in the ratio economic added value (of companies on the network) per unit environmental load, which can be plotted graphically as what has come to be called the E2 Vector. The E2 Vector enables benchmarking between a company's departments, between companies, between economic sectors and between different product-service mixes. This tool can have particularly value in the analysis, design and implementation phases of PSS development.

E2 Vector: the Eco-pool concept

With this tool it is possible to plot the environmental impacts of economic activities against the cumulative (financial) value that they create (see Fig. A2.4). Environmental load is used on the vertical axis. In the figure an imaginary Eco-pool for car use is shown (Goedkoop *et al.* 1999). Here a life-cycle has been used to define the pool, but this need not be so. Goedkoop *et al.* suggest using the Eco-pool as an addition to the 'profit pool'. Once the profit pool has been defined, an LCA practitioner will be able to generate an Eco-pool of the alternative business options a company has.

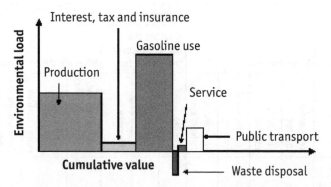

FIGURE A2.4 Imaginary Eco-pool for a car

The use of gasoline generates a relatively high environmental load. Other business opportunities, such as financing and insurance, or service and waste disposal, generate a much lower environmental load per unit of value.

E2 Vector: quantitative assessment

For the E2 Vector, Goedkoop plots cumulative *financial* value against cumulative environmental load. The result of these changes can be seen in Figure A2.5. The blocks form a slope that can be characterised with a vector, which connects the origin with the top right-hand corner of the last block.

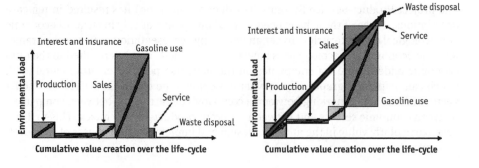

FIGURE A2.5 E2 Vector example

Source: Goedkoop *et al.* 1999

These vectors can be combined to generate the overall vector. A system with a vector that is less steep than the reference can contribute to unlinking, as the ratio between environmental load and value is better. This unlinking is shown in Figure A2.6.

Both the qualitative 4-axes expert panel (also described in this annex) results and the quantitative E2 Vector results in the Goedkoop study show that individual PSS can prove

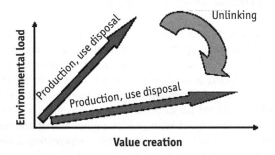

FIGURE A2.6 De-linking effect

Source: Goedkoop *et al.* 1999

beneficial to the environment in combination with creating (new) business. Moreover, the E2 Vector studies show a potential to de-link environmental pressure from economic growth.

Ecodesign: checklist for environmental assessment by econcept

The Ecodesign Checklist was developed in 1994 by Ursula Tischner in co-operation with Friedrich Schmidt-Bleek at the Wuppertal Institute. It has been tested in several applications and extensively revised by econcept (see Tischner *et al.* 2000). It may be used as a tool to identify weaknesses of an existing product or facilitate detailed development or redesign of new products (and hence can also play a role in most stages of PSS development).

The checklist contains a comprehensive list of questions on environmentally relevant issues of products along their life-cycle. But not all environmental aspects may be relevant to products. For instance, for a product that does not use any energy, the aspect energy input will not be relevant. Irrelevant aspects should be identified and be given the value 0. The remaining aspects can then be investigated thoroughly and evaluated 'step by step'. If there is not much time to investigate and if there are information gaps, data will have to be estimated. The list has already proved to be efficient in identifying the most important environmental issues.

The checklist can be helpful in detailing the design concepts further by systematically checking the environmentally relevant aspects that should be considered along the product's life-cycle.

After completion of the design phase the final check can show whether or not important environmental improvements have been overlooked. Additionally, the Ecodesign checklist allows the comparison of new solutions with the particular product. The subtotal of the evaluation shows which product is environmentally better. In the econcept checklist different aspects are not weighed against each other.

Ecodesign portfolio: selection tool

An ecodesign portfolio diagram is simply a matrix that plots the technical and economic feasibility of the developed design alternatives and ecological improvement potentials (see e.g. Tischner *et al.* 2000). Solutions are entered into the diagram according to the captions in the boxes (see Fig. A2.7). Those that are entered in the top right-hand box are those that will probably lead to an economic/ecological win–win situation and should be selected for development. Solutions that are assigned to the bottom right-hand box promise quick wins, with an emphasis on the technical and economic side. Those in the top left-hand box are very interesting from the ecological viewpoint but probably more for long-term strategists, as they are currently difficult to realise from the technical or economic viewpoint. Solutions in the bottom left-hand box should be removed, as they offer neither economic nor ecological advantages.

This type of diagram can be used in different versions with different criteria for a variety of problems. It can also be applied to questions of detail at the product development level: for example, for selecting materials. In this case the axes might stand, for instance, for 'material cost' and 'environmental impact of the material'. The tool is particularly useful in the various PSS idea selection steps in the different phases of PSS development.

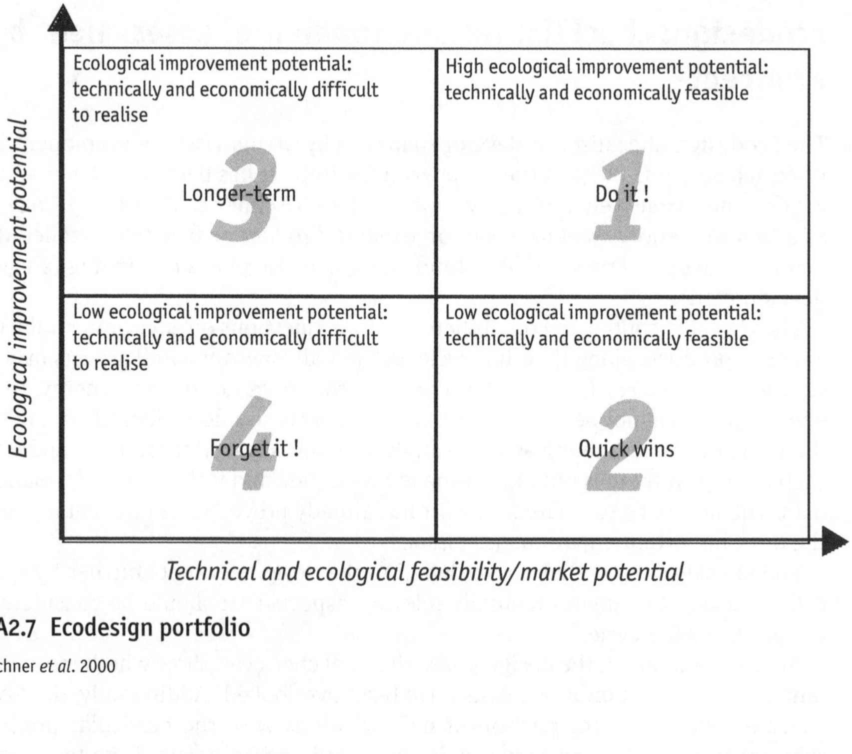

FIGURE A2.7   Ecodesign portfolio

Source: Tischner *et al.* 2000

Ethnographic research

Ethnographic research comes from social and cultural anthropology and aims to understand people in their natural social and cultural contexts (Wolcott 1999). The result of ethnographic studies is an adequate knowledge of high granularity on how people act and interact in particular domains. Such research fits particularly well in the analysis phase of PSS development.

However, these results include not only in-depth understanding of how people behave in certain social situations, but also (and ideally) why they do so, what motivates them, what is the meaning of this situation and what are the emotional and subjective experiences linked to these situations. As a rule, ethnography is a 'pronged activity' usually requiring field researchers who immerse themselves with the people they study. Applied ethnographic studies are highly useful in product development and design processes. They provide accurate as well as inspiring information about people's behaviour in the context of various domains ('contextual user profiling').

Gap analyses for services

Gap analysis is a tool for detecting service quality. Service quality can be measured as an input process involving the functional deployment of resources and activities. The output is the delivered service benefits. Consequently, a quality function deployment (QFD)-type input–output framework can be used to study services. Such a service quality framework is presented in Figure A2.8 (Dickson 1994). It is particularly useful in the analysis phase of PSS development.

Gap analysis has very close parallels with the positioning of the service and QFD. The task is for the service provider to identify and reduce the following gaps that have been identified by researchers as significant barriers to delivering a quality service:

- Gap 1. Management beliefs about consumer expectations are wrong. Management's benefit segmentation analyses are flawed

- Gap 2. Management operational specifications of the desired service do not match management perceptions of the target consumer's desired benefits and expectations. Management's QFD service specification matrix is wrong

- Gap 3. The delivered service does not meet management operational specifications. The implementation and control of service production script is basically flawed

- Gap 4. Promises do not match performance. The promoted positioning does not match the delivered service

- Gap 5. Consumer perceptions of the delivered service do not meet consumer expectations. Consumers are dissatisfied

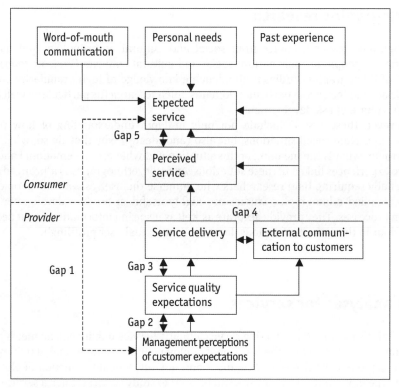

FIGURE A2.8 Service quality framework

Source: Dickson 1994

INES tool (Improving New Services): tool from the Eco-efficient PSS project

INES is a decision-support tool and a learning tool about the idea of sustainability at company level and about the impacts of a PSS idea. The tool is primarily used in the analysis phase of PSS development and idea selection, but also increases creativity (generating new ideas and adapting existing ones). It is possible to evaluate the PSS qualitatively and overall to gain a better understanding of the PSS. The tool is developed as part of the Austrian Eco-efficient PSS project, which was part of the Factory of Tomorrow project.

This Excel (Visual Basic) tool contains 67 questions for the comparison of the existing product and the PSS. There is no weighting possible between the three sustainability dimensions, but only within the categories (e.g. energy, waste). The final result is shown in a graph (see also Fig. A2.9).

Table A2.2 presents the categories for each sustainability dimension.

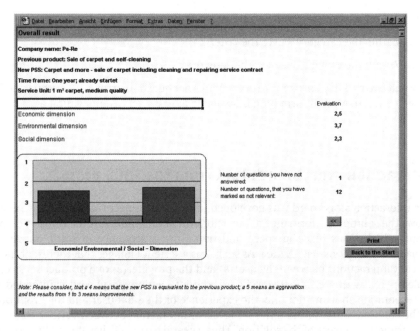

FIGURE A2.9   Screenshot of the final result within the INES tool

Environmental dimension	Economic dimension	Social dimension
• Material input • Energy use • Water use • Land use • Transport • Waste • Sewage water • Emissions • Environmental management	• Company key figures • Product-related figures • Macroeconomic figures • Relation to stakeholder	• Structure of employees • Social management • (Working) safety and health • Social justice • Equal opportunities • Gender issues • Human dignity • International justice • Customers

TABLE A2.2   Categories per sustainability dimension

The criteria are structured according to three levels:

● The first level contains the three sustainability **dimensions**

● The second level contains the **categories** mentioned above

● The third level contains the **criteria**

These criteria are qualitative or quantitative questions asking for, for example, percentage, change and value. An example of a 'level 3 criterion' is the question: 'How is the amount of greenhouse gas emissions changing with the new PSS?'

The aggregation is split into two steps:

1. Within the categories over the criteria
2. Within the dimensions over the categories

Between two and five answers are possibilities per question. Irrelevant criteria need not to be answered. More information is available at www.serviceinnovation.at.

Interaction storyboard: tool from the HiCS project

The interaction storyboard was developed in the HiCS project (Manzini *et al.* 2004). It shows the solution performance along a horizontal time-line. It is the translation of an event, which takes place in space and time, into a sequence of static images and explanatory captions (Fig. A2.10). As such, it is a series of images that represent the significant interactions between the user(s) and the provider(s) of a product-service.

Compared with a classical storyboard, the interaction storyboard is intended as a representation showing not only the experience of the final user and the 'front office' of the solution, but also the different levels of interaction between various stakeholders during the delivery of the solution. Thus, several vertically distributed lines of interaction show the synergies and connections, between different provider and user categories that constitute the architecture of the Solution Oriented Partnership. As shown in Annex 1, it is particularly useful in the PSS design phase.

MEPSS toolkit

The MEPSS toolkit allows industry to develop PSS using a formalised framework for innovation that should increase the chances of success and make sure that no core issues are disregarded in the innovation process. It is a full PSS development method.

The MEPSS methodology is accessible by using two main tools: a handbook and a web tool. The handbook gives an introduction, explains the design phases and guides the user towards relevant tools. The tool descriptions can be found in the annex of the handbook. The interim tools overview document of the MEPSS project consists of over 100 pages and shows that there is already a wealth of tools available for PSS development. The web tool provides content on all layers of the methodology. The navigation guides the user through the methodology. The web tool also functions as a download platform.

The handbook and the web tool were released in 2005 (van Halen *et al.* 2005; www. mepss.nl).

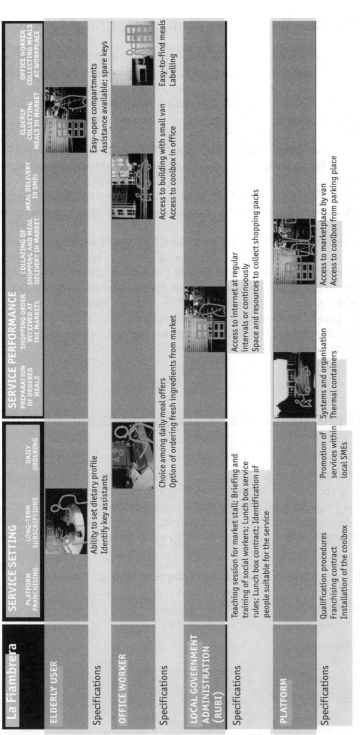

FIGURE A2.10 The interaction storyboard shows different levels of interaction between a core partnership providing the general solution organisation and local providers that manage various points of solution delivery where the user finally interacts with the service

Source: Manzini et al. 2004

META matrix for services: evaluation/assessment tool

The META matrix enables the rapid evaluation of the environmental impact of physical products (Brezet and van Hemel 1997). MET stands for materials, energy and toxic substances. On the vertical axis of the matrix, the phases of the product life-cycle are reflected. The filling-in of the matrix can be done qualitatively as well as quantitatively. The filled-in matrix is intended to give insight into environmental problem areas.

This tool was adapted to make it suitable for the analysis and benchmarking of services. Because the environmental impact of services wholly consists of the environmental impact of the products and support materials that are used with this service, it is not necessary to adapt the horizontal axis (M, E and T). There will be one added column, however, which reflects the Added Value to approach the EVR (Ecocost Value Ratio) model (Vogtländer *et al.* 2001; Brezet *et al.* 2001): hence the META matrix (refer to Table A2.3).

Compared with the MET matrix, more has been changed in the vertical axis. The life-cycle of a product is very different from the life-cycle of a service. With a service, production, use and disposal happen virtually in the same instant. In addition, the limitations of what belongs to the service system and what does not are not always as clear as with products. These system boundaries need to be determined at the start of the analysis and will be specific for every product-service system.

This tool is particularly useful in the analysis phase and the various idea and concept selection steps of the PSS design process.

Opportunity Recognition Diagnose: diagnosis modules of ProSecCo

Within the ProSecCo methodology **diagnosis modules** are available to assess the needs for support in the product-service development process. These modules are accessible via the *ProSecCo Solution Offering* (see www.prosecco-village.com).

The Opportunity Recognition (OR) Diagnose analyses the impact that an innovation will have on the existing company. The outcome of the OR Diagnose contains three spiderweb tables:

1. A spiderweb graph with six axes indicating the most relevant changes (0 up to 100%) in:
   - Distribution channels
   - Brand
   - Human resources
   - Organisation
   - Financial resources
   - Networking structure

META matrix	Examples	Material Input/output	Energy Input/output	Toxic substances Output	Added value
Transportation	● Truck ● Plane ● Ship ● Train				
Infrastructure	● Road net ● Telephone net ● Water net ● GSM net				
Buildings	● Offices ● Climate-controlled warehouse ● Shop				
Personnel	● Mechanic ● Office clerk ● Salesman ● Consultant				
Tools and support products	● Laptop ● Electric drill ● Telephone ● Camera				
Consumption goods	● Paper ● Water ● Detergents ● Chemicals				
Main service products	● Washing machine ● Copy machine ● Locker ● Gambling machines				

TABLE A2.3 META matrix

Source: Brezet *et al.* 2001

2. A spiderweb with three axes that plots the changes in the approach for the company developing the new PSS (in percentage from 0 to 100):
   – Change in strategy
   – Change in concept
   – Change in attributes

3. A spiderweb plot with five axes indicating the importance of the following innovation drivers for the PSS:
   – Customers
   – Competitors
   – Exploitation of internal capacity
   – New technologies
   – Regulations

Partnership co-ordinating tools: tools from the HiCS project

Three tools are presented in the HiCS project; each designed to support the co-ordination of the HiCS Solution Oriented Partnerships in terms of their progress towards objectives and the relationships between partners. The tools were developed by Andrew Burns and Stephen Evans and published in Manzini *et al.* 2004.

1. The PPF (Proposed Partnership Form) matrix allows the Solution Oriented Partnership to represent and plan the complex interaction of their relationships and activities, thereby aiding the separate planning of both

2. The LPS (Legal Progress Support) tool then helps Solution Oriented Partnerships co-ordinate the process of building and formalising the relationships between partners, and the sharing of costs, benefits and risks across the Solution Oriented Partnership

3. The MTG (Management Team Guidelines) tool provides Solution Oriented Partnerships with a mechanism and guidance for the co-ordination of the group's progress towards the goal of a Partner Based Solution reaching the market

These tools are specifically designed to be used throughout the life of a Solution Oriented Partnership. The PPF tool helps to force the discussion of different partners' ambitions, expected benefits, capabilities and potential responsibilities. It also helps identify partners that are missing and still required to make the Solution Oriented Partnership work. Later in the process it is used to incorporate new partners and can form the basis for business planning and legal relationship formation.

Perceived service quality model, e.g. for car sharing

Meijkamp (2000) researched the perceived service quality especially in the mobility sector focusing on car sharing. To measure the perceived quality Meijkamp constructed a conceptual model of the perceived service quality. The variables of this conceptual model are presented in Figure A2.11. Based on this conceptual model and the specific relationships, Meijkamp formulated hypotheses that were tested empirically (e.g. the hypothesis based on the relation between the 'overall perceived service quality' and the 'purchase intention' (Fig. A2.11) was: The overall service quality has a positive impact on the intention of contract extension). The tool is particularly useful in the analysis phase and the various PSS idea selection steps of the PSS development process.

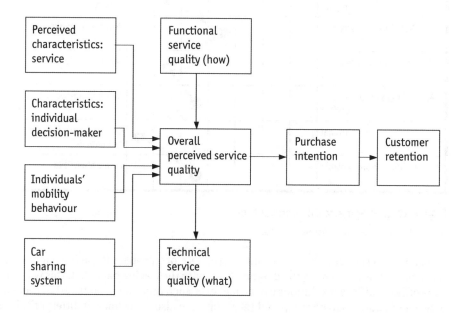

FIGURE A2.11 The conceptual model of perceived service quality in car-sharing systems

Source: Meijkamp 2000

Pragmatic Differential tool: selection tool

The pragmatic differentiation tool is a diagram based on semantics and can be used to generate a quality profile of potential solutions in comparison with existing products. First a list of opposites is entered into the diagram (positive and negative). For each criterion the object to be analysed is awarded a certain number of points on a scale between –3 and +3, depending on the user's judgement. Then the dots are joined up from top to bottom to give a zigzag line which represents the quality profile. The further the line lies to the right the better the solution (see Fig. A2.12).

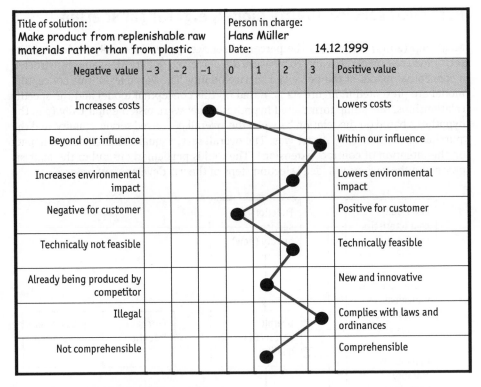

Title of solution: Make product from replenishable raw materials rather than from plastic				Person in charge: Hans Müller Date: 14.12.1999				
Negative value	– 3	– 2	–1	0	1	2	3	Positive value
Increases costs			●					Lowers costs
Beyond our influence							●	Within our influence
Increases environmental impact						●		Lowers environmental impact
Negative for customer				●				Positive for customer
Technically not feasible						●		Technically feasible
Already being produced by competitor					●			New and innovative
Illegal							●	Complies with laws and ordinances
Not comprehensible					●			Comprehensible

FIGURE A2.12 Pragmatic Differential tool

Source: this example taken from Tischner *et al.* 2000

A good idea is to draw quality profiles on a piece of transparent tracing paper with a thick felt pen (after copying the diagram form onto the tracing paper). In this way quality profiles of different solutions can be laid over each other and compared. If there are only a few solutions to be compared (2–3), one can also draw lines of different colours on one sheet. See, for a further description of this tool, Tischner *et al.* 2000.

Pre-Diagnose: diagnosis modules of ProSecCo

Within the ProSecCo methodology **diagnosis modules** are available to assess the needs for support in the product-service development process. These modules are accessible via the *ProSecCo Solution Offering* (see www.prosecco-village.com).

The **Pre-Diagnose** is available as a free rapid assessment tool for the first contact of the companies with ProSecCo. The result of the tools indicates which development approach is suitable for the present company/market situation. The user will answer more general questions and as a result will obtain 'tailored' cases. The tool is particularly useful in the introduction stage of PSS development.

Product-service life-cycle information management and acquisition

The project 'Environmental Life-cycle Information Management and Acquisition for consumer products' (ELIMA) provides a tool to gather information about the life-cycle of consumer products. This gives insight into how the consumer uses the product, and in turn this gives handles to find possible value-added services that improve the environmental life-cycle (compare the consumption chain analysis of MacMillan and McGrath listed in this annex). The tool provides a blueprint to facilitate the design and implementation of PSS. The result of the tool can be a PSS (product = consumer products; service = life-cycle improving services). So ELIMA offers a tool that enables sustainable PSS. Information about the project can be found at www.elima.org.

Progressive abstraction tool: creativity tool

An essential feature of progressive abstraction is the repeated question 'What are we actually aiming for?' This repeated challenging of the problem definition has the effect of gradually increasing the problem's level of abstraction. In this way the problem-solver is encouraged to look at the problem from different viewpoints and search for solutions at a more fundamental level. The tool is particularly useful in the idea generation stage of PSS development. To take the task of optimising a refrigerator as an example:

1st stage: how can refrigerators be improved in terms of their environmental compatibility?

- **Solutions**: thicker insulation; optimised refrigerating set; use of alternative refrigerants

- **Question**: what are we actually aiming for?

2nd stage: how, in principle, can refrigerators be designed to make them better and more environmentally benign?

- **Solutions**: divide the volume up into compartments with separate doors; access from above (as in commercial freezers); make components that are subject to continuous technical improvement (e.g. refrigerating set) replaceable; design with consideration to the optimum volume-to-surface ratio; operate in a cool place; use cool outdoor air to bring ambient temperature closer to cooling temperature; install permanently in the home (if possible next to an outside wall. This saves work when moving, and makes for better insulation, regular maintenance and a longer service life)

- **Question**: what are we actually aiming for?

3rd stage: what can be done to keep food fresh for longer in the household?

- **Solutions**: use refrigerators; store food in naturally cool places; use preserved food; only use durable food products; use food up quickly

- **Question**: what are we actually aiming for?

4th stage: what can be done to provide households with a sufficient supply of fresh food?

- **Solutions**: keep food fresh at home in larger quantities; keep food fresh in collective storages; have food delivered directly when needed (delivery service); make food supplies available close to households and around the clock (e.g. corner shop); cultivate fresh food at home

Having reached this point it might be possible to find a solution, a product/service or a business idea, which solves the problem at a higher level of abstraction, possibly making the initial problem altogether avoidable.

Profit pool (Gadiesh and Gilbert 1998)

Gadiesh and Gilbert described the profit pool concept in an issue of the *Harvard Business Review* (1998). This concept can be very useful for assessing whether it makes sense to extend a product offer with other value elements. The tool fits best in the analysis stage of PSS development. The idea behind the concept is as follows (see Fig. A2.13):

- Determine the ultimate function that a product or set of products and services performs for a user

- Determine what individual products and services make up this function throughout the entire life-cycle (e.g. for transport by car this means the production of the car, the sale of the car, the use of petrol, repairs, insurance, maintenance, etc., and ultimately the disposal of the car)

- Each of these activities generates a certain turnover and profit margin. For each activity the turnover is plotted on the x-axis and the profit margin on the y-axis. The surface area of the square that is produced indicates the total profit in that link of the chain

- The figure therefore shows at a glance whether there are activities associated with your own activity (e.g. sale of cars) with high margins and/or large profit volumes

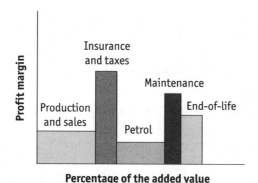

FIGURE A2.13 Imaginary profit pool of car driving

PSS Innovation Matrix

The PSS Innovation Matrix was developed by Lucas Simons in the project that led to the 'Innovation Scan for Product Service Systems' (Tukker and van Halen 2003). It can be used best in the idea generation stage of PSS development. On the y-axis of the PSS Innovation Matrix, the eight archetypical PSS discerned in Chapter 2 of this book are listed. On the x-axis the six most important ways of creating added value for a user are listed. These concern:

- Customer productivity: does the PSS increase the productivity or lower the costs for the customer by removing significant bottlenecks?

- Comfort (comfort and simplicity): does the new PSS make the product easier to use for the customer?

- More easily available (convenience): does the new PSS make the purchasing process easier?

- Reduction of risk: does the new PSS reduce perceived risks or uncertainties for the customer?

- Amusement value and image: does the emotional value or image of the new PSS increase the pleasure felt by customers?

- Adjustment to standards and values of the customer: does the PSS, for example, reduce the environmental burden caused by the product?

These two axes span the PSS Innovation Matrix (see Table A2.4). The tool can be used in two ways:

1. Generation of ideas
   - Select the two to three forms of added value that the customer finds most important for the selected market segment (x-axis)
   - Think of specific PSS for each of the seven categories of PSS option (y-axis), possibly using the techniques illustrated in the previous appendices

2. Test of completeness
   - Plot the ideas that the team had already generated in other ways in the matrix
   - See which cells are empty and analyse whether there is any good reason for this (for example, this form of added value is unimportant to the customer or the type of PSS is not feasible for your company in this market)
   - If there is no good reason why a cell is empty, think some more about PSS that would fit in this cell

Potential added value for customer PSS types	Productivity increasing or cost reducing	Comfort increasing	Lower purchasing thresholds	Risk reducing	Better emotional perception and image	Better fit with standards and values
Product-related service						
Advice and consultancy						
Product lease or hire						
Product pooling						
Product sharing						
Pay-per-unit of result						
Activity management/outsourcing						
Functional result						

TABLE A2.4 PSS Innovation Matrix

Qualitative 4-axes expert panel: assessment tool
(Goedkoop *et al.* 1999)

In Goedkoop *et al.* 1999, two assessment tools were presented. The one below is the qualitative assessment tool. The other, known as the E2 Vector, is a quantitative tool discussed earlier in this annex.

For the qualitative assessment Goedkoop *et al.* developed their tools in such a way that they include the most relevant issues for companies, consumers and society. As a result, they concluded that PSS must be assessed on four aspects:

1. What are the environmental characteristics at function fulfilment level and how do these relate to overall environmental load on society?

2. What are the economic characteristics at company level, and at the level of the business sector ('the pool')?

3. To what extent does the PSS match the company's identity and strategy?

4. To what extent would the market accept the PSS? These questions form the basis for our '4-axes model'

Each axis can be scored as neutral, positive (1, 2 or 3) or negative (1, 2 or 3). A plus score means: stimulating for introducing the new PSS. A negative score means the opposite. A neutral (zero) score means that the new PSS does not affect this item (see Fig. A2.14).

The tool is basically a specific elaboration of a Pragmatic Differential (see earlier in this annex). It is particularly useful in the PSS idea selection steps in the various stages of PSS development.

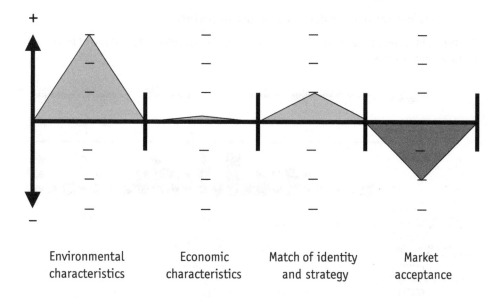

FIGURE A2.14 4-axes evaluation tool

Solution Elements Brief: tool from the HiCS project

The Solution Elements Brief is a tool developed in the HiCS project (Manzini *et al.* 2004). It breaks down the solution into elements that can be recomposed to give different final Partner Based Solutions. It helps to systematise and communicate the complex system. Its aims to simultaneously visualise the connections among elements and partners so that the solution can be designed, built and delivered (see Fig. A2.15). It shows:

- All the solution elements that are required to perform the targeted Partner Based Solutions (horizontally)

- The different options for each solution element (vertically)

- The contribution of each partner (which elements are already in its core business, which can be implemented and which connections with other elements require careful consideration)

- The elements that are delivered by specific partners

As shown in Annex 1, the tool is particularly useful in the PSS design stage of PSS development approaches.

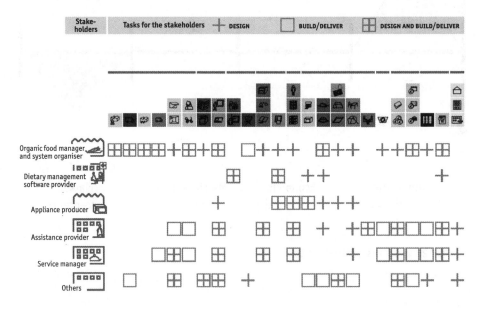

FIGURE A2.15 A Solution Elements Brief, showing the breakdown of solution elements and their attribution to each of the platform partners

Source: Manzini *et al.* 2004

Solution Scan: tool from the HiCS project

The Solution Scan is a tool for setting up a HiCS Solution Oriented Partnership (Manzini *et al.* 2004). The tool was developed by Helma Luiten, Tom van der Horst and Emma van Sandick. The aim of the Solution Scan is to make a company enthusiastic about the Solution Oriented Partnership methodology and about offering 'solutions' instead of single products. The tool allows a quick scan of the opportunities for a company to start or to join such a project. The tool is designed as a way to communicate the methodology and philosophy in limited time. It hence probably is most useful in the preparation and introduction stage of PSS development. The scan is divided into three phases:

- Phase 1 is the analysis phase in which the sources of innovation within the company and the market are defined

- Phase 2 is the idea generation phase. Phase 2 offers tools that generate ideas for potential Partner Based Solutions

- Phase 3 forms the conclusion and agreement on follow-up, and defines the transition to the next step in the innovation process. The results are listed and uncertainties for realisation are defined

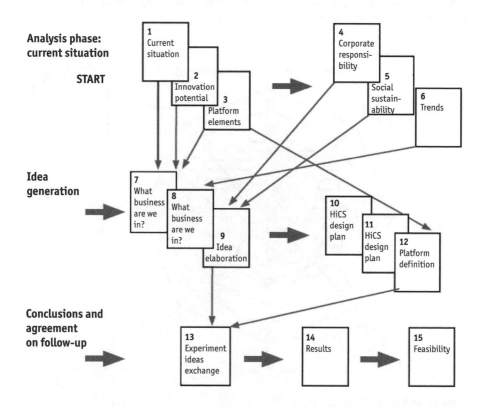

FIGURE A2.16 Outline of the tool sheets of the Solution Scan

Source: Manzini *et al.* 2004

The Solution Scan is a paper-based toolkit. A3 sheets are designed, one per tool, each with a dedicated layout. Each sheet is presented in a format that shows the steps that make up the tool, the questions that should be asked and what should be filled in. They are completed on the spot with the company in question. Figure A2.16 shows an overview of these tool sheets that make up the Solution Scan. The sheets are divided into three phases: 'analysis', 'idea generation' and 'conclusions and agreement on fol-low-up'. The figure also gives an overview of the interrelationships between the sepa-rate tools.

Spider diagrams

The 'spider diagram' is a generic tool for visualisation of performance of alternatives on a flexible set of criteria (see Fig. A2.17). The definition of the axis depends on the focus and scope of the planning task, user needs, and it results in a different emphasis for each exercise. The tool helps to visualise (comparative) assessments between PSS options and ideas in different stages of the PSS development process.

The 'spider diagram' may also be used in a workshop with relevant actors of product development. There are three steps to the process:

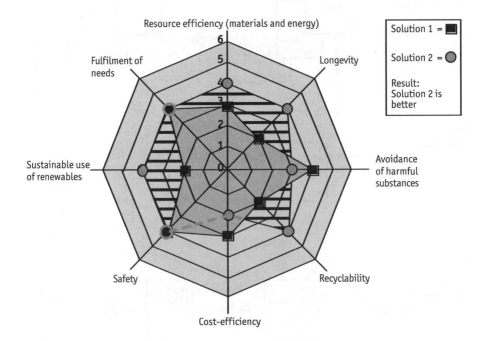

FIGURE A2.17 Spider diagram

Source: this example from Tischner *et al.* 2000

- Define the appropriate set of criteria and name each spoke of the diagram with one criterion

- Assess and grade the aspects according to the criteria (grade 0 = very bad at the origin of the spoke up to grade 6 = very good, along the axes from the centre to the outside)

- Fill in the results (marks on the spokes)

A line resulting from connecting the marks characterises the environmental profile of the solution. The further the line is located from the origin, the better the solution is.

It has to be noted that the 'spider diagram' is not a mathematical instrument. It does not make sense to use the size of the area within the environmental profile line as a measure for environmental compatibility. The size of the area depends on the order of the criterion on the steps. If the order is changed, the area differs. The distance from the origin is a measure for fulfilling the chosen criteria, not the area within the line.

Stakeholders' Motivation Matrix: tool from the HiCS project

The Stakeholders' Motivation Matrix shows the solution from the point of view of stakeholders' interest in taking part in the partnership. The tool was developed in the HiCS project (Manzini *et al.* 2004) and, as shown in Annex 1, is particularly useful in the design stage of the PSS development process. The matrix shows a checklist of motivations, benefits and contributions from each stakeholder's point of view, between individual partners and over the whole partnership (see Fig. A2.18). Cross-referencing the stakeholders (those already identified and those still needed) allows them to check what are or could be their respective motivations to evolve their current business; what each can bring to the partnership and what each gets out of the partnership; and what potential synergies/conflicts may occur between partners. The Stakeholders' Motivation Matrix is initially filled by the solution promoters as an input to the Solution Oriented Partnership methodology (HiCS project methodology) showing:

- Each solution promoter, their intentions, potential contribution to the partnership and expected benefits

- The target Solution Oriented Partnership

- The description of hypothetical partners still to be identified during the process

As more partners are identified during the building of the Solution Oriented Partnership, the motivation matrix is completed:

- Hypothetical partners are substituted by real ones

- Partners' contributions and expected benefits are adjusted

- Partner interactions, synergies and potential conflicts are investigated

Gives to...	Organic food manager and system organiser	Dietary management software provider	Appliance producer	Assistance provider	Service manager	Solution centre	Solution-oriented partnership
Organic food manager and system organiser	• To find new perspectives in the organic food industry	• Organic food market expertise to test the validity of the software	• Organic food market expertise to improve the performance of the appliances	• High-quality food products to be offered to customers	• New high-quality convenience meals for vending machines • A new service concept	• Knowledge and expertise from the organic food sector	• Organic brand identity • Expertise in organic supply management
Dietary management software provider	• A way to enhance the real value of the organic food offering	• To enter non-medical markets • To open and finalise research in new areas	• New criteria and dietary tools for the development of appliances for special food needs	• A way to better satisfy customer needs • Potential networking with food specialists	• Adds value to the service portfolio	• Expertise in the dietary industry	• Advice and dietary management through professional software
Appliance producer	• Competences in food processing	• Competences in food processing • Hardware appliances to be integrated with software	• To find applications for advanced food appliances • To enter the service dimension	• A dedicated appliance for customers	• A smart vending machine system	• Expertise and products in the white goods appliances sector	• Smart appliances for food processing • Brand identity
Assistance provider	• Specific knowledge of a very sensitive sector • Inputs and feedback from the reduced access to food context	• Specific knowledge of a very sensitive sector • A new area of business	• Cognitive and physiological feedback to better design the interfaces of new appliances	• To complete the present service offering		• Expertise in assisting people in a specific context	• Social dimension • Access to a specific context
Service manager	• Expertise in a specific market • Expertise in service management	• Feedback from the final users • Statistical databases	• Feedback from the final users • Inputs to integrate service and appliance design		• To expand the service portfolio • To extend the offering to new contexts	• Expertise and entrepreneurship in the vending machine industry	• Service management in specific contexts
Solution centre	• Catalyst in the design and development of ideas • Manage partner development	• To facilitate entry into new businesses • Support in the design and development of ideas	• To facilitate entry into new businesses • Support in the design and development of ideas	• To facilitate entry into new businesses • Support in testing of the solution idea with their customers	• To facilitate entry into new businesses	• To develop expertise in solution design • To obtain visibility as solutions experts	• Tools and expertise to facilitate and manage the partner-based solutions
Solution-oriented partnership	• Expand business and new market opportunities • To become a food solution provider	• Visibility and recognition to the end-user • Feedback from new clients	• New sales channels • Service expertise	• A new idea of service to be used to reach new customers	• A new service to be used to contact new possible context of business	• Opportunity to test a methodological toolbox • Expertise in the food sector	• To provide healthy, convenient meals in different contexts of reduced access to food

FIGURE A2.18 Final Stakeholders' Motivation Matrix showing all the partners, their contribution to and benefits from the partnership and potential interactions between them

Once complete, the Stakeholders' Motivation Matrix can form the basis of the business plan and the first formal agreement between partners.

Strategy Canvas for generating new value propositions
(W. Chan Kim and Renée Mauborgne)

W. Chan Kim and Renée Mauborgne (1997, 1999, 2002) wrote a series of articles arguing for a more radical approach to improve value propositions. Basically, they ask firms to radically reconsider the value proposition they put on the market, by posing the following questions:[1]

- Which factors that our industry takes for granted should be eliminated?

- Which factors should be reduced well below the quality standards of our industry since they are not seen as relevant by our customers?

- Which factors should be raised well above standard?

- Which factors should be created that our industry has never offered?

The key factors that affect competition found in this way can be charted in what they call a 'Strategy Canvas'—basically, a pragmatic differential which shows per factor the quality of the offering of the (average) competition and one's own firm, and which allows comparison with the quality actually valued by the majority of customers. Kim and Mauborgne suggest that via such analyses radical new offerings can be identified, that create a 'new game' in the market and make existing competition irrelevant. If such offerings also target the mass of buyers, by following current non-customers closely (and deliberately choosing to lose existing customers), and if companies do not feel too restrained in sticking to their own, existing competences, Kim and Mauborgne (1997) speak of 'value innovation'.

The Strategy Canvas is particularly useful in the analysis and idea generation stages of PSS development.

Sustainability Guidelines for PSS: tool from the MEPSS project

These guidelines were developed by Ursula Tischner and Carlo Vezzoli in the context of the MEPSS project (www.mepss.nl). The guidelines include all dimensions of sus-

---

1 Anderson and Narus (1998) follow a similar line of thought in their paper 'Understand what Customers Value', suggesting the compilation of a list of value elements, gathering (customer) data, validating the model created and understanding variance, etc.

tainability (environmental, sociocultural and economic) and give recommendations on how to design a PSS to be sustainable.

They have two levels: level 1 for PSS idea generation; level 2 for PSS design. Tables A2.5–A2.8 show an overview of the three dimensions with six sub-criteria each, and the full guidelines for PSS idea generation (level 1).

A. Environmental dimension	B. Sociocultural dimension	C. Economic dimension
System life optimisation	Possibility of consuming in a socially responsible manner	Market position and competitiveness
Transportation/distribution reduction	Health and safety	Profitability/added value for companies
Resources reduction	Living conditions/quality of life	Added value (customers)
Waste minimisation/ valorisation	Employment/working conditions	Long-term business development/ risk
Conservation/ bio-compatibility	Equity and justice/relation to stakeholders	Partnership/co-operation
Toxicity reduction	Respect cultural diversity	Macroeconomic effect

TABLE A2.5 Overview of the three dimensions of sustainability

A1. System life optimisation	Priority	H	M	L	N
Guidelines level 1					

- Can you offer services for **shared** use of products/infrastructures?
- Can you add to product/infrastructure offer, services for their **maintenance, reparability, substitution**?
- Can you add to product/infrastructure offer, services for their **technological upgradeability**?
- Can you add to product/infrastructure offer, services for their **aesthetic/cultural upgradeability**?
- Can you add to product/infrastructure offer, services for their **adaptation to new contexts (sight of use)**?

A2. Transportation/distribution reduction	Priority	H	M	L	N
Guidelines level 1					

- Can you use infrastructures for digital transfer/access to information?
- Can you look for partnership enabling **long-distance activities**?
- Can you look for partnership for **local resources use** (info/data transfer)?
- Can you look for partnership for **on-site production** (info/data transfer)?
- Can you add to product/infrastructure offer, services for their **on-site assembly**?
- Can you look for partnership to reduce/avoid products or semi-finished products **transportation and packaging**?

TABLE A2.6 PSS Sustainability Guidelines, A—Environmental (continued opposite)

A3. Resources reduction	Priority	H	M	L	N

Guidelines level 1

- Can you add to energy or material or semi-finished products, support services for their **optimal use**?
- Can you offer the access/availability to products/infrastructures through **payment based on the unit of utility/satisfaction**?
- Can you offer **collective use** of products/infrastructures?
- Can you outsource activities when **higher specialisation** and technological efficiency of products/infrastructures are available?
- Can you outsource activities when higher-**scale economies** are feasible?
- Can you look for partnerships aiming at the **use/integration of existing infrastructures/products**?
- Can you add to product/infrastructure offer **design of their adaptation to the context of use** aiming at resources optimisation?
- Can you add to product/infrastructure offer design services for their adaptation to use variations of resources requirements?

A4. Waste minimisation/valorisation	Priority	H	M	L	N

Guidelines level 1

- Can you add to product/infrastructure offer, take-back services aimed at **re-using or remanufacturing**?
- Can you add to product/infrastructure offer, take-back services aimed at **recycling**?
- Can you add to product/infrastructure offer, take-back services aimed at **energy recovery**?
- Can you add to product take-back services aiming at **composting**?
- Can you look for localised alliances/partnership aiming at **symbiotic/cascade** approach for **secondary resources use**?

A5. Conservation/bio-compatibility	Priority	H	M	L	N

Guidelines level 1

- Can you look for partnership aiming at decentralised **renewable/passive energy** resources use?
- Can you within services offer introduce products/infrastructure based on non-exhausting/renewable and biodegradable materials?
- Can you look for partnership aiming at the **use** of local non-exhausting/renewable and biodegradable **materials**?

A6. Atoxicity	Priority	H	M	L	N

Guidelines level 1

- Can you look for alliances with other producers aiming at **toxic/harmful resources re-use or recycling**?
- Can you add to product/infrastructure/semi-finished products offer, services for the **recovery/treatment** of the **toxic/harmful** emissions they are responsible for?

TABLE A2.6 (from previous page)

B1. Enable the customer to consume socially more responsibly (sufficiency)	Priority	H	M	L	N

Guidelines level 1

- Can you increase your customer's awareness of sustainability with new PSS?
- Can you offer more individual ways of fulfilling needs in a more socially responsible way, with new PSS?
- Can you enhance the transparency of your offer and how it contributes to sustainability?
- Can you avoid possible social rebound effects of your offer (socially counterproductive effects)?
- Can you create enabling platforms/increase the capacity of your customers through new PSS, e.g. let them participate in the design and production process?
- Increase customer's satisfaction, participation/involvement, motivation and awareness

B2. Health and safety (of employees, customers, stakeholders . . .)	Priority	H	M	L	N

Guidelines level 1

- Can you improve health and safety conditions
  - in production
  - in use
  - in recycling
  - in disposal

and generally/indirectly connected with the offer?

B3. Living conditions/quality of life (customers'/users' perspective)	Priority	H	M	L	N

Guidelines level 1

- Can you fulfil more socially acceptable needs or solve social problems by offering a new PSS?
- Can you do 'something good' for the individual and society as a whole, increase welfare on an individual and society level by offering a new PSS?
- Can you offer the new PSS with affordable prices for the specific target groups you are aiming at?
- PSS may focus much more on the needs and values of customers, e.g. through the possibility of customising PSS offers individually
- PSS may integrate customers directly in the generation of the PSS and with that increase value of the offer and satisfaction of the customers

B4. Employment/working conditions (employee perspective)	Priority	H	M	L	N

Guidelines level 1

- PSS may create better, more interesting and more secure jobs in PSS delivery compared with product manufacturing
- Can you improve quality of jobs, and secure jobs by new PSS offer?
- Will you be able to pay fair wages (regional standards) in the whole value chain of new PSS offer and offer adequate amount of working hours (regional standards)?
- Can you increase employees' satisfaction, motivation, participation through new PSS offers?
- Can you offer work in line with the capacity of employees and offer training and personal development if not?
- Can you influence also other companies in the value chain to care for good labour conditions, e.g. through new partnerships?

TABLE A2.7 **PSS sustainability guidelines, B—Sociocultural** (continued opposite)

B.5 Equity and justice *(society/global perspective)*	Priority	H	M	L	N

Guidelines level 1

- Does your new PSS help to avoid negative effects such as discrimination and exploitation of people, regions, countries?
- Can you influence also other organisations involved to apply acceptable social standards?
- Can you involve and respect minorities and target groups with special needs, such as parents, elderly people, disabled people, children, single people, illiterate . . . ?
- Do you have any opportunities to support partners in developing countries, e.g. through fair trade, partnership etc.?
- Can you help to support democratic structures through your new PSS, e.g. in developing countries?
- Can you help to increase communication and understanding of people through new PSS offers?
- Can you involve stakeholders, NGOs and others in the development of the PSS? Do you understand and listen to their needs and concerns?

B6. Respect cultural diversity *(society/local perspective)*	Priority	H	M	L	N

Guidelines level 1

- Can you increase stakeholder participation and satisfaction through new PSS, e.g. your neighbours, NGOs, the families of your employees, etc.?
- Can you offer them participation in decision-making in new PSS?
- Can you also increase their capacity?
- Can you offer more education and information to stakeholders through new PSS? Provide honest and adequate information to stakeholders, help to improve their education especially regarding sustainability issues?
- Can you use partnerships and synergies with other (stakeholder) organisations to improve the PSS offer?
- Globalisation is a challenge but nevertheless it is also important to have cultural and regional diversity. Can you support that with the new PSS?
- PSS can strengthen the role of the local economy because services are created at the same time and often at the same place as they are consumed. Can you use this effect?
- Can your PSS offer be adapted to the different regional cultures? Does it respect and support regional identity and local structures?
- Can you support cultural identity and diversity, e.g. customise your offer for different target groups?
- Can you increase diverse aesthetics and beauty through your PSS?

TABLE A2.7   (from previous page)

C.1 Market position and competitiveness	Priority	H	M	L	N

Guidelines level 1

- Can you improve/secure your market situation with a new PSS offer?
- Can you develop PSS that are better than the offers of your competitors, e.g. lower prices, better quality, meet customers' demands better?
- Can you fulfil demands of your customers that have not yet been fulfilled?
- Can you gain new customers by offering a PSS?
- If you look at the trends and how the market is developing, which PSS will be needed over the long run? Can you offer them already today?
- Can you profit from diversification through a new PSS offer, do business in a new field with new partners, become more flexible (especially important in saturated markets)?
- Can you improve your position in the value chain through a new PSS?
- Can you improve your image by offering innovative PSS?

C.2 Profitability/added value (companies)	Priority	H	M	L	N

Guidelines level 1

- Can you make your company more profitable (decrease cost/increase turnover) through new PSS strategies and therefore increase investor satisfaction/shareholder value, etc.?
- By analysing and redesigning the production and consumption system the PSS improvement can be beneficial for all participating actors, not just for manufacturers
- Can you optimise the value/production chain by offering a new PSS?
- Can you reduce the material elements in the system and therefore pay less for materials and products and increase the non-material elements in the system, but with a very efficient organisation?
- Can you solve some recycling/disposal problems through the new PSS and therefore reduce cost?

C.3 Added value (customers)	Priority	H	M	L	N

Guidelines level 1

- Can you save your customers money because your offer is cheaper than competitors' offers and can you also save other costs for your customers, such as disposal, measures to avoid risks, etc. (make sure you mention these effects in advertising)?
- Can you offer your customers more material benefit, e.g. creating more income, debt/tax reduction, increasing funding opportunities, saving cost, etc.?
- Can you offer customers more non-material benefit, e.g. satisfaction, take negative responsibilities out of their hands, offer highly customised solutions that are very valuable for the individual customer, etc.?

TABLE A2.8 PSS sustainability guidelines, C—Economic (continued opposite)

C.4 Long-term business development/risk	Priority	H	M	L	N

Guidelines level 1

- Can you increase your capabilities of being innovative and react more flexibly to changing market trends by introducing new PSS offers?
- Also consider long-term trends, when thinking about business development and try to understand how a new PSS offer will make you more flexible
- Do you have (or know) methods to measure the success of the PSS on the market?
- Do you have measures to learn from the success/problems of new PSS offers and use this knowledge for adaptation of the offer and new business development?
- PSS are often based on efficient information, knowledge and organisation management. Do you have the right skills and experts to manage that? If not, where can you find alliances?
- Can you reduce your liability risk through a new PSS offer?
- Can you reduce your investment risk?
- Can you avoid being hit by existing and upcoming legislation by offering new PSS, e.g. avoid product take-back and recycling legislation, avoid toxicity problems, etc.?
- Can you reduce the risk of damage to your image by offering innovative and sustainable PSS?

C.5 Partnership/co-operation	Priority	H	M	L	N

Guidelines level 1

- Can you search for partnership with other companies, organisations and even your customers to improve the PSS offer, or to generate new PSS ideas?
- Can you use simple and efficient ways to manage partnership and co-operation, e.g. ICT facilities etc.?

C.6 Macroeconomic effect	Priority	H	M	L	N

Guidelines level 1

- Can you generate positive economic impacts on communities and regions through the new PSS?
- Can you avoid possible rebound effects of the PSS offer?
- Can you internalise external cost through the new PSS?
- Can you contribute to diverse market structures through new PSS, and avoid monopolistic systems?

TABLE A2.8 (from previous page)

Sustainability evaluation tool: tool from the Sustainable Homeservices project

The goal of this tool is to find out whether a homeservice is more sustainable than the reference situation. The service should be compared with the 'existing situation', as if the service did not exist. The evaluation tool is a questionnaire and checks on all three dimensions of sustainability: society, environment and economy. To give scores a five-point scale is used. The tool is particularly suited in the various PSS idea selection steps in the PSS development process. It is available as a Microsoft Excel file via www.sustainable-homeservices.com.

The following categories are checked in the evaluation:

Society

- Equity (equity, fair trade, social exclusion, employment of the disadvantaged)
- Health (prevention and/or treatment of illness, mental/physical)
- Safety and security (crime, vandalism, risk of injuries)
- Comfort (noise/odour/pollution, saving time, convenience)
- Social contacts (self-help, communication, good atmosphere)
- Empowerment (participation, new channels towards decision-making)
- Information and awareness (training, awareness skills)

Environment

- Materials use (quantity, hazardousness, from non-renewables to renewables, use of recycled/recyclable materials)
- Energy use (quantity from non-renewable to renewable energy, energy efficient transportation of people and freight)
- Water use (quantity, re-use)
- Waste (quantity, hazardousness)
- Emissions (quantity and characteristics, including those related to transportation)
- Space use (space use, constructed space, green areas, natural habitats)

Economy

- Employment (job creation, securing jobs, long-term unemployment, type of employment, seasonal or not)
- Financial situation of the residents (savings, income, debt/taxes, funding)
- Regional products and services (diversification of services supply, opportunities for local producers/suppliers, marketing of regional products)
- Profitability for the company (short-/long-term profit, losses, funding, improved customer relationship)
- Profitability for the region/community (profitability at the macro level, economic efficiency of the service system)

Environmental, social and financial dimensions

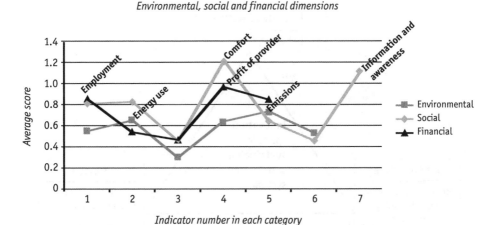

FIGURE A2.19 **Result of the homeservices sustainability evaluation tool**

An example of an outcome is presented in Figure A2.19. For each category the scores are given for the three dimensions of sustainability.

Sustainable Systems Triangle (SST): assessment tool

When designing sustainable systems, the SST framework suggests that designers look holistically for the innovative potential of (1) the devices/artefacts applied; (2) the physical and institutional context/infrastructure; and (3) the potential of new user practices and user learning (see Fig. A2.20). The tool hence fits best in the analysis and idea generation stages of the PSS development process.

We will describe two application examples for the tool (see Fig. A2.21):

- **The upgradeable oven.** To reach the envisaged sustainability improvements changes are considered in the technical device (D); the marketing and service infrastructure (I); and the user behaviour (do-it-yourself-service for the new design, U). Because the envisaged changes are radical compared with the existing oven system, D', I' and U' are depicted relatively far from their origins (the corners of the triangle)

- **Car sharing.** No or very small changes in the car design (D), large changes in infrastructure (I) and user behaviour (U)

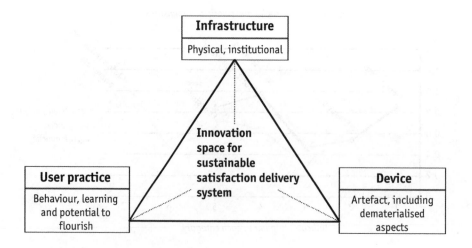

FIGURE A2.20 The Sustainable Systems Triangle (SST)

Source: Brezet *et al.* 2001

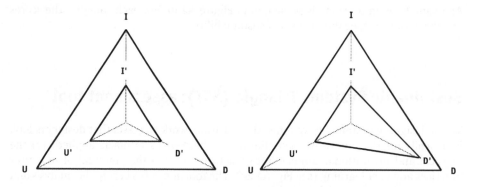

FIGURE A2.21 Examples: the upgradeable oven (left) and car sharing (right) in the SST Scheme

Source: Brezet *et al.* 2001

System Assessment: tool from the HiCS project

This is a sustainability assessment tool developed to check the Solution Oriented Partnerships developed in HiCS, both in early design phases and in the final solution phase (HiCS author: Paulo J. Partidário, INETI-DMTP; see for further information Manzini *et al.* 2004). The tool screens social, economic and environmental issues. The assessment process consists of ten steps:

1. Starting the assessment: goal definition

2. Definition of the system

3. Definition of the scope of the analysis

4. Definition of possible functional unit(s)

5. Definition of the assessment type (quantitative and/or qualitative)

6. Selection of indicators

7. Data management (input data, data assembling, performance of necessary calculations and inventory analysis)

8. Evaluation after assessment in each dimension of sustainability

9. Comparing solutions

10. Communicating results and conclusions (also useful for 'green marketing')

Figures A2.22 and A2.23 present results of the assessment of two sustainability dimensions.

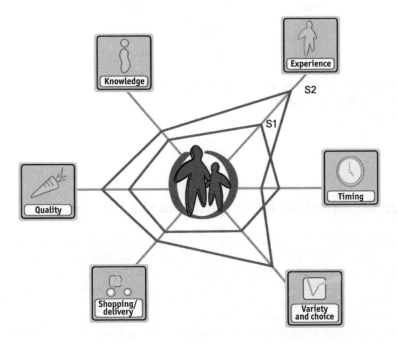

FIGURE A2.22 **Example of the social assessment of a new solution compared with a reference situation**

Source: Manzini *et al.* 2004

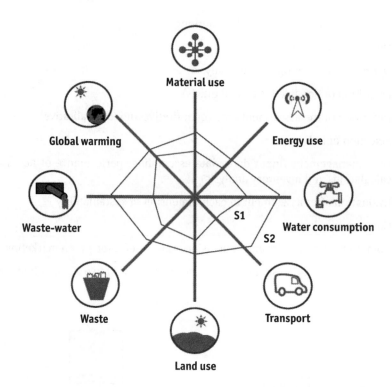

FIGURE A2.23 The environmental assessment of a given new solution compared with a reference situation

Source: Manzini *et al.* 2004

System organisation map: tool from the HiCS project

This system map tool is an approach to visualise business ideas (P, S and PSS). The system map consists of both a visualisation of the solution idea (an advertising-like image showing the solution) and a map of the general system organisation (Manzini *et al.* 2004). The tool was used during the second workshop of SusProNet; it is an outcome of the HiCS project and is also used in the MEPSS project. System map authors are F. Jégou, E. Manzini and A. Meroni (hics.ditec.polimi.it). It can play a role in all PSS development stages where a PSS must be visualised (e.g. the analysis and idea generation stage).

The map of the general system organisation uses icons for actors and processes, and lines for links in the form of material, financial and information flows. A distinction is made between primary and secondary actors. Very short texts in the map act as explanation. Figures A2.24–A2.26 clarify the layout of the tool.

FIGURE A2.24 Examples of the composition of icons for the actors and processes

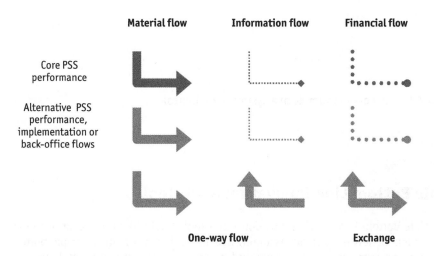

FIGURE A2.25 Composition of lines for the material, financial and information flows

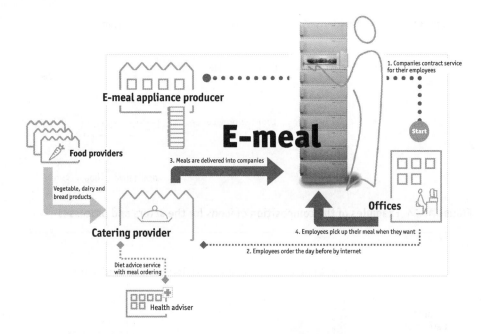

FIGURE A2.26 A worked example of a system map: E-meal

Triple Bottom Line Innovation Audit tool

The Triple Bottom Line (TBL) Innovation Audit tool should assist corporations in the development of new business ideas aiming at achievement of significant triple-bottom-line improvements (social, economic and ecological improvements). It is hence a methodology that covers the full new business development process. It was presented by B. Tuncer and M. Kuhndt of the Wuppertal Institute, at the Second SusProNet Conference, Brussels, 3–4 June 2004. The tool was developed for the ICT sector and concentrates on the initiation phase of the innovation process and supports recognition of sustainability improvement opportunities. At the same time, identification of required capabilities and institutional set-up to realise these options is undertaken.

The process begins with the identification of the needs for innovation. Business can foresee such needs in recognition of market opportunities or market risks. This stage is followed by the generation of new product-service mix ideas.

At the matching stage (see Fig. A2.27), an organisation can locate the innovation potential of these concepts and ideas using the 'TBL Significance Scanning Tool', which integrates stakeholder sustainability concerns. This would enable a comparison for social and economic value creation and environmental improvement potential. This tool also helps the organisation to place the idea in the context of the production and

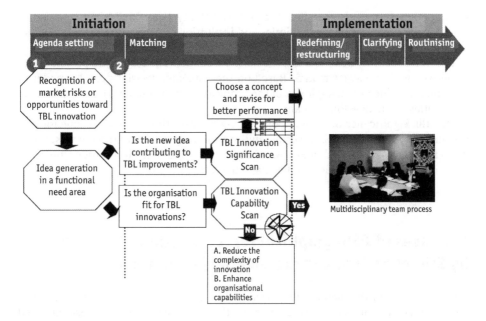

FIGURE A2.27 Overview of the TBL Audit tool

Source: presented by B. Tuncer, Wuppertal Institute, at the Second SusProNet Conference, Brussels, 3–4 June 2004

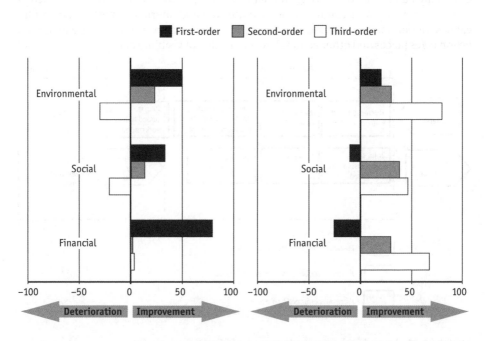

FIGURE A2.28 Possible outcome of the TBL Significance Scanning tool

Source: presented by B. Tuncer, Wuppertal Institute, at the Second SusProNet Conference, Brussels, 3–4 June 2004

consumption system. In parallel, the 'TBL Capability Scan tool' aims at assessing whether the organisational capabilities and institutions surrounding the organisation are suitable to achieve innovations with sustainability performance.

The 'TBL Capability Scan tool is a checklist-based tool. The results are presented in a spiderweb and in a SWOT matrix. Based on the outcome, decisions can be made: for example, to reduce the complexity of the innovation or to enhance the organisational capabilities of the developing team.

The 'TBL Significance Scanning tool' (Fig. A2.28) uses three checklists, one for each sustainability dimension. Each sustainability score is split up into three levels: micro, meso and macro, displayed in Fig. A2.28 as first-, second- and third-order scores. The authors suggest that this tool can be adapted to other need areas.

Use cases of PSS: graphical representation—tool adapted by School of Architecture and Design, Aalborg University

This tool is part of the methodology used to develop PSS at the school of Architecture and Design in Aalborg, Denmark. To envision the PSS, scenarios and use cases are used. Each scenario is composed of a number of descriptions of events (use cases) that describe the details of a sequence of action for each function included in a scenario. Use cases may be described in a diagrammatic way that shows the flow of events, actors involved, pre- and post-condition for each use case and alternative paths. The graphical description may also include further information such as the space in which each action takes places and other actions beyond the line of visibility of the service. The tool

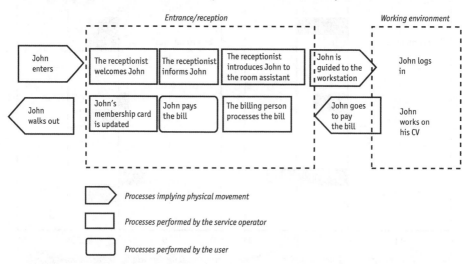

FIGURE A2.29 A graphical representation of a PSS use case

Source: presented by Nicola Morelli, Aalborg University, at the Second SusProNet Conference, Brussels, 3–4 June 2004

is particularly useful in the design stage of the PSS development process. Figure A2.29 gives an example of a basic graphical representation.

The representation above makes a distinction between three kinds of process in the PSS use case:

- Processes that imply physical movement

- Processes that are performed by the service operator

- Processes performed by the user

Validation of Life-cycle Economic Benefits of Partner Based Solutions: tool from the HiCS project

The goal of the methodology is to compare the life-cycle economic benefits of the HiCS Partner Based Solution with a suitable reference situation and, in doing so, to see if any cost reductions have been realised, and how. The methodology is designed for validating solutions on a pilot scale and should give concrete results with comparatively little effort. The tool was developed by E. Tempelman and P. Joore of TNO Industrial Technology; for a description, refer to Manzini *et al.* 2004. The tool helps in the selection of PSS ideas in the different stages of the PSS development process.

The validation only addresses the marginal or variable costs of the Partner Based Solution and no capital investment costs. In the validation the whole life-cycle is taken into account. The validation involves the following steps:

- Defining the functional unit for the validation (common denominator for all the costs in the system)

- Selecting a baseline for the validation; it is recommended to select a baseline that lies as close as possible to the actual situation

- Data gathering with a workshop approach

- Concluding the validation

This validation methodology is designed specifically for a comparative validation. It should reveal whether or not a certain Partner Based Solution is a step in the right direction and where the priorities for optimisation lie.

Value analysis/value engineering

'It is a systematic approach to identifying the function of a good or service, it establishes the value of its part, and tries to provide the function, or benefit, at the lowest possible cost without sacrificing quality or value' (Haksever *et al.* 2000: 187). In service development it could be useful to apply this tool after the elaboration of the service blue-print, combining the visualisation of each phase and thinking about it in terms of cost reduction. This is possible through some typical questions aiming at an understanding of whether the process can be simplified, integrated with the need, and so on (see Wells 1961; Falcon 1964; Heller 1971). The tool can play an important role in the analysis and subsequent idea generation stage of PSS development.

ViP approach (Vision in Product development): scenario method

The ViP approach aims at the development of an innovation vision of future products for a company or design consultant. The approach covers most of the stages of a new business development process. The following summary is taken from Brezet *et al.* 2001. The framework of the approach includes the following elements:

- The designer: responsible for his or her vision of the world and has, in the design decision-making process, sufficient space for free, personal and conscious choices

- The product. According to the designer the product represents an important value in the world. It is the result of a personal and free design process, led by opportunities (instead of restrictions) and, therefore, it is original. It can also be new and unusual, but this is not a requirement

- The context. A product, a user and their relation are not only part of a context, but are also being created by the context. The product–user relationship can be considered as an entity that should fit into the context, like an organism has to adapt to the ecosystem of which it is a part

- The company. The ViP approach expects the company to give the designer the necessary design freedom. This means that it will have to refrain from pushing the designer in certain directions, based on prejudices on 'how things are or should be'. In contrast, from the company an active and stimulating role in the design process is expected

- The user. The user is the object of the design but not the co-designer in the ViP approach. The reason for this is the thinking and feeling of users based on their past experiences and their present mental framework—that is, aiming at problem-solving instead of thinking in terms of new opportunities

- The interaction: the product–user relationship is to a large extent determined by the context. Therefore, it is important for the designer to first build an image of this context and the interaction process, before designing the actual product

Based on these elements, the ViP approach follows the next six phases in the design process:

1. Destructuring

In this phase it is important that the designer gets rid of all knowledge and insights that have created the existing product–user relationship. Fixation on existing knowledge will not lead to original solutions. All implicit assumptions should be reconsidered. For the designer, not only is the product the subject of study, but also the user needs and context variables that were important in the product creation process.

2. Creating a new context

In order to be able to determine which circumstances and factors are influencing the new product–user interaction, it is necessary for the designer to build a new context. For this, two strategies can be followed: (1) reformulation of the present context; or (2) description of the future context. In this phase, information retrieval is crucial, particularly focused on the aspects that emerged during the destructuring phase. Other domains should be taken into account as search fields, to enlarge the opportunities for new insights on the design problem.

3. Formulating the interaction vision

In this phase the designer defines the interaction vision, based on the new context. An interaction vision is a presentation or understanding of the interaction between a (future) product and a (future) user, as envisaged within the new context to create a new balance. An appropriate interaction vision: (1) has a clear and consistent relation with the context description; (2) is being formulated at a sufficient operational level for the further design process; and (3) gives certain original insights into the existing product–user relation. Particularly, the interaction vision might become interesting if it involves new characteristics that were not involved in the existing interaction.

4. From interaction vision to product vision

Based on the interaction vision, it is now possible to define the qualitative characteristics of the product to be designed: the product vision. They can relate to the product's meaning, function, value, style and so on. An appropriate product vision fulfils the following demands: (1) a clear and consistent relation with the interaction vision; (2) sufficiently operationalised; and (3) to a certain extent original, compared with existing products.

5. Turning the product vision into a product concept

Now, the product vision and the underlying interaction vision serve as a programme of requirements for the product conceptualisation. This step is principally not different from the 'normal' product development process as, for instance, described by Roozenburg and Eekels (1991).

6. From concept to design

Eventually a new product or product-system emerges from the design process, again using the standard tools and methods as described in Roozenburg and Eekels 1991. However, in many ViP-based projects the final result will be the product concept as generated in phase 5.

For further reading refer to Roozenburg and Eekels 1991.

References

Abdalla, A. (2003) *Concept Development and Realization of an Innovation Studio* (master's thesis; Soest, Germany: South Westphalia University of Applied Sciences; Bolton, UK: Bolton Institute).

ABF aktuell (2002) *Arbeitsmarkt und Berufsforschung im Referat ICF* (Hessen, Germany: Landesarbeitsamt Hessen).

Adriaanse, A., S. Bringezu, A. Hammond, Y. Moriguchi, E. Rodenburg, D. Rogich and H. Schütz (1997) *Resource Flows: The Material Basis of Industrial Economies* (Washington, DC: World Resources Institute).

Alderson, W. (1937) 'A Marketing View of Competition', *Journal of Marketing* 1 (January 1937): 189-90.

Amit, R., and P.J.H. Schoemaker (1993) 'Strategic Assets and Organizational Rent', *Strategic Management Journal* 14: 33-46.

—— and C. Zott (2001) 'Value Creation in E-business', *Strategic Management Journal* 22: 493-520.

—— and —— (2003) *Business Model Design and the Performance of Entrepreneurial Firms* (Working Paper; Fontainebleau, France: INSEAD/Wharton).

Anderson, J.C., and J.A. Narus (1998) 'Business Marketing: Understand what Customers Value', *Harvard Business Review*, November–December 1998: 53-65.

Andrews, K.R. (1965) *The Concept of Corporate Strategy* (Homewood, IL: Irwin).

Ansoff, I. (1965) *Corporate Strategy* (New York: McGraw-Hill).

Argenti, O. (2002) 'Urban Food Security', interview on www.fao.org/ag/magazine/0206sp2.htm, accessed 26 July 2006.

Azar, C., J. Holmberg and S. Karlsson, with contributions of T. Persson, R. Ayres, Th. Sterner and J. Nasson (2002) *Decoupling: Past Trends and Prospects for the Future* (for the Swedish Environmental Advisory Council, Ministry of Environment, Stockholm/Gothenburg: Chalmers University of Technology and Gothenburg University).

Baden-Fuller, C., and J.M. Stopford (1992) *Rejuvenating the Mature Business: The Competitive Challenge* (Boston, MA: Harvard Business School Press; London: Routledge).

Ballon, P., and S. Arbanowski (2005) 'Business Models in the Future Wireless World', in R. Tafazoli (ed.), *Technologies For the Wireless Future: The Wireless World Research Forum Book of Visions 2004* (Chichester, UK: John Wiley): 90-112.

Barney, J.B. 1991 'Firm Resources and Sustained Competitive Advantage', *Journal of Management* 17: 99-120.

Behrendt, S., C. Jasch, J. Kortman, G. Hrauda, R. Firzner and D. Velte (2003) *Eco-service Development: Reinventing Supply and Demand in the European Union* (Sheffield, UK: Greenleaf Publishing).

——, R. Pfitzner and R. Kreibich (1999) *Wettbewerbvorteile durch ökologische Dienstleistungen, Umsetzung in der Unternehmenspraxis* (Berlin: Springer Verlag).

Berger, C. (2002) 'Das Ende der Bürozelle', *Zeitschrift Karriereführer*, 10 March 2002; www.karrierefuehrer.de/arbeitswelt/buerozelle.html

Berkhout, F., A. Smith and A. Stirling (2004) 'Socio-technological Regimes and Transition Contexts', in B. Elzen, F.W. Geels and K. Green (eds.), *System Innovation and the Transition to Sustainability* (Cheltenham, UK: Edward Elgar).

Binswanger, M. (2001) 'Technological Progress and Sustainable Development: What about the Rebound Effect?', *Ecological Economics* 36: 119-231.

BMBF (German Federal Ministry of Education and Research) (1998) *Dienstleistungen für das 21. Jahrhundert* (Handlungs- und Förderungskonzept; Cologne: DLR-Drückerei, September 1998).

Brezet, J.C., and C. van Hemel (1997) *Ecodesign: A Promising Approach to Sustainable Production and Consumption* (Paris: UNEP).

——, A.S. Bijma, J. Ehrenfeld and S. Silvester (2001) *The Design of Eco-efficient Services* (Delft, Netherlands: TU Delft for the Dutch Ministry of Environment).

Brügemann, L.M. (2000) *Innovation of an Eco-efficient Product-Service Combination* (Msc thesis; Delft, Netherlands: Delft University of Technology).

Bullinger, H.-J., W. Bauer, P. Kern and S. Zinser (2000) *Zukunftsoffensive office 21: Büroarbeit in der dot.com-Gesellschaft gestalten* (Fraunhover IAO; Cologne: Verlagsgesellschaft).

Camp, R.C. (1989) *Benchmarking: The Search for Industry Best Practices that Lead to Superior Performance* (Milwaukee, WI: WI.ASQC Quality Press).

—— (1995) *Business Process Benchmarking: Finding and Implementing Best Practices* (Milwaukee, WI: WI.ASQC Quality Press).

Carson, R. (1962) *Silent Spring* (New York: Houghton Mifflin).

Castells, M. (2000) *The Rise of the Network Society* (Malden, MA: Blackwell Publishers, 2nd edn).

CEFIC (2003a) 'Facts and Figures: The European Chemical Industry in a Worldwide Perspective', European Chemical Industry Council, www.cefic.org, accessed June 2005.

—— (2003b) 'The EU Chemicals Policy Review: CEFIC's View', European Chemical Industry Council, www.cefic.org, accessed June 2005

CfSD (2003) 'Towards Sustainable Product Design 6', Centre for Sustainable Design, www.cfsd.org.uk/events/tspd6/tspd6_3s_cases.html, accessed June 2005.

Chandler, A.D. (1962) *Strategy and Structure: Chapters in the History of the Industrial Enterprises* (Cambridge, MA: MIT Press).

Charter, M. (2001) *Sustainable Services and Systems: Transition towards Sustainability?* (Farnham, UK: CfSD).

—— and U. Tischner (2001) *Sustainable Solutions: Developing Products and Services for the Future* (Sheffield, UK: Greenleaf Publishing).

——, G. Adams and T. Clark (2004) *Product Services in the Need Area Information and Communication* (SusProNet report; Farnham, UK: Centre for Sustainable Design, www.suspronet.org).

Chertow, M.R. (2000) 'The IPAT Equation and its Variants: Changing Views on Technology and Environmental Impact', *Journal of Industrial Ecology* 4.4: 13.

Chesbrough, H., and R.S. Rosenbloom (2002) 'The Role of the Business Model in Capturing Value from Innovation: Evidence from Xerox Corporation's Technology Spin-off Companies', *Industrial and Corporate Change* 11.3: 529-55.

Christensen, F.C.M. (1997) *The Innovator's Dilemma: When New Technologies Cause Great Firms to Fail* (Boston, MA: Harvard Business School Press).

——, M.E. Raynor and M. Verlinden (2001) 'Skate Where the Money Will Be', *Harvard Business Review*, November 2001: 72.

——, M.E. Raynor and S.D. Anthony (2003) 'Six Keys to Creating New Growth Business', *Harvard Business Review*, January 2003: 1-5 (Supplement).

CIAA (2003a) *Data and Trends of the EU Food and Drink Industry* (Brussels: Confederation of the Food and Drink Industries of the EU).

—— (2003b) *Annual Report* (Brussels: Confederation of the Food and Drink Industries of the EU).

Cleveland, C.J., and M. Ruth (1999) 'Indicators of Dematerialisation and the Materials Intensity of Use', *Journal of Industrial Ecology* 2.3: 15-50.

Collard, B., and A. DeHerde (1997) *Office Building Typology: Architecture and Climate* (Dublin: Energy Research Group, University College Dublin).

Collis, D.J. (1994) 'Research Note: How Valuable are Organisational Capabilities?', *Strategic Management Journal* 15 (Winter 1994): 143-52.

Cooper, T., and S. Evans (2000) *Products to Services* (Sheffield, UK: Centre for Sustainable Consumption, Sheffield Hallam University).

—— and K. Mayers (2000) *Prospects for Household Appliances* (Sheffield, UK: Centre for Sustainable Consumption, Sheffield Hallam University).

Correljé, A., and G. Verbong (2004) 'The Transition from Coal to Gas: Radical Change of the Dutch Gas System', in B. Elzen, F.W. Geels and K. Green (eds.), *System Innovation and the Transition to Sustainability* (Cheltenham, UK: Edward Elgar).

Davies, A., P. Tang, T. Brady, M. Hobday, H. Rush and D. Gann (2001) *Integrated Solutions: The New Economy between Manufacturing and Services* (Brighton, UK: SPRU, University of Sussex).

——, T. Brady, P. Tang, with M. Hobday, H. Rush and D. Gann (2003) *Delivering Integrated Solutions* (Brighton, UK: SPRU, University of Sussex).

Day, G.S. (1984) *Strategic Market Planning: The Pursuit of Competitive Advantage* (St Paul, MN: West Publishing Company).

De Bruyn, S.M. (1998) 'Dematerialisation and Rematerialisation', in P. Vellinga, F. Berkhout and J. Gupta (eds.), *Managing a Material World* (Dordrecht, Netherlands: Kluwer Academic Publishers).

—— (1999) *Economic Growth and the Environment: An Empirical Analysis* (PhD thesis; Amsterdam: Free University of Amsterdam, Tinbergen Institute Research Series No. 216).

De Geus, A. (1997) *The Living Company: Habits for Survival in a Turbulent Environment* (Washington, DC: Longview Publishing).

Deiss, R. (2001) *Information Society Statistics* (Luxembourg: Eurostat).

Dickson, P.R. (1994) *Marketing Management* (Forth Worth, TX: Dryden Press).

Doering, D.S., A. Cassara, C. Layke, J. Ranganathan, C. Revenga, D. Tunstall and W. Vanasselt (2002) *Tomorrow's Markets: Global Trends and their Implications for Business* (Washington, DC: WRI, WBCSD and UNEP).

Dosi, G. (1982) 'Technological Paradigms and Technological Trajectories', *Research Policy* 11: 147-62.

Dudda, C., S. Thomas and K. Schuster (2001) 'Functional Service Contracts for White Goods: Selling a Function Instead of a Product (Funserve)', paper presented at the *2001 eceee Summer Study Proceedings*, Mandelieu, France, 11–16 June 2001.

EC (European Commission) (1997) *Report from the Commission on the State of EU Agriculture* (Brussels: EC).

—— (2000) *Proposal for a Directive of the European Parliament and of the Council on the Coordination of Procedures for the Award of Public Supply Contracts, Public Service Contracts and Public Works Contracts* (COM[2000]275; Brussels: EC).

—— (2001a) *Economy-wide Material Flow Accounts and Derived Indicators: A Methodological Guide* (Luxembourg: EC, 2000 edn).

—— (2001b) *White Paper: Strategy for a Future Chemicals Policy* (COM[2001]88; Brussels: EC).

—— (2003) *Questions and Answers on the New Chemicals Policy REACH* (MEMO/03/99; Brussels: EC).

Ehrlich, P., and J. Holdren (1971) 'Impact of Population Growth', *Science* 171: 1,212-17.

Eid, U. (2001) 'The Roles and Responsibilities of Industrialized Countries in Assuring Sustainable Food Security', in *Proceedings of the International Conference on Sustainable Food Security for All by 2020*, Bonn, Germany, 4–6 September 2001 (available from the International Food Policy Research Institute, Washington DC, www.ifpri.org/pubs/books/2020conpro.htm#info).

Eisenhart, K.M., and J.A. Martin (2000) 'Dynamic Capabilities: What Are They?', *Strategic Management Journal* (special issue) 21.10–11: 1,105-21.

Ellger, C., and J. Scheiner (1997) 'After Industrial Society: Service Society as Clean Society? Environmental Consequences of Increasing Service Interaction', *The Service Industries Journal* 17.4: 564-79.

Elzen, B., F.W. Geels and K. Green (2004) *System Innovation and the Transition to Sustainability* (Cheltenham, UK: Edward Elgar).

EU (European Union) (2003) *Communication: Towards a Thematic Strategy on the Sustainable Use of Natural Resources* (COM[2003]572 Final; europa.eu.int/eur-lex/en/com/cnc/2003/com2003_0572en01.pdf, accessed 1 June 2006).

Eurostat (2002) *Material Use in the European Union 1980–2000: Indicators and Analysis. Theme 2: Economy and Finance* (Luxembourg: Office for Official Publications of the European Communities).

Factor 10 Club (1997) *Statement to Government and Business Leaders* (Carnoules, France: Factor 10 Institute).

Fahy, J., and A. Smithee (1999) 'Strategic Marketing and the Resource Based View of the Firm', *Academy of Marketing Science Review* 10 (oxygen.vancouver.wsu.edu/amsrev/theory/fahy10-99.html, accessed 27 July 2006).

Falcon, W.D. (ed.) (1964) *Value Analysis Value Engineering: The Implications for Managers* (New York: American Management Association): 9-24.

FDF (Food and Drink Federation) (2002) *World Summit on Sustainable Development 2002: Contribution by the UK Food and Drink Manufacturing Industry* (London: FDF).

FIEC (European Construction Industry Federation) (2003a) 'Construction Activity in Europe', FIEC, no. 46, Summary in www.fiec.org, accessed 1 March 2005.

—— (2003b) *FIEC Position Paper on the 'Common Positions' of the Council of Ministers* (Brussels: FIEC, www.fiec.org).

—— (2004) *FIEC's Initial Position Paper 'Social and Employment Issues' on the Proposed Directive 'Services in the Internal Market' COM(2004) 002* ('SOC' final 30/3/2004; Brussels: FIEC, www.fiec.org).

Fitzsimmons, J.A., and M.J. Fitzsimmons (1994) *Service Management for Competitive Advantage* (New York: McGraw-Hill).

Forrester (2004) '50% More Online Shoppers in 2004: High Street Shops Will Feel the Impact' (press release; Amsterdam: Forrester, 20 December 2004; www.forrester.com/ER/Press/Release/0,1769,973,00.html, accessed 30 May 2006).

Forum for the Future (2003) *Digital Europe: Making the Net Work. Steps towards a Sustainable Networked World* (London: Forum for the Future, www.forumforthefuture.org.uk/publications/Summarymakingthenetwork_page1482.aspx).

Frazão, R., and C. Rocha (2004) 'Product Services in the Need Area Base Materials. SusProNet report', *INETI/CENDES*, Lisbon, Portugal, 30 October (www.suspronet.org).

Gadiesh, O., and J.L. Gilbert (1998) 'Profit Pools: A Fresh Look to Strategy', *Harvard Business Review*, May/June 1998: 139-46.

Gattorna, J.L., and D.W. Walters (1996) *Managing the Supply Chain* (Houndmills, UK: Macmillan Business).

Geels. F.W. (2002a) 'Technological Transitions as Evolutionary Reconfiguration Processes: A Multi-level Perspective and a Case Study', *Research Policy* 31: 1,257-74.

—— (2002b) 'From Sectoral Systems of Innovations to Socio-technical Systems: Insights about Dynamics and Change from Sociology and Institutional Theory', *Research Policy* 33: 897-920.

—— and R. Kemp (2000) *Transities vanuit socio-technisch perspectief: Achtergronddocument bij hoofdstuk 1 van het rapport 'Transities en transitiemanagement'* (Maastricht, Netherlands: ICIS, Maastricht University).

Gibson, R. (ed.) (1998) *Rethinking the Future* (London: Nicholas Brealey).

Goedkoop, M.J., J.G. van Halen, H. te Riele and P.J.M. Rommens (1999) *Product Service Systems: Ecological and Economic Basics* (The Hague: VROM, EZ).

——, J. Krimphoff and S. Adda (2002) 'People-Planet-Profit Assessment of Product Service Systems', SETAC Europe Annual Meeting, Vienna, 12–16 May 2002.

Graedel, T.E. (1998) 'Lifecycle Assessment in the Service Industries', *Journal of Industrial Ecology* 1.1: 57-70.

Grant, R.M. (1991) 'The Resource Based Theory of Competitive Advantage: Implications for Strategy Formulation', *California Management Review* 33.3: 114-35.

—— (2002) *Contemporary Strategy Analysis: Concepts, Techniques, Applications* (Malden, UK: Blackwell Publishing, 4th edn).

Greening, L. (2000) 'Energy Efficiency and Consumption. The Rebound Effect: A Survey', *Energy Policy* 28: 389-401.

Haksever, C., B. Render, R.S. Russel and R.G. Murdick (2000) *Service Management and Operations* (Upper Saddle River, NJ: Prentice-Hall, 2nd edn): 187.

Halme, M., C. Jasch and M. Scharp (2004) 'Sustainable Homeservices? Toward Household Services that Enhance Ecological, Social and Economic Sustainability', *Ecological Economics* 51.1–2: 125-38.

Hamel, G., and C.K. Prahalad (1994) *Competing for the Future* (Boston, MA: Harvard Business Review Press).

Hammer, M. (2001a) 'The Superefficient Company', *Harvard Business Review*, September 2001: 83-91.

—— (2001b) *The Agenda: What Every Business Must Do to Dominate the Decade* (New York: Crown Business).

Hawken, P., H. Lovins and A. Lovins (1999) *Natural Capitalism: Creating the New Industrial Revolution* (New York: Little, Brown).

Hedman, F., and T. Kalling (2001) *The Business Model: A Means to Understand the Business Context of Information and Communication Technology* (No 2001/9, Working Paper Series; Lund, Sweden: Lund University, Institute of Economic Research).

Heijungs, R. (1997) *Economic Drama and the Environmental Stage* (PhD thesis; Leiden, Netherlands: CML, Leiden University).

Heiskanen, E., and M. Jalas (2000) *Dematerialization through Services: A Review and Evaluation of the Debate* (The Finnish Environment 436; Helsinki: Ministry of the Environment, Environmental Protection Department).

Heller, E.D. (1971) *Value Management: Value Engineering and Cost Reduction* (Reading, MA: Addison-Wesley).

Hertwich, E. (2003) 'Consumption and the Rebound Effect: The Consideration of Information and Communication Technology', *Proceedings of the SETAC-ISIE Case Study Symposium*, Lausanne, Switzerland, 3–4 December 2003.

Hinterberger, F., F. Luks and F. Schmidt-Bleek (1997) 'Material Flows vs "Natural Capital": What Makes an Economy Sustainable?', *Ecological Economics* 23.1: 1-14.

Hockerts, K., and N. Weaver (2002) *Are Service Systems Worth our Interest? Assessing the Eco-efficiency of Sustainable Service Systems* (INSEAD Working Document; Fontainebleau, France: INSEAD).

——, A. Petmecky, S. Hauch and S. Seuring (1994) *Kreislaufwirtschaft statt Abfallwirtschaft: Optimierte Nutzung und Einsparung von Ressourcen durch Öko-Leasing und Servicekonzepte* (Ulm, Germany: Universitätsverlag).

Hoffman, N.P. (2000) 'An Examination of the "Sustainable Competitive Advantage" Concept: Past, Present and Future', *Academy of Marketing Science Review* 4 (www.amsreview.org/articles/hoffman04-2000.pdf).

Hofstetter, P., and T. Ozawa (2004) 'Minimizing CO_2-Emissions per Unit of Happiness', in *Proceedings of the 3rd International Workshop on Sustainable Consumption*, Tsukuba, Japan, 21–22 October 2004, organised and published by SNTT and AIST.

Huppes, G., A. de Koning, S. Suh, R. Heijungs, L. van Oers, P. Nielsen and J.B. Guinée (2006) 'Environmental Impacts of Consumption in the European Union Using Detailed Input–Output Analysis', *Journal of Industrial Ecology* 10.3 (in press).

Illich, I. (1977) *Toward a History of Needs* (New York: Random House).

Inaba, A. (2004) 'The Interim Report of the Sustainable Consumption Project in Japan', in *Proceedings of the Third International Workshop on Sustainable Consumption*, Tsukuba, Japan, SNTT, AIST.

ISO (International Organisation for Standardisation) (2002) *Environmental Management: Integrating Environmental Aspects into Product Design and Development* (ISO/PDTR 14062, ISO TC 207/WG3; Geneva: ISO).

Jackson, T. (2004) *Chasing Progress: Beyond Measuring Economic Growth* (London: New Economics Foundation).

——, W. Jager and S. Stagl (2004) 'Beyond Insatiability: Needs Theory, Consumption and Sustainability', in L. Reisch and I. Røpke (eds.), *The Ecological Economics of Consumption* (Cheltenham, UK: Edward Elgar): ch. 5.

Jakl, T., R. Joas, R.F. Nolte, R. Schott and A. Windsperger (2004) *Chemical Leasing: An Intelligent Business Model with a View to Sustainable Development in Materials Management* (Vienna: Springer Verlag).

James, P., A. Slob and L. Nijhuis (2001) *Environmental and Social Well Being in the New Economy: Sustainable Services—An Innovation Workbook* (Bradford, UK: University of Bradford, TNO).

Jasch, C., and G. Hrauda (2000) *Ökologische dienstleistungen: Markt der Zukunft* (Vienna: IÖW).

Jégou, F., and P. Joore (eds.) (2004) *Food Delivery Solutions: Cases of Solution Oriented Partnerships* (Cranfield, UK: Cranfield University).

Johnson, J.V., and E.M. Hall (1988) 'Job Strain, Work Place Social Support and Cardiovascular Disease: A Cross-sectional Study of a Random Sample of the Swedish Working Population', *American Journal of Public Health*, 78: 1,336-42.

Kaczmarek, M., and F. Stüllenberg (2002) 'Decision Support by Model Based Analysis of Supply Chains', in S. Seuring and M. Goldbach (eds.), *Cost Management in Supply Chains* (Heidelberg, Germany: Physica Verlag).

Kammerer, M. (2002) 'Is New Work a Part of our Future or Merely a Marketing Gag by the Office Furniture Industry?', Presentation at *Orgatec Trade Fair*, Cologne, Germany, 22–26 October 2002.

Karasek, R., and T. Theorell (1990) *Healthy Work: Stress, Productivity and the Reconstruction of Working Life* (New York: Basic Books).

Kathalys (2001) *Vision on Sustainable Product Innovation* (Delft, Netherlands: BIS Publishers).

Kawakami, N., and T. Haratani (1999) 'Epidemiology of Job Stress and Health in Japan: Review of Current Evidence and Future Direction', *Industrial Health* 37.2: 174-86.

Kazazian, T., for WWF France (2003) *Il y aura l'âge des choses légères: Design and développement durable* (*The Age of Light Things is Arriving: Design and Sustainable Development*) (Paris: Victoire-Editions).

Kemp, R., and J. Rotmans (2004) 'Managing the Transition to Sustainable Mobility', in B. Elzen, F.W. Geels and K. Green (eds.), *System Innovation and the Transition to Sustainability* (Cheltenham, UK: Edward Elgar).

Khazzoom, J.D. (1980) 'Economic Implications of Mandated Efficiency in Standards for Household Applications', *Energy Journal* 1.4: 21-40.

Kim, W.C., and R. Mauborgne (1997) 'Value Innovation: The Strategic Logic of High Growth', *Harvard Business Review*, January–February 1997: 103-12.

—— and —— (1999) 'Strategy, Value Innovation, and the Knowledge Economy', *Sloan Management Review*, Spring 1999: 41-54.

—— and —— (2002) 'Charting Your Company's Future', *Harvard Business Review*, June–July 2002: 79-83.

Klein, B., R.A. Crawford and A.A. Alchian (1978) 'Vertical Integration, Appropriable Rents, and the Competitive Contracting Process', *Journal of Law and Economics* 21: 297-326.

Krutwagen, B., and E. Lindeijer (2001) 'LCI of Food in The Netherlands', in *Proceedings of the International Conference on LCA in Foods*, Gothenburg, Sweden, 26–27 April 2001.

KSI (Knowledge Network on System Innovations and Transitions) (2004) *Knowledge and Competences of Sustainable System Innovation* (research programme under the Netherlands BSIK programme, p/o DRIFT; Rotterdam: Erasmus University).

Labouze, E., V. Monier, Y. Le Guern and J.-B. Puyou (2003) *Study on External Environmental Effects Related to the Life Cycle of Products and Services* (Brussels: European Commission, Directorate General Environment, Directorate A—Sustainable Development and Policy Support).

Lasalle, D., and T.A. Britton (2003) *Priceless: Turning Ordinary Products into Extraordinary Experiences* (Boston, MA: Harvard Business School Press).

Lifset, R.J. (2000) 'Moving From Products to Services', *Journal of Industrial Ecology* 4.1: 1-2.

Lindblom, C.E. (1959) 'The Science of Muddling Through', *Public Administration Review* 19: 79-99.

Lippert, S., and K. Nowak (2001) *Veränderungen der Büroarbeitsplätze in der Zukunft. Realität und Zukunftsvisionen: Eine kritische Analyse von Büroarbeitsplätzen* (Projektarbeit SS/2001; Stuttgart, Germany: IPG Institut für Gestaltung der Planung, Fakultät Architektur und Stadtplanung, Universität Stuttgart).

Littig, B. (2000) *Eco-efficient Services for Private Households: Looking at the Consumer's Side* (Vienna: Institute for Advanced Studies).

Loh, J. (ed.) (2002) *Living Planet Report 2002* (Gland, Switzerland: WWF, www.wwf.org.uk/filelibrary/pdf/livingplanet2002.pdf).

Lovins, A.B. (1988) 'Energy Saving from More Efficient Appliances: Another View', *Energy J* 9:155-62.

Luiten, W.J., J. Hoogendoorn and T. van der Horst (2003) 'Sustainable Business Development: Business Models for Inherently Sustainable Systems', paper for the *Greening of Industry Conference*, San Francisco, October 2003.

Lutz, W., W.C. Sanderson and S. Scherbov (eds.) (2004) *The End of World Population Growth in the 21st Century: New Challenges for Human Capital Formation and Sustainable Development* (London: Earthscan).

MacMillan, I.C., and R.G. McGrath (1997) 'Discovering New Points of Differentiation', *Harvard Business Review*, July–August 1997: 133-42.

Manufuture (2003) Working document for the *MANUFUTURE 2003 Conference. European Manufacturing for the Future: Role of Research and Education for European Leadership*, Milan, Italy, 1–2 December 2003 (Brussels: European Commission, DG Research).

Manzini, E. (1996) 'Sustainable Product-Services Development: Pioneer Industries on Sustainable Service', workshop organised by UNEP-WG-SPD in the *INES Conference Challenges of Sustainable Development*, Amsterdam, Netherlands, 22–25 August 1996.

—— and C. Vezzoli (2002) *Product-Service-Systems and Sustainability, Opportunities for Sustainable Solutions* (Paris: Politecnico di Milano/UNEP).

——, L. Collina and S. Evans (2004) *Solution Oriented Partnership: How to Design Industrialised Sustainable Solutions* (Cranfield, UK: Cranfield University).

Maslow, A.H. (1943) 'A Theory of Human Motivation', *Psychological Review* 50: 370-96; psychclassics. yorku.ca/Maslow/motivation.htm, accessed 1 June 2006.

Maßelter, S., and U. Tischner (2000) *Sustainable Systems Innovation, Final Report* (Cologne: econcept for BMBF).

Matthews, E., C. Amann, S. Bringezu, M. Ficher-Kowalski, W. Hüttler, R. Kleijn, Y. Moriguchi, C. Ottke, E. Rodenburg, D. Rogich, H. Schandl, H. Schütz, E. van der Voet and H. Weisz (2000) *The Weight of Nations: Material Outflows from Industrial Economies* (Washington, DC: World Resources Institute).

Maylor, H. (2000) 'Assessing the Relationship between Practice Changes and Process Improvement in New Product Development', *OMEGA—The International Journal of Management Science* 29: 85-96.

Meijkamp, R. (2000) *Changing Consumer Behaviour through Eco-efficient Services: An Empirical Study on Car Sharing in the Netherlands* (thesis; Delft, Netherlands: TU Delft).

Miller, D. (1992) 'The Generic Strategy Trap', *Journal of Business Strategy* 13 (January/February 1992): 37-41.

Mintzberg, H., B. Ahstrand and J. Lampel (1998) *Strategy Safari: The Complete Guide through the Wilds of Strategic Management* (London: FT Prentice Hall).

MNP (Milieu- en Natuurplanbureau) (2005) *Milieubalans 2005 (Environmental Balance 2005)* (Bilthoven, Netherlands: MNP/RIVM).

Mont, O. (2001a) *Reaching Sustainable Consumption through the Concept of a Product-Service System (PSS)* (TemaNord 2001:526; Copenhagen: Nordic Council of Ministers).

—— (2001b) *Introducing and Developing a Product-Service System (PSS) Concept in Sweden* (Lund, Sweden: IIIEE, Lund University).

—— (2004) *Product-Service Systems: Panacea or Myth?* (PhD thesis; Lund, Sweden: IIIEE, Lund University).

Montalvo Corral, C. (2002) *Environmental Policy and Technological Innovation* (Cheltenham, UK: Edward Elgar).

Morelli, N. (2004) 'Developing New PSS: Methodology and Operational Tools', presentation at the Second SusProNet Conference, Brussels, 3–4 June 2004; www.suspronet.org.

Müller, H. (1995) *Service Marketing: Service-Kompetenz als unternehmerischer Faktor* (Berlin: Springer Verlag).

Myers, N., and J. Kent (2004) *The New Consumers: The Influence of Affluence on the Environment* (Washington, DC: Island Press).

Negro, G. (1992) *Organizzare la qualità nei servizi* (Milan: Il Sole 24 Ore Edizioni): 213-33.

Nelson, R.R., and S. Winter (1982) *An Evolutionary Theory of Economic Change* (London: The Belknap Press of Harvard University).

Nemry, F., K. Thollier, B. Jansen and J. Theunis (2002) *Identifying Key Products for the Federal Product and Environment Policy (Federal Services of Environment, Department on Product Policy)* (Namur, Belgium: Institut Wallon de développement économique et social et d'aménagement du territoire [IWT] and Vlaamse Instelling voor Technologisch Onderzoek [VITO]).

Nielsen, P.H., A. Tukker, B.P. Weidema, E.H. Lauridsen and Ph. Notten (2004) *Environmental Impact of Natural Resources* (Seville, Spain: ESTO/EU DG JRC—IPTS).

Nijdam, D.S., and H.C. Wilting (2003) *Milieudruk consumptie in beeld (A View on Environmental Pressure on Consumption)* (RIVM report 771404004; Bilthoven, Netherlands: RIVM, in Dutch).

OECD (Organisation for Economic Co-operation and Development) (2001) *Household Food Consumption: Trends, Environmental Impacts and Policy Responses* (Paris: OECD).

—— (2002) *Towards Sustainable Household Consumption: Trends and Policies in OECD Countries* (Paris: OECD).

Oldham, J. (2003) 'Policy Drivers and Barriers to Chemical Management Services: A UK Case Study', *Conference Experiences and Perspectives of Service-Oriented Strategies in the Chemicals Industry and Related Areas*, Vienna, Austria, 13–14 November 2003.

Paulk, M.C., C.V. Weber, B. Curtis and M.B. Chrissis (eds.) (1995) *Capability Maturity Model: The Guidelines for Improving the Software Process* (Boston, MA: Addison Wesley Professional).

Pine II, B.J., and J.H. Gilmore (1999) *The Experience Economy* (Boston, MA: Harvard Business School Press).

Porter, M.E. (1985) *Competitive Advantage: Creating and Sustaining Superior Performance* (New York: The Free Press).

—— (1990) *The Competitive Advantage of Nations* (New York: The Free Press).

—— (2001) 'Strategy and the Internet', *Harvard Business Review*, May 2001: 63-78.

Prepare (2000) Minutes of the Prepare TG 3S meeting, 2 October 2000, Cologne, www.prepare-net.org/topics_projects/index.html, accessed 1 March 2003.

Rafii, F., and P.J. Kampas (2002) 'How to Identify Your Enemies: Before They Destroy You', *Harvard Business Review*, November 2002: 115.

Reijnhoudt, J.C. (2000) *Dienstingang, het ontwerpen van een dienst op het gebied van kantoorinnovatie voor de handelsonderneming Ahrend inrichten* (MSc thesis; Delft, Netherlands: Delft University of Technology).

Reiskin, E.D., A.L. White, J.K. Johnson and T.J. Votta (1999) 'Servicizing the Chemical Supply Chain', *Journal of Industrial Ecology* 3.2–3: 19-31.

Riele, H. te, S.A.M. Duifhuizen, M. Hotte, G. Zijlstra and M.A.G. Sengers (2000) *Transities: Kunnen drie mensen de wereld doen omslaan? (Transitions: Can Three People Change the World?)* (Publication Series Environmental Strategy; The Hague: Environment Ministry).

Rip, A., and R. Kemp (1998) 'Technology Change', in S. Rayner and E.L. Malone (eds.), *Human Choice and Climate Change* (Columbus, OH: Battelle Press): 327-99.

RIVM (2000) *National Environmental Outlook 5, 2000–2030* (Alphen aan den Rijn, Netherlands: Samsom bv).

RMNO (1999) *Kennis voor een duurzame economie* (RMNO-nummer 141; Rijswijk, Netherlands: RMNO).

Roozenburg, N.F.M., and J. Eekels (1991) *Produktontwerpen, struktuur en methoden (Product Design, Structure and Methods)* (Utrecht, Netherlands: Lemma).

Rosegrant, M.W. (2001) 'Reaching Sustainable Food Security for All by 2020: Getting the Priorities and Responsibilities Right', paper at the *International Conference on Sustainable Food Security for All by 2020*, Bonn, Germany, 4–6 September 2001.

——, M.S. Paisner, S. Meijer and J. Witcover (2001) *Global Food Projections to 2020* (Washington, DC: International Food Policy Research Institute).

Rotmans, J. (2003) *Transitiemanagement: Sleutel voor een duurzame samenleving (Transition Management: Key to a Sustainable Society)* (Assen, Netherlands: Koninklijke Van Gorcum).

—— (ed.) (2000) *Transities and transitiemanagement: De casus van een emissiearme energievoorziening* (Maastricht, Netherlands: International Centre for Integrative Studies [ICIS BV]).

Sanne, C. (2001) 'Are We Chasing Our Tail in the Pursuit of Sustainability?', *International Journal of Sustainable Development* 4.1: 120-33.

Sawhney, M., S. Balasubramanian and V.V. Krishnan (2004) 'Creating Growth with Services', *MIT Sloan Management Review*, Winter 2004: 35-43.

Schmidt-Bleek, F. (1993) *Wieviel Umwelt braucht der Mensch? MIPS: das Maß für ökologisches Wirtschaften* (Berlin: Birkhäuser).

Segal, J.M. (1999) *Graceful Simplicity: Towards a Philosophy and Politics of Simple Living* (New York: Holt).

Simon, H. (1957) 'Administrative Behaviour', in *Models of Man* (New York: Macmillan).

Simons, L.Ph., A. Slob, H. Holswilder and A. Tukker (2001) 'The Fourth Generation: New Strategies Call for New Eco-indicators', *Environmental Quality Management*, Winter 2001: 51.

Slob, A., T. Tielens, M. van As and G.J. Ellen (2002) *Eindrapportage Definitiestudie Duurzaam consumeren en gedrag* (*Final Report Definition Study on Sustainable Consumption and Behaviour*) (Report 02-42; Delft, Netherlands: TNO Strategy, Technology and Policy).

Smits, R., M. Hekkert and H. van Lente (2001) *Transitiemanagement: Nieuwe rollen voor NOVEM?* (*Transition Management: New Roles for NOVEM?*) (report commissioned by NOVEM; Utrecht, Netherlands: Department of Innovation Studies, Utrecht University).

Stahel, W.R. (1998) 'From Products to Services: Selling Performance Instead of Goods', *IPTS Report* 27 (September 1998, Seville).

—— (2000) *Multi-client Study on the Shift from Manufacturing to Services, 1998 and 2010* (Geneva: The Product-Life Institute).

Stewart, G.B. (1991) *The Quest for Value: The EVA Management Guide* (New York: Harper Business).

Suh, S. (2004) *Materials and Energy Flows in Industry and Ecosystem Networks: Life Cycle Assessment, Input–Output Analysis, Material Flow Analysis, Ecological Network Flow Analysis, and their Combinations for Industrial Ecology* (PhD thesis; Leiden, Netherlands: CML, Leiden University).

Swank, C.K. (2003) 'The Lean Service Machine', *Harvard Business Review*, October 2003: 123-29.

TCO Development (2000) Report from the workshop on *Sustainable Workplace* (arranged by TCO Development within the Worklife 2000 Conference, Quality at Work; Stockholm: Bergendal).

Tempelman, E. (ed.), with P. Joore, T. van der Horst, E. Lindeijer, H. Luiten, L. Rampino and M. van Schie (2004) *Product Services in the Need Area Food* (SusProNet report; Eindhoven, Netherlands: TNO, 30 October 2004, www.suspronet.org).

Tessaring, M. (1994) 'Langfristige Tendenzen des Arbeitskräftebedarfs nach Tätigkeiten und Qualifikationen in den alten Bundesländern bis zum Jahre 2010. Eine erste Aktualisierung der IAB/Prognos-Projektionen 1989/91', *Mitteilungen aus der Arbeitsmarkt- und Berufsforschung* 27.1: 5-19.

Tischner, U., E. Schmincke and F. Rubik (2000) *How to do Ecodesign? A Guide for Environmentally and Economically Sound Design* (Heidelberg, Germany: Verlag form).

Trend conference (2002) *Consumer Trends 2003* (organised by Euroforum, Netherlands; www.consumententrends.nl).

Tukker, A. (2004) 'Eight Types of Product-Service: Eight Ways to Sustainability?', *Business Strategy and the Environment* 13.4 (best paper issue Greening of Industry Network Conference, October 2003, San Francisco): 246-60.

—— and T. de Bruijn (2002) 'Conclusions: The Prospects of Collaboration', in T. de Bruijn and A. Tukker (eds.), *Partnership and Leadership: Building Alliances for a Sustainable Future* (Dordrecht, Netherlands: Kluwer Academic Publishers).

—— and C. van Halen (eds.) (2003) *Innovation Scan Product Service Combinations: Manual* (Delft, Netherlands: TNO-STB; Utrecht, Netherlands: PricewaterhouseCoopers).

——, G. Huppes, S. Suh, T. Geerken, B. Jansen and P Nielsen (2006) *Environmental Impacts of Products: Literature Review and Input–Output Analyses on 500 Product Groupings for the EU's Integrated Product Policy* (Seville, Spain: ESTO/IPTS).

TÜV-Akademie Rheinland (2002) *Projectforum Service Engineering* (seminar report; Cologne, Germany: TÜV-Akademie Rheinland).

Valota, P., *et al.* (2002) *Report on Food and People with Reduced Mobility* (Deliverable 07 from the HiCS project; Milan: Associazione Consumatori Utenti [ACU]).

Van Gool, S., and M. Vermee (eds.) (2002) *Gfk Jaargids, Kerncijfers voor Marketing en Beleidsplannen* (*Key Figures for Marketing and Policy Plans*) (Dongen, Netherlands; Brussels: Gfk Benelux Marketing Services).

Van Halen, C., C. Vezzoli and R. Wimmer (2005) *Methodology for Product Service Innovation: How to Implement Clean, Clever and Competitive Strategies in European Industries* (Assen, Netherlands: Koninklijke van Gorcum).

Veenhoven, R. (undated) 'World Database on Happiness', www2.eur.nl/fsw/research/happiness, accessed 24 May 2005.

Vercalsteren, A., and T. Geerken (2004) *Product Services in the Need Area Households* (SusProNet report; Mol, Belgium: VITO, 30 October 2004).

Verkuijl, M., U. Tischner and R. Nickel (2004) *Product Services in the Need Area Offices* (SusProNet report; Cologne, Germany: econcept, 30 October 2004, www.suspronet.org).

Vlek, C., A.J. Rooijers and E.M. Steg (1999) *Duurzamer consumeren: Meer kwaliteit van leven met minder materiaal? (Sustainable Consumption: More Quality of Life with Less Material?)* (Research Report COV 99-03; Groningen, Netherlands: Centre for Environmental and Traffic Psychology, University of Groningen).

Vogtländer, J.G., J.C. Brezet and Ch.F. Hendriks (2001) 'The Virtual Eco-Costs '99. A Single LCA-Based Indicator for Sustainability and the Eco-Costs–Value Ratio (EVR) Model for Economic Allocation: A New LCA-Based Calculation Model to Determine the Sustainability of Products and Services', *International Journal of Life Cycle Assessment* 6.3: 12A.

Von Weizsäcker, E., A. Lovins and H. Lovins (1997) *Factor 4: Doubling Wealth, Halving Resource Use* (London: Earthscan).

VROM Raad (2002) *Milieu en Economie: ontkoppeling door innovatie (Environment and Economy: Decoupling via Innovation)* (The Hague: Ministry of Environment Advisory Council).

WCED (World Commission on Environment and Development) (1987) *Our Common Future* (Oxford, UK: Oxford University Press).

Weaver, P., L. Jansen, G. van Grootveld, E. van Spiegel and Ph. Vergragt (2000) *Sustainable Technology Development* (Sheffield, UK: Greenleaf Publishing).

Weidema, B.P., A.M. Nielsen, K. Christiansen, G. Norris, P. Notten, S. Suh and J. Madsen (2005) *Prioritisation within the Integrated Product Policy* (2.-0 LCA Consultants; Copenhagen: for Danish EPA).

Wells, L.D. (1961) *Techniques of Value Analysis and Engineering* (New York: McGraw-Hill).

Whaley, D., and J.K. Johnson (2001) 'Chemical Strategies Partnership', *New England's Environment* 7.3 (Spring 2001; www.environews.com).

White, A., M. Stoughton and L. Feng (1999) *Servicizing: The Quiet Transition to Extended Product Responsibility* (Boston, MA: Tellus Institute).

WHO (World Health Organisation) (1998) *GEMS/Food Regional Diets. Regional per Capita Consumption of Raw and Semi-processed Agricultural Commodities* (WHO/FSF/FOS/98.3; prepared for the Global Environmental Monitoring System/Food Contamination Monitoring and Assessment Programme; Geneva: WHO).

——/FAO (Food and Agriculture Organisation) (2002) *Diet, Nutrition and the Prevention of Chronic Diseases, Draft Report of the joint WHO/FAO Expert Consultation* (Geneva: WHO).

Wilkinson, L. (1998) *How to Build Scenarios* (New York: The Condé Nast Publications Inc./Wired Digital Inc.; www.wired.com/wired/scenarios/build.html, accessed 1 June 2006).

Williamson, O.E. (1975) *Markets and Hierarchies, Analysis and Antitrust Implications: A Study in the Economics of Internal Organisation* (New York: The Free Press).

—— (1979) 'Transaction Cost Economics: The Governance of Contractual Relations', *Journal of Law and Economics* 22: 233-61.

Wimmer, W., and R. Züst (2001) *ECODESIGN Pilot. Produkt-Innovations-, Lern- und Optimierungs-Tool für umweltgerechte* (Produktgestaltung mit deutsch/englischer CD-ROM; Zurich: Verlag Industrielle Organisation).

Wise, R., and P. Baumgartner (1999) 'Go Downstream: The New Profit Imperative in Manufacturing', *Harvard Business Review* 77: 133-41.

Wolcott, H.F. (1999) *Ethnography: A Way of Seeing* (Walnut Creek, CA: AltaMira Press).

Wong, M. (2001) *Industrial Sustainability (IS) and Product Service Systems (PSS): A Strategic Decision Support Tool for Consumer Goods Firms* (Cambridge, UK: University of Cambridge, Department of Engineering).

—— (2004) *Implementation of Innovative Product Service Systems in the Consumer Goods Industry* (dissertation thesis; Cambridge, UK: University of Cambridge, Department of Engineering).

Zaring, O., M. Bartolomeo and P. Eder (2001) *Creating Eco-efficient Services* (Gothenburg, Sweden: Gothenburg Research report).

Zeithaml, V.A. (1996) *Services Marketing* (New York: McGraw-Hill).

Abbreviations

ABC	activity-based costing
ADSL	asymmetric digital subscriber line
ASP	application service provider
B2B	business-to-business
B2C	business-to-consumer
BCG	Boston Consulting Group
BISS	Business Models for Inherently Sustainable Systems
BMVIT	Bundesministerium für Verkehr, Innovation und Technologie (Austrian Federal Ministry of Transport, Innovation, and Technology)
BSC	balanced scorecard
BSE	bovine spongiform encephalopathy
CD	compact disc
CED	cumulative energy demand
CEFIC	European Chemical Industry Council
CEO	chief executive officer
CFO	chief financial officer
CfSD	Centre for Sustainable Design, UK
CIRM	corporate infrastructure resource manager
CMM	capability maturity model
CMR	carcinogenic, mutagenic, repro-toxic
CMS	chemical management services
CO_2	carbon dioxide
CPU	central processing unit
CSR	corporate social responsibility
DES	Designing Eco-efficient Services
DMC	domestic material consumption
DOP	Denominazione di Origine Protetta
DSM	demand-side management
DSSN	Development Science Self Navigator
DVD	digital versatile disc

EC	European Commission
EHS	environment, health and safety
ELIMA	Environmental Life-cycle Information Management and Acquisition
EMAS	Eco-Management and Audit Scheme
EMS	environmental management system
EoLV	End-of-Life Vehicles
EPS	expanded polystyrene
EU	European Union
EuP	Energy-using Products
EVA	economic value added
EVR	Ecocost Value Ratio
FHE	Food, Health and a nice Environment
FIEC	European Construction Industry Federation
FMEA	failure mode and effect analysis
FP5	5th Framework Programme (EU)
GDP	gross domestic product
GNP	gross national product
GSM	global system mobile
H&S	health & safety
HACCP	Hazard Analysis and Critical Control Point
HiCS	Highly Customerised Solutions
HSE	health, safety and environment
HVAC	heating, ventilation and air conditioning
HVM	Human Vending Machine
ICT	information and communication technology
IDEFo	integration definition for function modelling
INES	Improving New Services
Innopse	Innovation Studio and Exemplary Developments for Product-service
IP	internet protocol
IPP	integrated product policy
IPPC	Integrated Pollution Prevention and Control
IPR	intellectual property rights
ISO	International Organisation for Standardisation
IT	information technology
IWSP	International Workplace Studies Program (Cornell University)
KPI	key performance indicator
LCA	life-cycle assessment
LCC	life-cycle costing
LCD	liquid-crystal display
LCP	least-cost planning
LDL	low-density lipoprotein
LETS	local exchange and trading schemes
LiDS	Lifecycle Design Strategies
LPS	Legal Progress Support
MB	megabyte
MEPSS	Methodology development and Evaluation of PSS
META	materials, energy, toxic substances, added value

MIPS	material input per unit of service
MPW	mixed plastic waste
MTF	Marrakech Task Force
MTG	Management Team Guidelines
NGO	non-governmental organisation
OECD	Organisation for Economic Co-operation and Development
OR	Opportunity Recognition
PC	personal computer
PDA	personal digital assistant
POP	persistent organic pollutant
PPF	Proposed Partnership Form
ProSecCo	Product-Service Co-design
PS	product-service(s)
PSS	product-service system(s)
PwC	PricewaterhouseCoopers
QFD	quality function deployment
R&D	research and development
REACH	Registration, Evaluation and Authorisation of Chemicals (EU)
rf	radio frequency
RIVM	Rijksinstituut voor Volksgezondheid en Milieu (National Institute for Public Health and the Environment, the Netherlands)
RoHS	Restriction of Hazardous Substances
SANE	Sustainable Accommodation for the New Economy
SBP	Solution Oriented Partnership Benefits Planning
SCM	supply chain management
SCP	sustainable consumption and production
SE&D	service engineering and design
SME	small or medium-sized enterprise
SOPMF	Solution Oriented Partnership Methodology Framework
SPSD	Sustainable Product and Service Development
SPSS	sustainable product-service system(s)
SST	Sustainable Systems Triangle
SusProNet	Sustainable Product Development Network
SWOT	strengths, weaknesses, opportunities, threats
TA	trend analysis
TBL	triple bottom line
TQM	total quality management
TRI	Toxics Release Inventory (USA)
UN	United Nations
UNEP	United Nations Environment Programme
UNESCO	United Nations Educational, Scientific and Cultural Organisation
UV	ultraviolet
VAT	value-added tax
ViP	Vision in Product development
VITO	Vlaamse Instelling voor Technologisch Onderzoek (Flemish Institute for Technological Research)
VOC	volatile organic compound

VoIP	Voice-over Internet Protocol
WBCSD	World Business Council for Sustainable Development
WEEE	Waste Electrical and Electronic Equipment
WP	work package
WRI	World Resources Institute
WS	workshop
WSSD	World Summit on Sustainable Development
WWF	formerly the World Wide Fund for Nature

About the contributors

Graham Adams graduated from the University of Sussex in 1970 with an Honours Degree in Mechanical Engineering. During his career he has worked in the fields of R&D in diesel fuel-injection systems, electronics and fibre-optic sensors, of which five years were in Spain, and seven years in Germany. In 1985 he joined Motorola to manage the Mechanical Design Group in the European Design Centre. During his time at Motorola he moved into quality systems where he successfully led a European team to obtain ISO 9001 followed by QS 9000. He then moved on to be the Global Environmental Design Manager for Motorola IESS, during which time he was responsible for developing the DFE tools used by the sector, and the integration of their use into the product launch process. He represented Motorola within EICTA and chaired the Supply Chain Management Task Force within it, after proposing the use of a common materials declaration standard for suppliers. The task force worked with the EIA and JGPSSI to agree a global standard, which also spawned the Rossetanet materials declaration initiative. In April 2002 he formed his own company, PlesTech Ltd (www.plestech.co.uk), helping companies integrate ecodesign into their existing engineering systems. and has produced software to help SMEs meet the requirements of WEEE, RoHS and the EuP. In addition he is the Co-ordinator for the South East England Environmental Business Association (SEEBA), and a trainer on the ERA 'Introduction to Design for the Environment for Electronic and Electrical Equipment' course.

Martin Charter is the Director and Visiting Professor of Sustainable Product Design at the Centre for Sustainable Design at the Surrey Institute of Art and Design, University College. Since 1988, he has worked at director level in 'business and environment' issues in consultancy, leisure, publishing, training, events and research. Martin is presently editor of *The Journal of Sustainable Product Design* and was the previous editor of *The Green Management Letter* and *Greener Management International* (where he retains Editorial Board involvement). Martin is a member of international advisory board of CARE electronics network, judge on the ACCA's sustainability reporting awards, an advisor on sustainable innovation to Hampshire's Natural Resources Initiative, an advisory board member of the Sustainable Trade and Innovation Centre (STIC) and SEEDA's Environmental Technology Taskforce. He is the author, editor and joint editor of various books and publications including *Greener Marketing* (Greenleaf Publishing, 1992 and 1999), *The Green Management Gurus* [e-book] (Epsilon Press, 1996), *Managing Eco-design* (Centre for Sustainable Design, 1997) and *Sustainable Solutions* (Greenleaf Publishing, 2001). Martin has an MBA from Aston Business School in the UK, and has interests in sustainable product design, green(er) marketing and creativity and innovation.

Tom Clark has wide environmental and management consulting experience across many industry sectors (including electronics) and countries, and specific experience in ecodesign. He has a high level of knowledge of environmental and sustainability issues gained from many years' experience, such as producing guidelines on ecodesign for the electronics and electrical industry for the Centre for Sustainable Design (CfSD) as part of its ETMUEL work; also carrying out a sector review of ecodesign application in the UK, identifying case studies and trailing the design guidelines.

Rui Frazão is a senior project manager at INETI-CENDES, the environmental unit of the National Institute of Engineering, Technology and Innovation, in Lisbon, Portugal. He has been involved in work on cleaner production, sustainable product development and sustainable product services since the 1990s. He has worked on various major projects in these fields, including MOSUS: Is Europe sustainable? Modelling opportunities and limits for restructuring Europe towards Sustainability; HAZTRAIN: Hazardous waste management training programme; and various sustainability projects with industry, including an eco-efficiency study with cement producers SECIL.

Theo Geerken is project leader for the Product and Technology Studies group which forms part of the Centre of Integral Environmental Studies at the Flemish research Institute VITO. This group is dedicated to research for both industry and authorities by applying methods and concepts such as LCA, Ecodesign, Substance Flow Analysis, Cleaner Production, Sustainability Evaluation and Technology Assessment. Theo Geerken is a civil engineer with a background in physics. He has industrial experience in the reprographic sector, with 16 years in research, product development and engineering, and integrating environmental goals into business practice. This sector is a classic example of PSS. He has been at VITO since 2000.

Ir. **Peter Joore** works as a senior project manager at TNO Science and Industry, co-ordinating multidisciplinary innovation projects in the field of sustainable product and system innovation. With an industrial design background, his main focus is on translating issues that are relevant for society into challenging new solutions, based on state-of-the-art technological opportunities combined with the accompanying organisational and service innovations. His area of work initially began in mobility, among other things working on the redesign of the interior of a Fokker aircraft, the development of signage for the new Hong Kong MTR metro, and the creation of the Mitka electric tricycle concept together with Nike and Gazelle. More recently, his focus has shifted to intelligent customised products to improve human performance: for instance, working on a tracking system for Alzheimer patients and on innovative playing concepts to improve young children's mobility. Besides his work at the Design and Manufacturing department of TNO, Peter works one day a week as a lecturer at the faculty of Industrial Design at the Technical University Eindhoven, a study that is focused on the development of intelligent products and systems, especially in the area of ambient care.

Helma Luiten is a project manager at TNO, Delft, the Netherlands. She graduated at the Technical University of Delft at the Faculty of Design, and then started working with Kathalys, the ecodesign centre of TNO Industrial Research. Since 2002 she has been working with TNO's strategy group on sustainable system innovation on a variety of projects on experiments for transition management.

Cristina Rocha (MSc) graduated in Environmental Engineering (Faculty of Sciences and Technology, New University of Lisbon) in 1989. She was awarded a postgraduate qualification in Sanitary Engineering from the same university in 1992. She currently holds a position as Senior Researcher at INETI (National Institute of Engineering, Technology and Innovation, Lisbon) and, since 1993, has been involved in national and international projects in the areas of Eco-efficiency, Environmental Management Systems, Ecodesign and Life-cycle Management and Product-Service Systems. In 1998/99 Cristina Rocha was a Research Fellow at Delft University of Technology/Design for Sustainability Programme where she developed a model for Product-Oriented Environmental Management Systems (POEMS). She has been involved in standardisation work for several years, working at ISO and at national level, and chairs the Sub-Committee on Environmental Management Systems and the Technical Committee on Social Responsibility in Portugal.

Erik Tempelman received his MSc in aerospace engineering from Delft University of Technology in 1994, followed by a PhD at the same institution. In his thesis, Erik explored the potential of advanced materials for sustainable transport. Based on his research he questioned the EU directives on car recycling, but he also challenged any purely technological operationalisation of sustainable development—still very much anathema in today's technical universities. He moved on to become a materials innovator at DAF Trucks, where he realised various successful applications of modern production technology. After four years, Erik went back to the world of sustainable development: at TNO, he undertook several projects in this field, of which SusProNet was one. However, materials science and engineering once again captured his interest. Leaving TNO, he briefly worked on advanced fastener materials for Nedschroef. Today, Erik is an assistant professor at the faculty of Industrial Design Engineering of the TU Delft. His field of work is production technology, especially as a driver for product innovation. Erik is an accomplished guitarist.

Ursula Tischner is founder-director of econcept, Cologne, Germany, and has a position as associate professor in sustainable design at the Design Academy in Eindhoven, the Netherlands. She studied architecture and Industrial Design in Aachen and Wuppertal, Germany, and specialised in ecodesign. From 1992 to 1996 she worked at the Wuppertal Institute for Climate, Environment and Energy in the field of ecology and design. At the institute she was engaged in theoretical and practical projects and wrote a guide for environment-friendly product design on behalf of the Austrian Ministry for Science and Research, which was published in 1995. After establishing econcept in 1996 she advises small and medium-sized companies (SMEs) on ecodesign and helps to implement environmental improvements. She edited (with Martin Charter) the book *Sustainable Solutions* (Greenleaf Publishing, 2001) and (with Eva Schmincke, Frieder Rubik and Martin Prosler) the book *How to do Ecodesign* (Verlag form, 2000). She also played key roles in major international projects in the field of ecodesign and product-services, such as Methodology Product Service Systems (2002–2004), the UNEP manual on Product-Service Systems, and together with Arnold Tukker took responsibility for most of the methodological work in SusProNet.

Arnold Tukker manages the research programme on Sustainable Transitions and System Innovation at TNO, Delft, and was the manager of SusProNet. He worked previously with the Dutch Environment Ministry on waste management and enforcement. At TNO he worked on issues such as life-cycle assessment and disputes on toxic substances. This work resulted in the book *Frames in the Toxicity Controversy* (Kluwer Academic Publishers, 1999), which acquired him a PhD in 1998. In the last five to seven years he has focused on participatory policy-making and governance of sustainable system innovations, among others, via a four-year project with one PhD on foresight for system innovations within the Dutch Knowledge Network on System Innovations. He has positions on editorial boards of *The Journal of Industrial Ecology*, *The Journal of Sustainable Product Design*, *The International Journal for Innovation and Sustainable Development* and *The International Journal of Life Cycle Assessment*, and is founding editor of Springer's book series on Eco-efficiency. He has published four books, 40 peer-reviewed papers and over 200 other publications on a wide variety of subjects. He currently manages the EU-funded Sustainable Consumption Research Exchanges (SCORE!) project, which supports the UN's Ten-Year Framework of Programmes on Sustainable Consumption and Production agreed on during the WSSD in Johannesburg in 2002.

Christiaan van den Berg graduated in Innovation Management at Delft University of Technology and works as consultant at research organisation TNO, department of Information and Communication Technology. For the SusProNet project, he organised congresses and contributed to the chapter on business strategies. Christiaan's expertise is on new business creation, future scanning and customer contact. He is mainly active in (product-)service industries such as telecom, assurances and energy.

Tom van der Horst has been involved in sustainable innovation projects since 1988. He has built up specific experience in a wide scope of research projects and innovation projects in practice in close co-operation with multinationals and SMEs. He is co-founder of the ecodesign discipline in many different cases in co-operation with the Delft University of Technology, and is behind the development of this approach towards sustainable product-system innovation. He is co-founder of Kathalys, Centre for Sustainable Product Innovation TNO/DUT. Currently, he is team manager of the business unit Innovation and Environment of TNO, co-founder of the Knowledge Centre for Sustainable System Innovation and Transitions (TNO/Erasmus University Rotterdam) and co-founder and former chair of O2 the Netherlands.

An Vercalsteren graduated in 1994 as engineer in electromechanics. Since 1996 she has been working as a member of the scientific staff at VITO where she built up comprehensive knowledge in the field of sustainable chain management. She has been involved in the performance of different LCA, ecodesign and eco-efficiency projects in which widely differing product types have been analysed, with both government and industry as target groups. She was project leader of the SusProNet project for VITO. She participates in various projects related to sustainable development.

Since 2002 **Martijn Verkuijl** has been working for econcept as a scientific assistant and consultant in the field of sustainable design. Martijn graduated in 2001 and has a Master of Science degree in Industrial Design Engineering at Delft University of Technology. Currently, his activities include the design of sustainable products and services, consulting companies on sustainable design and marketing issues, carrying out research projects, conducting training and education, and organising networks and workshops. In the SusProNet thematic network, econcept was responsible for the need area offices and for the general PSS state-of-the-art study.

Index